Publication of this work has been
made possible in part by a grant from
the Andrew W. Mellon Foundation.

A
Frontier Family
in
Minnesota
*Letters of
Theodore and Sophie Bost
1851-1920*

Published by the University of Minnesota Press,
2037 University Avenue Southeast, Minneapolis MN 55414
Printed in the United States of America.

Based on *Les derniers puritains,
pionniers d'Amérique, 1851-1920: Lettres
de Théodore Bost et Sophie Bonjour présentées
par Charles-Marc Bost,* © Hachette, 1977.

**Library of Congress Cataloging in Publication Data**

Bost, Théodore, 1834-1920.
    A frontier family in Minnesota.

    Includes index.
    Rev. and enl. translation of: Les derniers puri-
tains, pionniers d'Amérique, 1851-1920.
    1. Bost, Théodore, 1834-1920. 2. Bost,
Sophie, 1835-1922. 3. Pioneers—Minnesota—
Biography. 4. Swiss Americans—Minnesota—Biography.
5. Minnesota—Biography. I. Bost, Sophie, 1835-1922.
II. Bowen, Ralph Henry, 1919-    . III. Title.
F606.B75313        977.6'5    [B]        81-10401
ISBN 0-8166-1032-0                        AACR2
ISBN 0-8166-1035-5 (pbk.)

1.8 & Baker 12.30

The University of Minnesota
is an equal-opportunity
educator and employer.

The John K. Fesler Memorial Fund provided assistance in the publication of this volume, for which the University of Minnesota Press is grateful.

# A Frontier Family in Minnesota

*Letters of
Theodore and Sophie Bost
1851-1920*

Edited and Translated by
**Ralph H. Bowen**

**UNIVERSITY OF MINNESOTA PRESS**
**Minneapolis**

This book
is dedicated to
the future
of
EVE and NIKKO

"We'll cross the prairies as of old
The Pilgrims crossed the sea,
And make the West, as they the East,
The homestead of the free!"

Song introduced
to the Minnesota River Valley
by "The Singing Hutchinsons"
from New Hampshire,
about 1855.

# Contents

Introduction  xi

I. Off to America  3

II. A Wanderer in the New World  9

III. Westward to Minnesota  26

IV. Alone on the Claim  72

V. Waiting for Sophie  96

VI. The Honeymoon  130

VII. The First Child  147

VIII. The Civil War Begins  172

IX. The Lime Quarry  195

X. The Indian Uprising  211

XI. The New House  226

XII. "And the War Goes On"  237

XIII. The Death of Alice  257

XIV. Trees and Bees  268

XV. Alphonse Bonjour  283

XVI. Theodore in Europe  297

XVII. Another Alice  314

XVIII. Storekeeper in Excelsior  321

XIX. Back to the Land  329

XX. The Pioneers in Old Age  333

XXI. Echoes of War (1914-18)  344

XXII. "All Flesh Is Grass"  354

Postscript  357

Notes  361

Index  381

# Introduction

In many outward ways, Sophie and Theodore Bost were representative Midwestern pioneers. Their letters give us a familiar, if unusually vivid and detailed, picture of the Minnesota farming frontier in the 1850s and the ensuing decades. They shared with their Carver County neighbors the hardships of the first settlers in the Big Woods—the poverty, the severe winters, the discomforts of living in a one-room log house, the remoteness from neighbors and doctors, the virtual absence of leisure and recreation, the heavy labor of felling stands of giant oaks and maples, the bone-racking toil of pulling stumps and breaking the land, the unending round of household tasks. They eventually shared the triumphs and satisfactions too—pride in a newly fenced field, in a new frame house, in the family's first horse and buggy, in prizes won at the county fair. Despite the lean years that followed the panic of 1857 and the uncertainties of the Civil War period, despite killing frosts and July hailstorms that wiped out their beehives and destroyed their young fruit trees, despite the death of a small child from whooping cough, and despite the plagues of locusts that ruined their crops in the early seventies, the Bosts, like their neighbors, somehow survived, raised large families, built roads, schools, and churches, acquired pianos and sewing machines, went into business, and held political office.

Firsthand information about the externals of pioneer living is not hard to come by, and in this respect the most one can claim for Sophie and Theodore Bost is that they put down on paper with extraordinary completeness, liveliness, humor, and pathos the day-to-day successes and frustrations, the incidents of home and family life, the routine and the adventure of staying alive, without telling us much that is new about such things as money, weather, crops, livestock, food, clothing, and shelter. These matters and others of the same kind are already known to us with fair accuracy from the diaries, the account books, and (more rarely) the correspondence of a number of early settlers.

But here the special interest of this volume becomes apparent, for the pioneer generation, unlike our letter-writers, was not much given to introspection. The immediate demands of survival were too pressing, and the means of self-expression were almost always at a minimum, impoverished by meager educational opportunities, by limited social contacts, and by the dominance of utilitarian, dollars-and-cents concerns. For these understandable reasons all but a very few of the writings of Minnesota's pioneers deal almost exclusively with matters external to the writer's feelings. We are left to guess at the psychological impact of frontier existence, at the feelings of exile and uprootedness, at the anguish and despair that came from repeated defeat in the struggle with the climate, with illness, with loneliness, with natural catastrophes, and with business cycles.

These letters tell us a great deal about this psychic dimension of pioneering. Beyond physical obstacles and economic adversities, they provide what must be a virtually unique first-person account of how it actually felt to be an immigrant, an exile, a dweller at the forest's edge. We do of course have some (very few) letters and diaries that offer us a little of this kind of insight, and the emotional quality of life on the Middle Border has been given convincing literary expression by writers of the second generation, especially Hamlin Garland. But Theodore and Sophie were different from most of their neighbors in being unusually well educated and highly articulate. They came from families in which book learning and literary activity were taken for granted. Both had been brought up in an atmosphere of intense Protestant piety, which strongly encouraged introspection and self-awareness, as well as the frequent and intimate sharing of spiritual experience with parents, brothers, sisters, and children. Though they had left Europe (so far as they knew) forever, though they had crossed the Atlantic and the Mississippi, they never stopped feeling homesick for Switzerland and France. Sophie's letters to her own widowed mother and her sister Julie not come down to us, so it is difficult to be sure just how close she felt to them or to her brother Alphonse, but no one who reads the letters she and her husband wrote to his parents over three-quarters of a century (but mainly between 1851 and 1887) can doubt that both of the younger Bosts felt an affection almost amounting to worship for Theodore's father, Ami Bost, and great love also for Theodore's mother, Jenny Bost.

To these parents and their many relatives in Europe they wrote often and at great length, keeping them up to date not only on such subjects as the state of the crops and the health of the farm animals, but also—in even more detail—on their mental and spiritual state, on the ups and downs of their emotional lives. We are remarkably fortunate to have this searching record of the interior existence of a man and a woman as they struggled against a harsh environment and a culture that often outraged their European—and Christian—values. Even more precious is the privilege of coming to know, in astonishing depth and intimacy, the lives of two immensely appealing people, not remarkable for any public or material achievement, but extraordinary for their human qualities: their courage, sensitivity, tolerance, sense of humor, warmth, down-to-earth honesty, sense of duty, and ability to give and accept love. Their letters, wholly free of self-conscious or self-serving artifice, allow us to know them as few human beings ever have the ability to know one another.

From another point of view, too, the correspondence of Theodore and Sophie Bost should be of considerable interest to the scholarly historian and perhaps of even greater interest to the many thoughtful Americans of all national and ethnic backgrounds who in recent years have felt a growing desire to rediscover their "roots." Thanks to their attachment to their native culture, that of France and French-speaking Switzerland, the Bosts were able to place their experience on the Minnesota frontier in a broader and richer perspective than was possible for most of their neighbors who, at least in the early years, were mostly of old American stock from New England.

The Bosts had grown up in the emotionally charged atmosphere of early European Romanticism and had been especially affected by the great wave of evangelical piety that had such a profound effect on Swiss and French Protestantism in the first half of the nineteenth century. In fact, Theodore's father, Ami Bost, had been one of the leading figures in this Awakening (*Reveil*)—a powerful preacher, an influential theologian, a gifted composer of sacred music, and the translator of John Bunyan's *The Pilgrim's Progress* into French (his *Voyage du Chrétien* is still the standard version); he also set to music the fourteen short poems that Bunyan included in his text. Ami Bost's religious work was carried forward in Europe by the six of his ten sons who became Protestant ministers. His international reputation may be appreciated from the fact that Theodore heard his father's hymns and cantatas sung in St. Paul; also, a young Swiss friend of Theodore's reported in 1864 that one of Ami Bost's choral works, *The Apocalypse*, was performed at the dedication of a French Protestant church in Ottawa, Illinois.

Ami Bost—his baptismal name (a rather common one in French Switzerland at that period), suggests that his parents may have had Quaker sympathies—was born in Geneva in 1790, just as the French Revolution was beginning to remake the social and moral foundations of Europe. At the height of Napoleon's Empire he was a young man of twenty, and his native city-republic had been transformed (until after Waterloo) into the French *département* of Leman. Like his Huguenot ancestors, who had fled from neighboring French Dauphiné after Louis XIV's revocation of the Edict of Nantes (1685), Ami Bost was a man of strong convictions and unyielding determination. Like his son Theodore, he was an emotional Christian, more drawn to inner piety than to dogma. He had been educated in the schools of the Moravians, those gentle exemplars of eighteenth-century pietism, but his ardent, impulsive temperament, perhaps aggravated by the Romantic movement then rising toward its height, made him impatient of formalism and the rather tepid Deism then in vogue among the pastors of Geneva. He took his stand for a more intense biblical Christianity and a purified form of Calvinistic theology and church discipline. Not very surprisingly, the upshot of his vehement nonconformism was that the Geneva Company of Pastors removed him from their roster.[1]

Ill at ease in the official church, Ami Bost became an itinerant missionary in Alsace, in Germany, and in Switzerland, preaching, writing, converting, denouncing the complacency of the established churches, and living from hand to mouth—frequently, indeed, invited by the police to go elsewhere. During these years his phenomenal energy, irrepressible enthusiasm, and polemical zeal made him a principal leader of the religious revival that reached its height between 1828 and 1830 and continued through most of the following decade. To his evangelizing activities he added those of theologian, historian, journalist, and composer of music, publishing a number of solid tomes on the history of Christianity and writing several popular hymns and other sacred music without any apparent slackening of his other activities. His tirelessness and the sheer exuberance of his many-sided career are reminiscent of the great Methodist leaders of the preceding century, and the organizational side of Wesley's career may indeed have served as a model for his own. He was, to be sure, a Romantic, and his views on society and politics were far more radical than those of Wesley. Ami Bost consistently displayed strong sympathies for the oppressed and the disinherited and an instinctive hostility toward much of the *status quo* in church and state.

In 1826 the pastors of Geneva had removed his name from the official list; but by 1840, when he had become a well-known and beloved figure, they thought it fitting to restore his right to preach in his native city. One senses that this "rehabilitation" was more symbolic than substantial, for Ami Bost was still unable to obtain a ministerial appointment in Switzerland. He was now fifty years old. Since their marriage in 1814 he and his wife Jenny had raised and educated a large family; several of their children, including the six-year-old Theodore and his youngest brother Elisée, were still living with their parents. Ami Bost had no doubt used up the best of his youthful energies. Furthermore, the Awakening was beginning to be overshadowed by industrialism, science, revolutionary politics, and other secular concerns. So Ami Bost left Switzerland, resumed the French nationality of his ancestors, and accepted a pastorate at Asnières-lès-Bourges in central France; a little later he moved his family to Melun (just south of Paris), where he had been appointed Protestant chaplain in the prison administration. He enjoyed only a brief tenure, however, for his position was abolished in the wake of the revolution of 1848 because he had spoken up in defense of rebellious prisoners and had published an article denouncing the inhuman conditions that had provoked their revolt in the spring of 1848.

A wanderer once more, Ami Bost never again held a regular salaried position. He returned for a while with Jenny and the younger children to Switzerland where, in the neighborhood of Neuchâtel, his son Theodore, now an adolescent, first met (but was apparently not much impressed by) his future wife, Mlle. Sophie Bonjour, then a mischievous schoolgirl in pigtails. There, too, on the evening of February 26, 1851, Ami said good-bye— "with tears in my eyes"—to Theodore, the son he perhaps loved best of all, and put him on the coach that would take him to

## INTRODUCTION

Geneva; from there the boy (then just a few weeks past his seventeenth birthday) would take the train to Le Havre and thence a sailing ship to America. In his *Mémoires* the father recorded: "For several days it was as though I had been completely shattered in my inner being."[2]

For the next ten years or so Ami Bost lived in semi-retirement, writing his memoirs and several volumes of history and biography, and continuing to compose music. The aging couple lived for a time on the Isle of Jersey, then in Paris, then in Salies-de-Béarn, in Pau, and finally with their son John in La Force. Until the late 1860s, when he apparently began to lose his mental faculties, Ami Bost eagerly followed Theodore's doings, loaned or gave him substantial sums of money at several critical moments (where this money came from is not clear),[3] and repeatedly asked for additional details about "my American's" life in the wilderness. Most important, it was Ami Bost who decided that Sophie Bonjour was the right young woman for his son to marry and then, over a period of two years, convinced both of them, as well as Sophie's family, that his judgment was correct. Readers of these letters will not disagree.

Everything we know suggests that Jenny Pattey Bost was, in very different ways, an equally remarkable person. Five years younger than her husband, she was one of eight daughters; her father followed the trade of jeweler (*orfèvre*) in Geneva. One can readily believe that she bore the brunt of the family's many transplantations, and there is no need to embroider on the fact that — with little or no stable income and few close friends or sympathetic neighbors to fall back on, she managed to bear thirteen children and bring up eleven of them. She seems to have combined great courage and firmness with great sweetness and gentleness. Theodore and later Sophie certainly loved her very deeply. When, some years before his death, her husband's mind began to fail, Jenny became the only one to whom the children could turn when in difficulty, and it was she who somehow found the money to bring Theodore back to Europe for medical treatment in 1870-71. During these same years, she was the most important person, besides Sophie, in her son's life, and it was to her that letters — usually *double* letters, written partly by Sophie, partly by Theodore — came regularly from Minnesota; after her death, in 1874, the letters are few and far between. On Theodore's side, it is as though his mother's death finally severed the strongest of his emotional ties to Europe, for thereafter he thinks and speaks of himself almost exclusively as an American.

And so at last we come to the pioneers themselves. Theodore was born January 16, 1834, in Carouges, on the outskirts of Geneva. His childhood coincided with one of the relatively stable periods of the family's existence; they moved into Geneva in 1837 and stayed there until 1843 when he was nine. These years of childhood left him with an enduring attachment to all things Swiss; for much of his lifetime in America he continued to be a strong Swiss patriot—and sometimes a rather chauvinistic one at that. After the moves to Asnières-lès-Bourges and then to Melun he of course attended French schools and came to know France as a second homeland. In America he was always ready to take up cudgels in defense of French women or to express solidarity with France in time of war. He did not adopt his third nationality without mental reservations until the North committed itself to the abolition of slavery during the Civil War.

Something of the quality of Theodore's home life, as well as his closeness to his father, can be sensed from Ami Bost's *Mémoires:*

> For several weeks, or perhaps for several months, in the winter of 1837-1838, this little fellow [Theodore], then between four and five years old, would wake up regularly every night about midnight, get out of his bed no matter how cold it might be and come to my bed to kiss me; then, after a moment or two, he would go meekly back to his own bed.[4]

Family prayers and Bible reading of course played a large part in the Bosts' home, and there was a special session for the children every Sunday morning. The chief purpose of this gathering was

> to speak seriously and frankly with one another about our spiritual state and particularly to tell about any faults we were aware of having committed or any sins to which we might feel inclined. I contriubted my own share, restricting myself to things within the children's grasp—for example, when I had been guilty in their presence of impatience or carelessness, I blamed myself before them and if the situation called for it (while pointing out to them that they had perhaps provoked me), I asked their pardon. I always found that confessions of this sort had an excellent effect on my children. When they see us sin, they ought to see us humble ourselves for it.[5]

Theodore did very well in his school work, and one can readily see from his letters that he must have had a natural talent for writing. But around the age of thirteen he began to have severe headaches and had to drop out of school. Because the headaches seemed to be connected with his studies, it was decided that he should become a farmer. He himself had for some time wanted to do precisely that, and the headaches seem to have become less frequent once the choice of an occupation was settled as he wished, but in later life he did complain regularly of bad headaches, as well as acute pains in his back. While it is no doubt possible that both these ailments were psychosomatic in origin, it seems more likely that physical causes were present—perhaps something like what is now popularly called a "slipped disc." Theodore loved farming all his life, and as far as we can judge from his letters, he asked for nothing better than to be able to do heavy outdoor work; indeed, he took it as a personal tragedy that nature had not given him a sturdy frame and powerful muscles.[6] As it was, he repeatedly drove himself beyond the limits of his strength. He was rejected for military service in 1863 because he was found to have a hernia; for twenty years he simply would not admit that chopping down big hardwood trees and grubbing out their stumps was too much for him.

Just when Theodore decided to emigrate to America is not easy to determine. The idea may have been put into his head by his father's friend, M. Vaucher-Veyrassat,[7] to whose farm in Bellevue, not far from Geneva, Theodore was sent in July, 1848, to learn his future occupation. M. Vaucher was enthusiastic about the future of agriculture in the United States. We also know that while living in Bellevue Theodore became fast friends with at least two other youngsters about his own age: Charles Boissonnas, who did in fact go to America, and a certain "young Darier . . . [who] has two or three relatives who are good farmers and belong to a Swiss emigration society. . . ."[8] The following January Theodore was writing to his father:

> the other day I received the wonderful news about your coming here in the near future. . . . I think of you every night. . . . Today we read [your translation of] *The Pilgrim's Progress,* which interested us very much.[9]

We learn from another letter to his parents dated April 15, 1850, that his thoughts had been returning "to my old plan of becoming a missionary, . . ." and he went on to say that for this he would "give up all the plans we have had about my going to America or elsewhere. . . ." The same letter makes it clear that at that time

Theodore was not thinking particularly of becoming a pioneer on the western frontier, for he speaks of his father's coming to visit "the farm I would be managing"—managing, presumably, for someone else. It is probable, though, that Theodore's interest in farming was linked from the beginning with the recognition that— as the ninth son of an impecunious minister who had just lost his job—it would be unrealistic to think of acquiring land of his own, particularly in Europe.

At the end of July, 1850, almost exactly two years after the beginning of his apprenticeship, Theodore left the Vaucher farm because, according to his father's memoirs, he wanted to get to know other places and learn new methods. He went to work for a while on the estate of a rich landowner on the opposite side of the lake of Neuchâtel, but his treatment there was harsh enough to bring tears to his father's eyes,[10] and he quit in October as soon as the harvesting had been completed. It was apparently during the winter of 1850-51, which Theodore spent with his parents, that he finally got his father to consent to his going to America the following spring. Whether he had saved enough to pay his passage is not clear. Some of the money doubtless came from his parents' savings or was borrowed by them from friends or from their older sons. Ami Bost did, in any event, arrange in advance for his son to be taken in and taught American farming methods by an old friend of his, Pastor Fivaz, a former Swiss minister who had settled in Newark Valley, near Binghamton, New York; there he seems to have served as a kind of temporary guardian not only to Theodore but also to a number of other young Swiss immigrants.

Beyond this point we need not follow Theodore's wanderings in the New World, for his letters will speak for themselves.

Sophie Bonjour, the writer of nearly half these letters, also came from this fervently Protestant milieu. Her family seems to have lacked close connections with the clergy—her father was a schoolmaster—and, at least until near the end of her father's life, the Bonjours owned a little land and were in comfortable circumstances. At any rate, she and her sister Julie both received enough education to qualify as teachers, and they also worked as governesses in prosperous English and Scottish families. Her brother Alphonse, who later made his home with the Bosts in Minnesota and California, seems to have been something of a rolling stone as a young man; indeed there are suggestions that he left Europe because he had gotten into some sort of trouble. At about Theodore's age, he emigrated to Australia, where he tried his hand at sheep farming, gold hunting, and a variety of other occupations.

Reading Sophie's letters to Theodore's parents, one can sense that she too thought of herself as a pilgrim in the West. It must be remembered that her marriage was arranged through the good offices of Ami Bost and that when she married Theodore the day after her arrival in St. Paul, she had actually seen him only a very few times as a girl in her early teens. In their correspondence over more than two years he had spared her none of the daunting details of the life she would have to share with him in his rickety log shanty, and there can be no doubt that her decision to go to America was made with great reluctance and with grave misgivings under the persuasive urging of Theodore and his father. It is possible, too, that the Bonjour family's reduced circumstances following the death of Sophie's father in the fall of 1857 may have dimmed her hopes of making a more advantageous marriage in Europe.[11] The prospect of becoming a pioneer housewife was probably somewhat brightened for Sophie by the knowledge that she would be taking with her, as companion and household helper, a young orphan girl, Marie Moseman, who had been taken in by the Bonjour family; Marie never learned English and remained with Sophie until her death sometime around 1890.

Theodore and Sophie had exchanged many letters during their protracted "courtship," so it is perhaps not altogether surprising that they were no sooner married than they fell deeply in love. Their marriage was—to judge from all the evidence we have—remarkably tender, passionate, and harmonious for the more than sixty years of their life together. Though she was a fundamentally optimistic, cheerful, even-tempered young woman—in contrast to Theodore, who was subject to alternating spells of melancholy and exhilaration—Sophie never outgrew her homesickness. She was not much given to complaining, but we may be fairly sure that for her, Minnesota and (for the last thirty years of her life) southern California were always in some sense places of exile, an exile she willingly accepted as God's will, but an exile—a kind of Babylonian Captivity—all the same. These feelings emerge with special poignancy in the letters she wrote to Theodore's mother in 1870 and 1871 during the year-long visit Theodore made to Europe in search of medical treatment for his ailing back.

INTRODUCTION

Sophie, like other frontier wives, had her full share of privations and sorrows. Theodore's uncertain health, his inability (except for short spells, usually followed by weeks of invalidity) to do the heavy work of deforesting and "breaking" his land rapidly enough to provide more than an inadequate and precarious income for their growing family, a recurring cycle of bad luck—killing frosts, midsummer hailstorms, plagues of grasshoppers, prairie fires, financial panics that made their crops virtually worthless— these and a dozen lesser disasters threatened time and again to overwhelm her. The hardest blow was the death of her third child, Alice, the darling of the family, from whooping cough at the age of one and a half. Five other children, including a second Alice— all born at home with only Theodore, Marie, and sometimes a woman from a nearby farm to lend a hand—must have helped to tax her energies and test her fortitude. But in all she writes about these afflictions there is no hint of bitterness, no blame for anyone else, no self-pity. "The Lord giveth and the Lord taketh away: blessed be the name of the Lord." One is finally convinced that nothing could shatter her inner strength or her serene confidence that courage and perseverance would somehow prevail. Theodore, tormented by his unreliable vertebrae, his headaches and his hernia, tends on occasion to look for excuses, to dwell on the gloomy side, and to fear the worst. It is hard to avoid the impression that Sophie was the stronger and the more resilient of the two. Luckily, there was nothing wrong with *her* backbone. Yet she was very nearly as dependent on Theodore as he was on her. Perhaps the best way to sum things up is to say that as a pair of strangers amid the alien corn of Midwestern America, each would have been lost without the other.

Theodore was the second-youngest of the thirteen children born to Ami and Jenny Bost (of whom only eleven survived infancy). With the exception of Marie, who had five older and five younger brothers, all were boys. The oldest was Augustin (or Auguste); then came John, Ami Junior, Samuel, and Etienne, all born so early in the parents' marriage that Theodore thought of them almost as belonging to another generation. He felt much closer to his sister, who remained at home (except for brief intervals when she worked as a governess) until her death at the age of thirty-three, and to the younger boys, Paul, Théophile, and especially Timothée and Elisée with whom he had grown up. Inasmuch as the letters refer continually to Marie and to the nine brothers and their families, the reader will probably find it helpful to make their acquaintance in advance; further details will be given as needed in the notes.

Augustin served as minister to a number of Protestant parishes in France until he gave up active preaching at the age of forty-four to become a compiler of dictionaries, one on the Bible and another on church history. Like his father and several of his brothers, he was a good musician. He married twice and had four children by each wife; six of the eight grew to adulthood.

John was to become the most famous of the ten brothers, the outstanding "success" of the family. A highly gifted pianist and cellist, he had hoped at first for a musical career but decided to study for the ministry instead. Plagued by persistent headaches, he could not keep up with his studies and had to drop out twice, never finishing his degree. Later, however, as pastor of a small, unaffiliated congregation at La Force (Dordogne) in southwestern France he found his true vocation—social service and organized philanthropy. He became the center of a veritable whirlwind of activity, creating a series of asylums—eventually nine in all!—and leaving behind him an institution that must still rank among the leading exemplars of European philanthropy, the *Fondation John Bost*, which in 1973 had 1,068 patients and a staff of 539. Besides being a man of enormous energy and superb organizing ability, John Bost possessed great charm and sensitivity; he was a man of strong feelings and powerful eloquence. After a twelve-year engagement, he married Eugénie Ponterie, the daughter of a local nobleman, and acquired the family château. It was under his roof that Ami and Jenny Bost spent their last years, celebrating their diamond wedding anniversary in 1874 and dying within a few months of one another later that same year.

The next three brothers Ami Junior, Samuel, and Etienne, are referred to from time to time in the letters, but seem to have been less close to Theodore than the youngest sons. They were also perhaps less capable than John of assuming a position of family leadership when their father's powers began to fail some years before his death. Ami Junior became a successful merchant in Glasgow, where he established his own firm and, at the age of thirty-one, married Mary Cave, the daughter of an Anglo-Indian army officer. His wife brought him landed property in Ireland, where they resided for a time, but soon returned to Glasgow. He died at the age of forty-six after a change of residence to southeastern France had failed to restore his health. Samuel went to Calcutta as a missionary and there married Sophie Laguerre, who had come from France to be his bride sight unseen—rather like the other Sophie who came out to St. Paul to marry Theodore after a courtship by correspondence. Samuel later returned to France, held an assistant pastorate at Salies-de-Béarn (where his father and mother also lived for a time), worked with his brother John at La Force, served as minister in Chartres, and died at the age of fifty-seven leaving three children. Etienne became a tutor in a secondary school, then a pastor in the North of France, in Holland, and in Chartres. He married still a third Sophie (née Vivien), making it necessary for *our* Sophie in Minnesota to sign her letters "Sophie Théodore" or "Sophie T. Bost." Next in age came Marie, whose betrothal was closely followed by her lingering, painful, and heroically endured final illness.

Of the five younger brothers the eldest was Paul, an artist, a bohemian, and generally a misfit in the Victorian age. He studied to be an engraver, nearly succumbed to typhoid, dropped out of the Mission School in Paris, became an expatriate in England, dragged out an impoverished existence there without being able to bring any of his projects to completion, and married Alice Trew, who then had to support herself and their son Paul while her husband declined to worry about money, maintaining that it was his prerogative as an artist to be supported by society—in practice, his wife, his parents, and his brothers.

Théophile lived a more conventional life, serving as a pastor in Belgium, marrying Eliza Baker, an Englishwoman, fathering five children and raising four of them; he was a liberal Protestant and a man of some scholarly attainments. He published one book as well as a number of articles and pamphlets on religious and moral subjects. Theodore often refers to him with affection. But the names that occur most frequently are those of Timothée, his next-oldest brother and Elisée, his youngest brother who, except for Theodore himself, was to be the last surviving child of Ami and Jenny Bost.

In a family of preachers, musicians, and writers, Timothée, together with his elder brother Ami, had the originality to become a successful businessman. He spent most of his life in Glasgow where he had gone at the age of sixteen to join Ami Junior's mercantile firm. Eleven years later he again followed his brother's example by marrying a young woman belonging to one of the great families of Scotland. Isabella Lennox, called Bella, was the daughter of an Indian Army officer and was a first cousin of Ami Junior's wife. Timothée traveled widely on business, which took him to Poland and Canada among other places, and most of his eleven surviving children went to the far corners of the world to seek their fortunes. Timothée was strongly religious and had a kindly, generous nature. He put up part of the money for Theodore's trip to Europe in 1870-71, and a few years later advanced to Theodore the capital he needed to go into partnership in a general store when his physical disabilities made it impossible for him to go on doing heavy farm work.

Finally, there was Elisée, the youngest of the ten brothers. Born, as was Theodore, in a suburb of Geneva, he lived in various places in Switzerland, France, and the Isle of Jersey during his childhood, sharing with Theodore his parents' peripatetic existence. As a young man he studied theology at Montauban, served as tutor in several well-to-do families, and eventually became a pastor, first in Grenoble and then in Pouzin (Ardèche), where he spent the last forty-three years of his life. At the age of thirty-four he married Clémy Siefert of Lyon; they had seven children. Elisée had his share of the family's musical gifts and was a talented chess player.

From the death of their parents in 1874 until his own death in 1920, Elisée went on exchanging letters with his brother in America. He inherited and carefully preserved the letters his parents had received from Minnesota, leaving them to his eldest son Charles who in turn bequeathed them to their present owner, Charles-Marc Bost, who recently published a large selection of the correspondence under the title *Les derniers puritains, pionniers d'Amérique, 1851-1920: Lettres de Théodore Bost et Sophie Bonjour* (Paris, 1977).

The present edition includes translations of all these letters as well as some not included in *Les derniers puritains*, and is published by arrangement with M. Bost and his French publisher, Librairie Hachette. M. Bost has allowed me to consult a somewhat larger selection of the correspondence of which *Les derniers puritains* is an abridged version. These additional letters — some of which are included in this edition — have provided many new details, which have been incorporated in the notes. I am greatly indebted to M. Bost for allowing me to consult the manuscript of a

## INTRODUCTION

history of his family, which he has prepared for publication in France, and I thank him also for his patience in answering my many queries and for pointing out some errors in the first draft of this introduction.

It is also a pleasure to make grateful acknowledgment of the unfailing helpfulness of everyone at the Minnesota Historical Society, especially that of Bruce M. White, assistant editor of *Minnesota History*, who has given me the benefit of his very extensive knowledge of the state's early history, including the fur trade and the beginnings of settlement. Helen M. White very generously furnished me with a letter from Theodore, which she found in the course of her research on the Ignatius Donnelly papers in the Minnesota Historical Society. Earl W. Hayter, Professor-Emeritus of History at Northern Illinois University, has allowed me to draw freely on his encyclopedic knowledge of midwestern frontier farming. Mrs. Mark Knowlton of Excelsior, Minnesota, has passed on to me many interesting reminiscences of the Bost family, especially of Theodore's son Alphonse, and has permitted me to consult a number of pertinent documents and photographs. Finally, I wish to thank Theresa M. Weaver for her expert assistance in typing and retyping the manuscript of this book. Elaine Kittleson and other members of the secretarial staff of the Northern Illinois History Department have likewise contributed much to the preparation of the book for the publisher.

Ralph H. Bowen

DeKalb, Illinois
October, 1980

A
Frontier Family
in
Minnesota
*Letters of
Theodore and Sophie Bost
1851-1920*

EDITOR'S NOTE: Italics have been used to indicate that a word or phrase was in English in the original text. This happened more and more frequently as Theodore and Sophie became Americanized. When words were underlined in the original text, this is indicated either in brackets or in a note.

# I

# Off to America

These early letters allow us to follow Theodore's first steps away from his family, home, and school. Leaving Melun on July 14, 1848, at the age of fourteen, he went to live with the Vaucher family in Bellevue, not far from Geneva. Ami Bost had just lost his position as Protestant chaplain in the French prison system, and it may be that this worsening of his parents' economic prospects had some bearing on his decision to become self-supporting. At any rate, he was not thrown entirely on his own resources from one day to the next, for the Vauchers were close friends of the older Bosts and even took them in for a while the following year. Theodore seems to have been happy in Bellevue; he liked outdoor work and there were at least two boys of about his own age with whom he made lasting friendships. These letters show him keeping up close ties with his parents and his brother Paul. They also reveal him as a warmhearted, imaginative, idealistic young man, serious and conscientious but at the same time something of a dreamer. This was more than an adolescent trait. It helps account for his lack of material success, as well as his appeal as a person.

## M. Vaucher to Ami Bost

Bellevue, June 26, 1848

. . . I am very well pleased that Theodore is taking up farming as his occupation. It is, after all, the most secure, and before long I am certain that it will be considered one of the most honorable, especially if the farmer is at the same time an educated man. . . . In America agriculture is flouishing in a remarkable way, and there is no doubt that as soon as men with scientific training can be found in sufficient numbers, the capital will be available for clearing and improving the eight million *hectares* [about 18 million acres] that are merely awaiting the men and the money to enable them to be put to use. . . .

3

**Theodore to his parents**

Bellevue, April 15, 1850

Dear Parents:

I was speaking with M. Vaucher the other day about my old plan of becoming a missionary, and I told him that if some society were willing to send me out to a station where I could improve the physical well-being of the heathen, I would give up all the ideas we have had about my going to America or elsewhere. My only regret, I said, would be that when you're old I couldn't welcome you as a visitor to the farm where I would be the manager, but I added that making a big pile of money means nothing to me. I shouldn't want to be obliged to preach nor to do a great deal of literary work because I know very well I'm not cut out for that. But I could spread the Gospel just as effectively by working. I don't know whether you understand what I mean. If I were to do this, I'd want to learn to do a little carpentry and perhaps also some masonry. I already know a little about homeopathy[1] and I would try to learn more about it. Then, while the missionary with whom I was working went all over the place preaching the Gospel, I would teach them how to cultivate the soil, build houses, and look after livestock if they don't [already] have any. What would please me best from all points of view would be to live far away from the harassments of the world, which I find harder and harder to bear as time goes on. I have had an idea along this line: if Paul should be willing to go out as a missionary, I'd prefer to be with my own brother than with some stranger, and I hope that he and I wouldn't quarrel.

It remains to be seen, and it seems to me very doubtful, whether any society would agree to make use of me in this way without requiring me to study a lot of books in some institute. M. Vaucher has told me that he wouldn't be surprised if some society accepted me, recognizing in me someone who wishes for the spiritual and bodily well-being of his fellow creatures, which is my very sincere desire. I have of course asked God to guide me and give me counsel in this project. And you pray for me too, dear Parents, and give me your advice in the next letter you send me. . . .

On July 30, 1850, Theodore took leave of the Vaucher family and left Bellevue. This is what his father wrote in his memoirs: "He came to the conclusion that it would be good to go elsewhere and learn other methods and to find a place, where, later on, he might set himself up permanently. At first he came home to us to rest for a few days from the strenuous work he had been doing (threshing, plowing, mowing, caring for the oxen, horses, cows, and pigs—and not a single one of these chores seemed to arouse in his mind the slightest distaste). Then he found himself a job working for a rich land-owner on the opposite side of the lake [of Neuchâtel]. Since my son could not be lodged in the landowner's own house, he lived at an inn, or rather a tavern, in the village of Cudrefin, almost directly across from us. . . . In the quiet of the evenings we would let our thoughts turn affectionately toward our dear Theodore . . . how many times did I not sing to myself with tears in my eyes this prayer which I composed especially for him:

> Shelter him beneath Thy wing,
> O Jesus, our unfailing God,
> And hide him in Thy bosom!

"But when the outdoor work was finished in October Thèodore came to spend the winter with us, still turning over in his mind (but without saying much to us about it) the idea that I already rejected once but that I now accepted without hesitation the moment he put it to me again—his idea of going to America in search of work, land, and freedom!"

Ami then wrote to one of his former colleagues, Pastor Fivaz, who had been running a farm for some years in the state of New York. The latter replied that he was willing to take Theodore in and help him.

## Pastor Fivaz to Ami Bost

Newark Valley, Tioga County
New York State
December 25, 1850

Dear, good, old, and faithful Friend:

I received your letter this afternoon, and this very evening I am answering it in agreement with my wife and son. We will wel-come your Theodore to our house, our family, and our farm. We have an extra room in the house and he may have it for his own. Although he already has done farm work for two years in Europe, which is very good, he will still have to go through a complete apprenticeship in American agriculture. My son, who had spent two years [farming] in Germany, still had to learn the trade from the bottom up like everybody else.

At least your son will not have to learn from costly experi-ments paid for out of his own pocket, and we will teach him to avoid this kind of experiment altogether, for we have already lost our tails in the fight. Of course, contrary to nature, we have grown new ones, but we won't let ourselves be caught in the same trap again. Here, as in Europe, there are fields, pastures, cows, horses, sheep, plows, cultivators, and so on. We make use of crop rotations, etc., but the relationships among all these things are very different. Since last May we have had in our home a young man of twenty-six, M. Recordon, who comes from Rances, near Orbe.[2] Since then he has worked without wages alongside my son, even though he was already an experienced farmer. In general, the Americans do not pay wages to a foreigner, or scarcely any, unless they see that he is skilled in their methods of work. Accordingly, we recently obtained a place for Martin, a young man from Orbe, in an American family but without pay for the first year. Therefore, it is on those terms that we will at first receive your dear son, but you can rely on us in this respect: as soon as your son deserves to be paid wages, we will not want to see him work without pay, whether we keep him on here with us or whether we place him later in one of the respectable American families of our neighborhood. He will easily learn English, even while living with us, because of our day-to-day dealings with the Americans. He will have, as often as can be arranged, a horse and buggy which he can use for his errands and visits. In short, we will treat him like our own son and like the son of my dear Bost. I can't say more than that. The sooner he can be on his way here, the better. I understand that March would be the earliest time he could leave. By the end of February we begin to collect sap for making maple sugar, but at least he would get here in time to begin spring plowing.

He mustn't load himself down with too large a trunk unless he wants to bring a lot of books with him, but we have books of all kinds—on religion, agriculture, history and so forth. . . . Although, like everyone else, he will have to dress up on Sunday, there will be no need for fine clothes the rest of the week. He will not need more than six to ten shirts, two of fine quality and the rest of durable material, a good blue denim blouse for summer work in the stables and other chores, two jackets for winter. In Switzerland they sell knitted jackets, quilted, I think, and warm, for very little money. I seem to remember that they are gray and the cloth is woven on a loom. A second one made of the heavy cloth they produce here in America would also be very desirable. Since it will be cold during the ocean crossing and since the American winters have days that are good and cold, he will need a good overcoat or cloak. [Also,] woolen trousers and a pair of canvas ones for summer. It is by no means necessary that all this should be new. Let him bring whatever he now has. But I do insist on the blouse

and the jacket; my wife has knitted some for us, and we couldn't
get along without them. Also two or three pairs of hobnailed shoes.
Linen or cotton stockings, and some heavy ones of wool, but not
too many. Boots are better made and cheaper here than in Europe.
In general, people bring too much baggage, for everything can be
bought here except for the jackets, blouses, and carpet slippers. In
general, everything made of woolen cloth is expensive and of lower
quality than in Europe. I tell you this not only for your son's information but also for him to pass on to his two traveling companions.[3]
I may have gone into too much detail, but this, in general, is what
one should bring from Europe. . . .

 . . . And now [I will say that] I believe your son is doing
the right thing to come to America with no money in his pocket.
Difficult as it is to get a start in life in Europe, it is easy here for
an honest, intelligent, and industrious man to make his way. A
good hired man can earn from $120 to $150 a year, that is to say,
more than 600 to 750 French francs, in addition to his meals, laundry, and so on. But an apprenticeship is necessary before one can
equal an American worker. It will not take your son long to recognize this. A cabinetmaker or the like can earn a dollar a day with
room and board in addition. It's true that he will then be unem-
ployed for part of the winter. During the haying and harvest season
a hired hand receives the same wage (the dollar is worth 36½ batz
[in Swiss money]). This results from the scarcity of laborers, for a
man's expenses are not in proportion to these high rates of pay.
Hence, after a few years they are quite easily able to buy a farm.
These are a few details for your son. I will just add that he mustn't
expect to find Europe in America. Let him save his comparisons
for a time when he will know more about the New World. The
things that are valued over there, even in farming, are of little use
here. A man would soon ruin himself completely by sticking to
European ways. As for the rest of the story, he himself can write
to you about it once he's here. . . .

"The departure," writes Ami, "was decided on with a suddenness that was almost frightening, even though we had in fact been expecting it. At ten o'clock
on the evening of February 26 [1851], my Theodore climbed up into the
coach that had stopped before the door of our house, traveling at first to
Geneva! I could not make myself realize the true magnitude of this separation,
but the moment was no less cruel for all that. As one grows older, one's sensi-
bility seems to grow duller, but this is probably true only in certain respects,
for a person feels the same tenderness as before; it is only that the organs by

which the feelings are expressed seem to atrophy, and one then experiences great sorrow without tears. That was how it was with me. Without seeming outwardly to be deeply affected, for several days it was as though I had been completely shattered in my inner being."

# II

# A Wanderer
# in the New World

Theodore was just a few weeks past his seventeenth birthday when he went to Le Havre to board the sailing ship that was to take him to America. After a stormy six-week crossing during which he suffered almost continually from seasickness and dysentery, he landed in New York on April 20, 1851. He stayed briefly with the Fivaz family in Tioga County, New York, as his father had arranged—but apparently left much sooner than expected for reasons of which we are ignorant. He then worked for a few months on the farm of a family named Ball near Dover, New Jersey. In November of the same year we find him in Canada at "La Grande Ligne," a Swiss-run Baptist mission and agricultural settlement some thirty miles south of Montreal. Located in open country not far from the Richelieu River, the mission consisted of classroom buildings, dormitories for about forty boys and the mission staff, a church (the only structure still remaining), and a number of farm buildings. The mission was headed by another friend of Ami Bost, Mme. Henriette-Françoise Odin-Feller. Theodore was given a job teaching French.

**Theodore to his parents**

Grande Ligne Mission
Near St. John's[1] —Can. East [Quebec]
Saturday, January 15, 1853

Dearest Father and Mother:

It is your opinion, dear Father—and my principal reason for mentioning it is to excuse the conduct of those who have played some part in pushing me into this—it is your opinion that people allow money to play too big a part in ushering in the Kingdom of God. This is an idea that has often occurred to me and one that gives me more and more pain.

But what you say about the apostles and their not making these continual appeals for money proves only one thing, which is

9

that the Christians of those times were more fervent and devoted than those of today, so there was no need to ask in order to receive; besides, it proves that their way of life was different from that of the present. St. Paul says that the members of the churches ought to share their worldly goods with those who teach them, but where will you find church members who do this outside the United States and a few of the free churches in France? Besides, the missionaries here are not part of constituted churches, but of churches that are yet to be formed, and how would they live if they were not supported by someone? Those whose health is good enough travel continually in their missionary field and could not, like St. Paul, preach the Gospel while working for a living, because they must always run after people, whereas people went running after St. Paul.

In addition, for the time being all the schools at this mission are free, and yet the instructors have to be paid. I don't find any mention of schools in the Epistles, but schools are just what cost the most. In this house there are at present about fifty people who have to be fed. Mme. Feller, who is in charge of the mission (I don't know whether she gets paid or not); M. and Mme. Normandeau are paid $200 [a year]; M. and Mme. Roux get $200; I get $80; and M. Cornette gets $60; also there are four or five domestic servants, three day laborers, thirty two boarding students, and always a few visitors. And at that the wages paid are just barely adequate. The former, those who are paid 200 *piastres*,[2] have to pay the establishment $100 for their board; thus they have left only $100 for books, travel, and clothing for themselves and their wives. So the result is that my pay, tiny as it is, is still better than theirs because I get my board free.

I agree all the more readily with your arguments because there is very little one can do down there [Australia]. I don't want to let myself be carried away by my own impulses—which run strongly toward traveling, it's true—and my mind can still grasp the rational arguments presented to it and decide to remain quietly here where I am. For the time being, then, dear parents, don't worry about me. I've never had any intention of leaving in the next year or two, and between now and then many things can happen.

. . . As for coming back[3] to Ireland, I'll think about it, dear Parents, but for the present I believe it is my duty to stay here in America. Here a person is free of all chains and if, as I still hope, I can once get a farm of my own or a large one to manage, I shall be a great deal more free than in Great Britain. Here a man can try out whatever ideas he may have; he can enter any occupation that appeals to him, and I have seen farmers who own more than a thousand *arpents*[4] go out to work for their neighbors by the day with their horses, something no one would think of doing in England. If I want to make some changes on my farm or try out some invention, I don't have to worry about what my neighbors will think. And besides, agriculture is a large-scale affair in America but not in England. As for wood, you can burn as much as you want, and, in short, you can do just as you like on your own farm, whereas in England you have to conform to custom.

And now, dear Father, you tell me that "when the time comes, it won't be hard to find more than one young woman of merit, etc." To be frank, I will make no bones about saying that there has been more than one occasion when that would have been enough to bring me back [from America] because there is a great scarcity of worthy young women in America, but let's look ahead a few years: if there should be a whole swarm of cute little tykes, what could one do with them in Europe? Look how limited the opportunities are! But here I don't despair of carving out a future for myself, and in that case, what a future there will be for the little ones! (Today, you can see, I am building castles—not in Spain, but in America!)

. . . Yes, dear Mother, I shall be nineteen tomorrow, and how many of those years have I neglected to make good use of! May the coming year be better employed! How many things have happened in the last two years! . . .

January 29

In my next letter I will tell you about some well-located land, fertile and covered with standing timber, at $1.50 [an acre] in the State of Vermont. In ten years this land will have at least tripled in value so that, even without farming it, the interest on the investment would be more than ample. For now, good-bye—how I would love to see all of you living here on a good farm! (This land is about fifty or sixty miles from here.)

Your Theodore

At the end of April, 1853, Theodore left the Grande Ligne Mission and went to Burlington, Vermont, where he earned his living by teaching French.

**Theodore to his parents**

> Burlington
> Vermont, United States
> September 6, 1853

Dearest Parents:

Tim has probably already told you about my change which (contrary to your expectation, as well as my own) hasn't turned out as I had thought. I wanted to get back onto a farm again and here I am still teaching, but it is altogether different from La Grande Ligne. . . . In fact, by working four hours a day every Monday, Wednesday, and Friday, and having the other days free, I earn more than at Grande Ligne, not counting my room and board there, and I get far less tired and have no worries. If my pupils don't get along well, that's their worry, and it isn't any longer my job to teach them how to succeed. I hope to have more work soon, but I prefer for the present not to tire myself too much. I am beginning to get my strength back splendidly, and I do a lot of walking on the shores of Lake Champlain. In my letter to Tim, I told him that I was think of taking a room with Mrs. Worcester, in whose family I am giving lessons, but since she has just taken in more students, she doesn't have a room for me any longer, so she has recommended me to the house where I now am. I pay $2.50 a week, not including my laundry, which costs me about twelve cents a week. In one way I'm glad I left Mrs. Worcester's place, because everyone there had tiny appetites like fashionable young ladies, and I found this embarrassing. In this house where I am now there are about fifteen heavy eaters, and this puts me more at ease. The owners are good Christians and have already done a lot to help me. Since I got here, I've found a great many people who have been very obliging.

Every Monday, Wednesday, and Friday at eight o'clock in the morning I give a lesson to three young ladies (seventeen to nineteen years old, two of them quite pretty), and they pay me $8 a month. At nine o'clock another lesson to two girls (fourteen and eighteen, not bad looking), and tomorrow I shall start giving lessons at Mrs. Worcester's place from 11:45 A.M. to 12:30 P.M. and from 2:00 P.M. to 3:00 P.M., [making] six hours a week [at her house]. For these six hours I will get only $2, but I also profit from the arrangement because if I did not teach at this school I would have to go to a great deal of trouble to find students elsewhere in town;

this [connection] gives me some professional standing. For twelve hours of lessons per month (three per week) I ask $6 for two students, $8 for three, and $10 for four. . . .

## Theodore to his parents

Burlington, Vermont
January 28, 1854

Dearest Father and Mother:

. . . A rather brilliant future seems to be opening up for me here, and I'd be pleased if three-quarters of the young men back in the old country could say as much.

If you are just an ordinary workman, your position is already better than in Europe, not only because workers are paid high wages, but also because they are considered and treated as human beings if they show they deserve to be so treated. There is nothing of that envy of the lower classes for the higher classes, and if I were to return to the old world, I'd have a hard time believing myself inferior to some property owner just because he was richer than I was. But that isn't exactly what my brilliant prospects consist of. In the western states, and especially in the southern states, there scarcely exists such a thing as a *French Teacher*, and New England (Vermont, Massach[usetts], New Hampshire, Connect[icut], and so on) drain off their surplus teachers into those other states. One of the two young women who taught English at the mission has refused $1,100 for a two-year [contract] to teach music and French, and like everyone else here (except my employers) she advises me to go South.

I am content with what I have here, even though I have nothing left over for extras, and if I see that it is my duty to stay in Burlington, I'll stay here without complaining. But I feel that I'm wasting my time here, that I could make more money in the South; and since a person has to think about the future, I see no reason why I shouldn't move to the South. A *Teacher* who is no better than mediocre can earn $400, $500, and even $600 a year, and often more. I'm not letting myself be carried away by imaginary visions of happiness down there; it is really a question of whether or not that is the path I ought to take. I am asking God's guidance and since, as it seems, he has blocked my path in Europe, He will also block my path in the South if such be His will. A number of young men from the mission are also thinking of going South, and then, after saving their money for a few years, they plan to go *far in the west* to buy a few hundred acres of land in what, back in Europe, we call America. That is really the only course that is attractive in America. Living in the Eastern states means living a little better than in Europe, but a young man who comes to America as we imagine it back home should go a thousand miles inland.

It is breathtaking what giant strides American civilization is taking: the West [Midwest] is visibly filling up with people, and if I don't return to Europe or if I don't devote myself to spreading the Gospel, as some would like to see me do, I believe the best thing would be for me to do the same thing as my friends from Grande Ligne. It would be an important step to take, especially because of the long distance from here, but as for you and me, we would be at about the same distance for writing and receiving letters, perhaps a few days longer. There is just as much, and perhaps more emigration from Vermont to [the West of] America [as there is] from any European country, proportionately speaking; about a month ago, thirty families left from a single village in the northern part of this state to go out to Iowa and buy land. These lands, which belong to the government, are sold for $1.25 an acre.

In many ways the life of a pioneer, who has to clear the land before he can cultivate it, is terribly hard. His struggle is that of civilization against nature, of civilized people against savages in some places, and of people against wild animals almost everywhere. This struggle is terrifying, especially for people who are no longer young. As for myself, I have no illusions about its difficulties; I can foresee what I'd be up against for the first few years, but, after all, when one is young and full of vigor and has a strong sense of where one's duty lies, one will be able to overcome the obstacles. Besides, if you expect to harvest a crop, you have to sow it first, and if I hope to have anything to live on in my old age, I shall have to work for it while I'm young. I believe that a young man with a little money, working with other young men who know the country and, like those from Grande Ligne, are good Christians, will do very well out there.

All this is what I've been turning over in my mind, but I don't yet have my heart set on it; it would be a new path for me, and for the moment I haven't decided to follow it. I'm leaning that way a little, but if I find that this road, too, is closed to me, I won't shed any tears over it, I can assure you. Although I very much enjoy adventures once I see that I can't avoid them, I should be just as happy if I didn't have to get mixed up in too many of them, especially violent adventures. So it isn't a hunger for excitement that is driving me. I can reason about such things more coolly than most young men of twenty.

And once again, dear Father and Mother, let me say a few words particularly to you. I would like very, very much to see you again, but if God doesn't want that to happen, then I don't want it either. When I first came to America, I had hoped that before now I could have been of some help to you, but I have found that this country was not what I had expected it to be. If God blesses the work of my hands, I'll be able to help you someday, but I think (though I'm not sure of it) that in order to do that I'd have to go South. If I had known that there are five *French Teachers* besides myself in this small city, I never should have settled here. Still, let God's will be done. But good-bye, dear Parents, I must hurry in order to get this letter in the mail—my warm greetings to everybody. Did Ami get my letter? What is this dear brother of mine doing at the moment? Good-bye again, and may God watch over all of you.

Your most affectionate
T. Bost

**Theodore to his parents**

Burlington, Vermont
April 6, 1854

Dearest Parents:

You tell me, dear Mother, that it is taking a risk to be baptized in such cold water,[5] and you ask me if there are never any bad results. I have never heard of anyone getting sick afterward. As for myself, when I saw the faces being made by a forty-year-old man just ahead of me, I said to myself: All right, it looks as though you're in for the same thing, so get a grip on yourself! I stepped down into the water, which actually seemed fairly warm, and took about ten steps with M. Normandeau; but then, as they were singing the hymn and M. Normandeau was saying, "Brother, by reason of the love that God has awakened in your heart, I baptize you in the name of the Father, the Son, and the Holy Spirit," I could think of nothing else but the water. When he raised me up again, for example, I felt sure that I was going to make a horrible face because the water running down my back might have been warmer, but I made a heroic effort of self-control, so that the other boys wouldn't think I was cold at all. Since they had all been in my classes, they still took their lead from me to a great extent, and this encouraged them to step down into the water. But there was only one who came off really well; this was a very likable boy of thirteen. M. Normandeau hesitated for a moment before baptizing one other boy who had never, except for one time, been in the water before. His heart was beating so wildly that M. N. could count the pulses through his clothing, but said he, "God will help him," and he pushed him under. The expression on the boy's face was really something to see! Then we went and got into dry clothes in a tent that was open to the sky, the thirteen-year-old boy along with me; we came out with fewer clothes on than before, but we were sure our emotional state would keep us from being cold. As for my physical constitution and my general health, they tell me that I am *strongly built* and in *very good health,* which is perfectly true in comparison with the 113 students at the school, who are all between seventeen and thirty-five years old.

For the moment I have no more than three or four projects floating about in my head, but in spite of what you may think, I am not especially absorbed in any of them. The amount of work I have to do keeps me from all worry and should put your minds equally at rest on this score. In the first place, I can stay on here or else go South. But what I fear in this connection is that given the strength of my Christian feelings I would be prompted both by human nature and by conscience to commit the crime of helping slaves to escape, or at least of not preventing them, and with their infernal *mobs,* the chances of getting along there for such a lawbreaker would not be very good. Again today I've just been reading notices advertising the sale of 200, 250, and the like, slaves. The other day four fugitive slaves passed within a few miles of this place, pursued by their masters. The local people stopped the latter and furnished a team of horses to the former, so they got safely to Canada. Hurrah for the *Green Mountain Boys!* In the West they did even better some two weeks ago and tore down a jail where a fugitive slave was being held, but one of the leaders is in prison because it is against the law to help a slave.

And now, to come to the end of my letter, the House of Representatives has passed a bill that will give 160 acres to any person who wants to settle in the West, and if he lives on that land for five years it will belong to him. In this way, anybody will be able to acquire a farm, and no one will have a right to more than 160 acres—this is to prevent *monopolisation* (I don't know if this word is French or not). If this bill can get through the Senate, it will soon be in force, but it is feared that it will not pass, because the Senate is fairly aristocratic. In any case, I am not thinking of going out there in the next four or five years, inasmuch as it isn't a bad a idea to have put a little money aside before going to settle in the West. As for California, it is, as you say, a splendid place to farm, but (I don't know exactly why) I am not very much tempted to go there. Everything must be in proportion, so that if you can earn a lot, you will also spend a lot. In addition to that, the mixture of populations—Chinese, American, British, German, French, Spanish, Italian, and so forth—must make the region rather turbulent. Oregon might suit me better: it is a little colder (which I prefer), though it is warmer than where I am now.

If I could get a position as *Teacher* in Virginia, I think I would take it. I don't like the thought of having to wait a long time before I can save the several hundred dollars I would need to settle myself on a farm. It's a pity you're so determined to stay in Europe because I think you would like this country very well.

Well, then, good-bye, dear Father and Mother, brothers, sisters, aunts, uncles—cousins, and friends! May God bless you and keep you! Pray for me so that I may be able to do God's will. Good-bye.

> Your most affectionate
> Theodore Bost

**Theodore to his parents**

> Burlington, Vermont
> June 3, 1854

Dear Parents:

Strangely enough, almost every time I sit down to write a letter, I find myself in a situation that won't be settled until several days after the letter has been sent off.

Perhaps I'll still go South, though I am even less tempted to do so than I was six weeks ago. I don't know whether you have heard anything about the passage of the [Kansas] Nebraska Bill—

maybe not, seeing that events in Europe are important enough to take up your whole attention.[6] Therefore, I'll try to tell you in a few words what it's all about.

In the territories ceded by France to the United States [the Louisiana Purchase] it had been stipulated by the treaties [*sic*] that slavery could not be introduced above the thirty-sixth parallel of latitude, and up to now this principle has been respected.[7] But [Franklin] Pierce, the President, and [Stephen A.] Douglas, a Senator who aspires to the presidency, incited and paid by the South, have discovered that it is contrary to the principles of liberty and the Gospels to hinder the whites from oppressing the blacks, and they have worked to such good purpose that they have been able to secure passage by the Senate and the House of a bill that allows the *Slaveholders* to go and settle with their slaves in all the Territories of the Union. This means that several hundreds of millions of acres have been opened to slavery. This is not to say that slavery will in fact be established over that whole area. The Northerners are beginning to get angry and are moving into these territories on a large scale; they are directing new immigrants from Europe into the same regions. When the time comes to transform these Territories into States, everyone will cast his vote for or against slavery, and if the majority is against it, they will tell Pierce and his ilk to go hang themselves.

Oh, well, it seems that a person can work off his bile by letting loose with a string of big words, but what real good does that do? I am indignant to see a nation that calls itself Christian behaving in this way while screaming at the top of its lungs about the despotism under which the British are supposed to live.

I can't keep from rejoicing when I learn that some slaves have reached Canada by means of the U.G.R.R.—the *Under Ground Rail Road,* an imaginary railway invented to account for the way in which the slaves make their escape. Thirty arrived in Canada four or five days ago, which means a loss of at least $30,000 for the South, and a good thing, say I, and too bad it wasn't more. Another slave—escaping, I think, from Virginia—managed to get a hold on a piece of lumber protruding from a ship and was able to go on hanging from it for two or three nights without anyone's noticing. He was tossed up and down with every motion of the sea water during this whole time. Finally when he was completely exhausted he cried out for someone to come to his aid, and the people actually had a hard time locating him. The arm by which he had been hanging had been scraped bare of flesh right down to the bone, but no one paid the slightest attention to how much he was suffering and he was taken back to the state from which he had come. Even in the face of this sort of thing there are still some Americans so lacking in humanity as to assure you that the Negroes are perfectly happy and don't want to be free! There was still another slave who got as far as Boston where he was recaptured by his owners, and even though there were several riots, he was taken back to the state he had come from.[8]

In spite of the hatred of violence that I feel at the present time, I should get untold pleasure from holding one of these butchers still while his slaves tickled him with a whip. This would even be showing the slaveholder real charity, because it would rid him of the idea that the blacks are not human beings. But however things turn out, the day will come when they will be punished, and if not at the hands of man, then at the hands of One who will never let them escape!

I think after all that if nothing turns up in the next few days I'll go out and find some work to do on the land. That will be good for my bodily health as well as for the health of my soul. In these times a man can easily earn $14 or $15 a month over and above his board, etc., and although it is a long time since I've done any really hard work, I think I should be able to earn that much or almost as much. I could have an understanding that for the first week I would do only as much as I am capable of doing until I again get used to heavy labor. I am impatient to get a little piece of land where I can be my own boss, but those little pieces of land are not easy to find except in the *Far West,* so I'll have to work for wages for a while before I'll be able to get one. Still, that's all to the good because it will give me time to choose my occupation after mature deliberation and after learning what God wishes me to do. Sometimes, when I think of the poor Canadians, and often too of the poor Savoyards,[9] I'd like to be in a position to enlighten them, especially the latter. It's a pity that Savoy can be so beautiful and yet be plunged into such darkness; for this reason I've been glad to learn that they are beginning to make some headway with missionary work there.

Perhaps there will soon be some big news, inasmuch as people here expect a war with Spain over Cuba, which the Americans of the southern states of the U.S.A. would like to have as another

*Slave State.* Do you know that there is talk of recalling the American naval squadron from African waters so the slave trade may be resumed? This makes me grieve for the Americans because they are heaping up such a terrible store of divine wrath by their conduct. Christian people here are deeply afflicted by this state of things and are working might and main for the good cause. But for the present evil is getting the upper hand over the good and will do so until God teaches them to let His will be done, for He too has some right to be heard in these matters, though the South denies it to Him. There is a great deal of excitement here about all this, but before long everything will peter out again. The Northerners aren't able to keep their minds on one idea for very long at a time. The Southerners persevere in their evil ways, and the Northerners do not hold fast to the good; for this reason I believe God will do without them and will act by Himself.

And now let me thank you all for your letters. I may be far away from here when you receive this one, but such is man's earthly lot. Good-bye, dearest Parents, and pray for me always. *Au revoir.*

T. Bost

In the summer of 1854, when school was out, Theodore left Burlington and returned to the Swiss mission at La Grande Ligne.

**Theodore to his mother**

> T. Bost
> St. Johns, C.E.
> August 11, 1854
> (mailed the fifteenth)

Dearest Mother:

I've taken a job here for two months peddling religious literature for a Bible Society. The work is hard and there are lots of painful moments, but I do my duty as best I can. So far I haven't actually been beaten, but I've been on the receiving end of an unending stream of insults, which is good for me, seeing that it proves to me that I am following the right road. The worst part is having to go about on foot in the terrible heat we have been having this summer for nearly six weeks now, between 26°R. [Réaumur, or 90.5°F.] and 32°R. [104°F.] in the shade; a number of observations have put it even above 35°R. [111°F.] in the shade, but I rely only on the lower figures.[10] The nights are stifling and I can't drink the water, so for three weeks I've been tortured by thirst. You can't get any good wine here, and I don't like to add brandy to my water as everyone here advises me to do. I drink as many as ten cups of tea per day — tea containing as much pepper as anything else, so as to give it some flavor, according to what people say. I can hardly wait for the hot weather to finish, but we'll get at least another two weeks of it. The other day, in the course of one of my rounds, I asked for a bed for the night. They didn't show it to me until I was about to turn in: it was nothing but a box five feet long — I am five feet nine inches tall — and four feet wide, in the bottom of which they had put a little bag of feathers covered with a piece of linen that seemed of very dubious cleanliness. The man who showed it to me said in all seriousness: "It's a bit short for you, but you can just make yourself into a triangle." I was feeling sick, but the idea of making myself into a triangle kept me laughing right up to the instant when I fell asleep. I had no light of any kind, so I searched in vain for the sheets; anyhow, there weren't any, and I finally had to be content with a piece of woolen blanket. I slept fairly well, but all my joints were stiff when I woke up. In general, the Canadians have no independence of mind and that makes it hard, not to say impossible, to sell Bibles.

I think, too, that I'll be able to finish my two months [at this job] — I shall already have finished one when this letter goes into the mail. I will have saved about $20, I think, and this should be just barely enough to pay my way out to the West. Still, my three years here are far from having been wasted; it's true that I haven't saved any money, but I've gained a lot of experience: I've learned to know the country and its people, their customs and their language, all of which will be very useful to me; and on top of all that, I have undergone enough small tests of character to know that I can patiently endure the trials and the numerous disappointments of this life. I have learned to forgive injuries and to count on nobody except the poor when I needed help. These trials have been hard, sometimes very hard. I haven't told you about them for fear of causing you pain, but now that it's all in the past and I have gotten the hang of how people live in this country, I can tell you all this. People have discouraged me from attempting anything and have given me no help at all, even when they could easily have done so. I have tried my best to do the right thing, but now I see my way clearly, and with God's grace I shall not go on making so many stupid mistakes.

In all my thinking about the West I know I am building all kinds of castles in Spain, and yet I am fully prepared to find the stones hard. I am somewhat accustomed to disappointments, so that if my castles should crumble, they won't crush me under their ruins. (I think I am becoming quite an orator.) I am beginning to be an American; I am no longer eager, as I was three years ago, to clear a piece of land and then live on it to the end of my days; I am becoming a *go ahead man,* and my sole ambition is to get out into the wide-open spaces. I've taken my time reaching this decision to leave the East, but if it pleases God to let things come to pass in this fashion, I shall not let much more time go by until I move on from here.

Good-bye, dearest Parents, or rather *au revoir* if such be God's pleasure.

Your most affectionate
T. Bost

At the end of the summer of 1854, Theodore went to teach in a new institution, the Hedding Literary Institute, which had just been established in Ashland, New York, a small village in the Catskills. The principal was the Rev. Thomas B. Pearson, Professor of Moral Philosophy and Evidence of Christianity. The faculty numbered eleven persons, offering instruction in mathematics, civil engineering, natural sciences, ancient languages, literature, music, anatomy, physiology and hygiene, drawing and painting, and decorative arts. Theodore was Professor of Modern Languages.

**Theodore to his parents**

Ashland, Green County
New York
February 6, 1855

Dearest Parents:

It seems to me that only a month ago I was only twenty years old, and now I'm twenty-one! What a lot of changes have occurred in these last four years! To begin with, I was at home, young, very young, knowing nothing at all about the world, and now I am several thousand miles from home, still young but more experienced, having been a farmer in New York State, a missionary-schoolteacher in Canada, a *French Teacher* in Vermont, again in Canada a peddler, a fisherman, etc., and now once more a

*French Teacher* in the State of New York with the virtual certainty of being 1,200 miles from here in eight months! Uncle Sam's farm is a big one, especially if you consider that after I've arrived there [in the Midwest] I'll still be less than halfway from here to Oregon.

What you say, dear Mother, about the rise in land prices, which might prevent me from buying any, has brought back to me the ideas I had about America when I was in Europe. You needn't worry on this score. The Territory of Minnesota, the place I want to go, covers 166,000 square miles, which is 106,000,000 acres; it is about 400 miles square, extending from 46° 30' to 49° north latitude, and in one place to 50°. If I can't find enough land there, and if you can lend me enough money, I can go out and buy you a few more hundred million acres just by going a little farther to the South or West. It is only five years since Minnesota was declared a Territory, and I think it will probably be admitted to the Union as a State next year. I have bought a book, *Minnesota and Its Resources;*[11] it is very interesting, very impartial, giving the bad side as well as the good, and seeking only to attract those who have strength, courage, and goodwill, but giving assurances that such people will succeed. The climate is like that of [eastern] Canada but much more uniform. Often there are several weeks when everything moves by sled, which is an enormous advantage to those who have grain or merchandise to transport, and for healthy young people, the cold weather there can be nothing but a benefit; in fact, I will go even further and say that this cold weather is life-giving. The thing that does a person harm in Canada is the continual instability of the temperature, with changes of as much as 30 °R. [67.5 °F.] in the space of twelve hours in winter, and I don't know how much in the summer. In Minnesota the first hard frosts come later than here also. . . .

You can see that I am eager to get back to working the land, but at the same time I want, if I do go back to farming, to take some of my friends from Canada out to Minnesota with me to form a sort of colony of Protestant Christians and build ourselves a church—or rather, not to be an exclusive congregation but to consider every Christian a brother, naturally without drawing any distinction among sects, and to recognize no other power than that of God in our church. At the same time, we should always be ready to listen to the advice of more advanced Christians and to follow it. We Baptists take an active stand only against the power of the minister *as minister* and not [simply] as a Christian.

Perhaps you think me too independent, dear Father; but it seems to me that if every Christian does his duty in everything that concerns him, keeping close to the Bible and listening to the counsels of other Christians, then there is no need for a power to be instituted among them to make the whole machine run; and if, on the other hand, you put the slightest power into human hands, it seems to me that unless you go on to become a Jesuit there is no place on this slope where you can reasonably come to a stop. For some time now I have thought about preparing for the ministry, but I no longer see any need to do so. If I go out to settle in the West, I think I will be able to do just as much good without being ordained. I am repelled by everything that is too much bound up with ceremony, and in all formal ordinations it seems to me that there is a whole multitude of things that are at odds with biblical simplicity.

The only two ceremonies I love are baptism and communion, administered with biblical simplicity and without the long faces people are in the habit of putting on in the second of these, even when that long face is not very much in harmony with their inner feelings. As for baptism, I can see beauty in it only when it is done by immersion; otherwise I see in it only an imperfect symbol of cleansing, and I don't see in it any trace of the notion of burial.[12] I hold all the more firmly to the former because I seem to observe in many Christians an unforgivable laziness. In order to earn two or three dollars they would take all sorts of risks, but when it comes to obeying one of God's commandments, which seems a bit difficult for them sometimes, they quickly take cover under the excuse that obedience to this one commandment won't save their souls. Furthermore, they well know that no one has ever contracted the slightest illness from being baptized even in the terribly cold weather of the winters we have here. Certainly there are a great many things more important than baptism, but that's no reason for closing ones eyes to this commandment.

But . . . enough of all that. I don't know why I always turn my letters into inventories of all my thoughts. Once I get going on one of these subjects I can find no stopping place except by coming to an abrupt halt. One thing I would like to know is whether in Europe the Methodists shout and scream in such an outrageous way as the American Methodists do while a few others are trying to pray. It is shocking sometimes to listen to them; it is so scandalous that you want to stop up your ears. And they tell me that I can't see the beauty of these exclamations because there isn't enough of the spirit of God in me! It would be all very well if their shouting came from the heart; in that event I'd forgive them for preventing me from hearing the prayer; but [their cries] come from the lungs rather than from the heart. This keeps me from attending their prayer meetings because I always feel nauseated when they are over. I feel sure you'd agree with me completely if you ever once listened to them.

It's after midnight, and I must go to bed because tomorrow morning I must get up early, at 5:30, and take this letter to the post office. Could you not send me from time to time some French newspapers in exchange for some from here? Good-bye, dear Parents, may God be with you all.

> Your most devoted and loving
> Theodore

My friendliest greetings to all my brothers.

# III

# Westward to Minnesota

Four months after his twenty-first birthday, Theodore gave up school teaching with relief and headed for the frontier. His thoughts had been turning toward Minnesota for some time, but his decision was probably precipitated by the fact that the Hedding Institute had run into serious financial difficulties, so that the faculty's salaries were far in arrears by the spring of 1855. French had never been a popular subject there, so Theodore's classes had remained discouragingly small and his salary correspondingly low. With his meager savings and some money he was able to borrow from a female colleague, he had barely enough to pay his railroad and steamship fare—but not to buy much food along the way—to St. Paul. He left Ashland by stagecoach early on a Monday morning at the end of April and reached Chicago the following Saturday, May 5. By the next Monday afternoon, May 7, his steamboat, the *Golden Era*, had entered Lake Pepin and it must have tied up in St. Paul that evening or early the following morning. Penniless and exhausted, he set out to find a job—any job.

**Theodore to his parents**

> April 30, 1855
> En route by way of
> Oakhill and then? . . .
> then at St. Paul

Dearest Parents:

Well, here I am on my way West. I left [Ashland] this morning, Monday, at seven o'clock and had dinner in Acra at one. . . . Now, at seven in the evening, I am here in Oakhill, the railroad station across the river from Catskill. I crossed the Hudson in a small boat. The river is three-quarters of a mile wide here, but that isn't exactly a marvel for me after seeing the Richelieu and the St. Lawrence.

No doubt Timothée has written you that the Trustees have rented the Institute for one dollar [a year] to Mr. Pearson and the business manager. We could all of us bring suit, which we would win, to obtain payment of our salaries for the entire year, but since the Trustees don't have a penny to their names, they wouldn't be able to pay us. Inasmuch as Mr. P. didn't need eleven teachers for only sixty students, he has dismissed six of us, and two others are leaving in addition. During last month's vacation I spent $25 for clothing, etc., thinking I would be staying on there for the whole summer; but this money—though I need it badly at the moment—hasn't been wasted because these clothes will last me, I think, a long time. The Trustees still owe me $16 over and above the money they caused me to spend unnecessarily and in addition to the hardship of being thrown out of work.

I have made up my mind to make a clean break with the eastern part of America and go out West to see if I don't have better luck there—I hope so. Besides the $25 I had left, I borrowed $6 from the business manager and a lady named Teucher gave me $5 more, but I will send this money to her when I can because the lessons I gave her were more a pleasure for me than hard work. Yesterday they were asking me, "Where will you go?" "I don't know." "What will you do?" "I don't know." And that's the truth. But I intend to keep going straight West and work at whatever turns up. One of my American friends who overheard my answers as I've just quoted them said to me, "You are one of those who will succeed because you talk this way; but all the same I wouldn't want to be in your shoes just now." "I'm not worried a bit," I told him, "God will provide." I made part of today's journey in the company of this American, who was one of my fellow teachers, and only when I took final leave of him did I begin to feel really and truly alone, utterly alone, but I didn't shed any tears over that, even though I am a person who weeps easily and even though I am leaving some very good friends. May God bless them all!

Catskill is 35 miles south of Albany and 160 miles from New York City. Ashland is 50 miles to the West in the Catskill Mountains. Just now the weather is quite cold. Nowhere between Ashland and Catskill did I see any leaves on the trees. In an hour I leave for Albany and go from there to Buffalo at the tip of Lake Erie; then, if pleases God, I'll go by railroad over—or rather, beside and above—Niagara Falls and will go on into Upper Canada

[Ontario] and on to Detroit (Michigan), to the west of Lake St. Clair. After that God will show me what I am to do and where I am to go. I plan to be traveling five days and nights without stopping, but I have the strength for it. In the European trains a person can sleep, but in this country, where more passengers get on every five miles, making a big uproar and waking everybody up, and where sudden bumps and lurches of the train toss you up in the air without warning, there is little chance of getting any sleep. I am writing in pencil, not having a portable inkwell, but I hope you'll be able to read this letter just the same. I would like also for you to keep it in a safe place because, some day in the future, I should like very much to reread my first letters from America and especially this one which describes such a great change in my life. Up to now I haven't really been in America, but in a kind of second-rate, aborted Europe, or however you choose to express it.

This morning I was feeling a little sorry for myself, thinking that I was about to take leave of my cultivated friends and that from now on I shall be thrown entirely among common people. I was surprised to find how much more aristocratic I am than I was three years ago; I hope that I shall soon be able to correct this fault. There are riff-raff in all classes; there were two among our teachers, and there are plenty of them everywhere you go. These two, after insulting the lady teachers, went after me, saying that Americans have a perfect right to insult foreigners whenever they feel like it. I didn't deny that this was so, but hit one of them (who had learned how to box) right between the eyes, knocking him flat on his back. He threatened to kill me, and I laughed in his face. The whole faculty was disappointed that I had called it quits after just one blow and thought I should have kept it up. Nevertheless, the committee told me they hoped I wouldn't strike him again. I replied to them in a strongly worded letter, and they admired my reply. I don't exactly see what they found in it to admire because it was a long diatribe against the Americans. It appears that the other two came out of the incident with a strong reprimand from the committee because they've left and haven't come back. I am positive that if I hadn't hit him, they would have thought I was admitting myself to be in the wrong, and they have shown enough common sense to see that it was something really serious that made me use my fists. Since this incident, all the teachers, both men and women, have shown me a great deal more friendship than before, and so have a lot of students. This is how you have to behave here, even among Christians. If a man [doesn't defend himself], he is called a coward and no one considers him worth very much. If he makes other people respect him, no matter how, he is a fine fellow . . . and there is some truth in this way of looking at it. In a country and at a time in which everybody looks out only for himself and nobody looks out for other people, everyone has a right to stand up for himself. We ourselves are the only neighbors we have, and, though it troubles me very much, I quite often have to act on this principle. But enough for tonight; before the week is out I'll have enough news to fill up this letter . . .

Wednesday morning, in the Ohio woods

Yesterday, when we arrived in Buffalo, we missed the cars (second class) that go by way of Niagara Falls, and, since I didn't want to pay the $13 it would have cost to go on to Chicago in first class, I've taken the line that follows the shore of Lake Erie. It is a glorious day and everything is green here; I'm sending you a violet from these woods, not so much for itself, but just because it seems like a nice gesture. But good-bye for now: the cars are half a mile from here where I left them awaiting the arrival of another part of the train. To fill in the time I have been for a walk in the woods — the country around here is magnificent. When we get to Cleveland, on Lake Erie, I'll eat my first meal since Monday noon. Good-bye.

Half an hour later

Last Friday a [railroad] bridge 1,200 feet long was completely destroyed by fire. We all had to get out of the train and, making a detour, cross the river on foot, and now we are waiting for a train coming from Cleveland. I lunched in the temporary station at one end of the bridge; I had a little cake and two hard-boiled eggs. The country gets more and more beautiful as we go along. The number of prospective settlers, both foreigners and natives, on their way out West is unbelievable. There are 400 on the express train that has just left. In second class, where I am, we have three or four hundred. At the moment they are crossing the footbridge in the village where we are; a flock of sheep bars the way — the whole scene is laughable. . . . Speaking of burned bridges, the number of accidents is frightening. Yesterday in Buffalo I saw them picking up a man who had just been run over by a locomotive and had his arm badly crushed. This caused a few minutes' excitement, then it was all over and people stopped talking about it because they are used to this kind of thing; but as for me, it makes me shiver just to think about it.

The railroad advertisements say that you can go from Buffalo to Chicago, second class, in twenty-three hours. I think these must be "sterling hours"[1] because we've been on the road for sixteen hours and have covered only about 190 miles, with 570 miles or thereabouts to go; besides, we'll probably have to wait half a day for another train. In the meantime, I will end my letter and go look for my poor old trunk, which has been taking a great deal of harsh treatment from the Americans.

Saturday, Chicago
at the Southwestern end of Lake Michigan

It's odd what sort of impressions your mind receives when you're very tired. I am worn out and very disheartened [bien noir]. I need to spend a Sunday in church where I can be close to God.

Sunday morning, on board the Golden Era,
on the Mississippi River

The view of this river, with its innumerable islands, is magnificent. But the boat vibrates too much, so I can't write properly. I will include more details in my next letter.

Sunday evening

I've just realized for the first time since I boarded the steamboat that I haven't yet seen the Mississippi at its widest point. From the time we left Galena in northern Illinois until now we have been continually making our way among these islands. Several times we have stopped to take on firewood, once or twice in Iowa and once at an island belonging to Wisconsin. The oddest thing is that except for these islands you hardly see any of the country itself. The river is enclosed between two series of cliffs [bluffs], each about a hundred feet high and heavily wooded, and nowhere are they low enough to let you see what is beyond them. People say that at their summit begins a perfectly flat plateau.

Every mile or so we stop to let off settlers at places that have only two, three, four, or half a dozen houses, all of them just built. On leaving Galena we had five or six hundred migrants on this floating pigsty of a New and Splendid Steamer Golden Era! What rascals the Americans are! They rob the foreigner and they rob each other, all the while remaining "good Christians." It would give me great pleasure if I could get my hands on our purser for just five minutes, long enough to teach him not to collect higher fares than he is entitled to from immigrants. I will write soon to Glasgow with more details—many, many more.

I am weak with weariness, having had only a few hours of sleep in the last eight days and having begun to eat only last night. Today I am eating my head off. I paid the extra fare as a cabin passenger [rather than a deck passenger] in order not to arrive half dead at my destination. For a trip of 560 miles I pay $7, which includes my room and meals. The food is excellent, and the sleeping arrangements would be fine if there weren't so many of us: 150 other cabin passengers sharing the accomodations with me, sleeping on mattresses laid flat on the floor of the saloon (you may as well say, on the floor itself); and then, naturally, there are the *deck passengers* who sleep outside in the open air. If it pleases God, tomorrow night or Tuesday morning I shall be in St. Paul. Pray for me because, though I am fairly courageous, I find my position—alone and homeless as I am in America—a little bit forlorn. If one of our family or one of my Canadian friends should be waiting to welcome me, I wouldn't exactly be moved to tears of sorrow. *Adieu.*

Monday afternoon

Just now we are on Lake Pepin, which is fifty miles long and two, three, or four miles wide. A very pretty lake, but still closed in by hills like the rest of the Mississippi valley. We'll get there tonight, I hope, and tomorrow I'll begin making some calls. I will go and see the editor of a newspaper to whom I wrote some time ago and who sent me a very polite reply. . . . [The remainder of the letter is missing.]

**Theodore to his brothers, Ami and Timothée, in Glasgow**

St. Paul, May 26, 1855

My very dear Brothers:

I am addressing the envelope containing this letter to you, but the letter itself is for my parents; you may read it too and then send it on to them afterward. You will see why I am sending it first to you.

Dear Parents, may God be praised! I've finally found a job,

a rather strange one from some points of view, yet I hope a fairly well-paid one. But what a lot of agony I had to go through before I found it! On my arrival here I put up at the hotel from which I wrote to you, paying $6 a week, and yet it is far from being a good hotel. I shared my room with another fellow; there was no window; the sheets were clean only in places; there was no chair; and so on. . . . There are many worse ones, but the food is so bad that working men can't stand it very long.

So I stayed one week, but when I came to pay my bill, I had only $5.93. A Swiss young man lent me seven cents, and I handed over my money to the hotelkeeper without saying a word. He, judging from my air of indifference and from my good clothes, which I had put on for the occasion, seemed to think I was at least as rich as Rothschild. A young man had told me to come back in two days and he would give me a job. So I stayed on at the hotel, since I had to stay somewhere, without a cent in my pocket. Hence I was unable to write to you, because one must put five cents in postage on letters to France. Nor could I write to Ashland because domestic mail also requires stamps. I kept on wearing my fine clothes so as to make people believe in them, as they say in Canada; and although hotel bills are supposed to be paid every week, they let me stay a week and a half without paying. During that time I walked between fifteen and twenty-five miles a day without finding any employment. One day I went with a Baptist minister to see the postmaster, but he didn't need anyone. I went to see a merchant, but he had no openings; at the sawmill, too, all the jobs were filled; the carters already had too many workers; the same with the farmers no help wanted! No money to leave town and no money to stay! Unable to pay my hotel bill and unable, by the same token, to leave in order to find cheaper lodgings—because then they would have learned that I had no money—I was getting desperate, and I would have come back to Europe to fight in the Crimean War rather than remain in this land of America where people make money on such a vast scale! I suffered a good deal for all these reasons, yet I was obliged to act as though I didn't have a care in the world. If I've got to suffer, I told myself, I'd prefer to be miserable in Europe; there, at least, I would be among my relatives. And frankly, if I had to go through four more years like the last four, I would sign on as a soldier rather than remain here.

In the end a Baron de Freudenreich,[2] a Swiss, who has taken a strong interest in me, told me I had already had so much hard luck that I couldn't possibly have much more and that I would soon begin to have a run of good luck. I am fortunate in having a more solid basis for my hopes than belief in good or bad luck. The next day he told me to go see a certain M. Burnand (not Bornand), a Vaudois;[3] but when I got there this gentleman had just left for New York.

So then he said he would introduce me to Captain Dodd,[4] a road-building contractor who works for the government. I went to see him right away to ask for employment as a common laborer, and I came into his office just at the moment when about forty men were signing a labor contract. When I saw what the terms were, I hesitated because you had to agree to stay on the job until the road is completed this coming November, working the whole summer from sunrise to sunset either at cutting down trees or at pulling them up by the roots, or else at digging ditches alongside the new road; I was to sleep outdoors under a single blanket that I would carry with me every day the same distance our road-making had advanced. The food, naturally, would be more or less good, and for five months no one would need a change of clothing! Always the same clothes, day and night for five months—that would be no joke. I waited until the men had left the room and then told Captain Dodd that I would like a job where my head and legs, which are good, would be of more use to him than my arms.

Baron de Freudenreich supported my arguments, and Dodd finally said he would take me on for a few days on trial, so as to see whether I would actually be able to keep the workmen's accounts, whether I was sufficiently up-and-coming, etc., and that afterward he would pay me a wage at least equal to that of the workmen. They earn $25 for every twenty-six days of work, plus their food and shelter; the shelter doesn't amount to much, it is true. It would be my job to call the workmen [to meals] when the horn was blown at midday and at the end of the day, and to keep records of each man's earnings; perhaps, too, there would be some surveying and measuring for me to do.

I am by nature hardworking, and when it comes to walking, he won't find one American in a thousand, perhaps even ten thousand, who can beat me at it. I shall have to live under the same conditions as the rest of the crew, sleeping outdoors. It may be that we shall have tents, and I hope God will grant me the blessing of good health. Next Thursday I'll take my Bible, some extra pairs of socks, an undershirt, a suit of good clothes, and a pair of working trousers, and leave with the whole crew to where they are beginning to make the road, seventy-two miles from here. We shall all travel on foot, and I can hardly wait to see those Irish and Germans trying to keep up with me and Captain Dodd. The hardest part of my job will be to look out for Dodd's interests without getting on the bad side of the Irish; they hate all overseers, and the latter have to be continually on their guard; sometimes they [the Irish] take it into their heads to beat up a supervisor. But Dodd will soon straighten them out. They have agreed in their contracts not to quarrel or get into fights, and if they lay a finger on me, the Law will deal with them! But I hope they'll behave like men. Besides, if my arms are not equal to the task, which I suspect will be the case, I can always fall back on my legs, which will quickly get me out of danger.

My hotelkeeper is standing here in front of me as I write; his eyes seem to be devouring me; his nose and his chin almost touch. Well, what of it? I show no concern, and if he tells me to get out, I'll say "All right." I think the Baron will help me out in a pinch. But all this is very painful for me. I simply could not stay any longer in the Eastern states—the labor market is glutted. And out here it seems to be the same story!

In order to emigrate to America and do well here one must either have money or belong to the very lowest class in Europe—be poor, very poor, before leaving, knowing what it is to suffer from hunger. Otherwise I should never advise a young man to come here looking for work; it's too hard and monotonous. This is the first time I've written to you in this mood; I don't like to write to you when I am feeling discouraged, and when I wrote to you before, I always tried to make myself feel happy. But for several months now I have suffered too much to be able to go on writing to you in the same vein for fear that you may encourage other young men to come here. Someone who wants to be a teacher may come and be successful, but I know people who have tried that line of work and have done nothing for fourteen years. Others, too, may find work, but if they have no money, the chances are a hundred to one that they won't get anywhere either. A young man who has a few hundred dollars can do very well for himself, but if not, the odds are all against him. This is my considered opinion, and before coming to it I struggled against it for four years. Life is hard in America, and there are very few pleasures to be had if you are single and have no family with you. Perhaps it will cause you some pain to find me thinking like this, but I would rather give you the whole story, once and for all, about the little trials and tribulations of living in America. If I were the only one whose affairs had gone badly, I wouldn't say anything—but how many there are! It's true that if a man perseveres, he may very well succeed, but it is far from certain. And by making the same effort one may achieve an equally good station in life without leaving Europe.

This Baron de Freudenreich is from Berne, a handsome man, six feet two or three inches tall, the former manager of the Alpina settlement, the one where M. Suchard [5] from Neuchâtel worked for so long, and he has already found good positions in this country for a considerable number of young Swiss. When you meet a man like that along your way it is a real pleasure. The road on which we are going to work goes from Mendota to the Big Sioux River [which flows into the Missouri at Sioux City]. You won't find Mendota on any of your maps, but it is south of St. Paul, how far exactly I don't know.[6] I know there is a distance of seventy-two miles involved, but I'm not sure whether it's from here to Mendota or from there to the Sioux River. The road we are going to be building (the length of which I've forgotten) will go through forests, across the prairies and rivers, and will be a great thing for this region. The government publishes an announcement that on a certain day it will let the contract to build a certain road to contractors, and the one who offers to do it for the least money gets the contract. At first I thought that was silly, but it is fair enough. The successful bidder hires his men and makes such arrangements as he sees fit to make, just so long as the road is finished by a certain stated time.

Well, I will now turn to other subjects. The temperature [*sic*] [7] here is extremely dry this year—no rain since the month of November and only a few inches of snow that stayed on the ground about six weeks. This is normal enough for the winter, but there are always the spring rains. As a result, the Mississippi and all the other rivers are very low. Three or four steamboats have gone aground on sandbanks; they get them moving again by long beams, pulleys, and various mechanical contrivances—it's interesting to watch. People fear for this year's harvest if it doesn't rain soon. The temperature here is 94!

The other day the Winnebago Indians, who have promised to leave all of the territory to the east of the Mississippi, passed through St. Paul, several hundred of them in all. They went down the Mississippi, starting from below the Falls of St. Anthony, in their canoes, a distance of eighteen miles as the river flows. Most of them went and gathered in front of the Capitol in St. Paul, and while their Chief held a discussion with the Governor, they started up a war dance that lasted for three hours. Most of them were wearing nothing but a small loincloth; others, in addition to this strict minimum, had on leggings cut from trousers that began at the ankle and reached to a little above the knee; only a few—not including the dancers—had blankets; in general, the women and girls were decently clothed. All the dancers were horribly painted, with their heads covered with feathers and their tobacco pipes stuck into the tresses of their hair. Their dancestep was like trampling something underfoot. With their bodies bent forward and their legs always bent at the knees, they moved forward, striking the ground twice at each step, first with the right foot and then with the left, then jumping again on the right foot, all in a very rapid tempo, shouting "Oo oo, oo oo, oo oo," and so on and so forth. When they got to the middle of the circle where the musicians were, they let out blood-curdling screeches and then turned laughing toward the outside of the ring.

The music was performed on two old butterbarrels with skins stretched over the open end, two tambourines, and five or six rattles fastened to a stick, all following the tempo, or rather giving the beat to the "Oo oo, oo oo" of the dancers; as a result, the chanting they produced was almost frightening for its monotony. Some of them had remarkably handsome legs; during the dancing, or rather the trampling action, it was a pleasure to watch the rippling of their leg muscles, which always occurred without any muscular movement at all in the upper part of the body—only the legs were moving. Several had very attractive faces, and their skins were so light that they must be descended from French Canadians. After three hours of dancing the group broke up and they paddled their canoes back up the Mississippi. It was a pleasant sight to see the line of canoes moving over the water, with the women paddling along with the men.

The poor Indians! It filled my heart with sadness to see them going away. They are headed for a region where there is very little game and where the Sioux have threatened to kill them if they intrude, but the government is forcing them to go just the same. The authorities forbid the sale of strong liquor to Indians, but one day while walking in the woods I saw approaching a drunken Indian whom three or four others were trying to restrain. He wanted to fight. When I saw the state he was in, I made a sharp turn to the left, letting them go past; then I continued my stroll. Inasmuch as I was a lone white man, he might have had designs on my scalp, and I am too attached to it to get along easily without it.

Yesterday I went to see the Falls of St. Anthony, but whether it was boredom or fatigue or just that I've seen so much water lately, I couldn't see any beauty in them at all. There wasn't much water; just a stretch half a mile wide and big piles of *logs* and trash from the sawmills that had come to rest just on the lip of the falls. I found all that so mean and tawdry that I went on for another eighth of a mile, sat down on a log, took off my shoes and stockings, and washed my feet—isn't that a down-to-earth detail! —and this right in the middle of the falls of the "mighty Mississippi." I let my feet hang over the falls, which was very refreshing; in fact, that was all the benefit I got from that twenty-mile hike. When I had read descriptions of these falls I had been prepared to see another Niagara, but even though I haven't seen the latter, I don't hesitate to state that the Falls of St. Anthony are nothing but a pale copy of Niagara Falls.

It's true that for some time now the beauties of nature have had little effect on me, and yet when I think of the Alps and our Swiss lakes, I often have a hard time keeping the tears from coming. This happened to me just the other day while I was reading a few words about the Alps. But, though I am often discouraged, I am determined to go marching straight ahead; I intend to do my duty, and God will do the rest. I don't want to hurry things but to walk in the path of faith, hoping that my position will soon be more clear and less unpleasant. Probably the soldiers in the Crimea would give a lot to exchange places with me.

I have just had an interruption. I was writing in the barroom of the hotel, and I spoke with Dodd's clerk about my money. He promised to see to it. I told him that I didn't even have any postage stamps, and without comment he handed over four with a request that I should write a letter to his sister for him. I've never seen her and don't know the first thing about her, but anyhow I'm going to sit down and write to her as if I were her brother. He is too lazy to do it and told me to just tell her whatever came into my head. I haven't done much writing in English, having never studied it, but never mind, I can already write it pretty well—almost without making mistakes. It's a good idea to know how to do a little of everything.

I am thankful to God for having solved, at least for the present, my money problems in this way. I hope I'll be able to repay all my debts in a month or two, provided Dodd doesn't go bankrupt (he has done so before this, like my dear friends at Ashland), or provided that after having given me a trial he doesn't find that there is one employee on his payroll he can do without. The Americans are a rascally lot, but whatever happens, they can't kill me; and anyhow even if they kill me I couldn't be more wretched than I am—though a person can be happy on this earth if he does his duty.

These misfortunes have done me good by bringing me closer to God. When something good comes along, I am tempted to rely only on my own strength and to forget to pray, thinking that I must help myself before praying to God for His aid; but this time the weight of my troubles was a little too much, so I have been praying more than I usually do. It does one a lot of good to pray. Even if you don't see any tangible results, you are happier after a good, long prayer.

Thousands of pigeons are flying over the city continually. People [who come out] from the city and people inside the city shoot into the thick of them, and every three or four shots a pigeon veers to the left or to the right, lowers its head, and falls dead to the ground. Sometimes they fall into the river and drown after being killed by the lead pellets. The poor creatures! To have to die twice! There are also many wild ducks, prairie hens, and quail. The river is full of excellent fish. I was mistaken when I said I was twelve or thirteen hundred miles from New York; we are actually fifteen or sixteen hundred miles away: 144 from New York to Albany, 298 from there to Buffalo, 543 from there to Chicago, 171 from Chicago to Galena, and 405 miles from Galena to here. It is amusing to hear people newly arrived from the East speaking about the *western* Great Lakes, for those lakes are now all to the east of us.

I hope it rains between now and Thursday. Since it has to rain sometime, I hope it comes before we set out on our journey, because [if it comes later] it will make the ground soft and we will get our clothes and blankets wet. After five months [*sic*] [8] of this life, I think I know something about what America is like and how pioneers have to live, and if ever I return to Europe I'll know what I'm talking about. One thing that may be of interest to you is that they use gunpowder to blast away rocks right in the city streets; they cover the explosive charge with long, heavy planks and then— boom! Nobody gets excited except a few horses that take the bit in their teeth; the men pay no attention; the ladies let out little shrieks; a few curious bystanders stroll over to look; and then the workmen start preparing another charge. . . .

I'm using a tiny script for this letter, but that's because I have so much to tell you. If I could only find the right words to express my feelings, I'd speak of the emotions I have when I think of you. But I don't like to see emotions written down on paper. One can describe a landscape and the thoughts it gives rise to, but I can never express myself as I'd like to when it comes to describing my feelings. I can call up from memory with astonishing vividness places like Plainpalais, Bourges, Asnières, Melun, Bellevue, Serrières and Neuchâtel, Cudrefin—especially the latter places where (although you didn't know it then) I was thinking a great deal about coming to America.[9] I wanted to leave, and yet I was afraid to go; I felt a need for more activity, a need to develop my abilities, and that I have been able to do, at least up to a point. When I'm forty, I'll be as fully developed as other men are at eighty if things keep on going as they have been. Everybody thinks I'm twenty-five or thirty or even older. When my hair has turned completely white, I'll send you a lock, or rather a whole swatch, because my hair curls like candles.[10] I am a little worried that I may suffer from toothache this summer; I have been having some bad ones these last few days. I cured them by giving up tea drinking again, by taking three doses of medicine in one gulp,[11] by putting ice in my mouth, by scalding my cheek, by rubbing it with a piece of linen, and by sticking pins up under my gums. True, all this is painful enough to get rid of the even greater pain of the toothache. If I don't write again soon, you may conclude that the flies and mosquitoes have eaten me alive in the woods. I don't know how we'll manage this summer with relatives[12] of that ilk.

It is an impressive and beautiful sight to see the steamboats— each one with two engines, some with a single millwheel [paddlewheel] in the stern, others with wheels at the sides. The lowest deck above waterlevel is for the poor immigrants and the livestock; the hold is for merchandise; the second deck, eight feet above the lower one, is for the *cabin passengers;* eight feet higher still and covering only a fourth of the boat is the pilot house, and on top of this cabin is the rudderwheel. And despite this great height, boats carrying 200 passengers and a heavy load of freight can get through shallow places with only thirty-three inches of water, and they do get through even if they have to scrape the bottom—a sandbar was built up this year downstream from Lake Pepin; at that spot there were only thirty to thirty-three inches of water.

When shall I be able to write to you again? And where shall I be then? Shall I be completely committed to that eminently pioneering occupation, roadbuilding? I'll keep you up to date on all that, if it please God, although I may have nothing better than a pencil to write with—but when you go to war, you have to live like a soldier. Please, all of you—write to me often; you keep me company that way. The enclosed violets come, as I have told you, from Ohio; the grass (wild hay) is from one of the Mississippi islands belonging to Wisconsin. Timothée may have the hay; one violet is for Papa and the other is for Mama. I expect your never-ending thanks because these are such magnificent gifts; they cost a lot and are worth a lot. But good-bye for tonight, dear Father, Mother, brothers, and sisters; I am very tired from having walked a long way today, then writing this long letter, writing the one for the clerk, another to the postmaster at Ashland, another to a young lady of the *Faculty*—not a *love letter,* I assure you. but rather one of friendship. . . .

Saturday morning
It has been raining hard all night, so already one of my wishes has come true; if this goes on for another two or three days as it did last night, we shall have had enough rainfall for the entire year. After that will come a hot spell and working will be a real delight. True, for the lumberjacks, all this makes little difference since the rain doesn't make the wood much softer. But the farmers who are good Christians can't help thanking God for this blessing, for in all Episcopal churches and in several others, they have been offering up prayers for rain.

Rereading my letter, I find that I've had some rather harsh things to say about America in some places, remarks that may be particularly unjust inasmuch as I have found what may turn out to be a very good situation with rather good pay and nothing to spend it on; my outlays for clothing, especially, will be small. But perhaps it's better to say what one thinks. It is a fact that a young man who has relatives in Europe, and no *home* in America, can get thoroughly fed up with life.

Good-bye to all of you, dear Father, Mother, Sister, dear Mary [the wife of Theodore's brother Ami]—since this letter will be sent by way of Glasgow—and pray for your faithful and loving

Theodore Bost

**Theodore to his parents**

My tent
Nine miles from St. Peter
July 15, 1855

Dearest Parents:

Having a little time on my hands, I'll write to you in advance.[13] Today is Sunday, the only day I can get any rest. This week the workmen will get their pay, and then I'll know how much I am being paid per month. I am not much worried about that because, even if I am paid no more than the workmen, I have the big advantage of being able to go anywhere I please and can thus find the best location for pitching my tent.

But before I start bringing you up to date, I almost feel that I should ask your pardon for always talking so much about myself, about what I am doing or may do. This causes me a twinge of pain whenever I think about it, when I realize what a strong inclination I have to talk about myself. I believe this may have something to do with the kind of company I'm in; each one tells all about what he has done, and everyone listens attentively. Then when the first has finished, another begins, and so on until everybody has had a turn. The Americans think it is natural and good for a man to blow his own horn and boast of his ability to do anything under the sun. Of course, this doesn't mean that I agree with them.

The crew consists of about a hundred men. We have two camps: one for the loggers and stumppullers and one for the pick-and-shovel men, the graders, and the bridgebuilders. I am always with the loggers, since it is my job to blaze the trail. At present we are following a different route [from that on our official maps] because the government surveyors have made one stupid mistake after another. I am following the old route, the one laid out by Captain Dodd; I try to guess where it makes what seem to be bad detours and why; then, when I think I've got to the right spot, I shout as loud as I can. One of my assistants responds with a single shout from the spot I had started from and then comes directly to where I am, blazing the treetrunks as he comes while I keep on shouting. In this way we are building the road quite straight, since I can make my voice carry a half-mile. Besides having the good effect of enlarging my lungs, this sometimes give me the occasion for a good laugh.

The other day, after I had been feeling quite ill, I set out on one of my shouting trips wearing nothing but my light summer pants. Hundreds of mosquitoes were soon swarming all around me so that I was obliged to keep waving my arms continually. One of the workmen, who knew nothing about my method of marking the route by shouting, heard me yell for ten minutes at a stretch without any apparent reason and saw me make wild motions all the while; he thought for sure I'd gone crazy and went running off in terror to find the cooks who, for a joke, pretended to take him seriously. I overheard him stating his opinion and saying how sorry he was for me, and it was all I could do not to burst out laughing; but when he saw the *bossman* coming out of the woods from the direction where I was shouting, they made so much fun of him that he went running at top speed back to his work. The *bossman* of the lumberjacks is a young British-Canadian, only nineteen and a half years old, the strongest man in the crew and one of the handsomest young men I have ever laid eyes on. Next to him the strongest is a young Swiss from St. Gall, a placid, good-natured youth. After him there are still another three men who are stronger than me, but they are all friendly. As for the rest of the crew, discontented and angry as they are at Dodd, they often make trouble for me, and this means I have to take a domineering tone with them that I don't like. The other assistants and the Captain himself swear like Frenchmen, if not as much as Germans or Irishmen; and inasmuch as I don't want to swear, I am forced to be very abrupt with them and threaten to fire them if they don't do as I say. In fact, in dealing with any of these fellows it is a good thing to be handy with your fists because they are like animals. I do less work than at first because I don't want to kill myself.

I have been sick for a whole week, so I have been sparing myself as much as possible since then. My fever, which settled in my head and was very painful, was the result of having to wear such heavy clothing in the woods during this extremely hot weather, of my having been struck on the head by a falling branch three inches thick, and, above all, the way the crew behaves and the bad-tempered, domineering tone I have to take with them in order to keep the workmen in motion. I have been sleeping and dreaming almost continuously for almost a week; furthermore, at that time [the Fourth of July] some crazy young idiots came in and fired off their guns in the hayloft where I was asleep on the floor. That drove me almost out of my mind, but a few days afterward I was able to eat and drink again. Mrs. Dodd took very good care of me when she saw that I was really sick, and on July 4 she made me lie down on a bed, but I couldn't bear to sleep indoors. I hate the idea of getting undressed; the most I will do is take off my boots. What a strange thing habit is!

One thing that was painful for me, just a little while ago, was to have taken fright during a thunderstorm; I, who never have had the slightest fear of storms, was all atremble for some minutes before it broke. I don't know whether it was because of the nervous condition I've been in for the last several weeks or my lack of trust in God, but I was terrified. The storm struck with incredible violence in the middle of the night, with bolts of lightning coming very close; and the shock, coming on top of the rain's heavy impact, broke the horizontal bar at the top of our tent. It's true that I wasn't the only one who was frightened, and in order to restore some semblance of order I had to make the men laugh. Since that night we've had a number of storms, but we've gotten used to them and are no longer astonished to see big trees being felled by lightning.

Every week we move our camp, advancing about two and a half miles each time. The tentmen go on ahead to clear enough space for seven tents, leveling the ground and digging a little ditch on both sides of the line [of tents] to carry off the rainwater; they dig one or two wells, each one about four or five feet deep, in addition to the wells they dig all along the road so that the men can have water to drink while at work. Then, when *Moving Day* comes, we load up two wagons with the cookstove and our supplies and tents and blankets; and finally we make all our arrangements for the night. Once the camp is in order, we spread hay and unroll our blankets on top of it; then every man stretches out on his bed, the nights being too hot to have anything over us. If it weren't for the mosquitoes, we'd sleep outdoors, but we are forced to stay inside, keeping fires burning outside to prevent them from coming in. And when that isn't enough, we make fires, or rather smudgepots, inside. In addition, I have a *mosquito bar*, some very gauzy cloth that Mrs. Dodd gave me, which gave me pleasure and has been very useful. I sleep underneath it with two of the *bosses*—foremen, that is.

There has been and still is what I'd call *"claim fever"* in the camp. I think I've already told you that wherever the land has not been surveyed it is not yet on sale. Anybody can stake out 160 acres and farm them without paying a cent to anyone. Every workman may occupy one of these lots (or *claims*), which is a very good idea because everything sells for such a high price and a man can make a great deal of money. And when the land is *"in market,"* he can easily pay the $200 for his lot. Everyone wants a claim along the road, on a lake, or on the edge of a marsh in order to have [wild] hay; and everyone will soon be able to get what he wants, but no one has the patience to wait. So every Sunday, twenty or thirty road workers go on scouting expeditions.

I went on one yesterday, which briefly caused a relapse of my brain fever, with chills and shivering; I almost lost consciousness. I either skirted or walked all the way around five lakes in less than five hours, walking twenty-three miles through the woods and swamps, through nettles five or six feet tall—a sign of very rich land—and through places where nothing grows but bushes. We went loping along like famished wolves, saw a deer, then five pretty lakes, each about a mile long on the average; we saw a number of *loons,* a kind of aquatic bird that resembles the *outarde,* ate great quantities of wild currants and gooseberries, saw some dams built long ago by beaver in a place where the Indians make their maple sugar, and observed a party of about thirty Indians with twelve horses camping in a marsh. I lay down at full length on the ground among them to rest while they talked to us in the Indian language, which must have been highly edifying both for them and for us. I drank a little brandy containing rhubarb and some other root extracts at a *claimer's* cabin I came to, ate my supper, and lay down on the ground for an hour. The fever left me then and I got back to the camp around six o'clock in the evening, with my two thick flannel undershirts and my two pairs of trousers as soaking wet as if I had fallen into one of the lakes.

I'd like very much to take up a *claim*, but I think I'll give up the idea because everything is too far from the road we're building, and that is a very important consideration. I prefer to wait, but if I find a *claim* near a lake, near the road, or near a marsh with brush growing on it, I will get it if I can. When there is only brush, you just have to cut everything at ground level, burning the bushes if they are big enough, and then you get a yoke of oxen and start plowing. But for plowing on the open prairie you need two yokes of oxen. With a good *claim* and a man to help him, a person can make a great deal of money; and the sooner I can get established, the better it will be for me. My brain is weary, and when I have a place of my own I'll be able to get a little rest and work all the harder the rest of the time. Everybody keeps telling me I have been working much too hard these last few weeks, and I'm beginning to think that everybody is right. I haven't been so thin for six years, and if I didn't feel that I am better now than before I was sick, I'd give up this job and find something else to do. But in the last few days I have begun to get back my strength, and my color is better; my diet is limited to bread with a little molasses and some coffee, which is all I can manage to swallow. This life is a harsh but attractive one, [I mean] the life of a pioneer who clears the forests, and ours is even worse because we have to move on to another location with different food and water almost every day; we sleep badly and work very hard, even if we don't feel in shape for it. Still, when you look at the product of your work, you feel it's worthwhile.

More than twenty *claims* have been taken up close to our road during the last few days, and next spring hundreds more will be made. This is the road builders' reward. Those who are actively clearing the land will enjoy pleasures that are still sweeter, though not so great—including that of watching their crops grow in place of the brush. Yesterday I saw a magnificent vegetable garden in the middle of the woods. The owner, a Scot who arrived last winter, cut off two or three acres of brush, plowed the land, and now he is looking forward to a splendid harvest of corn, potatoes, cabbages, onions, beets, etc., etc., which he can sell for at least $500. Practically no work is required for their cultivation; there is not one single weed, and the earth, which contains a great deal of humus, retains plenty of moisture. I could almost imagine myself in the Junction Gardens in Geneva,[14] but a look around at the lakes, the Indians, the forests, and the marshes covered with first-class hay standing five feet tall made me soon recall—what I had indeed not forgotten—that I was far from Geneva and in the New, the very New World. Speaking of Geneva, the Swiss who are working here tell me that Geneva is especially beautiful these last few years. Is this true? Oh! "When shall I ever see my beautiful Switzerland again?" is what you often hear the Swiss people around here saying, and I say that myself quite often. But still more often I think of No. 25, rue Chaptal, in Paris.[15]

I have just had to interrupt my writing to stop an Irishman from stealing some bread. He is insolent as all-get-out. I had to shout at him and call down "Thunder" upon his head; this is the strongest profanity I have resorted to up to now, and sometimes it is hard for me not to imitate the Captain and his assistants: these rough Irish boors don't understand gentle language. But I mustn't swear, all the same, because it makes me feel physically sick when I lose my temper and get excited; but it does my soul good when I am provoked to anger because that makes me wish for peace. My Irishman has just returned with two fish he caught with his bare hands in the little stream near which we've made our camp; he has forgotten his ill temper and is all smiles. What a strange bunch of people they are!

The Engineer came today to survey the ground we have cleared, and he says that Dodd is losing about $500 a week. That's not exactly what you'd call making a pile of money. I am unhappy about it on his account, because he already has more than enough trouble. Almost all the workmen hate him because he is continually cursing them and doesn't abide by his agreements with them, so they say. In this they are right, even though I always take his side in front of the men. I have no idea how this road-building project will turn out. We have only finished about a fifth of it, and already half the money voted for this road has been spent. But here I fall back on that generous and delightful American proverb: *"If he pays me, all is right enough."* It's true that everybody has enough troubles without worrying about other people, but how far that principle is from the teachings of Christianity!

The woods here consist almost entirely of basswood, with a few oaks, sugar maples, huge elms, and so on. We often find swarms of bees in the hollow trees, but it's still too early in the season to get much honey from them.

Sunday, the twenty-third

Still another week has gone by and the workmen haven't been paid. We have had a week of rebellion; for two days all the men refused to work, demanding their money, and the Captain has discharged about ten of them. It was wrong of him to do that, and he has told them so many lies to cheat them and to avoid paying them that I took the workers' side against him and contradicted him despite the signs he was making to me to hold my tongue. I told the workmen that they had put in their time and had a right to their money. This could cost me my job, but I had it in my head that "the workman is worthy of his hire," and, in spite of temptation, I did my duty. Since that time he has done his utmost to catch me in some mistake or other, and he tells one lie after another to provoke me. If he tries to fire me in order to replace me with somebody who will agree to let him swindle the workmen, I shall do all I can to stay and will tell the workmen the whole truth about his dealings. The Chief Engineer is against him and will help me if I want him to, but I hope the Captain will mend his ways when he realizes that he hasn't lost as much money as he had thought. I will save the other page [of this letter] until the day he pays up, and that will be a day to remember, as I already foresee.

August 11

Today was payday and a strange one—even a little too much so. The Captain behaved very badly: he fired about twenty workers without paying them off; another twenty picked up and left without collecting even half of what was due them; and fifteen more, to whom he had sworn that he wouldn't pay a cent, have left with all that was owing to them. This was a gang of Irishmen who took the clubs they had continually been threatening to beat me with and went to call on the Captain, finally making him understand that it would be unhealthy to let them go unpaid any longer; so he, like a cowardly clown, paid them in full even though they hadn't worked anywhere near as well as the rest.

But the best part of the business is naturally the way it affects me. I asked him how much he intended to pay me per month; he replied that he would come and talk with me about it the next day and would also give me his instructions for making the road inasmuch as he was planning to be away for three weeks. I thought that sounded rather fishy, but didn't say anything. The next day [there was] no sign of Dodd, nor the day after, nor the days after that. Since I knew he was only ten miles from here, I sent word to him that I needed money and had to see him before his departure. I had been ill for two weeks and in all that time had been unable to eat anything at all. Because bacon and beans are not proper food during these extremely hot spells, I wanted to buy a little milk or butter or some potatoes or anything at all that I (and the rest of us) could digest. Furthermore, since the men were talking about killing him whenever they had the chance, I wanted to settle up my accounts with him. He sent me back his answer: if I was worried about my money, I could leave immediately, and if I waited until he got back he would fire me. This is the only way he has left of getting out of his difficulties—fire any workers who have worked well without paying them.

I have fallen ill in his service; on a number of occasions I have put my life in great peril, have been obliged to pick up a knife to compel a man to let me blaze the trail as I wanted to; I have spent whole nights running errands for him through the woods in the midst of terrible thunderstorms; and I have done my duty in every respect so far as his interests are concerned. All I've received in return are a couple of sets of work clothes and a visit from a doctor, and now he says that he owes me nothing. Very well, *all right Sir, all right!*

His wife gave me $5, and, weak though I was, I started off to walk to St. Paul along a road that had been marked but not yet made. I left with a heavy heart because all the workmen sympathized with me and shook my hand, trying to cheer me up and saying that Dodd is nothing but a rascal and that he will get himself killed one of these days. This is something I am glad to tell you, dear Parents, to disabuse you of the idea that I have a violent nature—all the workmen wished me well and told me that many times they had wanted to beat the daylights out of Dodd and some of his foremen on account of the pointless malice they have habitually indulged in; and that they saw me as Dodd's representative, as someone carrying out his orders. Even the Irishmen who meet up with me now are glad to see me.

But to get back to my departure from the camp. The first day I walked thirty miles without even seeing a house. The woods were soaking wet, and I had mud up to the tops of my boots. I had to keep jumping about without stopping for a distance of sixteen miles on account of the thousands of mosquitoes that would have alighted on me the instant I stopped moving. I was exhausted when at last I came to a house where I spent the night after eating a good supper with milk in my coffee (which was made with good, clear water), potatoes, and other good things. Oh, my dear Parents! I don't think I'm a greedy person, but I was so happy to get a good meal that I was almost glad I had left Dodd. But I was determined to stay with him, sick and weak as I was; I would even have put up with a small wage rather than lose my job. But inasmuch as he has fired me, well, so much the better! Besides, I soon felt much relieved on moral grounds. As long as I stayed with him I was falling into evil ways; he had a great influence on me, as he does on everyone, and I lost my courage, which turned out to be much more an animal feeling dependent on the state of my health than I had supposed. He sometimes intimidated me and kept me from upholding the truth and the rights of the workmen. At the same time, I gave him plenty of reason to be annoyed with me, and so, to get even, he tried at first by despicable lies and strong oaths to make me throw up my job. Among other things, he said to me in front of the men that I had given a voucher signed with Dodd's name to a man named Mieliton and that this man had never worked for him. I denied having done any such thing, and he swore that he had seen it with his own eyes, and that he had gone to the storehouse and had seen the voucher signed in my handwriting for a man whose name I had spelled M.i.e.l.i.t.o.n. Several days later I went to the storehouse; there I was told that he had never set foot inside the place and that there was no voucher for a man of that name. This is only one detail in a thousand, but it will show you what sort of man I had to deal with.

People here (Baron de Freudenreich among others) ask me why I and the sixty men who had been fired didn't simply kill him; the men were just waiting for someone to lead them, and Dodd's knives and revolvers would have been of no help to him against such a big gang. My reply was to tell them that I was too much of an innocent and could never have brought the thing off because I am too kindhearted. Perhaps extremes meet in me without producing a happy medium. The Baron, to whom I gave your message, is an excellent man, but he is opposed to the doctrines and ways of the Methodists. As for myself, I prefer to leave with God the decision to take away Dodd's life if that pleases Him. I know that He hears the cries of the workmen who haven't been paid their wages, and that in one way or another He will pay me. I have the inclination, if you are willing and able to lend me some money, to go and settle near St. Peter, and then we shall see whether he [Dodd] will pay me or not. Nobody really likes him, but there are a few who don't actually detest him, and he is making some slight effort to increase the number of the latter. But I am straying still further from the story of my journey.

The second day I made another thirty miles, but only sixteen miles of this was in wild country where there were no houses, and the roads were better. I was able to get some rest. In the evening I reached the open prairie where, for the first time in two months, I could feel the wind on my face. What a pleasure it was to take in great gulps of fresh air! I understood why we had all been sick and why such a large number had deserted the construction crew because of illness. We were being smothered in the woods where there was no breeze to refresh us. Since then I've been eating like a wolf. On the third day I reached St. Paul. There, on the following morning and much to my surprise and my even greater joy, I met the same young Swiss who had come out here with me two months ago; he too had just arrived in the city. So that now makes two of us out of a job, he being sick besides, and neither of us has yet found work. Oh America, land where people gather up money by the handful, you are a better place for scoundrels than for Christians, no matter what they say! But money doesn't necessarily bring happiness, and even in my penniless condition I am happier than Dodd because I know that I've done my duty and because, unlike him, I don't have to carry pistols and knives. I am ready to do that which God expects of me—go to the North Pole, to the South, to New Orleans, or to Oregon, overseeing slaves in Cuba or being myself a slave, a storeclerk, or a hired man on a farm. May He guide and assist me, for He knows what is best for me.

I found here three or four letters that were listed in the newspapers as having arrived for me, including your good letter of July 12 which reached me at a moment when things seemed at their blackest. It quickly lifted me out of my melancholy and encouraged me to entrust myself to the arms of the Lord. The sympathy of one's friends, and especially that of Christian parents, is a precious thing. Never had I felt this so deeply as I did that day. It is a consolation to me to know that I was not alone in my sufferings and that others were thinking of me when I labored.

Then, too, your offer of money won't cause me any annoyance either. If we weren't so far away from each other, I would quickly ask you to send me $100 or $200 which would give me the wherewithal to spend the winter on a *claim* and clear it of timber, but it [the money] would come too late and it would be better to wait until early next spring. Then I could, without any fear, assume responsibility for whatever amount of money you might send me. I say "without any fear" because a person can only come out ahead when he buys and farms land. I thank you, dear Father, for the offer you've made to lend me this money for one to two years without interest. I hope I needn't take advantage of your generosity and that I can pay you the interest starting with the first year. If you can lend me $1,000, I could perhaps take two quarter-sections (two quarters of a square mile), which would give me a farm one mile long and half a mile wide. If there is less money, half that amount of land would be enough, and this is why: the best land is wooded or is in *openings* in the woods. However, that costs more to clear, even though after a few years it gives much better crops. In any case, the least you can get a quarter-section for is $200, and you need $150 for a yoke of oxen, $50 for a wagon and cart, $50 for other tools, $100 to build a house tight enough to spend the winter in, $50 to furnish it, and about $200 for spring planting. I make no allowance for food, but I've put the prices of the other items a little too high, and I'll feed myself out of what's left over. All this adds up to $800, and if you lend me $1,000, I'll have $200 with which to buy another quarter [-section], but naturally you'll understand that I'd be satisfied with less.

The Baron tells me that in order to get off to a good start you should have not less than $800 because then you can go ahead and clear enough land right away, whereas with less money you can't improve your land very much during the first years. There is no lack of good locations, and I know a number of fine *claims* whose owners will be giving them up or will be forced to abandon them because it is said that all the land near St. Peter is to be put up for sale in the fall and that when this happens the owners will have to pay $200 [to the government], which many of them will be unable to do. I had thought that Dodd would pay me well, and I had already cut a stick of red cedar that I intended to give to Elisée[16] this fall since I had expected to earn as much as people in comparable jobs are paid—$60 to $70 a month. I will keep this stick for better times. I found it near a pretty lake, and the red cedar is itself handsome in addition to the fact that it comes from Minnesota, which is indisputably beautiful country. If I see you again I shall have a great many little adventures to tell you about, but in a letter they would take up too much space.

Your letter took less than a month to reach me, and this is very good; your next one may very well come as promptly, but after that—unless I spend the winter somewhere else—they will take a little longer on account of the snow and ice. I was very sorry to learn of the death of Ami's little girl.[17] All things pass away, and if some live on to a greater age, they are no less close to death for all that. When will my turn come? And you, dear Sister, you too have been very ill—so each of us has trials to undergo—and thank you very much for your fine letter, which has done me so much good. Thank you, dear Etienne, for your good letter. My congratulations on your marriage,[18] and my warmest brotherly greetings to this new sister—except that you don't even give me her baptismal name—and my best wishes for a happy future—all these greetings from your most affectionate brother from Cudrefin, etc., including St. Peter and the Lake of Bienne.[19] And my thanks to you, dear Father, dear Mother, and dear Elisée for your good, your wonderfully good letters. In times like those I have just been going through, a few letters are worth hundreds of dollars. Do you think this paper is too heavy? It is the lightest I've been able to find here. If it's too heavy, I can cut off the margins and make it lighter that way.

Good-bye, dear Parents. Address your letters to St. Paul, Minnesota, and they will always know where I am. God knows where I'll be when this letter gets to you, but it will surely be on its way before I've found a job. My journey from Ashland cost me $28, everything included, for a distance of about sixteen hundred miles. I have read *The Lamplighter*[20] in English, and I like it very much.

Elisée, I am still wearing some of the whiskers I let grow while I was in the woods—three hairs per square mile. Good-bye, dear Parents. I am doing the best I can and I say my prayers.

P.S. Yesterday I saw Dodd drunk in a billiard parlor, and after telling me three or four lies he gave me $25. So here I am, rich as Croesus. He told me he had been satisfied with my work—for this I thank God. Thanks to the Baron I expect to get a job today. Good-bye, everybody! May God be with you as He is with me. This time I've written enough to pay five cents postage on—have I given you enough to read?

**Theodore to his sister Marie**

St. Paul, Minnesota
September 7, 1855

Dear Sister:

You, too very well deserve to get letters from your brother in America, don't you? And inasmuch as for several days now I have been feeling happier, I'll take advantage of this moment to write to you. Just as it causes me a great deal of pain to write when I'm despondent, so it gives me much pleasure to communicate with all of you when I'm contented and happy, [a state of mind] that I've all too rarely experienced since I set foot in Minnesota. As I wrote to Tim, I have a job selling lumber. I take comfort at least from the thought that soon I shall have passed through all imaginable occupations and that then I shall naturally get back to my sheep[21] or my pigs, as you prefer, which I will try to stay with from then on. Meanwhile I am not getting any thinner and am even putting on a little weight at the rate of about a pound a day (six per week); I will leave it to you to figure out how much I'll weigh in a hundred years. If I go on this way, in only ten more days I'll weigh as much as I did two years ago, and in a few months I'll be as strong as I was then. My troubles and worries have done me more harm than anything else because, now that I have a job and have received all your letters, I feel ever so much better. But instead of talking so much about myself, I want to tell you about this region and its people.

I'll begin with the Indians. For the most part, they have very handsome faces; there are even some who look like Father Salicisse of Geneva. It's true that there are numerous exceptions, especially among the Chippewas, but it takes the exceptions to prove the rule. The *squaws* are marvelously ugly; I've seen only one or two that were passable; they all walk exactly like Chinese women, and in the woods I could always tell by their footprints whether it was a man or a woman who had used the trail before we came along. They are all dirty and covered with *body lice,* a kind of vermin unknown to me until I found myself covered with them [on Dodd's road]. The way these *body lice* made their way into the camp will give you an accurate idea of the moral standards of our workmen. I was furious with them. The Indians are beginning to be *troublesome,* and people expect that some battles will be fought not far from here between the Sioux and the Chippewas, and the Red River *Half Breeds,* who have just left St. Paul with a quantity of provisions and a lot of livestock.

                                    In the city, Saturday morning

I have just run into one of my old friends from Dodd's road crew who told me that Dodd wants to see me. Then he told me that the owner of that vegetable garden I saw in the woods shot at a squaw, after warning her to get out of his field, and wounded her badly. I don't imagine she'll go back there again, but I fear for the life of Forsyth, as he was named, because the Indians don't take such things as a joke. He has collected the names of five or six hundred people on a petition asking that they [the Indians] be removed from that district. Another bit of news: my former workers have been fighting among themselves since I left the camp. People around here fight so much that little notice is taken of it when they do, and I suspect that Dodd's wish to see me is not exactly in proportion to his desire to do me a good turn. You may be sure that I've taken no pains to recruit workers for him and that I've spoken frankly about him to his friends—all of which would probably entitle me to feel the weight of his fists. Dodd weighs 212 pounds and is terribly strong, so I'm in no hurry to see him; but if he wants to get hold of me because I've been talking about him, then I'll have to do the best I can. Perhaps I'll try to find out which of us can run faster before I find out which is stronger. But one sure thing is that I won't stop saying what I think of him. Another time he'll be careful not to harm those who help him.

This leads me to some comments on the Americans in general. I admire them for their *sang-froid.* They are inclined to leave the other fellow alone, and they want other people to leave them alone too. They don't expect anyone to give them any help and would take offense if you offered to help them. However difficult their position may be, they always feel sure they will be able to deal with it, as able as anyone else. And at all times they will remain calm and unruffled. You have to annoy them a great deal before they fly into a rage, and even then they are still calm, though in a deadly sort of way, whereas we French or Swiss, and I especially, lose all our self-possession when we get angry. I know that when I was on the road crew and alone against a gang of workmen, although my voice remained perfectly steady, my legs shook and my knees knocked together like drumsticks, whereas on similar occasions my *bossmen* were as calm as though you were coming to greet them as a friend. Just the same, though, if I were really backed up against a wall, I would be calmer than they are, but at the same time I would be inwardly shaking with fury. It is in this respect that I believe French or Swiss blood to be superior to Anglo-Saxon blood. We have so much life in us that we always jump around too much and waste our time and strength to no purpose unless something quite extraordinary occurs to make us concentrate all our forces on a single goal, and one can see this in all sorts of ways. When there is a great deal of work to be done, the Americans get through it more rapidly than the French; the latter try to hurry, but have their minds on something else all the time, so they work more slowly than the Americans. But if there is a truly staggering task to be done, the tables are turned. When I say all this I am speaking from experience and from a great deal of observation. Hurrah for passionate people! I can forgive them for going astray and even for having evil passions, but I can't excuse the Americans for remaining phlegmatic all the while that they are slaves to their passions. It's disgusting to see people, who seem always to be masters of themselves and always calm, giving themselves up to sin without making any effort to resist it. I can't understand how someone can sin willfully and in full awareness of what he is doing.

What nice people we have here! Only two fistfights in the last half-hour, one between an innkeeper and one of his guests, the other between two young men: these two rolled right into the Mississippi while they were fighting and kept on fighting as they swam. Bystanders pulled them up onto a steamboat by their hair, and they started fighting again. The onlookers separated them, and then everybody began to argue about which of them had put up the better fight and that's how the affair ended. For me this atmosphere is terribly disagreeable! In such a case, if someone were to strike me and I had to stand up for myself, I would fight as hard as possible and do my opponent as much harm as I could because these bullies, picking fights with everyone and battling with someone every day, need to suffer a little in order to enjoy life, and you won't find many Americans willing to take the pains to deal out heavy blows for long at a time. But what a topic of conversation, my dear Marie! Forgive me—I hardly know what I'm saying because my mind is so upset by my troubles that often I don't know until it's too late that I've been behaving badly. Living among such people as these, a young man like me can hardly prevent himself from imitating them, and although God preserves me from committing any grave sins, it is still true that my heart prompts me to commit little ones (little, that is, from a human viewpoint). I boast, I sometimes get angry, and I feel that I am far from being master of myself. Nobody here helps me to behave well, and it is almost considered a sin to be a Christian. Naturally, their mockery doesn't prevent me from trying to act like a *"pious chap,"* as they call me, and I always want to pray more. But keep on helping me with your prayers, all you members of the family in Paris, because the old Enemy, though wounded, is not dead.

Undoubtedly you know, dear Marie—and here I respond to a "hint" contained in one of your most recent letters—that the American women have very handsome faces, the same calmness as the men, but without ever behaving in a disgusting way as so many of the men do hereabouts. Often they are very beautiful, and I could sit admiring them for hours on end. If another feeling creeps in, it isn't my fault, but—always a lot of "buts"—I don't know if it is because I am no longer capable of falling in love or if it is really the fact that they have very few lovable qualities. For four years now I haven't seen a face that I found truly attractive. Only one—and she is married—is everything I'd like to find in a Christian young woman, pretty [*jolie*] and capable enough of loving so that she will help her husband, even when things are going badly with him. In general they are beautiful, very beautiful, but not *jolies:* a husband might be very proud of them, but he couldn't love them very much. Husbands and wives here seem to marry because you've got to marry someone, the men because they need somebody to look after the servants, the women because they want fine dresses, carriages to ride in, etc. They all live as happily as their hedonistic nature allows, but without enjoying life as much as we do, and without loving as much, *by far.* If you take away from a Frenchwoman her smile, her eyes, and her liveliness, her beauty will, comparatively speaking, disappear, whereas an American women would still be beautiful. But hurrah for the French and Swiss girls! Come and tell me whether I'm dead or alive!

If you could read all I feel in my heart, you'd see that I do nothing to foster these feelings of anger, hatred, and restlessness that trouble me so much. I don't feel that I am *at home*; I have to struggle against everyone. I have to make my way alone, without any friends around me; everybody is absorbed in his own business, and the only young people who might become good friends are dissipated and debauched; hence I get out of their reach *"in double quick time."* When I am with a lot of people I like, I am myself; but at present, and whenever I'm not with friends, I am no longer myself and boredom makes me malicious. In all the past four years I have been happy only for a few weeks before and after my baptism, and for a few weeks at Pointe-aux-Trembles;[22] but then I was wonderfully happy. I don't expect to be happy again for a good long time; a half or a quarter of that happiness would be enough for me, and I think that perhaps I'll soon reach the quarter-mark again. I felt happy when I began writing this letter, but then the two fistfights made me depressed. What a civilization! What fine Christians! Even though I am nothing but a *"damned foreigner,"* as they call me, I don't think that is a bad thing. Little Switzerland is worth the whole United States—you remember the man from Geneva who once said that Paris is a little Geneva! This is a dark picture of the States that I am drawing for you here, but it is a faithful one, and in order to love the United States you have to live on a farm— your own or someone else's—because American farmers are much better than city people. But in order to have a great deal of love for them, you have to be far away; then you can like them because they let you alone and are not the kind of neighbors who will be always trying to get the better of you.

When God grants me the blessing of having a home of my own, I should like very much to see you, and I promise never to get angry with you. You can paddle yourself around the lake in your *bark canoe*, assuming I'm not able to paddle it alone, which would be very strange. We can go fishing together, and then in the wintertime—for you are going to make a long visit—I'll take you for rides on a bobsled. If I'm still a *bachelor*, I won't promise to show you a house that is kept in perfect order, but you'll excuse that, won't you, knowing what sort of fellow I am? In any event, we'll have to wait for a year or two because for the first two years *log cabins* aren't very comfortable, even for men. For me it would be delightful, but for a young lady like you, accustomed to living in fine houses,[23] the idea of coming here to sleep in a *log cabin*

without any windows—and the *logs* have long open spaces between
them—with a bark roof that only lets in water when it rains, a floor
[of earth] 9,000 miles thick, a bed made of one or two planks and
a blanket, exotic food—that idea, I repeat, would be a very funny
one to do—supposing one can speak of "doing" an idea. By the
way, do you know that I've lost my ability to speak! It tires me
excessively to work out the implications of an idea, whatever it
may be, and often in the middle of a conversation I stop talking
and begin to think and think and think, having nothing more to
say because my thoughts are so different from those of the Americans. But you'll find that with a few days of practice I'll be able to
speak on certain subjects like, for example, the one that ends on
the middle of this page.

I've just thought of something else. Do you know, or have
you ever given any thought to the fact, that all the leading newspapers of the United States are controlled by Unitarians: The *New
York Daily Tribune, Times, Herald, Gleason's, and Ballow's Pictor-
ial*; and also that they write the most interesting books: *The Lamplighter, Hot Corn,*[24] etc.—all these are published by Unitarians.
*The Lamplighter* struck me from the very first page as the work of
a Unitarian. Probably you have noticed that the name of Jesus and
the word Savior don't occur even one single time in this book. It's
very odd that there should be so much intellectual superiority in
this not-so-very-numerous sect. No Methodist or Baptist has ever
been President of the United States, whereas three or perhaps six
Unitarians have been elected. The influence of this denomination
on the masses is becoming more and more important even while
the membership of the sect is getting smaller. But I must go to bed,
dear Marie. It's Saturday night, I have worked hard today, and I'm
very tired. I hope the next letter will bring me news of Elisée's success and that he will have passed his baccalaureate examinations.
Good night, and may God be with you, Marie, and with all of you.

Good night.


Sunday morning

For several days now it has been terribly hot. The month of
August was chilly, but September is very warm. Someday when I
send you a newspaper from one of those Southern states, read the
advertisements. You'll always find some announcing sales of Negroes, rewards to whoever catches fugitive slaves, etc., as well as

insults to the Abolitionists in the editorials, paeans of praise for those who kill them — in short, I promise you that it will be worth taking the trouble to read them.

Every Sunday I think about Bellevue. Once I was on my way to spend the Sabbath on Mount Mussi, and my heart suddenly contracted in anticipation of the thought that someday I should have to leave that beautiful country. In calm, clear weather we could hear the bells of Thonon and Evian, which made the beauty of the lake and of the Alps even more awesome and magnificent. How lovely our Switzerland is, Marie — don't you agree?

The natural beauty of America is much inferior, but this country is also beautiful in some ways. You would believe this if you had been with me on that trip up the Mississippi which I described to Tim. At the beginning we were continually going beneath the foliage of wild vines; the woods were splendid, abounding in fairly good wild plums. To complete the scene, imagine an Indian chasing a [swimming] deer in his canoe, try to visualize the wilderness we were in, and you will have an idea of the mental picture I had formed of America. I have found it to be entirely different from what I had thought it would be. But what good does it do to complain? I hope that in a few years I'll have a lot of money. St. Paul grows more attractive day by day. It is situated, as you know, on the left bank of the Mississippi on a plateau that is a *"rolling prairie"* in the full meaning of the word. In addition, the authorities level out all or almost all the ups and downs of the terrain, frequently lowering the grade of the street by eight or ten feet and leaving it up to the owners to find a way of getting up to their houses. Ravines are being filled, and regular embankments are being built along the river, whose banks are still largely in a primitive state: steamboats tie up to the first stump they come to or the first big rock they find on the shore. Have I told you that a couple of miles from here there is a cave[25] several miles long? As a matter of fact, now that I think of it, I'm going back there tomorrow with a candle and some matches, and I'll give you further details when I get back.

Sunday evening

That cave doesn't really contain anything very interesting. There's just a small stream that has hollowed out a bed in the rock. You have to walk the whole way bent double. Well, anyhow, I've seen the famous cave. My day was quite upsetting because I again ran into that man from Dodd's road crew who [the road worker] wants me to go back with him to collect the wages owing to me. I don't want to go there at all; I'd rather lose the money than have any more dealings with Dodd. Besides, this other man is so immoral that I couldn't accept his help. He also told me that one of my former assistants back in the camp, who resented my having been placed over him, had poisoned Dodd's mind against me in order to get my job. Last Sunday he got a good beating up himself, along with his brother, from a workman who refused to recognize him as a superior. I assure you that I thank God I escaped from that gang; I am a little surprised that I got out of it alive because a foreigner is always hated by the Americans, especially if his position is higher than theirs.

Another thing that has contributed to my agitated condition is listening to music in the churches. It has an overwhelmingly strong effect on my whole constitution; it makes my blood pound in my head and makes me desire a great many things; but, thanks be to God, it has finally helped me to see that God knows better than I do what is good for me and that, if He sometimes makes me undergo periods of gloom and suffering, it is only for my own benefit. I have been able to pray more today, or rather this evening, and I am less distracted. I feel too that if I were closer to God, I'd be more compliant with his will and more content with what He gives me. I wish that some of my friends in Canada could be here with me so we could pray together and talk about God, and I hope that one or two of them may come before long. I also wish Sunday came more often, I feel so good as soon as I set foot inside a church. Only in the midst of trials and tribulations does one realize how precious the Christian religion is. Tomorrow, if it pleases God, I'll finish this letter and send it off right away; then in three weeks I'll send another to our parents and will send one every month to [all of you in] Paris. This, along with my letters coming by way of Glasgow, will keep you up to date on my doings. Good-bye for tonight, and may God bless you all. Pray for me always that God will give me spiritual riches rather than material wealth. The body can get along without riches so long as the soul is close to God. Good night!

Monday morning

If you don't believe it can get hot in Minnesota, you ought to be here right now. What a heat wave! I have a half-dozen workmen [to oversee] today, and you can be sure that the sweat is really pouring off us. So much the better—it will be very good for our health. Furthermore, I am beginning to be a fairly good salesman, which pleases my boss. I've sold $75 worth of boards, and that's only one *item* in his business. He is a Frenchman from Lyon who came here five years ago and has prospered.

The bell has just rung for dinner and I'm on my way. Again, good-bye. And good-bye once again—I've just had my supper and have come back to write a little more before going to bed. So good-bye, dear Sister, dear Parents, and dear friends—may God bless you abundantly.

Think always of your very affectionate

Theodore Bost

**Theodore to his parents**

Still St. Paul, Minnesota
September 23 & 30, 1855

Dearest Parents:

It's now five years since we were at Serrières [on the Lake of Neuchâtel]; but now we are all far from there. You have aged by five years and I by at least ten, for a man who is all alone in America experiences a great deal and ages rapidly. I'd even say that I've aged too fast, or rather that too much has happened to me in this time; my character has developed under forced draft, as it were, instead of maturing naturally, so that I often feel torn by two sets of impulses—those of a young man of twenty and those of a man of thirty.

The reason I begin my letter with this little discourse is that I am beginning to understand why you may be uneasy on my account. At one time I write to you in one frame of mind, another time in a different mood, and that's because of the different circumstances I am having to contend with. I want to reassure you about one thing: I am determined to correct the faults I have. My chief failing, I think, is my violent temper; but when I am on my guard I am so fully in control of myself that everybody thinks I'm a good-natured, timid fellow. At night, there's a big difference, as my bedmate can tell you. The first few nights he took me for a ninny he could push around, so he tried to assert a claim to three-quarters of the bed. I didn't say anything, but finding myself crowded in the middle of the night, I brought both feet into action (he tells me) with the result that he wound up outside the door. Since then he hasn't bothered me at night. In the daytime he has always been friendly enough, and we get along together very well, as we do with all the other clerks. So tell me, was I at fault in giving him that kicking? In a country where everybody does just as he pleases, isn't a person allowed to defend himself and stand up for his rights?

Yesterday, for example, one of the men stole some lumber worth about 20 fr. [$4]; the lumber didn't belong to me; and yet I can't excuse him for having taken it. It's true that he has done no wrong to me personally, but if I see that fellow again, ought I to leave him alone or ought I to try to have him arrested? He should pay for his lumber or else he should be punished. Who will take action if I don't? The law? There's only one *policeman* in the whole city, and where can I find him if I see this man around town? The only thing I can think of is to put on a very bold front, speak in a harsh, firm tone, and, if that doesn't work, I suppose I'll have to resort to force. "You'd be doing the wrong thing," say you, but wouldn't I be doing a still worse thing to let a thief rob everyone without ever being punished?

As the Americans see it, everyone should look out for himself and punish those who do him an injury just as the law would punish them if it could. And as a matter of fact, why should I get a man sent to prison for a number of years when I can produce better results so far as the individual is concerned by giving him a good thrashing? These ideas, you will say, aren't very Christian; but I can't bring myself to believe that a Christian ought to act in this country the same way he would act elsewhere. With us in Europe, if a man lets other people walk all over him, he soon gets justice because in our country people are capable of feeling remorse. But here, the more a man is beaten down, the more people take advantage of him; they treat him more like a beast of burden than a man. I do the opposite; but often my blood boils in my veins when I see the Americans robbing and mistreating the poor, simple Germans. It would give me a great deal of solid pleasure to see them get the comeuppance they deserve from those poor Germans. In this sort of situation the Americans are brutes rather than men, and it's a waste of time to talk to them about humanity. Should they let it be said that instead of freeing the Negroes, they should make all foreigners slaves? And yet Dodd told me precisely that. He is the right arm of the governor of Minnesota and has hopes of rising high in the world.

Speaking of Dodd, and to bring this long chapter to an end, all the original workmen have left the road job, which cannot be completed this fall. Poor Dodd! I saw him the other day; he had a very long face, but he didn't say anything to me. As soon as I had seen him, I went off to look for the road workers who had been taken on first and sent him about a half-dozen who wanted their money, but I don't know whether they were able to get any. I don't need to tell you that I'm not at all content with my present mode of life in a town where people are all the time fighting, where there is no good company, no life at all apart from business. No hymns are sung in people's homes; there is no music or anything that could make life less of a burden. Political life consists of calling the other candidate a rascal, a thief, and a liar; and the other candidate responds with even more insulting language if he can. The only one who doesn't indulge in these insults is the candidate of those who are opposed to the extension of slavery into the Territories: this is all to his credit. The Know-Nothings[26] have no influence here at all.

If it weren't for the fact that the long winter will soon be upon me, I would leave St. Paul and make a trip on foot around the places I hear most highly spoken of for the fertility of the land and for the other advantages they offer the farmer—places like Crow River, St. Peters [sic], Cannon River, which are the ones that have most recently attracted attention; I ought to go and look over the two I haven't yet seen. Well, the bell is ringing for church, and I must be on my way; if it pleases God, I'll be with you again in an hour.

Back again. I attended a good service by our pastor, Mr. Forbel. His sermon was in simple language, unpretentiously delivered. All the better! It is a good thing to be free of the kind of pomposity one finds at the Presbyterian church where last Sunday we had a sermon on geology and zoology which made me think of "the square of the hypotenuse" in the account of the priest [Lacordaire] whom Papa mentions in his *Mémoires*—all just to prove that he'd been to college.

No matter what happens, I hope that early next spring I can take up a *claim*. I will make the necessary arrangements to begin the preemption process; then, if I have no money, I'll hire out for the summer and will try to have saved up $200 by fall so I can buy the land from the government when it is put on sale.

For a month or more a man has been selling watermelons here every day; he grew them on an acre and a half of his *claim*. He just planted them outdoors, never transplanted [them] into fertilized beds, never took the least trouble with them, and they are magnificent. People say they are good, but I much prefer the other kind of melons which grow equally well. You can buy a good melon for five or ten cents. On hot days many people can be seen walking around eating melons. Being too poor to buy one, I eat only those given to me by others, but these taste just as good as though I had bought them. This is convenient and perfectly acceptable. One day I was eating someone else's melon when another man came up and said *"Excuse me,"* and then, taking half of what was left, went on his way. I'm not yet American enough to see nothing amusing in such notions of independence.

The weather has been wet for the past several days; last night the rain came down in buckets and endangered the houses that have been built along the streets they have dug out to level the terrain. This weather is not at all to my boss's liking because timber from the upper Mississippi can now come downstream, the sawmills can get all the logs they want, and this will drive down the price of lumber which my man is now able to sell as dear as he pleases. How hard it is to make everyone happy at the same time! I don't feel very well today, but this suits me better than not. I generally have an excess of vitality that leads to fatigue and boredom; but when I'm off my feed I can think more calmly about things, and that makes me happier.

When I get my *claim* I will be able to put all my strength to good use. If I can persuade my Canadian friends to join me, we can establish a little settlement off by ourselves, which would be much more pleasant than being all alone, as well as more advantageous. I have written to Cornu and Louis Pollens; the former is a good Christian though younger. Toupoint, Bourdeaux, and others might also come. If this all works out, it would be very good. Naturally, I hardly dare build many hopes on it because up to now not many of my plans have come to anything. It is true that I ought to leave it to God to make plans for me while I work merely to do His will.

Incidentally, I don't believe I've told you where I'm sleeping. It's a shed about a hundred feet long, at one end of which are a wooden bed and a not-very-soft mattress, four or five blankets with no sheets, a chair, and a desk. The shed is full of merchandise, grain, and rats; every night my boots and those of my roommate fly for immense distances through the air aimed at the rats, but we always miss them. On the other hand, they scamper all over us during the night—very enjoyable! We get up at half past six or seven o'clock and go to bed between eight and ten. Since I have to stay in the warehouse all evening and since the place is not very conducive to meditation, I undress around nine o' clock and do gymnastic exercises until my friend has finished writing his letters; then we crawl under the blankets, each on his own side of the bed since the first nights. My friend can't bear to be all alone in the evening—that's why I have to be there to keep him company.

To give you some idea of the number of nationalities in St. Paul, I will list for you the places of origin of Mr. Rey's clerks. He comes from Lyon, his chief clerk is from Belgium, another is from the southern states, another from Prussia, another from Germany; I am from Switzerland; and then there are two French Canadians—all foreigners but one, and even he is a Southerner and hence more or less hostile to the Northerners: he is the one with whom I share a bed. I get my meals at the Merchants Hotel where the food isn't bad.

I don't know whether I've told you that those people named Flowers who founded the colony at Fort Atkinson[27] are the same young men who made off with £15,000 which didn't belong to them; but this didn't prevent them from being welcomed everywhere in America as good church members.

September 30

By the way, one of my former workmen who came here last Tuesday told me that the whole crew, with Dodd himself taking the lead, have written me a letter asking me to come back and explain a number of things that Dodd doesn't understand. But this letter has never reached me for the very good reason that Dodd never mailed it, considering that he isn't crazy enough to want to hear me take my solemn oath that the pay slips I left with the workmen are correct. He has been trying to convince the workmen that I made a lot of mistakes; they, in turn, have been telling him that he fired me because I was too honest and was unwilling to rob them; this is just what he wants to hear! The poor wretch! The best part is that this workman got Dodd to pay him for nearly all the time he had worked on the basis of a reckoning which Dodd later claimed was false, although it actually wasn't, and he [Dodd] sent a constable to arrest this man because he had paid him almost all that was due him. The man was not arrested, however, since he couldn't be located; but he is furious, all the same, that Dodd is trying to have him arrested like a common thief. What a brazen rascal this Dodd is! Still, if he takes anyone to court, he'll get the worst of it; with my records and my word against him, he would have no way of proving his rightful claims even if he had any. It's a wonderful mix-up! I don't harbor any grudges against him; but rather than stand by and allow him to go on stealing from his men, I'd prefer to see him punished. But God knows better than I do when and how He ought to punish him.

I think it's time to go to church, so I'll be on my way.

After dinner

I've been to church, but couldn't pay attention to the sermon because I was too preoccupied. At least I was able to turn my worrying to some advantage by blessing God during and after the service for my having lived through so many happy times and in so many lovely places. The truth is that at Grande Ligne and at Pointe-aux-Trembles I did have some very good times; and almost everywhere I've been there were natural beauties to enjoy; I have become aware, too, that if my imagination is the source of many melancholy moments, it also enables me to get more intense enjoyment from many happy occasions. The mental images I have of the beautiful St. Lawrence, of Lake Ontario, of the Richelieu River, of Lake Champlain, Lake Erie, Lake Michigan, the Mississippi, the prairies, the forest, my pioneers' road, etc., etc., will always be fixed in my memory. After the service I took a stroll to the top of a low hill from which I could see the Mississippi, the prairie, the woods, and St. Paul itself: everything is still in a primitive state. Even the city is in an *opening* on the prairie; the streets have been marked out with the scythe and the ax. I was just telling myself that the picture I had made for myself of an imaginary America didn't come up to the reality I was looking at, when all of a sudden an American came up and asked me the price of the land thereabouts. Always dollars, dollars, dollars! I told him politely that I had no idea, and then I hurried out of the vicinity of that dollar-obsessed individual. How many opportunities for enjoyment they lose by seeing nothing in nature but dollars or the means of making some!

Good-bye, dearest Parents—write soon and pray always for your

Theodore Bost

**Theodore to his parents**

St. Paul
Tuesday, November 20, 1855

Dearest Parents:

It would have been a much greater joy to be writing to you from my own house; but that would have delayed the mailing of this letter by several days and I didn't want to do that. I'm going to tell you in as few words as possible about what has happened this past week. I left here, I forget which day last week, and went up the Minnesota River as far as Chaska. Striking out from there each day, I crisscrossed the whole surrounding area, visiting a number of *claims*. I saw one I could get for $300, and I heard about another one six or seven miles (so they told me) from Chaska. I started out to have a look at it, and after I'd walked two miles I found that I was still nine miles from the *claim*. Then I went farther upstream to Louisville, but I didn't much like what I saw there, so I came back. I walked eight miles through marshland to Shakopee, which I reached at four in the afternoon. From there I left on Friday morning the sixteenth to fetch the money from here to pay for the $300 *claim*; the next day, being in a hurry, I returned to Shakopee by the stage, arriving at four in the afternoon. Then I went four miles on foot through the marshes and got to Chaska just at nightfall. But I pressed on and reached this *claim* the same evening (Saturday, November 17) in order to tell the *claimant* not to leave on Monday as he had planned to do. I lost my way in the woods but finally came to a fence after I had floundered around for a long time looking for a landmark. It led me to an old German-Swiss woman—*"nicht ferschté"*[28]—who offered to put me up for the night. Despite the rather slovenly and dirty condition of the house, I accepted, understanding or pretending to understand her German and sleeping (with my clothes on) in the same bed with one of her sons and a not very interesting population [of vermin], slept a little, had breakfast, and resumed my wanderings—I had no compass—and finally located the father of the *claimant* who told me his son wouldn't sell his *claim* on a Sunday. I reassured him on this point, and on Sunday, November 18th, I finally got to the son's house; I told him I didn't want to transact any business on Sunday either, but that I hoped to strike a bargain with him the next day. I spent a very pleasant day with him and his wife. We went to church together, or rather to the schoolhouse a half-mile from there. They hadn't finished making the door, and you could see the sky through holes in the roof; the place was very cold, though there was a good stove with a stovepipe running out through the door opening. We heard a good sermon; the preacher christened (baptized by aspersion)[29] the two little girls in my man's family; this made one of them cry (very piously, no doubt). It is quite true that the external aspects of religion are of little importance compared with the great interior transformation; but it did give me pain to see administered to anyone and everyone a rite that ought to be reserved for true Christians. But as to that, everyone has a right to his own opinion.

I spent last night with them, and the next morning, November 19, after breakfast we walked around the whole *claim* and then came back to the house. I paid him $300, got the sale witnessed, and then left at one o'clock that afternoon for St. Paul. It was cold and I didn't feel at all well. I had seventeen miles to walk before nightfall. So I began to sing and finally enjoyed, for the first time in two years, one of those blissful moments when I felt as though I were in Heaven. I hope to enjoy many more such moments this coming winter.

At six in the evening (yesterday) I arrived at Gibson's inn. I spent the night there with a large crowd of [stagecoach] passengers, including in particular a *gin-tleman* [*sic*] and two ladies. One of these, as she came in, executed a series of very odd maneuvers, walking in circles and S-curves and taking little steps and hops to one side or the other until she collapsed on the settee. Her husband, who had trouble keeping his legs under him, told me she was suffering from toothache!!!

I left the following morning, Tuesday the twentieth, setting out for St. Paul at seven o'clock, right after breakfast. It was snowing hard, and the bad roads across the prairie were covered with ice. I had to go by way of Minneapolis (because the Mississippi was too full of big cakes of ice to allow the ferry to cross at Fort Snelling). So I crossed by the suspension bridge, which is four or five hundred feet above the falls (but farther to the north), had another look at the falls, which were prettier than the last time I saw them last spring on account of the chunks of ice, and I got to St. Paul at two o'clock this afternoon, having walked twenty-seven miles in seven hours without trying to hurry and over very bad roads. This evening I felt fine, though a bit tired from all the moving around I've done this past week. Tomorrow (the twenty-first), I'll get all my belongings together, buy various items for the *claim* — and then I'll start out for *home*.

Now I must tell you what I've already bought, but before I do that I must thank you from the bottom of my heart for lending me this money. I am setting out at last for a place where I'll have land of my own, free and able to work for myself and at the same time for you. It was too late in the year to take an uncleared *claim*, since winter has already begun in earnest and since I can't do any building, well digging, etc., during the very cold weather. Besides, it would cost a great deal of time and money to make a cabin tight enough to hold in some warmth and give me a place to store my potatoes. Furthermore, the available *claims* are a long way from any settlement and hence, for the time being, not so desirable. But the *claim* I've just bought was occupied by a railroad engineer who thought he'd like farming but got tired of it. He built himself a good cabin from tamarack logs, twenty-three feet long by thirteen or sixteen feet wide, with a cellar six feet deep and twelve feet square; [he left me] sixty bushels of potatoes, three of rutabagas, a good stove and stovepipes, kettles, and so on; also three tons of hay, ten or fifteen bushels of Indian corn, 200 fence rails (in addition to those in the fence that already encloses one and one-half acres of cultivated land), an excellent well, 160 acres, of which twenty are in natural meadowland and the rest in good timber (and easy to clear in some places). Naturally, I'll still have to pay $200 to the government when the land is put on sale, as well as about $12 to finish the house and about $30 more for tools, beds, blankets, etc.

The *claim* is four miles from Excelsior, [a town on] Lake Minnetonka, four and a half miles from Chaska, and five miles from Shakopee, which is on the Minnesota River. If it pleases God, I'll build more fences this winter, and perhaps I can get the use of a neighbor's oxen to haul some logs to the sawmills, where they pay a fairly high price for good sawing logs, a big advantage to people who live near a settlement.

Another good point of this claim is that the people roundabout are English or American,[30] either Christians or at least churchgoers, ready to lend a hand to their neighbors and to protect one another's *claims,* so that this *claim,* though not the very best, is in any case one of the best I've yet seen. Maybe when Spring comes, I'll sell it at a good profit and take up another one farther west. Nearly all the *claims* have the shape of a perfect square [with its sides running] from north to south and from east to west, though the boundaries have only been roughly marked out up to now. When I have the time, I'll go all around the present boundaries, carving my name on the trees in place of that of the former owner. There are lots of partridges and a few deer, and this will relieve the monotony of the potatoes and bacon. Since I'll be doing my own cooking, I won't bake bread, which would take too much time and be too much trouble. I'll do my cooking in the evening while I'm repairing the cabin or writing letters.

In my next letter I'll send you a sketch-map of my *claim* so you can get an idea of the spot where I've pitched my tent. If I stay here two years, I'll probably go on and stay the next twenty, and if I'm here two years, I'll get this claim in apple-pie order—it has all sorts of possibilities for being very nicely improved.

But, dear Parents, I have one of my very bad headaches and some pain in my teeth. It is getting difficult for me to go on writing, so I think I should bring this letter to a close—especially considering the fact that I am sitting beside an American who, in a fatherly way, cautions me that long letters are always a bore, and that the shorter a letter is, the more pleasure it will give. So I am inclined to take his advice and adopt that method of pleasing you, but do write me a long reply because, so far as I'm concerned, the longer the letters I receive, the better I like them. Address your next letter to:

Theodore Bost
Chanhassen, Carver County
Minnesota Ter[ritory]

Good-bye, then dear Family—write to me as often as you can. I know that—scattered far and wide as you are—that won't be easy. Good-bye, dear Papa, good-bye, dear Mother; may God bless you abundantly and render to you a hundredfold all that you've done for me.

Good-bye, dear Sister—if it pleases God, you may come over

here to make my butter and watch me work. I hope God will restore you to good health before you come here. Good-bye, dear
Elisée—so you're now a theology student! Aren't you having a lot
of fun, ha, ha! Good-bye, dear Auguste, and also your wife and
family. Good-bye, dear John, Samuel and Company, dear Paul,
Théophile, and Elisée. Good-bye to you all. May God bless you all.
Good-bye to all the Swiss relatives!

Your very loving brother and son,
Theodore Bost

Good-bye.

If this letter is a long time getting to you, it is because—with
the [Mississippi] river no longer navigable—it has been necessary
to set up a stagecoach company, and they take longer to make the
trip downriver than the *Steamboats*.

# IV

# Alone on the Claim

Theodore to his parents

Chanhassen
Minnesota Territory
December 2, 1855

Dear Parents:

If you don't find my handwriting very clear it is because I am using my knees for a desk as I sit on an upturned keg; my penholder is one I whittled myself. So now I am in my own house, and I'm really leading the life of an unmarried settler. I haven't yet been able to do very much except store my corn, explore my *claim*, cook, cover up a few holes in the house where the snow was coming in as merrily as you please, and attend to a number of other little chores. Last Tuesday, when I moved in, the snow was two inches deep on the floor. The stove, along with the pots and pans, was all that had been left behind; the beds, chairs, benches, and tables had all been taken away. I asked God to bless my entry into possession of this *log house* and then borrowed a neighbor's oxen to go and fetch my things from Shakopee.

The next night I put a little hay on the floor, spread four old suits of clothes over it, took off my boots, put on my warmest clothing, rolled myself up in a double pair of woolen blankets, and slept very well. I got up good and early. Then I started my cooking activities, which are very simple: I have two tin plates and some knives and forks. I boil six or seven potatoes and peel them; next I fry up a good big piece of bacon and brown my potatoes in the bacon grease; then I eat my whole meal using my knees as a table. Sometimes I fry the potatoes in butter, but since it costs thirty cents a pound, I use it sparingly. Sometimes, too—as I did to-day—I make a boiled dinner of bacon, potatoes, and rutabagas; this is for special occasions when I want a good soup. When my stomach demands something different, I'll humor it because it's bad policy for a farmer to stint himself on food. One of these days I plan to go down to Excelsior, [which is] on the very pretty lake called Minnetonka, and bring (using my neighbor's oxen) some basswood *logs* with which to make a tight ceiling. It has been cold the whole time, and it did me no good to build a fire; I couldn't get warm anywhere except in bed.

When I've finished repairing this *log house*, I can use my evenings to make chairs, beds, tool handles, tables, etc., at my leisure. Yesterday evening I did part of the sewing for a mattress in which I shall put corn husks as soon as those I've selected have had a chance to dry; then, when I've made a bedstead, I'll be perfectly comfortable. As soon as I am a little richer I plan to buy a cow and will put her in the *log house*. . . . I'll try to keep her warm and feed her well: I have plenty of potatoes, and if she doesn't like them, tough luck for her!

Here is a rough sketch of my *claim*, the sides of which run from north to south and from east to west. . . .

On Sunday we all go to the Unionist temple, so that all Christians here belong to this church—this ought to be done everywhere. . . . .

I see the West as the ideal place for people to live. . . . Those who are born here grow accustomed to effort at an early age and develop their faculties in all sorts of ways. Then, when they are grown up, they leave their parents and set out to clear some land on their own. They marry, and their children are old enough to help them just when they have cleared enough land to need their children's aid, but don't have enough to need hired hands. In the meantime, they have had to learn a little about all kinds of trades—mason, carpenter, cabinetmaker, farmer, gardener, cook, hunter, physician, etc. They learn to like their neighbors and to make themselves respected. They love their families; they have good friends; and yet, if need be, they can live alone for a long time and say, in the manner of Louis XIV, "I am the world." [*Le monde, c'est moi*][1] At the same time, cheap newspapers keep them informed of every tidbit of news, and the paper that tells us of the taking of Sebastopol[2] also tells us the color of Queen Victoria's dress and that Napoleon [III] kissed her on both

cheeks, details that are all very interesting—the last one especially—very touching.

But I must get to the most important point of my letter, and I
don't quite know how to begin because I have so little experience in
such matters. And it is only after a great deal of thought and prayer
that I have decided to do nothing about this except what you, dear
Father and Mother, think will be best for me. I ought to get married, and the sooner the better. I am very happy as I am at present,
but all these little household chores take a great deal of time—time
that could be devoted to men's work. It doesn't make so much
difference in the winter, but in the summer when I'll have the cows,
pigs, hens, etc., to take care of, it will be more inconvenient, and if
I could find a good, strong girl to marry, I would be relieved of
these little chores and my outlay for food wouldn't be much greater,
while there would be big savings in other respects. Furthermore,
though I know that marriage isn't always a paradise and that it
necessarily entails cares and responsibilities, it seems to me that a
farmer is happier when he can feel that he has a partner who will
care for him than when he has to come home to an empty house.

All this is only an introduction. Now comes the great effort.
No doubt you remember that at one point in my life I was in Neuchâtel, and you also no doubt noticed that it was not for nothing
that I went calling on my Aunt Narbel and that in fact one of my
reasons for visiting was her big daughter Marie.[3] I was sincerely
fond of her, and I think that she didn't exactly find me repulsive
either. I often asked her in fun whether she didn't want to come
with me to America, and she, also in fun, answered "Yes." Now if
you are willing, and if she too agrees, [could we not] change these
jokes into reality? I haven't written to her since I've been in America, and if she should refuse, it wouldn't surprise me at all, but
enough time has passed so that her refusal would not plunge me
into the [depths of despair]. But if she should accept my proposal,
I should be very happy. I have naturally seen here in America a
number of delicate young ladies and a few husky farm girls, but I
haven't found any who have both the good manners of a young
lady and the tastes and physical strength a farmer's wife must have.
If you agree with my ideas about all this, I wish you would speak
to Marie, and perhaps to her father too, to find out what she thinks.
The first two years would perhaps not be very comfortable, but
little by little the bird makes its nest, and I wouldn't like very

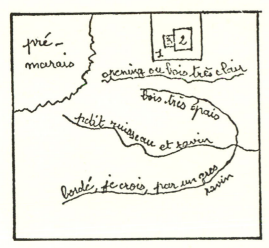

*1. C'est le jardin d'un acre et demi défriché.*

*2. C'est la maison où j'habite.*

*3. C'est le shanty [1] où eux habitèrent l'été dernier, communiquant avec l'autre logis par une porte.*

**My claim.** My garden (1); the house I live in (2); the claim shanty where they [the previous occupants] lived last summer (3).

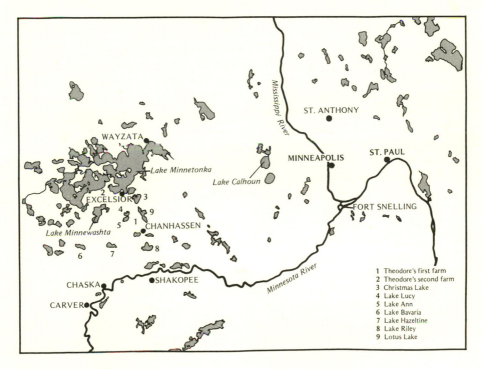

| | |
|---|---|
| 1 | Theodore's first farm |
| 2 | Theodore's second farm |
| 3 | Christmas Lake |
| 4 | Lake Lucy |
| 5 | Lake Ann |
| 6 | Lake Bavaria |
| 7 | Lake Hazeltine |
| 8 | Lake Riley |
| 9 | Lotus Lake |

**Chanhassen and vicinity**

75

much to spend two years building it all by myself. . . . So far as food and shelter are concerned, we'd have all that . . . by next year when the garden will be well in hand, . . . and if the scenery isn't as beautiful as in Switzerland, . . . still, on this score, there is a good deal to be said for my *claim*; the woods are surely very beautiful in summer, and we are quite close to a lake. . . . But I repeat: for the first two or three years, life won't be as pleasant as it will be later on; and yet, unless Marie has changed, I think it would agree with her well enough. You can see that I am taking life seriously and that my attitude is positive; but I will leave it to the novelists to express poetic sentiments about love because, if I feel love in my heart, I prefer to show it by my actions and not on paper. I felt love for Marie, I haven't loved anyone since then, and I think that if she were here I should feel even more love for her now on account of her simple manners, her excellence as a house-wife, her cheerful ways, and, I believe, her Christian faith. I say "I believe" because in those days I myself had scarcely any firm ideas about what Christianity means, and I didn't discuss it much with her. My dear Aunt Narbel told me that she thought she [Marie] was a good Christian.

The reason I've never discussed this with you is that I thought I ought to wait, and until now I was hardly in a position to marry. But now it would be pleasant and useful to have a good wife, and of all the girls I've ever known Marie is the only one who has made a good impression on me and the only one who combines the qualities of a well-bred young woman with those of a farmer's wife. No doubt there are a great many who are burning with eagerness to lavish their attentions on chickens and cows, but after a few months the little woman would want to go to dances or spend her time gossiping with the neighbors, and so on. So it's now up to you: if you know of anyone who would suit me better, that's another story and I'll do as you think best. If not, write to Marie, and if she agrees, make the necessary arrangements as soon as you can so she can come as soon as possible.

It is getting rather late, and I want to read a few chapters [of Scripture] and enjoy a few good moments of communion with God before I go to bed. So good night, dearest Parents—may God watch over you and keep you in good health. Pray for me that He may guide me at this time and that He may cause everything to work out for my well-being.

Good-bye, dear Father, dear Mother, dear Brothers, dear Sister, dear cousins, relatives, and friends—and remember your very loving brother, son, and friend

Theodore Bost

**Theodore to his parents**

Chanhassen<br>Thursday, December 20, 1855

Dearest Parents:

Today [having been chosen] by the Governor to be an occasion for giving thanks to God for all the blessings He has bestowed upon us during this past year, I am abstaining from work, not so much on account of that as because I don't want to offend my neighbors, who consider this day as sacred as a Sunday. As for myself, I think all the days of the week ought to be regarded as *"thanks giving days."* In addition, I sang some hymns this morning and spent some good moments in prayer.

My situation has changed a little for the better since I last wrote to you. I have moved into the old cabin, which is eight feet square, four feet high at the north end, and seven feet high at the south end. Before moving in I took some earth from the cellar, mixed water with it, and then threw it with all four fingers and my thumb between the *logs* of the cabin walls, so that now I am cosy and warm, and in the morning when I wash I have hardly any ice in my room instead of seeing my drinking water turned to ice at a distance of eighteen inches from the red-hot stove.

This cabin is now my bedroom, living room, dining room, pantry, etc., and if I stay near the door and pay attention, I can spin around three times in a row, pivoting on my heels, without knocking anything over. Seated on my (empty) nail keg, I can do everything I need to do without getting up; I tend my fire by leaning over to my right, where I also keep my kettle, etc., within arm's reach; then, by leaning over to my left I write you this letter on a table where I keep my lamp, a tin can (in which I've put my ink, since freezing cold cracked my glass inkwell), a cup, etc.; then, still perched on my keg, by leaning over backward I land on my bed which serves me as a backrest. Speaking of the bed and table, I've made myself a bed—how handsome it is!—and a table—oh, what a beauty! The former is so strong that last Sunday, when I was cautiously getting out of bed, it suddenly gave a cry of distress and let me go crashing down onto my old trunk which let me fall to the floor after having inflicted a fine V-shaped wound on my heel, except that the cut was I-shaped in depth. When I looked around, I saw that my bed had followed me down and that, even though it had not suffered an inch-long cut, it had dislocated, or rather fractured, a hip; I have applied several bindings to it, but every night when I begin to crawl into bed it starts to complain and tries to throw me to the floor. But by clinging to the roof and to some pegs driven into the *logs* I give it a good shaking until it understands that it must take me in; after which, holding my hat in one hand and hanging on to a *log* with the other, I wave the former until my lamp is blown out. The next morning, by taking the same set of precautions, I get my feet into my carpet slippers and there I am, fully dressed!

When one of my neighbors learned that I had cut myself this way and that I had spent a whole night without being able to sleep on account of the cold, he came over to see me, bringing some tools with him. Since I had spent the whole night looking up at my roof and the stars as well, we set to work together to fix up the little cabin where I now live. It's worth a great deal to have good neighbors. I have some others who live about a mile from here who give me buttermilk to make my pancakes with and give or lend me many other things as well.

Today I was in Smithtown, at the western end of Lake Minnetonka. From the top of the hill that runs along the edge of the lake I was able to guess where the *town* was, and, as I went down the path leading to it, I was impressed by the lake's beauty. Though I am used to seeing great expanses of water covered with ice, it seemed to me that this frozen lake had an unusually mild and tranquil aspect. The broken, heaped-up ice you see in the St. Lawrence has a kind of beauty but isn't pleasant to look at. Lake Champlain, too, is quite beautiful when frozen over, but it is almost too big and the banks have been deforested to make room for human habitation. But Minnetonka is still wild—not exactly wild, but not civilized; that is to say, there are woods all around it rather than fields dotted with stumps.

As these thoughts were going through my mind I came to the village, which is quite attractive. They have planted trees everywhere, the streets are very clean, no one has fallen ill there so far, the people are all Christians and have never had any lawsuits among themselves. Of course, I should add that the entire population so far consists of a man, his wife, his mother, and his children. Their house and *store* make up the whole village. These are now built of *logs*, but in a few years the town will have more houses because the *storekeeper* has the lowest prices of anyone between here and St. Paul and perhaps in all Minnesota outside St. Paul. I bought about thirty pounds of flour, pork, etc., and went home singing as I climbed the hill, which is the steepest but shortest way. "The steep slope of this mountain . . ."[4]

The roads are hard going, poorly laid out, deep in snow, and [so bad that] I was obliged to cut across the fields for about two *miles*. Four *miles* going and four coming back makes eight miles and in addition I lost three miles by taking a wrong turn, which makes eleven. Then my load began to seem very heavy because of the bad walking—the upshot of all this was that I worked up a great sweat and my two flannel shirts got as thoroughly soaked as they did last summer. Yet at the same time my moustache (?)[5] and mouth were covered with ice, and my eyes, suddenly watering in the bitter cold as I came out of my cabin, formed teardrops that turned to ice in the corners of my eyes. That was the part I liked the most. In a short length of time one sees enough to talk about for years, and when a person is strong and healthy, the colder it is, the better he feels.

Oh, if you could only see how beautiful the weather is! The moon tonight shines more brightly than I've ever seen it, and it is almost full, just as it was on the fourteenth of July, 1848, when I said good-bye to you to go to Bellevue. It's so cold that the *logs* in my big house make continual crackling noises, and I have great difficulty keeping warm even in my little cabin, but there is a certain grandeur about this frigid silence. Outdoors everything is quiet, and the dry leaves that still cling to the oaks don't make the slightest sound. The thing that impresses me most strongly is that instead of feeling lonely in such complete solitude, I seem rather to be surrounded by friends, and it seems to me that God is close and all around me.

The day after tomorrow is Christmas! And then New Year's! The weather is utterly magnificent. I just got back from the *meeting*. There I learned that last night in Shakopee—six miles from here in a low-lying area—they had a temperature of thirty degrees *below zero* Fahrenheit! Being on higher ground, we must have had a higher reading than that. On the way back my knitted nose protector froze onto my face. But when the sun shines brightly, this cold weather is splendid. I am happy this evening, having sung [hymns], read, and prayed.

January 1

I expected to spend the day by myself, but a boy came and made a call on me . . . and then, later on, he came back to help fell some trees. I celebrated the holiday yesterday by using butter instead of lard in my pancakes. By the way, you mustn't scold me if this ink is pale; the reason is that it has been spoiled by freezing and unfreezing so many times, and I can't find a new bottle in any of the villages around here.

Happy New Year to all of you, dear Parents, and may God heap blessings upon you, may He sustain you in your old age, dear Father and Mother, and may He make your life easier than it has been up to now.

Your most affectionate
Theodore Bost

On Tuesday, January 29, 1856, Theodore became a naturalized American citizen at the Capitol in St. Paul. This cost him one dollar. "I wouldn't have done it if it hadn't been necessary to hold a claim," he wrote.

**Theodore to his parents**

Chanhassen
Minnesota Territory
March 13, 1856

Dearest Parents:

Now that I know what it is I have to say, I can write it with joy and without hesitation—I'll try to be brief.

Your first letter, dear Brother,[6] hasn't reached me. It went down with the *Pacific*. The second one came almost three weeks ago, and I waited for the first one to know how to answer. The third and fourth came yesterday afternoon, and—a sign that I'm not yet fully Americanized—they kept me from sleeping last night. You'll easily understand this when I say that I didn't know which of the Bonjour girls was Julie and which was Sophie. I had always had the [mistaken] idea in my head that Sophie was the older of the two, and, although I like and respect the older girl, I wasn't aware of the great difference [in age] between M. N. [Marie

Narbel] and her, and I'll admit that it was a little difficult for me to give up an old attachment in order to fix my choice on a young woman whose merits were not (in my opinion) so very much greater. Although I may seem rather frivolous, I am really very constant, I believe, where the affections are concerned; and I repeat, it wasn't easy for me to give up my Marie—all the more difficult in that I considered myself almost obliged to give my preference to her if she still had any memories of me, even if I didn't love her passionately; besides, it would have given me pleasure to make her happy. But the idea of having sickly or feebleminded children has always terrified me, and I regard it as a duty to avoid doing anything that might have that result. Recently there has come into my hands a paper giving many examples of such children born of marriages between cousins; and besides, the granddaughter of the wife of the former owner of my *claim*—also the child of cousins—is deaf, and people say that was the reason. This thought, prompted by duty, has influenced me more than all the arguments based on my own [chances for] happiness, though I confess that the latter had a strong appeal; and once I had decided to break with the past, these arguments kept me gazing up at the stars through the holes in my roof.

But I'm afraid I may still not be exactly correct in my ideas about Julie and Sophie, because the latter was such a mischievous little thing that I fear she may not have been the one who turned into the reasonable, affectionate young woman you've told me about. The elder sister was a big, strong girl whom you seemed to like better than the younger one, and right up to yesterday evening I had thought she was the one you were suggesting for me. I could live happily with her, too, though not as happily as the one I called "the mischievous little thing," the one I now think is the girl you have in mind. While I'm on the subject, ask her if she isn't the same one who, at the age of thirteen or fourteen at Aunt Narbel's, as she was about to go off to bed that last night, suddenly said to me, "Give me a kiss," and then, just as I was going to take her at her word, gave me a little slap on the cheek, turned her back on me, and ran away. If she's the one and if she will give me the great happiness of coming here, we shall see whether or not she'll have to make amends for both the slap and the refusal of the kiss. There are other things about her that I could add, but let it go for now.

. . . As for the "finer things" of life, these have been splendid this winter. During the past six or eight weeks I've been suffering from acute dysentery (caused by the food). All this time, both day and night, I've had the beautiful heavens for a roof, a foot of snow on my floor, and the air around me warmed to thirty-three degrees below freezing. I am physically tough when I'm happy, but I don't think I should subject anyone else to this kind of life. If Sophie's answer is "Yes," I'll get right to work and build all sorts of pretty little houses. Then, on the subject of domestic servants, I can easily design my house so as to have well-separated bedrooms. I can't give you any answer about servants' wages; servants are extremely rare hereabouts, there are no older women, and the younger ones get married to farmers as soon as they arrive. If Sophie can afford it, she would do better to bring one with her from Europe, someone who wouldn't play us the mean trick of leaving us in the lurch after we had paid for her passage. I have just been told that a servant's wages are between $2.50 and $3 a week, not including board, and that they all do exactly as they please.

As for the formalities of getting married, I don't know where I can find out what we need to know—I get lost in anything that has to do with legal forms and requirements. I'll do my best to get the information.

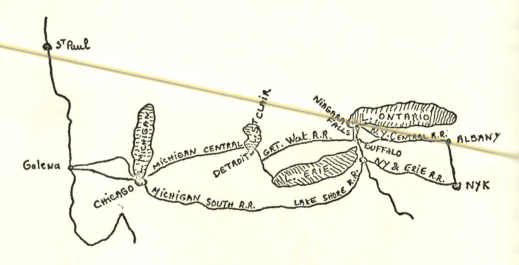

Routes from New York to St. Paul

I give you above, from memory, a map showing the two railroads one can take to get here. The New York Central is more popular than the New York and Erie Railroad, although the latter is better for those who tire easily, the seats being wider by several inches—six, I think—but the New York Central is more dependable. The Great Western has the advantage of going over the bridge at Niagara Falls just a few hundred feet downstream from the falls and is a good deal more direct than the Lake Shore [line]. I believe, though I'm not completely certain, that when you take the Great Western you have to change at Rochester. In any event, the conductors are very polite to ladies and will give any information desired.

The Michigan Central is better and goes through a more attractive region. From Chicago, take the train to Dunleith, which is on the Mississippi. When I came here last year, Dunleith didn't exist, but now that the *cars* go to the Mississippi, a city has been founded where the trains stop. From there to St. Paul, take the mail *steamers* or the People's Line—a line that is being organized to force the mail boats to lower their fares. Once aboard any of these fine boats, she can make herself *at home* and rest to her heart's content.

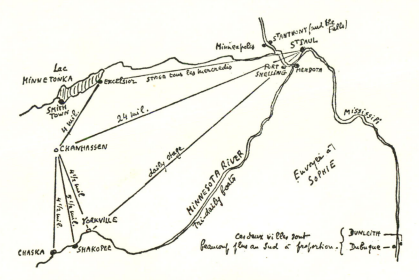

**Routes from Chanhassen to St. Paul**

ALONE ON THE CLAIM

From St. Paul to Chanhassen there are three ways to travel: (1) take the stage to Excelsior; this leaves every Wednesday from St. Anthony—and from St. Paul to St. Anthony there are two coaches every day; or (2) the *Daily Stage* from St. Paul to Shakopee; or (3) the *semi-weekly tri-daily boats*[7] that go up the Minnesota River and from which one can land at Yorkville, three miles from here—this is the most comfortable way to come, but is the least regular in respect to schedules. But there is talk of starting a regular line next year, or rather this year as soon as the ice has gone out of the river. It is about 1,700 miles from New York to St. Paul, 300 to 400 of which (from Dunleith to St. Paul) are by water. One can make the whole trip in four or five days. In any event, one must travel first class; the second-class accommodations are wretched. The fare varies a good deal, but for $30 to $40 one can make the whole trip from New York to St. Paul. Take a *through-ticket* and register all baggage for the entire journey. Bring as many books as possible—they are expensive and hard to find in America. For at least a month in winter one has to stay indoors to keep warm, so there is plenty of time for reading. Besides, if Sophie comes, and especially if she brings a servant, she will have plenty of spare time. Bring very warm clothing and shoes and also—here's the farmer speaking again—a few pounds of alfalfa and sainfoin to sow; there's none to be had here. Chanhassen is thirty miles (twelve leagues) *West of St. Paul.*

Good-bye, dear Tim, may God bless you and send you at least a good answer.[8] I'll write a longer letter soon. Good-bye dear Father, Mother, sisters, brothers, and so on. May God be with you and with me.

Theodore Bost

P.S. Nothing but lack of money would keep me from improving the house and maintaining my wife properly, but I'd like a thousand times better to have no livestock and work like a Negro than to feel that my wife wanted for anything. If God gives her to me, and she is happy with me, I'll be happy. These last five years have already taught me how to be happy even though poor.

Good-bye and answer right away.

Saturday, the fifteenth

They tell me there is no way of getting married at a distance, but that the formalities here are very simple when the bride and groom are both present.

## ALONE ON THE CLAIM

In a second letter to S. (if I write again) I couldn't easily hide from her my [original] preference — this has already made many difficulties for me in writing this [first] one. Perhaps you were thinking it would be easy for me because I didn't know Sophie very well, but it seems to me that I remember such a great difference between the two sisters that I could no longer speak in the same way to one as to the other. As for Sophie's face, I have almost no recollection of what she looks like. You say she is strong, but I had been thinking of her as frail and very lively; in any event, she would find that I too have different manners and a new and broader pair of shoulders. What shall I do if I am still mistaken about which is which and am confusing J. with S.?

You say that Mama doesn't recommend S. as highly because she prefers Julie's more restrained manner. But that's not the way I am inclined. Mama can be happy enough just living to do her duty, but I need more than that to be happy. I won't thank you yet, but will wait to see whether Sophie accepts; but then I'll do so with joy. Where is S.? Have you written a single word about that? Is she in England? In France? How old is she? You say I should tell her that I've chosen her because she is more suitable for me than Julie on account of her age; yet at the same time you tell me that J. is the same age as me.[9]

If Sophie refuses (which I hope she won't do), I shouldn't think I had any obligation to resume relations with M. N. I can very well change ships once, as the Canadians say, but the idea of coming back after having once left doesn't appeal to me.

If S. accepts, give my best thanks right away to the Bonjour family and accept also my liveliest thanks for your interest in her and the trouble you've taken to arrange this marriage. When I think that I'll have to wait almost three months to get an answer! What a long time to wait! Perhaps, though, I'll get it sooner because the Mississippi won't be frozen much longer, the snow will no longer be delaying the trains, and I hope our mailman, who deserves to be an Irishman,[10] won't — as he has done in the past — leave our letters to gather dust for a whole week in St. Anthony, bringing only the newspapers on the excuse that there was too much for him to carry!

I spoke of writing a second letter. But isn't there a possibility that Sophie might start out — if God should give her to me — a few days after you had written me a letter telling me to begin getting the house ready? Does my sister Marie no longer think of coming to live with me? I've been waiting a long time for a letter from Mama. Affectionate greetings to the whole family.

**Theodore to his brother Etienne**

Chanhassen
March 23, 1856

Dearest Etienne:

I now answer your first question: "Chanhassen" means "maple sugar" in the Sioux language,[11] and the name was given to this *township* by the wife of a man who, just this past week, went off in pursuit of a couple of Sioux who had stolen a *racoon's* [sic] skin from him; but the Indians, when they noticed his carbine and the size of his arms and legs, gave up their skin—not their own, but the coon's—and returned it to the owner. Lake Minnewashta means "Good Water," and Lake Minnetonka "Big Water." These lakes are the most beautiful sight I've seen in America, the prairies and the forests being less beautiful than I had expected. I believe Lake Michigan and Lake Erie are magnificent, but when I saw them I was too downhearted to appreciate them properly. . . .

The Mississippi is not as pretty as the St. Lawrence, and yet the many islands in it as well as the banks of the river are covered with magnificent trees in whose shade grow enormous wild vines under which one may stroll at one's ease. Deer very often swim across the river, and the Indians with their canoes and *paddles* add still more interest to the scene. At long intervals you see a small *log house* belonging to a hardy lumberjack who has settled on government land to cut wood which he sells to the *steamboats;* then, when he has saved enough money, he leaves his cabin for good and goes up to the top of the *bluff*—which is in my opinion the real bank of the Mississippi although it is almost always a half-mile, and sometimes three to four miles, from the water's edge—where he stakes out a *claim* and makes a home for himself.

Another view that remains engraved in my memory is one from the *Big Woods* of glorious memory [where Dodd's road ran]. For an hour or two I had been following an Indian trail when all of a sudden I came out on the shore of a pretty little lake about two miles wide and three or four miles long. The lovely virgin forest surrounded it on all sides; a short distance away a deer was grazing on the grass at the water's edge. But for me the most beautiful thing was that there was no house in sight, not a sound to be heard other than the cry of some wild swans. The fish swam right up close to me looking for food.

There have been other interesting things. I was standing on a small hill between this lake and another one perhaps twenty feet away—the mound had been built by beavers. . . . A few hundred feet father on [there was] a fine stand of sugar maples used by the Indians who had left behind a sort of house made of branches and reeds. It has been given to me only a few times in the past five years to admire nature; ordinarily it weighs upon my imagination like a heavy burden, a burden such as I never was conscious of in Switzerland. This results, I think, from being surrounded at all times by people who have no imagination nor taste. When you live among people who regret that so much water flows over Niagara Falls, making it impossible to build sawmills there, and when the same people, contemplating a beautiful forest, ask themselves whether one could fatten hogs there, you finally come to the conclusion that in their country there is nothing beautiful.

So, my dear Etienne, you have your own house and, without having described it to me, you want me to give you a description of mine. The one I'm living in is eight feet on each side, eight and a half feet high at one end, and five at the other, the theory being that the roof has enough pitch to keep the rain from running through into the house. The floor is made of basswood *logs* split in the middle and with sufficient space between them so that I never need to sweep the floor. A door opening to the southwest is so well made and so well adapted to the region that in time of war one could take aim and fire a rifle through it without doing any damage. I've used a great quantity of newspapers, corn husks, mud, etc., but all to no avail—a refreshing breeze persists in blowing through it no matter what I do.

For the astronomer, too, my bedroom has incomparable advantages. The roof is so well designed that you can see only one star at a time unless you put your eye up close to one of the thousand or so holes. Also, the east door that opens into my parlor has so arranged matters with the east door of the said living room [12] that one can see the sun and moon through both of them at once.

I could say more on this subject, but I'll turn instead to my living room. The floor is made of oak boards that have been coated underneath until a week ago with ice or frost an inch thick produced by the dampness of the cellar and the infinite warmth of winter. The weather having turned warm and sunny a week ago, all this ice has fallen to the floor of the cellar, which is six and a half feet deep. The living room is twenty-three feet [long] by thirteen feet wide; the walls are made of tamarack *logs*, a low-grade species of coniferous tree that loses all its leaves in winter and is often found in marshy places. I have about twenty of them growing on my marshland. These *logs* have their chinks filled with mud on the outside and plaster on the inside, which is supposed to keep the house fairly warm. The ceiling above this twenty-three foot by thirteen foot area consists of six or seven tamarack rafters which are waiting patiently for someone to put boards over them. Such as it is, it (my living room) has one window facing south, two facing east, one facing west at the north end of the wall; also there is a door at the west end and another at the east end. The garret or attic, or what will become one when I get around to installing the ceiling, has one window facing south and one north. I'll put in partitions to make three or four bedrooms because it's too hard to heat such a large space.

Well, now I'll tell you about my oxen. The right-hand one is smaller than the other. I'm going to describe my first day's work with them. When I bought them, they hadn't been trained to work but were obedient to one's spoken command, or so I was told. Fine! I hitched them to a small *log*. "Get up!" I yelled confidently. No response. "Get up!" More silence. "Get up!" I shouted again. This time the little one looked at the big one, which shook its head. "Get up!!!" I screamed in desperation, accompanying this shout with a prodigious whack from my stick. The result was stupendous. In an instant their tails were in the air, and I was trying unsuccessfully to hold them back. The *log* leaped high in the air and rebounded, followed at a long distance by your poor brother; but all of a sudden the *log* refused to go any farther because it had met and embraced one of its friends under the snow and the shock of this embrace threw my big ox to the ground while the little one made a *demi-pirouette*. I had been yelling "Oh, oh, oh, oh, oh, oh!" the whole time, and when I caught up with them I kept on shouting "Oh, oh, oh," accompanying these cries with my walnut stick. And I brought to bear so many striking proofs of my superiority that they humbly lowered their heads and declared themselves vanquished. For the first week I had recourse to the same arguments, interspersed with repasts of potatoes and corn, and now that they see how I combine force with generosity, they follow me everywhere with pleasure and fear. Leading them, I walk very fast: (1) because their horns prick me from behind, and (2) because the [sedate] schoolmaster's pace which oxen find so pleasing is deeply displeasing to me.

My woodland consists of sugar maples on the east, maple and basswood to the north, and beyond that, where most of the timber is, I have a number of fine oaks, some of them more than four feet in diameter, some walnut trees, some flowering shrubs, basswood, maple, red oak as well as white and black, red and white elm, etc. But as for beech trees, I don't know of anyone who has ever seen any in Minnesota, and in all my explorations I myself have never seen any. I have done some felling and burning of trees this winter, and one incident showed me how highly skilled I am: one day when I chopped into my boot, the ax blade sliced in twice (among other times) with great force, cutting through trousers, boot, and stocking, but I managed not to cut myself; whereas other people who had made only a couple of attempts managed to cut themselves each time.

Well, you're a married man,[13] so you tell me, and to judge by your letter you're not sorry; you have a sweet, good-natured wife, you have a house and garden, livestock to take care of, and many friends. You have made yourself such a comfortable niche in life—and still you haven't forgotten me! When I received the news of your marriage, I was happy to know that you're happy, but I was still having such bad luck that it gave me pain to learn in detail about your good fortune. I was so depressed, so disheartened, that—although I was far from wishing other people were less happy—I rebelled against the thought that I should be so wretched while others were happy. Those times are past, thank God, and I trust they will never return. They were times of severe trial for me, unaccustomed as I then was to misfortune; but they taught me to find happiness in circumstances where others would think they were miserable.

Probably you will find out before I do whether and to whom I am to be married, and on that subject I have a few things to say to you. . . . After five years in America I know I can be happy with a young woman like M. N., and, provided she is as happy as I am, we shall both be happy.

. . . You ask me what plants can be grown here. Up to now the most widely planted crop has been corn, but if winter wheat turns out well—something that hasn't yet been tried—people will grow a lot of it. Spring wheat is beginning to be produced in quantity, and I plan to sow enough for the needs of my family—if I am to have one. People also raise oats as well as potatoes, rutabagas, beets, and the like. There are not many horses because these cost an enormous amount of money and can't be used in the woods. There are a great many, and some superb ones among them, in St. Paul. Oxen are the animals mainly used for hauling and plowing. In the pine forests there are some enormous oxen, but these cost over 1,000 frs. [$200] a pair. When they start to pull, the yoke, the chain, or the *log* has to move. The cows are far inferior to our fine Swiss animals and are relatively far more expensive to buy. Their Porcine Majesties are just as clean and well mannered as in Switzerland; the dogs and cats behave about the same as ours do. But there is one strange thing, . . . all these animals have an extraordinary fear of Indians. Some people think this is because of their smell; horses will take the bit in their teeth if they are not used to being in the presence of Indians, and dogs can hardly be restrained from tearing away their blankets and leaping at their throats.

As for the Indians, I've seen no good-looking ones among the Sioux or the Winnebagos; the Chippewas are much more handsome. The moral standards of the first two tribes are far from exemplary, seeing that people point out as a curiosity a squaw who is known to be virtuous! The poor girl! Everybody gaped at her as if she were an animal in the zoo! Both men and women have very small hands and feet; the women are short and stocky, whereas the men are more slight in build. I have seen hardly any that I think are stronger than I am, but they have the edge on me when it comes to endurance in walking or running. Their eyes are beautiful, but they have an empty look—they don't seem to be thinking about anything. Since they steal and are covered with lice, almost everyone chases them away from their houses, shouting "Pacotchi!" ("Get out of here!"). They always have such an odd and would-be majestic manner that I burst out laughing whenever I see them, which makes them laugh too. Poor people! How they persist in their wretched way of life! What a strange gift, as the Deerslayer[14] might say!

I've just realized that today is Easter, the day we used to hunt for eggs in our garden in Geneva, a holiday in Europe but not observed here where no one gives it a thought. But why should we not celebrate this anniversary of the resurrection of Jesus when we make so much noise commemorating the Declaration of Independence on the Fourth of July?

Good-bye once again. *Au revoir!*

Your most affectionate
Theodore Bost

**Theodore to his parents**

Chanhassen
Minnesota Territory
Sunday, May 18, 1856

Dear Parents:

. . . I just stopped writing to kill a squirrel that wakes me up every night gnawing at the rags I've stuffed into the cracks in my door; just now he was busy doing it on the outside when, from the inside, I put the muzzle of my rifle two inches from his head—well, he's dead, and that will teach him to come and try to do in the daytime what he was doing at night . . . This letter will be very short because I am extremely tired and my hand shakes too much.

I got back from St. Paul a week ago and am feeling much better on account of the change in my diet I had in St. Paul and also on account of some homeopathic medicine and several glasses of strong liquor I drank in order to buck myself up. This week I've been burning [branches and brush] where I've been chopping down trees, and yesterday I plowed my garden patch to sow wheat.

A neighbor told me yesterday that my oxen couldn't plow this land, which had been plowed only once before, but I hired the son of my neighbor to the west to hold the plow while I led my young oxen, and by four o'clock in the afternoon we had plowed more than half an acre. I say "we" because I pulled, whacked, and yelled while the oxen were tugging, veering off, and snorting, and my young helper was pulling, pushing, sweating, and trying to keep the plow from being entangled in every stump or clump of bushes. They heard me yelling half a mile off. At first my oxen didn't want to pull straight ahead; the incorrigible small one pulled sidewise like anything; then in the afternoon he began to pant and almost collapsed, while the big one, quite unperturbed, stolidly went about his work. Yesterday morning the little one was so crazy that he kicked me a dozen times, and on account of that I made him work twice as hard.

Ordinarily the plow brings up the subsoil if one plows more than six inches deep, but yesterday we couldn't bring any up, which shows that once my land is well cultivated it will produce more than other people's. I am far behind in my work, so I'm thinking of hiring a man for ten days or so—the *logs* in my clearing are too heavy for one man, and besides, spring having come two weeks late this year, everything is behind schedule. I leave my oxen yoked day and night. This past week I've been letting them run loose, and when I need them I go looking for them where I think they may be; I've hung a bell around the big one's neck (he's as quiet as the other is wild); the little one gets tired of walking straight ahead and starts to circle around the big one, who rarely goes more than a mile from home. My cow hasn't had her calf yet, but I'm expecting it any day now—and then, instead of drinking plain water, I'll have some good milk. You people who can have it whenever you want it can have no idea how much I long for it. Pork and potatoes and soup made from odds and ends get terribly dull after a while.

I'm sending you a few violets from my *claim* instead of some of the flowers we don't have at home [in Switzerland] because it's better to remind myself that my world is something like yours. Only these violets have no smell.

Yesterday evening when I was through plowing I stretched out on my bed to rest a few minutes; when I awoke, the moonlight was streaming into my cabin. I got up and went out for a breath of air and stood there for a few moments looking around at the landscape. The trees are beginning to put out leaves, and the *whip-poor-wills* were almost frantically repeating their cry. My fire had spread from the clearing and was burning the dead leaves in the woods; a few big maples, rotten but still standing, also caught fire, their branches falling one after another, and then the trunks themselves came down. My oxen kept at a respectful distance and, being tired, had no wish to take to their heels as they usually do when the fire gets close. After looking for some time at this charming scene, I took off my boots and slept the sleep of the dead until six o'clock this morning, almost twelve hours without interruption, I was so tired from shouting, whacking, pulling, etc. . . . Just the same, this is a good occupation: I feel happy when

I'm tired; one can always find something to laugh at. I'm scarcely aware of the privations I have to put up with.

Speaking of privations, I'm getting very impatient to have a reply to my proposal [of marriage to Sophie]. I'd be terribly disappointed if I couldn't have Sophie after having yearned for her—I'd even say *expected* her—these three months past. Besides, I'd prefer to have her arrive here in the summertime when the vegetation is at its best and the countryside looks like something other than a desert. I realize that in summer I'll have less time to spend with her, but I'd always be close to the house, and she'd surely hear me even if she couldn't see me. It seems to me, now that I'm getting the farm into production, that we could get along very nicely, having plenty of everything and improving our position from year to year. This year the house will be warm, I hope, and next year the interior will be more attractive. I think I shall have to dig another well: the existing one has been almost filled in by the terrible frosts we've had this past winter—the earthen walls have collapsed.

I'll stop here for today; in a couple of weeks I'll write again, if it pleases God. I'm off to church, where I'll hand this letter over to the postmaster.

Good-bye, dearest Parents—Father, Mother, brothers, sisters, etc. . . . and dear Sophie Bonjour. I won't say much about her in this letter because I don't know if she's coming or not, and until the doubt is resolved, I can't bring myself to write about her. *Adieu* to everyone.

> Your most devoted, weary, and happy
> Theodore Bost

**Theodore to his father**

> Chanhassen, Minnesota
> Sunday, June 29, 1856

Dearest Father:

Here is another letter, but it will be my last one until I have had an answer from M. and Mme. Bonjour. After hoping for such a long time, I begin to be afraid, and I don't like to write when my spirits are low. My dear Sophie—I say "my" until I have proof to the contrary—can tell you how dejected I was last Thursday: I was expecting a letter from her, and all I got was a letter telling me of Marie's illness. It's true that Mama, Samuel and his Sophie, and

Auguste send me good letters, but [the news of] Marie's illness made me despondent and so I felt completely discouraged.

I can see that this year I'm going to have to do what many newcomers do—be satisfied to watch my neighbors enjoy their large, rich fields. I haven't yet been able to get my field plowed and have only an acre and a half planted. If it pleases God, I'll be able to plow two acres this week and plant them to potatoes and buckwheat. It takes four yokes of oxen to break the land and tear up the roots of small trees, and the older *"settlers"* have made arrangements this past year to help one another; the new settlers don't yet have any oxen and so have to be content with admiring other people's fields. That causes me more pain on your account than on my own because I'll have enough to live on (if I buy meat) with what I can grow on my one and one-half acres, and I'll have more time to work on my house and get more land ready for planting [next year].

Here are the answers to the two questions you asked in your last letter. The best way to get from St. Paul to here is to take the *steamboats* (one almost every day this year) as far as Chaska. *Cars* is the term used to mean the railroad, like *"chars"* in Canada and *wagons* in England; anyway, there is a railroad from Chicago to Dunleith. The *cars* are *wagons* about sixty feet long, heated in winter. Every traveler ordinarily takes a whole seat (two places), and the men are polite enough to remain standing so as not to disturb the [unaccompanied] ladies unless they are invited by the latter to sit down, which the ladies never do without being introduced. Generally there are lots of vacant seats, and you can have all the room you want. Traveling is very pleasant in the States. Not only are the *cars* and the *steamers* very luxurious, but the hotels you stay in are as comfortable as a private home: you can go in and out as you please without anyone running after you to demand payment. On the Mississippi only, it is customary to give twenty-five cents per trunk to the boy who carries them on and off the boat. You talk about "preparations"—I had forgotten that in Europe a trip is a very serious matter; as for myself, if I were to sell my farm and return home, I'd put on decent clothing, take my money in my pocket, and leave without any baggage, not even an overnight bag—that way it's so much more convenient and economical of time. It's true that I'm not a young lady.

I've come to the bottom of the page and must close now. Every week I impatiently await a letter—not from Sophie's parents, for they will not have received my letter until just recently—but the one that will tell me what answer they've given to my dear Sophie.

Good-bye, dearest Father. My best greetings to the whole family. I'll write next week to Salies [-de-Béarn].[15]

May God be with you.

Theodore Bost

# V

# Waiting for Sophie

**Theodore to his father**

[Written in early July, 1856]

At last, dear Father, I've finished a map [for Sophie] which
has given me as much trouble as yours did, but you go to such
pains for me that I should put myself to a little trouble for you.
To begin with, I must thank you for getting me so completely entangled with Sophie. I know very well that it's a lot harder to dis-
entangle oneself, but at least so long as I'm in the net I enjoy life
more than I would if I weren't in it. You may be sure that I shall
have enough courage to survive a "break" if there must be one. As
a matter of fact, for five years now I've been able to do without
happiness—more or less, you might say, like the Gascon's horse
that died just when it had learned to live without eating. Still, I
hope there will be no need to return to practicing my obligatory
indifference [to pleasure], which was more apparent than real.
So don't worry, dear Father—I believe you more than I do her.
She does her level best to make me think she is not as you portray
her, and every word of her letters completely refutes what she
says. You deserve a good scolding for telling her that I'm waiting
to welcome her to my "cabin open to all the winds" before I've
had a chance to fix it up. If you write me that she's leaving a week
after the date on your letter, I'll undertake to get the house in
perfect order during that time and meet her in St. Paul. You won't
find any of those lazy good-for-nothings, such as you have in
Asnières, around these parts! And furthermore, [I don't think
much of] your notion of letting her read everything I've written

96

# WAITING FOR SOPHIE

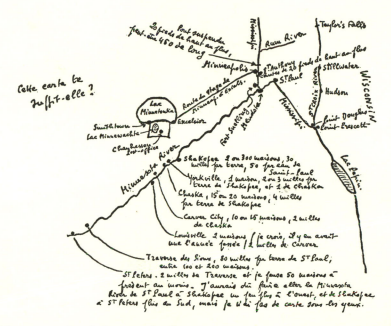

[Without a map I can't show you the distances, but I give you figures, which will do just as well. Strictly speaking, Chanhassen is the house belonging to the Lymans, who have a big farm; he is our *post master*. Mrs. Cle[a]veland gave the *post office* the Indian name Chanhassen (maple syrup), and the whole township is beginning to be known by this name. My place is about thirty-two miles from St. Paul, six from Shakopee, five from Chaska, four and a half from Yorkville, six or seven from Carver, and at a comfortable distance from the German town. What we call "La Germanie," "L'Allemagne," "Germany," "Deutschland" is an ill-defined area that begins three miles west of my place; it has been settled by a bunch of Germans whom we have nothing to do with except for politics. However, since they are not very intelligent in that field, we are going to try, if possible, to have ourselves included in another county.]

**From St. Paul to Chanhassen**

to you! Because looking down from the battlements of her castle[1] she keeps giving me digs for which she seems to be getting the information out of my letters. Hence I'm very pleased that you are getting her to send me letters [of yours] in which you praise her — maybe, between the two of us, we'll succeed in convincing her that she is what she is. You tell me to keep up my patience, that she's more worth waiting for than Rachel.[2] A fine way to make me patient! The result will be to make me swim across the ocean to take in tow the steamer that's bringing her to America. I'm going to ask her what you've been telling her about me. I'm worried that your fatherly affection may have painted too bright a picture of some aspects of my character. But, not being as modest as she is, I haven't yet told her the awful truth about myself. Anyhow, it would be hard to do because there isn't anyone who could give a perfectly accurate description of my character.

Good-bye, dear Father and everybody. May God bless you and all of them.

Theodore Bost

**Theodore to his parents**

Chanhassen
Minnesota Territory
Sunday, late September, 1856

Dearest Parents:

Your last letter gave me much pleasure, although I had been hoping for better news about our dear Marie. Thank you, dear Sister and dear Mother, for your good wishes in connection with my marriage, and thank you, dear Father, for the trouble you're taking to "wind things up." Try to make yourself as seductive as you can, because the suspense becomes painful when a fellow is obliged to wait four to five months for any answer at all from the parents. Are they afraid I'm too isolated? But, just as I am now, I have two neighbors within half a mile, whereas M. Vaucher [in Switzerland] didn't have anybody closer than a mile away; and if Sophie and I should want to, we could build a house between these two neighbors, the Maxwells and the Moores (the latter have just bought the Hobsons' farm); but it seems to me that I'm already close enough to other people so that it's not exactly like living in a desert. As for the question of money, I think I already have enough to get along as I have been with this *claim*, though if I had a little more, I could develop it more rapidly and get a larger income from it. I am more and more firmly convinced that a person can make money out of a claim because, even though I haven't, so to speak, raised anything this year, I could sell my *claim* with everything on it for enough to repay what I owe you and have two or three hundred *piastres* [dollars] left over. The price of *real estate* is rising faster and faster.[3] The corn, dear Mother, is very fine here; mine was over eleven feet high and was not field corn of the coarse variety. I had only a fifth of an acre in corn, but I expect to have between 800 and 900 bushels of shelled corn, not counting five or six bushels that the squirrels have eaten.

I have $200 in the bank at 12 percent a year which I could invest at a much higher rate of return in my *claim*. But if this land is *in market* before I've been able to realize the value of my next year's crops, I'd be in a bad squeeze.[4] I'm also thinking of going to see one of my neighbors and arranging to have about twenty more acres broken with his help, which could cost me $120 — $6 an acre. It's a high price, but crops are selling for a very good return.

In Carver they have chosen me, along with Lyman, Powers, and Adams,[5] to represent the *Chanhassen Precincts* at the Republican Convention in Minneapolis. The Republicans are opposed to slavery, whereas the Democrats are in favor of extending it [into the Territories]. I wasn't able to attend the meeting on account of the rain, but I'll compensate myself by going to St. Paul where I'll stay with a friend and bury my nose in reading matter from morning to night.

Good-bye, dearest Father. May God be with you and bless you for all the good you have done. Good-bye, dear Mother and dear Sister. May God be with you.

Think sometimes of your happy hermit,

Theodore Bost

**Theodore to his brother Théophile**

Chanhassen
Sunday, November 28, 1856

Dearest Philo:

Winter is here, and with it the long evenings — hence I have time to write. I've just learned from Tim of your marriage, on which I congratulate you. I hope you'll live happily with your Eliza (that's her name if my memory is correct), whom you ought to bring here so I can make the acquaintance of this new sister you are giving us. I suppose she speaks French, because it would be quite difficult to be married to a girl who speaks nothing but English when the young man has had, as you tell the story, so much trouble making himself understood by her father in that language.[6] I wish I could have been there when you were talking with your father-in-law. I recall the time when I was afraid of making mincemeat of English and all the embarrassments that caused for me. Now I tear it to shreds without pity, and if the people I'm talking to don't understand, I modestly conclude that they don't speak the language.

So, then, that makes five of the Bost boys who are married; who'll be the next? I will, I hope, because although I'm not the eldest, I'm certainly the one that needs a wife the most urgently. And yet I'm happy as I am; I feel so serene after five years of troubles, so free after so many tricks of fate, that I bear my woes patiently; and I await my Sophie with as little impatience as possible. You are lucky, Philo, not to have had difficulties with the father as Tim and I have.[7]

Today I have more leisure than usual for the following reason: You may know that last summer I was employed to assess the property of the residents of this district, which led me to travel all over the region. In the course of these wanderings I came across a pretty lake, Clear Water Lake, which is about two miles by three, almost square, with a sandy beach and a pretty island in the middle. Not being a poet, I can't explain to you what a charming effect that lake had on me, but if I hadn't already taken up this claim, I'd have taken one fronting on this lake. When I got back here, I told several people that this lake would be a marvelous location for a *country seat* (summer cottage), and two of them, Cleaveland[8] and Adams, came over to see me early Wednesday morning to ask if I would go with them as guide, interpreter, etc., etc. . . . Like a true American, I didn't take long to make up my mind: I bolted my breakfast, turned my oxen loose together with my cow and my calf, wishing them *bon appetit*, snatched up my rifle, and we were off. Five miles from here we had to strike out across the fields with no guide but the sun. I soon realized that I had dropped down too far to the south but I said nothing about it, and after we had worked our way back toward the north we came to a place where ten men were busy *raising a barn*; . . . since I knew them all, I [knew where I was, so we] soon came across a road leading to the lake, which is almost entirely surrounded by Swedes. We went into the *store* where they were selling the meat of a deer that a twelve-year-old Swedish boy had just killed. From there I took them a half mile farther south to the house of another Swede who had killed a deer while it was swimming in the lake a week before. Having asked him how much he wanted for his claim, which I thought was too much, I went to the farm of a Tyrolese where I had recently stayed overnight. From him I felt sure of getting a better bargain, and, to the great satisfaction of my friends, who didn't understand a word of the

French we were speaking—the Tyrolese and I—the deal was concluded: about 150 acres for $550, the price of the land having already been paid to the government, which is very cheap.

Then we went a mile to the west to spend the night—they stayed with a young Swede who lives on a peninsula at the southwestern end of the lake, and I, along with another young man [named Bingham], who was with us, put up at the house of another Swede who also lives on the shore of the lake. These Swedes are almost all *close communion* Baptists, excellent people, industrious, and good at carpentry. Most of their houses are built with a floor . . . made by splitting tree trunks (usually basswood) so as to make planks about two inches thick. It's good to see the accuracy with which they do this work. He too [Theodore's host] had killed a deer, and our supper consisted of venison, potatoes, coffee, and cranberries. His house is built in the midst of the trees that surround the lake where the deer come down to drink. After supper we were startled by the cries of his wife and their little girl; on going outside the *log house* we found it was only a deer that had frightened them; it had passed by quite close to them, and they hadn't been able to see it coming because the moonlight hadn't been bright enough. We went to bed, and then the next day, after a magnificent breakfast, we paid them forty cents each for our meals and beds, and I bought for myself two *raccoon skins* and two *muskrat skins* for a dollar.

We came back here with my friends, and on the way I negotiated another deal for them with an old German while the two Americans looked on without knowing what to say. This time I got an even better price than the day before, that is, 110 acres for $275. When it was all settled, I said good-bye to them and continued on my way toward the west with young Bingham, who wanted me to show him a part of the country where he might stake out a *claim*; so we went through the woods following the marks that had been made on the trees to blaze the trail. We got lost in a marsh after we had been walking for four hours. . . . Then we went a mile or two south, finally coming upon a sort of road along which we hoped to find a place to spend the night. Not having had any dinner, and with *poor prospects* of getting any supper, I was looking for game and after a few minutes I saw a pheasant. . . . Knowing myself to be a poor marksman, I didn't dare aim for its head for fear of missing it altogether, so I aimed for its body, which worked so well that the bullet left behind nothing but the head and a piece of leg. I burst out laughing and asked young Bingham what we should do; he decided that there was too little to be worth the trouble of cooking it, and I decided that this time I had outsmarted myself. After walking an hour, we came to a house where there was a dead deer; going inside, we found that it belonged to some Germans, had supper with them and breakfast [in the morning]. The American paid them $1.25 for the two of us. . . . A neighbor had found and tied up my oxen, but hadn't been able to catch my cow, which is still at large unless Cleaveland rounded it up when he got back. I'll see him in a few hours and find out what he's been doing. And this is why I'm at leisure to-day . . . long live America!

All right, now, own up! Wouldn't you rather be in a half-savage country, living as free as the wind in the fields, treating everybody you meet as though they were old acquaintances, than live as you do, surrounded by chimneys, gaslights, omnibuses, etc. . . . ? But let me give you some details about my house that was so cold last winter. I've put in a ceiling and built a partition in the middle [of the larger cabin]. This gives me a bedroom about ten by sixteen feet and seventeen [*sic;* "seven" is probably meant] feet high, a window on the east, one on the south, and a door into the north room; the stove is in the middle of the bedroom, the table is between the south window and the stove, my bed is behind me, and my tool chest is underneath it. I'd like very much to add: *and a nice wife* [is ] beside me, but that happy day hasn't yet arrived. It's cold outdoors, but the sun is shining, which overcomes nine-tenths of the effect of the cold. Inside my room the stove is try-ing to glow as brightly as the sun, but can't quite succeed. What an advantage it is to have wood on one's *claim*! In half an hour I can chop enough wood to keep the stove going, and it's a big one. I let it burn all day long and it costs me nothing.

Well, I've chattered enough for now. I hope you'll follow my good example and let me know what you're doing in Bati-gnolles[9] where I'm sending this letter without being at all sure you'll get it. *Adieu,* dearest Philo, whom I haven't seen, I believe, for over eleven years. Congratulations again and my best wishes for happiness with your new wife. I pray for you both; you pray for me too. Send my greetings to everyone in the family who's not in Paris, and embrace for me those who are there, if any. Auguste and Elisée have written to me, and I haven't yet answered; tell them again that patience is a great virtue and that I've had to wait for them on occasion also.

Why don't you come and see the sights around here with your young wife? Perhaps for the same reason that has kept me so long in America—lack of money. Why don't we Bosts go out and make a lot of money!!!!!! But never mind, we are just as happy as many people are, and much happier than the rest. In addition, we have what many lack—the hope that one day we shall all be reunited at the feet of our Savior.

Good-bye once again, dearest Brother. Give your wife my very best greetings and remember also your brother in America.

Theodore

## Theodore to his mother

Chanhassen, Minnesota
Sunday, November 23, 1856

Dearest Mother:

No, I am not neglecting you because of Sophie. It's just that the days are short and I don't have much time for writing—so let's have peace.

Winter is here, and it was time, after all. We have had two snowstorms, one last Wednesday and one today. I wouldn't be surprised if today's snow weren't still here right up to next March. However, we could still have a few more good warm days. We have had a few days that I considered rather chilly, but I hadn't thought—as I found out later—that it was -12°R. [5°F.]. It's strange how one gets used to anything, and besides, 20° or 30°R. here seems hardly any warmer than 4°, 5°, or even 10°[R.] in Europe;[10] it is true that your feet freeze, but your teeth don't chatter. I have made a big pile of *logs* just outside my door; because they were too dry they are hard to chop up, but I want to have a good supply of wood on hand for the very cold weather. What are you thinking of when you write that I can warm myself by splitting wood? Last winter it was all I could do to keep from freezing while I chopped wood. In any event, I can't split the wood until I've chopped it into short lengths, inasmuch as I burn nothing but tree trunks and have nothing but an ax to cut them with. I can hardly believe that last year in my little cabin I burned more wood in an hour than we used to burn in a whole day in

Serrières, taking the living room and your bedroom together. My harvest has been very small on account of the small size of my field; and grasshoppers and squirrels have eaten up at least $12 in wheat and $5 in corn; also, grasshoppers have eaten my potatoes, onions, turnips, etc. So I have acquired a pair of cats who, I hope, will provide me with a dozen or so more by next summer—and then the squirrels had better watch out! As for the grasshoppers, I can only hope they will never again do so much damage.

But aside from this, I am as pleased as can be with my *claim.* The soil is better than on my neighbors' land and better than the soil of the prairies and *openings.* Everything was growing marvelously when the grasshoppers came and ate everything down to the ground and even below ground level. My corn gave a good yield, but since I hadn't planted much I don't have any to sell. (One of my cats is sitting on my shoulder, and the other is trying to rub out my words as fast as I write them.) I haven't been able to work as hard this year as I had hoped to do because the continual waiting for an answer from M. Bonjour has often drained the strength from my arms. Then, too, I wasted a lot of time cutting brush in a field of mine when I thought I was going to be able to get it broken—I did this three times.

The $30 the county owes me are for the work I did this summer when I *"assessed"* this district; I don't know how you would say what I did in French: I estimated the value of the livestock, the *improvements* and the tools of every inhabitant and gave the list to the commissioners who decide how much the owner has to pay in taxes. This year the county tax amounted to 2¼ percent, and the school tax, on account of the gross stupidity of the directors, went up to 3½ percent, which makes a total tax for the year of 5¾ percent. Everybody is furious, but there's no help for it. I think that next year it will be no more than 3 percent. Everything I own was valued at about $400 since the *claim* itself is not counted in as long as the government hasn't yet been paid for it . . .

What M. Bonjour said has made me feel like my old self once again.[11] I really was a little irritated by his silence, because I could see no reason for it. In this country marriages are quickly decided upon, and a father would never think of opposing his daughter's marriage. I had forgotten that I am not the only one who loves his parents and that other parents besides mine also love their children, and I was coming to think of M. Bonjour, not as the man I

know, but as my imagination was determined to represent him—
that is, as a father who was taking a long time to make up his
mind, giving no thought to his daughter or to me. I see now that I
was mistaken, and I can only love and respect him for his decision.
All the same, it's very odd that in Europe people think a child is
gone forever if it goes more than three leagues from the family
home! Here people speak of a journey of 1,000, 2,000 or even
3,000 *miles* as something not at all out of the ordinary.

Yesterday I spent the evening at the Adams' house where we
sang hymns and two or three of Papa's songs. I could hardly recognize the tunes, they have been changed so much to make them go
with the English words.

Since the Mississippi River is still busy putting on its winter
clothing, the mails haven't yet begun to go by stagecoach. So here
we are, shut in by the ice for another year, until next spring. Trade
will be dead except for [that of] the farmers. But I am in a hurry,
all the same, for railroads to be built in Minnesota; they would be
profitable in a few years' time despite the great distances and the
small number of inhabitants, especially merchants. As for the
visitors, they are all afraid of the winter climate and are taking advantage of these last few days of open navigation to go down the
Mississippi, unaware that they are running away from a region
where the sun shines nine days out of ten without a cloud in the
sky and where the cold weather, even when extreme, makes you
happy as a lark. Someone asked a man from the Red River of the
North if he wouldn't prefer St. Paul to living up there: "Oh, no,"
he said, "it's much too hot in St. Paul!" Someday I must go up
there and make a tour of the country, an immense territory where
the waters empty into the northern seas and into Hudson's Bay,
where there is hardly any commerce and no form of communication except by oxen and horses. Every year hundreds of them
come down to St. Paul with their *"Red River carts,"* wagons with
two wheels, built entirely of wood, loaded with furs; they return
home with blankets and supplies. The Selkirk *settlement*[12] is a
thorough mixture of French Canadians, Swiss, British, etc., and
especially half-breeds, generally half French Canadian and half
Indian—they all have magnificent black eyes, much more ex-
pressive than those of pure-blooded Indians, whose eyes are bright,
but empty of all thought or expression.

Tomorrow, Sunday, I'll have to work a little because I can't
avoid it: I've forgotten to cut my wood supply and take hay to my

livestock, so I don't have any choice. Hereabouts people are very strict about Sabbath observance, and so am I, believing as I do that it is more dangerous not to observe the Sabbath than to overdo its observance. . . .

I have only now realized that you won't receive this letter until several days after New Year's. So I wish you all a Happy New Year. May God be with you and all the rest of our family—Father, brothers, cousins, aunts, and so on. What a lot of things a person can do in just one year! May we always do only that which is good and advance every day in the knowledge and grace of our Savior.

Good-bye, dear Parents, may God be with you.

Your
Theodore Bost

**Theodore to Sophie**

Chanhassen
December 21, 1856

My very dear Sophie:

Must I, then, go back to being formal, using the *"vous"* form of address with you [rather than the familiar *"tu"*]? I suppose I should, inasmuch as I've been lectured to from two sides on the subject, and yet I can't quite bring myself to do it. As is my way, though, I'm going to defend myself for something I didn't do. In *your* [*votre*] letter from Paris—bah! I'll defend myself some other time; I don't have time today. I can only say that if I did start calling you *"tu,"* it was not "without permission," though a certain young lady may not have remembered. The reason I continue to use *"tu"* is that at this very moment—God willing—everything may have been decided and, I hope, in my favor—and in that case I couldn't very well use *"vous"* with my future wife. But if it has been decided that I shall have to find myself a wife in this country, I really don't know whether I'd have the courage to write to *you* [*vous*]: it's a lot easier to go from friendship to love than from love to friendship, and I wouldn't get much consolation from that second word.

I'm complaining again, as usual, because your [the *"tu"* form is used here and in the remainder of the letter] last letter was too short, and also because your letters are becoming *few and far between*, which doesn't do much to relieve a hermit's loneliness. I feel jealous every day when I visit the neighboring families, *such as they are;* everybody feels sorry for me, even though I don't feel excessively sorry for myself. But when I come home in the evening to a cold house, finding the fire out and unable to light it again, I have no other recourse than to throw myself on my bed while my neighbors are enjoying one another's company, laughing occasionally, talking, and reading, and I tell myself that if my Sophie were here with me, I would be far happier than all the rest of them put together, if she could be happy with me. Do you realize that little by little I've gotten so used to the idea that you are surely going to come, even though all your letters conspire to drive that idea out of my head, that I can't imagine what I'd do if you didn't come?

It's bad enough to be all alone, even in the summertime, when the days are long and I can work and move around outdoors; but at present, from four in the afternoon until ten at night, I have only a few newspapers to read and the stove to stoke with wood—six hours of solitude every day, not counting stormy days which always put me in a black mood, as at the present moment when snow is coming down, driven by a terrible northwest wind which I feel and hear all the more because I'm on top of a hill. When you wrote to me, you were sitting beside my dear father, but I'm writing to you from beside my red-hot stove, my melancholy but very necessary companion to whom I must now give something to eat. There, I've just filled it up, and in ten minutes I'll have to fill it again. There is some satisfaction in knowing that I have too much wood on my land.

Many people, the Maxwells among others, can hardly wait to see you, and I don't have the courage to tell them that everything isn't already decided. But here a whole year has slipped away since the time when I was hoping to be married in the spring. And yet, though each day has seemed like a century to me, without exaggerating at all, the last year has gone by very quickly.

How does it happen that you've received from Paris the first letter in which I was so impudent as to call you *"tu"*? I must admit that, after all, when I think how bold I was, I begin to think I'm not *the most bashful young man you ever saw*, though everybody says that's what I am. Oh, if you could only see what *courtships* are like here in America, you'd never talk about impudence! So don't be surprised if from time to time I give you cause to call me impudent—it's been too long since I've lived with really modest young people.

## WAITING FOR SOPHIE

My father talks to me of sobriety (in the moral sense) and praises me for being more prudent than he is, etc. Alas! If he only knew what I'm like in the depths of my soul, he would know whether or not I'm moderate in my desires—but who can be moderate at the age of twenty-three (which I'll be in three weeks)? It is true that, more than most young men, I can restrain my imagination, but that doesn't really make me any more moderate. Oh, how I wish I could know for sure that you're coming! That would allow me to get through the winter with joy while waiting for spring to come. I fear for my own interests in connection with your staying with your family, with your sister, who is so flatly opposed to your leaving, and with your parents, who aren't at all in favor of your going. Although my father hasn't written me a word about his visit to your father, I have the conviction that the outcome depends a great deal on you, and how can I manage to persuade you to come? I neither can nor want to mislead you with an imaginary picture of this country, which is inferior to Switzerland from every point of view, but it sometimes seems to me that you would be happier here with me than in Europe—assuming you would have been "sweet on me" over there—because here people's family lives are all the more intense for living at a distance from other people; besides, people are calmer and less distracted by wars and famines; the husband lives more completely for his wife and the wife for her husband. But my fire is going out (speaking with reference to my stove), so I must go coax it back to life. What a pity to be interrupted in the middle of such a fine flight of eloquence!

Hurrah! I've just made a really big discovery!!! It's evidently a slip of the pen, but that's your hard luck. How dare you scold me for saying "*tu*" when, at the end of your letter, you speak of giving me a good slap on my cheek—and instead of saying "*votre*," you write very distinctly "*ta*." At first I read it "*la*," but the "t" is too clear to leave me in any doubt. "It's going too far" [as you wrote] —it's definitely going too far and I'm going to tell Papa. Ah, my young lady wants me to get a scolding from my father, yet she allows herself to fall into the same mistake I made! Well, now, you mark my words—I'm not going to forgive this offense except on condition that it's to be repeated; as a believer in homeopathy, I remain true to my principles—but, speaking seriously, wouldn't you call me "*tu*" when you'd decided to come?

The *"vous"* is too sedate for me, and all the people who have loved me have called me *"tu"* or would have if my situation had allowed it; that's why I've always attached so much importance to something you consider insignificant.

But I must stop writing, dear Sophie. Shall we be as far from one another next Christmas? As for that, we're about to begin a new year that will be decisive for the two of us. Oh! Let us pray to God to show us the way we must go, and may He give us [grace] to follow His will, whatever it may be. Naturally, I shall bless Him if this year brings you to me, but I hope I shall also bless Him if He refuses me that happiness. *Adieu, adieu*, dearest Sophie—may God give you no end of blessings, not only for this coming year, but for your whole life to come. *Adieu*, dear Bonjour family: father, mother, brother, sister. May God be with you all.

Once again, good-bye, my darling—and don't forget your devoted hermit,

Theodore Bost

**Theodore to his father**

T. Bost
Chanhassen, Minnesota
January 4, 1857

Dearest Father:

I'm finally getting around to replying to your good letter that was enclosed in the one from Sophie. I would have answered right away, but I wanted to wait a few days, seeing that Sophie sends my letters on to you. First of all, I'll answer your question:

*"Land in market"* means land that has been surveyed so that the drawing, or *"plate,"* has been sent from Washington to the *Land Office within the boundaries of which* the land is located. I paid nothing for the land in my *claim* for the simple reason that the land itself didn't belong to the *claimant*; in the same way, if I should sell my *claim*, I'd ask a high price, not for the land itself, but for the right I have acquired to buy this land at the price of $1.25 an acre. When I bought this *claim*, the *"plate"* of the township hadn't yet come back from Washington; otherwise the *claimant* would have preempted *[préempté]* (put down his money first) and kept the land. Nevertheless, if I did not prefer to keep my $200 in the bank for the time being, I would use it to acquire the *"title"* in case I need to do so. Once the government has been paid

for the *claim*, it is called a *farm*, but not many people around here have paid up.

The Democrats are for the extension of slavery, and the Republicans are against extension at the very least. It had been decided that slavery could not exist north of 36° 32′ (or 32, 36),[13] and this boundary was repealed two or three years ago.[14] Because people from the North have the right to go into the southern states with their cattle, the Southerners ought to have the right to come North with their slaves—that's what known as democracy in this country. We Republicans are opposed to the extension of slavery into the Territories, and many of us are in favor of the abolition of slavery. In the last election Buchanan, a Democrat, was the winner, so we can expect to see Kansas come into the Union as a slave state, as well as Utah with slavery and polygamy, and then let anybody say that the United States isn't a free country!!!!

So now that I've answered your questions, I will talk about my doings. What a fine Christmas I had! [I was] carrying buckets full of dirt from morning till night! Then, on December 31, I froze my right big toe and spent the afternoon of New Year's Day with young Maxwell reading some uninteresting book, and I laughed when I thought of the good old times, of the Christmas trees, the presents, and so on. I at least expected a letter, especially one from Sophie, written from her parents' house and bringing the news that they've given their consent, but I received none at all, perhaps because the *mail contractor* who carries the mail from Dubuque to St. Paul only brings it [on here] when he feels like it. The newspapers pay him compliments every day, and he is going to be dismissed. The last we heard, there were three or four tons of *mail matter* waiting to be brought here from Dubuque. Still, it would have been a marvellous New Year's Day if only Sophie had written me that she's coming! I'd like to see her father in my shoes for a month or two—maybe then he'd give me an answer. Have you written to me since your visit to him?

How I would love to see you again, dearest Father! Does an eight-day sea voyage scare you so much that you'll give up forever the thought of seeing our beautiful vegetation and our strange way of living?

This winter has been much milder than last year's. We've had only three or four really cold days. December 31 was one of the coldest, and my boot got filled with snow; my toe was frozen badly enough to raise a big blister on it. I wrapped it in a piece of cloth, and I haven't looked at it for two days. I think it has healed up.

My fire isn't particularly hot, and yet I don't feel chilly. I'm especially warm at night, and I'm grateful for that when I think how much things have changed since last year. And yet my situation can still stand a lot of improvement; for example, when I come home in the evening half frozen to find the fire out, unable to wait an hour for the stove to get red-hot and another hour for the whole cabin to warm up, I often wish my Sophie were here—not to build the fire, but to keep me company. I suppose that in Europe marriage is only one of life's pleasures, but here it is—if not the only one—at any rate one of the greatest, and for this reason I can understand why the Americans get along so well with their wives: even the least attractive of them still increases the comforts of a house by a great deal. Don't think that I am always in "a fine state of moderation"—sometimes, indeed, I am terribly impatient to receive any answer at all, but especially a favorable one.

When you get this letter, it will be almost six years since we said good-bye to one another—how many more years will go by until we see each other again? Will it be before the great Day of Judgment which will reunite us for eternity? How fortunate we are to have that hope before our eyes! And yet, for over a year now I have had less desire to die than I had three or four years ago—not that I am less ready, but I enjoy life more and I have no more of those gloomy spells that prevented me from doing anything.

And now, dearest Father, may God be with you and all those around you. Give everyone my affectionate greetings. Good-bye.

Your Theodore Bost

**Theodore to his mother**

Chanhassen, Minnesota
February 5, 1857

Dearest Mother:

It's nearly three weeks since I received your letter, so I'll explain why I didn't answer right away. There has been a succession of little mishaps, and I am now staying at Mrs. Maxwell's house, unable to write to you from my own place.

My cow has gone the way of the calf. The calf died of a jab from the cow's horn and the cold weather, and a little later my cow died in half an hour—poisoned, I believe. She got loose for two days and died the following day. It was very painful for me to watch her dying in such convulsions, but I bore this trial as I ought to bear it; in any case, she has fed me well this past year.

Another reason for my delay is that in order to avoid the danger of losing my *claim* I have to build a cabin in which I must live for one week in order to preempt; I went down to Minneapolis with a neighbor, and the officials refused to let me pay for my *claim* because one of them had made a stupid blunder when he gave me my *statement* last year. Even though it was all their fault, I was obliged to hunt up a lawyer and pay him $5 to draw up another *statement*, and in two or three weeks I hope to be able to preempt my *claim*. It is a disgrace to have officials like that, and if they give me any more trouble, I intend to read them a lecture and send it to Washington. If it pleases God, I hope I shall soon be done with this *claim* and be able to call it a farm.

So, dear Samuel and Sophie,[15] you haven't forgotten me either! Shall we meet again one of these days here below? I hope so, because the kind of life I live is rather hard if you never see your brother or sister, your father or mother, or . . . ! But I must have patience! I'm not dead yet, and lots of things can happen in the course of a year. I have a feeling that this one is going to bring me a great many new things. Whatever happens, I'll try to glorify God and behave like one of His children.

Despite the loss of my cow, if I should sell my claim and everything else I own, I would have between $300 and $400 even after repaying you your money. What handsome fortunes are being made hereabouts! Just now you can lend your money on land mortgages at 4 percent a month; or, by finding notes backed by good cosigners, you can get interest of 2½ percent a month, or 30 percent a year. But I have a bad headache, and I don't have much time to spare.

I'll conclude, then, by thanking all of you for your sympathy and by begging you to write to me often and to pray for me always.

All my love to our whole family.

Good-bye, dear relatives in Salies.

Your Theodore Bost

**Theodore to his father**

> T. Bost
> Chanhassen, Minnesota
> February 21, 1857

Dearest Father:

To give you some idea of how much I can endure, I'll tell you that the *"shanty"* where I am now living is almost exactly as good as the open air. The holes are so enormous that I have given up trying to close them. (I'm speaking about my preemption *shanty* and not about the house where I formerly lived.) Two weeks ago we had a cold snap four degrees colder than the freezing point of mercury. Poking my nose out of my blankets in the middle of the night, I could feel snow falling on my face. Thinking that the weather had turned warmer, I went back to sleep. The next morning I saw that what I had taken for snow was only my own breath that had turned into frost and fallen in my face when I rolled over in my bed. I got up and tried to light the fire, but the wood was so cold I couldn't get it to burn and was obliged to run and take shelter with the Maxwells to keep from freezing. Several days later there was a big thaw, and when I went home to my own place in the evening I found my bed covered with water, but I crawled in just the same and awoke the next morning feeling fine but wet from head to foot.

You know, of course, that I have decided to preempt this land so I can get ownership of my *claim* and that in order to do this I had to build another cabin. You also know that I went down to Minneapolis to do this preempting, and that, on account of a clerical error, I was unable to complete the process at that time. I was going to go again the following week, but then I read in the newspaper yesterday that the *Land Office* was closed and I don't know when it will reopen. Sometimes it seems to me that I have more bad luck than other people, but God does everything for the best, and besides, He has given me a good piece of land.

But to come to the main question that concerns us, I haven't yet come to the point where I'm willing to "give up" Sophie. If I gave her up, it would only be for her sake, seeing that the present state of affairs must be at least as painful for her as it is for me.

Rather than give her up, I would prefer to leave my claim next spring, lose myself for several months with surveying parties in the unexplored parts of Minnesota (Doum!) [?], and then go spend the winter in France to see if my presence might not do more good than my letters. The expense would be fairly great, but I know I can earn enough in a year to indulge myself in that pleasure. Besides, it has been six years since we last saw each other, and it's time we got together again. The cost of the trip could even turn into a gain, in fact, if I can borrow money in Europe, promising to invest it only in real estate or in mortgage loans.

As for the two girls who are neighbors of mine, "one is pretty and the other is good"; they are surely the best I could hope to get, but both prefer fellows of dubious morals to Christian young men, simply because the former have "*more of the devil in them.*" I have almost come to the point of quarreling with them over their taking communion and then keeping company with young wastrels, but it seems that their Episcopalian principles allow this. It's true that the Christian young men of this neighborhood are the sons of farmers, shoemakers, etc., and are opposed to slavery while holding puritanical views; whereas they [the girls] are the daughters of Episcopalian *aristocrats* and are consequently friends of slavery and enemies of Puritanism. As for the sister of one of my neighbors (Powers), she is in St. Paul and, I believe, *engaged.*

But, dear Father, even if I thought it right to marry one of these young women who live next door, I couldn't consult you first because in this country the girls want nothing to do with long engagements. So neither they nor I could wait for letters to go back and forth between here and Europe. But in any event I should be very careful not to marry anyone who was not a Christian girl, [but would choose] one who would do honor to our family and also be a good wife. Still, I don't like to think about such possibilities. I would rather go on believing that God will give me my Sophie. I only hope you will tell me frankly whether or not you think it would be better for Sophie to break off our relationship now.

I have just decided to build a new house, a good solid one, at the southeast corner [of my property] and less than a quarter of a mile from two others on a well-traveled road. The expense would be fairly small, and the advantages would be very great from all points of view, especially if my dear Sophie comes.

I spend nearly all my evenings visiting one or another of my neighbors. You will already have learned that my calf froze to death, even though I had put it in the stable, and that my cow is dead — from what cause I don't know. All this has made me quite discouraged.

The *Lamplighter* and other books have been lent to me by various people. The Americans are very eager to read about everything new, particularly in the *newspapers*. Good-bye, good-bye. *My love to Sophie* and to all the others. Good-bye once again —

Your Theodore Bost

**Theodore to his father**

T. Bost
Chanhassen
Minnesota Territory
Sunday, May 24, 1857

Dearest Father:

Since I have a little free time for writing, I'm going to describe for you an experience that has become commonplace for me but may be of some interest to you.

Sunday, June 7

Exhaustion prevented me from telling about the scene I had in mind, which was merely an immense fire, covering two or three square miles, that almost suffocated the ladies I was driving to Excelsior in my oxcart. The prairie fire burned over an area of about 300 *perches*[16] during my overnight absence and forced me to spend seven hours the next day putting out the fire that had spread to my stable — you should have seen how I had to work!

Today I'm very weary, having done a great deal of work for [my neighbor] Powers this past week, so you must excuse the brevity of this letter. The weather is terribly hot, which is surprising because for seven months any kind of warmth has been unknown hereabouts; the trees are almost covered with leaves, and the mosquitoes, no-see-'ems, deerflies, *gnats*, etc., are having a carnival; last night I was awakened by being bitten about twenty times. This reminded me of my responsibilities, so I got up at four in the morning and hung over my bed the symbol of summer — my mosquito netting; then, since it was Sunday, I went back to bed instead of starting my day's work, amused myself for a while swatting gnats, and then dropped off to sleep until around eight o'clock, delighted to have a day of rest. After a lordly breakfast, I equipped myself with a broom in order to chase away the insects I was sure I'd run into on the road and started off to my old house to see how my garden was growing. No sooner had I got into the woods than I could see that the broom would be of no use, so I cut a couple of leafy branches and went trotting along barefoot through the brush, etc., threshing about me to right and left till I got out of the thickest part of the woods; then I went on up the little hill where my house is. There I discovered with transports of joy that the grasshoppers had saved me the trouble of weeding my garden—not an onion, radish, or beet was left, practically no beans, melons, etc., etc., and when I asked the thousands of grasshoppers why, they answered me with their incessant "trrrrrrrrrrr."

So I've moved again, and instead of living on the northern edge of my *claim* I am now at the southwest corner near a well-traveled road and in sight of several houses, which is splendid. Besides being the chief architect and builder of this house, I take delight in living in it. All your fine kings, princes, etc., don't sleep any more proudly than I do. My house! How huge it is! It consists of one room thirteen feet by fifteen feet, with a garret of the same size; the bedroom has one door opening to the south, one window on the east, and one to the west, as does the garret. It isn't yet plastered [chinked], or rather mudded, but in this scorching weather it is a great blessing to let the air circulate more freely between the *logs*. The dooryard is really delightful. Ten feet from the door I have two oak trees (*red oaks*), one of them two feet thick, casting shade . . . I was almost getting poetic. . . . Outside the west window I have another big red oak and two basswood trees about twenty feet away. At the northeast corner, about fifteen feet from the house I have a sugar maple whose sap quenched my thirst while I was building the house. For years an old dead oak has been held up by the maple, and I, fearing that it would come down on my head someday, attacked it (the oak) with ax and fire, and it was finally brought to the ground by a thunderstorm, missing the house by twenty feet, while I was at work on the roof. I am really very pleased with this house, especially the location. . . . My dear Sophie hardly writes to me at all anymore, but I'm going to write to her in no uncertain terms to teach her not to be so jesuitical.

. . . Good-bye.

Your pioneer,
Theodore Bost

**Postscript by Marie Bost, added
to a letter from Theodore forwarded by her
to their father (February 5, 1857)**

. . . I've just sealed the letter for Theodore, and I enclosed in it a bookmark embroidered by my own feeble hands with the word "Hope." I thought it would please him to receive something civilized, even without counting the *intention* and the *meaning*.

I still suffer a good deal, but the atrocious pains that make me scream have lessened and I sleep a little at night; but I still can't get out of bed or out of the armchair where I have to stay motionless. . . .

Thank you for your little messages. . . .

Your daughter,
Marie

**Theodore to his mother and sister**

Minneapolis, M.T.
June 25, 1857

Dearest Mother and dear Sister:

Three days ago I received your letter telling me about the aggravation of our Marie's illness, but I prefer to believe she's better than think that God has called her to Him, though in that event, dear Sister, your sufferings would indeed be at an end. I have trouble understanding that you can be so ill—I who am a hale and hearty young fellow who has never been really sick in his whole life nor even seen serious illness in those around him. But you are in the care of our dear parents and that must be at least some slight compensation for your sufferings.

I was finally able to preempt [my land] yesterday. I came down here with Sarver, one of my neighbors, and we *"proved"* for each other. The officials at the *Land Office* again tried to make difficulties for me, and consequently I was very careful not to call the *Receiver's* attention to the fact that I haven't paid him the $4 to which he was entitled for having *located* my *Land warrant* (what a long time it would take to explain to you what all these terms mean!),[17] but inasmuch as his hair splitting has forced me to pay out $8.50 that I would have preferred to keep, I hope he won't feel too much impoverished without his $4.

So now I am free to live elsewhere than on my *claim* if I should have occasion to leave it. What a lot of headaches people have with their *claims*! The *Land Office* is always full of lawyers, with clients who argue with one another, but without shouting. How many times do "$5" find their way into the lawyers' pockets for consultations lasting five minutes! The officials wanted me to make use of them [the lawyers] to make out my documents at the rate of $5 each, which would have come to $10; but a very nice man who is opposed to slavery—naturally, the officials are *for* slavery—made out the two papers for $2.50 each; this, with my other $4, has saved me a tidy little sum.

I wish I had the time to tell you mile by mile about my twenty-five mile journey here from Chanhassen, but I'll have to do it in summary form. For the first four or five miles the road was terribly muddy, with water often up to my knees on account of a phenomenal rain that has raised all our lakes by four or five feet. After that there were fifteen miles of brush, lots of grasshoppers—I killed hundreds of them with one stomp—and for miles and miles we walked from one heap of them to another, crushing them happily. They are still only a quarter- to a half-inch long, but they devour everything; hence poor folk are obliged to sell out their *claims* for a song. Six miles from here we saw a stag running as though we were chasing him, but we had already seen too many deer to get excited over him. A mile farther along we saw two lakes, each one several miles across, and they were so pretty I wish I'd been able to send you one.

The Mississippi is beautiful just now. I crossed it yesterday on the suspension bridge, built high up over the falls; then, after doing my business in St. Anthony, I went a mile downstream and crossed again by an 850-foot wooden bridge that goes from one bluff to the other in five or six (I think) arches. The falls are very beautiful just now, except that thousands of logs are stranded on the rocks and that smacks too much of civilization. Minneapolis is growing fast.

My love to everybody,

Your very devoted
Theodore Bost

**Theodore to his parents and brother Samuel**

T. Bost
Chanhassen, M.T.
August 23, 1857

Dearest Relatives in Salies:

For nearly three months now I've had no news at all from Switzerland, and I begin to think it would really be better for me to break off relations with a girl who would only marry me to oblige somebody else. [Otherwise] I'd be asking her to make a sacrifice of which she might later repent, and that would also make me sorry for having accepted it. Poor Sophie — she should have begun by reading the fable about the miller, his son, and the donkey,[18] and then she would have saved me a lot of disappointment and herself a lot of unpleasantness. Anyhow, if I must forget her, I'll try to do it.

Meanwhile, this [uncertainty] puts me in a very awkward position. Fanny Maxwell is the only girl hereabouts that I could love, but — always supposing she were willing to marry me — I hesitate to tie myself in that way to such a family. I don't like to put my reasons on paper in detail; but the word *"débauché"* [dissolute, loose living] could be used in a general sort of way, and on top of all that, they wrinkle up their noses when they speak of *"parvenus,"* of the miserable Yankees, and so on and so forth. For six weeks I had stopped going there, but Mrs. M. then went around complaining about me to the neighbors and I started going again if only so she could say that some "religious people" came to visit her. Still, I don't know what attitude to take when I see that she considers herself flattered by the things that Irishman[19] goes around saying about her — it makes her laugh with delight [to hear them].

It is really disgusting to see a lady who wants to pass for a Christian behaving this way. These Anglo-Saxons can't free themselves from their stupid stiffness except by throwing themselves into total licentiousness. She is just as kind to me as before, but I don't accept many favors from her anymore and try on the contrary to pay back the ones I am already indebted to her for. And when all is said and done, I don't think she intends to do anything bad, but she has no kind of principles and simply acts on impulse. If I were going to live with Fanny at a distance from her family, that would be a different matter; she has a noble soul and a much more elevated nature than the other members of her family, so that she yields easily to good influences; she weeps frequently (perhaps from vexation) . . . and she likes the company of good Christians—in contrast to the rest of the family. But to live with her here would mean bringing in the rest of the family all the time, along with the crowd of *débauchés*, the hard-drinking young fellows who hang around them. For a long time I've tried to keep to a *juste milieu* between this family and the Americans [New Englanders], but I find that hard to do. I prefer the sometimes foolish austerity of the Yankees to the loose living of those who call themselves Southern aristocrats. These latter profess great indignation against the immorality of French women, but they also have precious little to say for themselves when I tell them that if all the deeds people believe hidden were made public, others besides French women would be convicted of the most flagrant immorality.

You write to me about politics, dear Samuel, and I could tell you a lot of things about this country, governed as it is by 200,000 or 300,000 slaveholders. I hope Minnesota will enter [the Union] as a state opposed to slavery, though the Buchanan administration is doing all it can to prevent it.[20] Even supposing that I had the inclination to throw myself into politics and that I had so few conscientious scruples that I'd be successful, I couldn't be elected to Congress for at least ten and a half years at the earliest, not having as yet quite finished the process of becoming a citizen and having to be one for ten years before being eligible to run for Congress. What a pity! They really need at least one conscientious young man among their members! But I will write no more tonight. May God bless all of you, dear family, and dear Marie especially, and you too, dear Sophie [Samuel's wife], who are perhaps quite ill at this very moment;[21] I hope, nevertheless, that my dear sister and the two of you will soon be well. Good-bye once again!

Yours,
T. Bost

**Theodore to his father**

Shakopee, M.T.
Sunday, November 15, 1857

Dearest Father:

This is going to be a really splendid letter—I feel it in advance—but since I am half out of my mind, I don't know what I can do about it. I've just received your letter of October 15 from Lyon, and I want to write to you in complete candor, come what may; I'm too tired and vexed with all these uncertainties to think of sparing other people's feelings.

I had believed for a long time that Sophie was not being altogether sincere with me and that caused me pain; but not having any proof, I didn't dare act on my suspicions. If instead of telling me she had no desire to get married [to me], she had told me she preferred somebody else, I wouldn't have complained—I find it quite natural that others should be preferred to me, but it isn't right to behave in this underhanded way. And then [there have been] all these postponements, as well as all these things she says she has been told to the effect that a girl wouldn't be valued by a young man if she said "Yes" right away—all this has often led me to think she is something of a coquette, but perhaps I'm mistaken.

As for me, I much prefer a girl who gives herself in complete confidence to one who drags things out endlessly in order to test me or to make herself seem more desirable. I know that some people put a higher value on whatever has cost them more trouble to earn, but this is not true of me. Furthermore, [the situation] almost drives me to tell lies, and I have sometimes been afraid that I might have deceived Sophie. I love her as much as ever, and I would love her as before if she were to come here; but—although I have always been sure she would make me happy—I've never thought she would be less happy than I: call that pride if you like, but it's a fact. I can never marry a young woman who thinks she's better than I am and shows by her actions that I should be ever so grateful to her for becoming my wife. You see that on this point I've become an American: "Nothing for nothing" is their principle.

But to finish on the subject of Sophie: if she consents to come, or if I come to bring her, and if she agrees—not to please you or me, but as much for her happiness as for mine—then everything remains as I told you in my last letter. But if she were always to have the notion at the back of her mind that she has given up a better prospect in order to do a favor to you and me, then the whole thing is a failure. If we marry, I'll give myself to her as she gives herself to me, and although I know I'm not much good, I can't say that I'd feel sorry for the girl who takes me for a husband. This point of view will astonish her (and you too, perhaps), but I feel it is my duty to let my pen run freely; I don't want to waste my youthful years in correspondence, feeling as though I were on a bed of thorns. Neither would it be proper to promise more than I can fulfill.

So much for the prologue and the first point. Let's go on to point two.

If you are able to make sure that Sophie continues or wants to continue this "other love," then I can't come, however much I'd like to see you; both you and I have too much need of money to spend it that way. So once I receive a frank, or hard but clear, answer to that letter, an answer without any "ifs," I shall, God willing (in case Sophie refuses), have an hour's serious conversation with Anna Maxwell during which I'll have occasion to say some big words and probably listen to some rude ones. That hour will reveal what her character is because she is a mixture of two things— perfect nobility and the incredibly lax standards of certain Episcopalians whom I don't know whether to call Christians or good-for-nothings. I'm sure she isn't as bad as she makes herself out to be, but her nature is so proud and obstinate that she cares little what people think of her as long as she acts according to what she calls good principles. Hence it would not be on account of her character that I would resort to strong language, but on account of her principles and her friends, and once I start talking to her about them, I anticipate a volley of artillery fire, but it doesn't scare me at all.

I admit that the odds are almost completely against me, but if my principles alone can't overcome them, I shall consider myself lucky not to get her. All her "friends," her relatives, her heredity, her upbringing, and even her passions push her to marry a young Irishman who, like nearly all libertines, has a few brilliant qualities (?) [sic] that make the ladies admire him. These are qualities I don't want to possess because they are foreign to my nature and because I want people to see me just as I am, or rather I want to improve the traits God has given me and stamp out the bad ones without trying to be a lady-killer and going around meowing like a tomcat. After all, without flattering [myself], those persons who have loved me and still love me are worth more than those who admire him; and even if that were not so, my conscience is clear in this respect. If I had half the money people say he has and if I loved Anna [Fanny Maxwell] enough to propose to her right now—I'm not going to—I wouldn't have any doubt at all that I could conquer the fortress after that hour of conversation because I know she thinks more highly of me than of him, but I don't blame the poor girl for wanting a little more comfort than I can offer her.

If I don't ask your opinion about all this, it's because all that would take too much time. Furthermore, I know what you want for me, and, if it pleases God, whatever girl I marry, you will have no reason to be ashamed of her. Your portrait, dear Father, is in their pretty little living room (the Maxwells'), and Mrs. M. admires it and thinks that your expression seems to be *"soverly* [*sic*] *good."* [22] So don't be afraid your son will take a wife from that family who could cause you shame. No, she is trying to behave well, and if she is blinded, it's the fault of her upbringing.

Well, this has been a long *speech*; but, as on the preceding page, I wanted to get it all off my chest.

So now you understand, dear Father, what I meant when I spoke of writing a splendid letter today. It's not often that I say everything that's on my mind, but this time I thought I had to speak clearly and a little boldly, and I think I've done the right thing. I wrote yesterday to S. B., before I had gotten your last letter, and I want you to write to her at once in whatever terms you please.

Monday morning

My thoughts are the same as they were yesterday. It's hard for me to realize that we were not meant to have everything happen just as we'd like it here below. May God lead me and us! Good-bye, dearest Sister—I ought to be happy knowing that others suffer more than I do and don't complain. Pray, all of you, that everything, all these affairs, end happily in the near future. Good-bye, dear Brothers, dear Samuel and Sophie and your children. God be with us all. Good-bye, dear Father and Mother.

Your Theodore

**Theodore to his father**

T. Bost
Shakopee, M.T.
December 20, 1857

Dearest Father:

Inasmuch as I wrote to you last week, I have no reason to write again at length; but having received yesterday your letter of November 18, enclosing one from Sophie to you, I hasten to reply.

After I had read her letter I could think of no one but her, and A. Mxl. [Anna Maxwell] vanished. Even in those moments when I despaired of Sophie's ever coming and so gave myself free rein to look elsewhere for a companion, I viewed the possibility of marrying Anna almost with terror. Her nature, though noble, is so crude and irritable that I feared the prospect of a life filled with quarrels. Thanks to God, I am saved for the moment from all that. But I am still full of doubts about Sophie. Is it wise and, in addition, generous, to accept a sacrifice that seems to be so hard for her to make? It is very poetic to say: "Having renounced happiness, I shall be better able to live a life of devotion," but is it possible in practice to do that? And if I saw that she was unhappy here, would I be consoled by the thought that she was pining for another young man whom she had rejected only from a false sense of duty?

I had been badly hurt to learn that she had so quickly formed an attachment to another young man before she even received my answer to her letter refusing my proposal and that had more than a little to do with my turning my affections toward A. M. Thank God I didn't take the bull by the horns as you feared, and I no longer have any desire to do so. How will all this end? If, as I asked you to do, you have shown Sophie my next-to-the-last letter, isn't she now angry with me in her turn, and won't that lead to still more of that letter writing of which I am already so tired—just as I suppose she is.

Good-bye, then, dear Father, and good-bye, my very dear Sophie—I'll wait to hear from you before I write again. Good-bye, dear family in Salies and elsewhere. May God bless you all as we begin this new year.

Your Theodore Bost

**Sophie Bonjour,** *fille*, to Ami Bost

Hofwyl
December 25, 1857—Christmas!

My very dear Friend:

Finally, as you put it, chaos is being cleared up. May God be praised! Mama will write tomorrow to Theodore to give him this answer, so long delayed—it is an unconditional "Yes," you may be sure, and I have given it less reluctantly than I had anticipated. Theodore's slightly impolite frankness really pleased me greatly. I admire him for his dignified and noble self-respect, for the way he got a little indignant at what he took to be coquetry, even insincerity, on my part. Fortunately I can assure him with my hand on my heart, that I don't feel myself guilty of such serious faults.

When I came home from Scotland last fall, I wanted to be off [to America] to be with him, [but] my father's unwillingness and the impossibility of talking with him about my going away, placed me in a false position which no doubt caused the vacillations he naturally attributes to lack of will power on my part. It's true that the more I saw the obstacles getting stronger, the more I stopped thinking about what had not yet been able to take shape as the purpose of my life, and when in the spring I said "No" to his proposal I did so without any regret other than that which I felt from sympathy with him. Must I confess it yet once again? I found very quickly—even too quickly—consolation in a deep and sincere love. You know, dear M. Bost, what sorrow it has caused me to make a break [with this second suitor]. But neither will you forget that I *did* make the break out of deference, in the first place, to the wish expressed by Mama much more than for love of Theodore— these two things have accordingly been almost totally separate in my thoughts. However, by reason of the one, the other has become much more painful to me. If I were to refuse your son now, it would not by any means be in order to accept the one I gave up after a few weeks of correspondence. Mama knows and believes this, and you don't doubt my word either, do you? I have won your confidence by five years of trust and candor, and, if I felt differently, I wouldn't hide it from you. There is still much, much sadness in my heart—you won't hold this against me, will you? After undergoing all these distressing conflicts, I have come to feel so keenly what a privilege and what happiness I enjoy in having the love of a mother and sister that I understand less than ever how I can possibly leave them. This thought troubles them too, but their all-too-natural regrets do not make me afraid to make the sacrifice: I am completely confident about marrying Theodore, and I believe I can say that he can be completely sure of me. I have made mistakes which I have no thought of concealing, either from others or from myself, but these wrongs have been committed more against myself than against Theodore, and I think I've paid for them in full.

Now is not the time to dwell upon those long days of pain. I have suffered a great deal, but I deserved it, and I hope it's over. God has been good and merciful, even in punishing me. You know, dear friend, that I told you this at the very beginning and in the midst of my most painful struggles—I felt it only in a vague way at that time, as though it were something in the future; but now I see it vividly. I needed a severe lesson to teach me to hold fast to the

Lord and to expect no strength save from Him—yes, I needed to be humbled, even in my own eyes, and I have been, and I thank a good and tender Father for it while supplicating him not to spare me any trials if they should be needful to keep me in the path that leads to Him. Dear friend, pray to Him as I do that above all things I may be His child—I desire this more sincerely than ever!

Now that I have really told you all that is in my mind, let me speak of practical things. Mama is to write to Theodore; she will give him her consent, and, as for the journey, she will tell him that if he wants to come here, he may leave right away; otherwise I'll go there. For my part, I shall write to him as though he expected me to come. But Mama, and I too, want very much for him to come to meet me in New York, which I think would mean an absence of only two weeks for him and not involve too great an expense. She will tell him what she intends to give me to take to him—at least 1,000 fr.—and then, if we want it later, a part of my inheritance to get us off to a good start.

For some time now we have thought it would be a better idea for me to bring one of my relations than just anybody (you understand all the drawbacks of a servant who can leave you on the spur of the moment or be unsatisfactory), and if you remember my young cousin Julie, who was adopted some years ago by my parents and lives with us, I'm sure you'll say, as Mama does, that she is just the one to go with me! She is strong, energetic, very clever at all household tasks, and would be as helpful to me as any servant could possibly be. Besides, she is very fond of me, I am fond of her, and would stand almost in the position of a mother to her. It's true that we have not yet spoken of it either to her parents or to her, but they would be only too happy to have her so well placed. And, as for her, she would follow me, I think, to the ends of the earth without even thinking there was any special devotion involved.

So there are a great many problems more or less solved. I'm happy I can give you pleasure as we come to the end of a year that has been so stormy toward its close. Your first urgings were very embarrassing to me, as I have already told you only too clearly, but please believe that I am deeply grateful for the tenderness with which you have promised to do nothing that would mean too great a sacrifice for me! Yes, *this* has been a sacrifice, but I am very far from imagining that it gives me any additional claim to Theodore's gratitude or to that of any member of your family. I feel strongly that I should instead first ask him to forgive me, and then [I should ask the same of] you, who have tried with so much affection to bring me into your family, one whose sympathy and concern I value so highly. Thank you, dear friend, for not having despaired of bringing me to my senses nor doubted the goodness of my heart at a time when I gave you so little reason to believe in me. You will tell T., won't you, that I haven't been as guilty toward him as he must have believed and that he may restore me to his esteem? Not the least in the world do I want to conceal from him the struggles I had to undergo before I could rid my heart of that which never should have crept into it; but if I have been at fault, have I not also made reparation?

Mama asks me to give you her greetings (not Julie! She is almost in despair at the outcome of this business. My dear, dear sister!). And Mama is terribly eager to meet Theodore and would find it very difficult to resign herself to his not coming. At least you will be there at the worst moment of our trials, and I hope to show you that I'm worthy of Theodore. Could you not send us a portrait of him? Lend it, I mean—more for Mama's sake than for mine?

Farewell, dearest friend,

> Your ever affectionate
> Sophie

**Sophie Bonjour to Marie Bost**

> Hofwyl
> January 15, 1858

Dearest Marie:

Did you call me your dear sister? I am already that, so far as my affections go, and I'd like to prove it to you every moment of the day, sitting down beside that bed of pain where for so long you have been waiting for a sign of God's will as to your future. Oh, how your unhappy existence reminds me of the condition in which for a whole long year I saw my dearly beloved father whom the Lord has now called to His glory! I should like to give you the benefit of all I learned in that sickroom, visited by trials, about how to comfort a beloved invalid, but you have better care than I could give you despite all my good intentions, and above all you feel yourself under the protection of our heavenly Father, who in-gives us to the trial He requires of us. What infinite mercy, and flicts pain only for a certain time and matches the strength He gives us to the trial he requires of us. What infinite mercy, and what a sweet privilege it is to know that He is moved by compassion toward us! Desiring only our sanctification here below, He wants us to be forever happy beyond the grave. When life seems hard to bear and the road seems dark, what floods of light does He not send to light our path! Weak and worthless as I am, does He not put up with me patiently, and may I not praise His mercy and bless His ways? Alas, when we see those we love afflicted with trials, it seems to us that the greatest blessing of all would be to see them delivered from these—is this due to a lack of faith? I can hardly believe this is true, and so I pray to God that He will make you well, dear Marie: we should be happy indeed if He would give you back your health.

Shall we talk about Theodore? When I think of his loneliness, of the way he had to suffer on account of me, I assure you that I am at a loss what to say. I'm afraid I never can *make up* for the debt I owe him. With the Lord's help I nevertheless hope to become what he has hoped I'd be to him, and I think that is the highest and noblest desire I can have, for considering the long time he has waited for me, it is inevitable that he will have built up expectations which I am very much afraid I shall be unable to satisfy. But never mind! He shall educate me to be as he wants me; though I have no great merits, I am at least willing to let myself be shaped, and I know that if that's what T. wants, I can become anything in the world that will please him, and that's something, at least, isn't it dear Sister? And when your brother tells you he is happy not to be alone any more, and happy to have me, you will also love me a little for love of him.

Will you kindly give your brother Samuel and your dear sister-in-law my greetings and thanks for their desire to write to me. I should like to know and love in person all the members of your family, and I haven't given up hope of this. T. has no intention of staying in America the rest of his life. If circumstances permit him to return here, I shall be glad, whatever happens, to feel a real bond between us (him and me) and all those we are leaving in the mother country. And in any event, we shall all be united up there, and that is one rendez-vous we shall not fail to keep.

Good-bye, dear Marie, may the Lord bless and watch over you. Believe in the sincere affection of

Your future but already devoted sister
Sophie

# VI

# The Honeymoon

As things worked out, Theodore did not go to Europe to be married, presumably because he didn't have the money. Nor did he go to meet Sophie in New York. Her arrival there, about June 1, would have coincided with Theodore's busiest season on the farm; he would have had to spend money to have his livestock taken care of in his absence; and he may not even have had the money for his railroad fare at that time of year since he would not yet have had any produce to sell.

Sophie was to have taken with her a young cousin, Julie Borel, but at the last minute Julie's father withdrew his consent to his daughter's leaving Europe. In her place Sophie brought a young woman sixteen years old, about whom practically nothing is known except her name, Marie Moseman, and the fact that she had been a servant in the Bonjour home.

Ami Bost accompanied Sophie and Marie to Le Havre and saw them aboard ship at the end of May, 1858. No account of the Atlantic crossing has survived, but it must have been fast, for the travelers arrived in St Paul on June 4. Theodore met them there, and on the following day he and Sophie were married after a courtship-by-correspondence that had lasted two and a half years.

**Sophie to Ami and Jenny Bost**

December 3, 1858

Dear Mama and dear Father:

Yes, dear Mother, we did get the letter with two pages written by our poor Marie, and if we haven't mentioned it, it isn't that we haven't been deeply moved by receiving what may be almost the last lines she'll ever write.[1] Theodore was very anxious that she should get our photograph. You will see that our Dodo

130

## THE HONEYMOON

[Theodore] seems to have grown very thin; in fact he is thin, and his lack of color worries me sometimes when I happen to be more than usually aware of it. The poor dear has been through too much, and, though he bore his hardships nobly, he still shows the marks of them. Fortunately, all that is over, and I love him too much not to be good for him. In a few years we'll send you our portraits again, and you'll see, if it pleases God, that my husband's face is as full of good health as my own—that will be a great day for me and for you too, dear Parents, will it not?

. . . I feel sure we've already told you about our honey tree in one of our previous letters. But let me say first that I don't think you give Theodore enough credit for his skill and intelligence in discovering this treasure-house of sweets. Anyhow, it's not everybody that has such good fortune; among our neighbors, many of whom have often gone out to hunt wild bees, there isn't a single one who has found any, whereas my Dodo has never gone except in his spare time and he never fails to find some. I'll let him tell you how much honey we got out of the tree because I've forgotten and don't like to be always interrupting his reading as I've been doing this evening. He got stung only twice, and I didn't get stung at all although I came up very close to watch him.

The rains have made it impossible for me to have any wild raspberries or strawberries for the simple reason that it has rained every time I could have gone out to gather them. We have also some wild plums and grapes, as sour as can be. I believe that little by little many kinds of fruit trees will be introduced and acclimated in this region; for the time being everything is very new. But Theodore and I are young enough so we can wait for a few years, and even without complaining very much.

Now it is winter with long evenings and many stormy days when we have to find things we can only do indoors, but anyhow there will always be plenty to do. I save up jobs for poor Dodo, and when he doesn't feel like working, I'll find things to talk about! Then spring will come! Then it will be marvelous to live much of the time out of doors after the long virtual imprisonment of winter. I will have my Swiss vegetables to plant and care for, my flowers to cultivate, and so many other things. . . . I look forward to it all with great pleasure, and I'd feel even happier if clouds of mosquitoes didn't darken a little these pictures of rural bliss. Then, too, we'll probably have a cow, and this will be magnificent for my cooking. I'm sure, dear Mother, that you'd be delighted with the crusty rolls made with buttermilk that they bake around here. Usually I have good luck with them. If dear Father weren't so afraid of being seasick, I'd even go on hoping that someday you might come and set yourselves up near us. You'd be delighted with our stoves, which are very convenient, and with just a little money one could live very comfortably. The cold weather people tried so hard to frighten me with hasn't yet shown all it can do this year, but it's doing pretty well just the same; today (this is December 3) we have had – 14° [R. or 0° F.], which I only learned this evening, and yet I had been outdoors and not *extra* warmly dressed. We'll have to see whether I'll be as brave in the middle of winter. People have been telling me that I won't get through the worst weather without being sorry I ever came here, but this was the Maxwells and they are always grumbling about something or other.

We saw the comet in all its splendor, dear Sister Sophie, and I have often asked myself whether you have been admiring it every evening as we have, except that when it's evening here it's morning where you are.

The religious revival that has been evident in your part of the world hasn't had much effect here. Almost all our neighbors are Christians, but I don't know if it's charitable to add: as long as there's no question of money. In New York I read several tracts relating to the revival and heard some allusions to it in conversations and in a sermon.[2] The people I stayed with were very devout and rejoiced very much in this new life of the spirit; we talked about it together and with Dr. Buck, who seemed very indignant that some people in Europe don't believe in the genuineness of so many conversions. I didn't have opportunities to see or find out anything more about these matters, which must cause so much rejoicing among those who love the Gospels.

You have often asked us about our minister's wife [Mrs. Sheldon].[3] I saw her once and may see her again because we are thinking of going to church in Excelsior where he lives. Excelsior, you know, is five miles from here; the minister preaches there in the morning and then rides on horseback to Chanhassen in the afternoon. I think Mrs. Sheldon is a pleasant person to know, but even if I saw more of her, her time is so fully taken up with her five or six children that I could scarcely take any pleasure in her company. I often see Mrs. [William] Sarver,[4] who has the prettiest little baby in the world, and the Maxwells, where I sometimes enjoy myself very much. The eldest daughter, Fanny, who is married to a Mr. Hinds, is now staying with her mother with a delightful little ten-month-old boy. Mrs. Powers has a little girl of the same age, and I often go to see her, so that my liking for children is fully satisfied. The other women of the neighborhood are too far away for me to visit them often, but I am on excellent terms with everyone, and that's all that matters to me.

Perhaps this letter will reach you right around New Year's Day, so I want to enclose in it all our most tender and deeply felt good wishes for you, dear Father and dear Mother, and for all our brothers and sisters. May the Lord give you peace and bring us all together again someday at the foot of His throne. This is the hope and prayer of your most affectionate daughter and sister,

Sophie T. Bost

## Theodore, then Sophie, to the elder Bosts

Chanhassen, Minnesota
February 10, 1859

Dearest Parents:

How long it is since we've had any word from you! What's the reason? If you only knew how disappointed I am every time I go to Shakopee for the mail and find no letters!

Dear Father—if you only knew how often I've thought of you these last few months! I don't know why it is, but I am a person who very seldom dreams and I've dreamed about you a great deal lately. Maybe it's because of your poor health, which makes us worry. Last night I dreamed that I was embracing you as a son embraces his father and that wakened me—how I wished my dream had been real!

And you, dear Mother, you may be very sure that we, and especially I, will not forget you. I am always praising you to Soso [Sophie]. I think it's very consoling to be able to talk with her about my dear old parents. So you see that—far from coming between us—my love for her brings me even closer to you.

But we have a little bit of news to tell you. If all goes well, Soso and I will be the mother and father of a new little American Bost [Bostillon] early in September. It may be rather early to talk about it, but I know you'll be so glad to get this news that we didn't want to wait any longer to let you know. It will be really delightful to have a little darling in the house, and it seems so natural at the same time, just as it does to be married. I think I must have been intended to have a wife (a very philosophical idea which proves that I am as much a son of Adam as any other man). So, dear Parents, if it pleases God, you will soon be the grandfather and grandmother of a little American.

And now I'll reply, dear Mother, to your repeated questions about the religious revival in the United States. If I didn't answer before, it's because I didn't quite believe in the truth of the reports about it in the newspapers. Coming at the same time as a terrible business depression, it smacked to me too much of mercenary religion, and I was very skeptical about the real Christianity of the converts, especially around here where people are such slaves to fashions and fads. Still, it appears that in all the cities there have been a great many genuine conversions, even including some sailors from the fleet. In rural areas the religious activity has been much less strong, probably because the farmers, being more isolated, cannot attend so many meetings and also because the farming population of the eastern states is, or at least claims to be, already devoutly Christian. Here in our region there were a number of conversions two years ago, but none this past winter. Religious movements are still very active in many places.

The business outlook is still very dark for us Minnesotans. This makes me sorry for you, dear Parents; after drawing for you so attractive a picture of Minnesota, it is painful for me not to be able to send you better news. The frightful rise in land prices having stopped, or rather collapsed, all the investors have withdrawn their capital from the territory, so at the moment we are in a bad slump. However, the capitalists will soon see that they can make more money and do the country more good by setting up manufacturing of all kinds. We have magnificent pasturage for sheep, but since there are no woolen mills, nobody raises any. We have magnificent forests containing all sorts of wood, but no barrel factories, wagon factories, etc., etc.

But, dear Parents, I feel sure you will want to be patient for a while—isn't that so? We'll save all we can, and I promise you that as soon as we have good outdoor weather, I will work hard this winter while most of our neighbors are doing nothing at all. In a few days I'll make a trip to buy a cow—I want to get a good one cheap, which is hard to do, even at a time like this winter.

Farewell, dearest Parents—I have a very bad headache and can write no more. Just received a good letter from Tim and Bella. Good-bye, Good-bye.

Your Dodo

Dearest Parents:

It's my turn to write to you, even though Theodore has already told you about everything even halfway important or special in our recent doings. The prospect of having, if God blesses us, a new little treasure to cherish in a few months' time is a source of great happiness for me. Still, I try not to let my heart become too much attached to this hope because we might be disappointed for one reason or another. I have no mother here to advise and help me in these circumstances, so novel for me, and sometimes I am afraid that I've let my hopes be aroused too soon. Hence I almost wanted to keep our lovely secret for another month or two. It was Theodore, all proud and happy, who took it on himself to be sure in place of me, and I don't care enough about making a mystery out of nothing to make an issue of it, especially since he explains that habit has not made you indifferent to such news, dear Parents, and says that you will be very happy to rejoice with us. As for the chance of losing our baby, perhaps during childbirth, we are not much concerned about it—and what would be the use [of worrying]? Sufficient unto the day is the evil thereof, and I may add that I very often find this true and that, as you doubtless know, dear Mother, it isn't a bed or roses to be an expectant mother—for the last two months my health has been completely upset. No need to go into details, and I wouldn't complain except that it makes me so nervous, often melancholy, and even worse than that.

Fortunately, I know that all this will pass, and I know that the spring weather will give me back my strength and my usual good health; hence I am terribly impatient for spring to arrive. Theodore has provided me, so far as he could, with everything under the sun, and more than strict economy would have permitted at any other time, but this doesn't make up for the lack of vegetables, which I miss very much. At the moment my dear boy has gone to take home Anna Maxwell, who came to spend part of the evening with us—am I not brave, dear Mama, to let my husband go chasing around this way with that pretty girl he pretends he was courting before our marriage? From what she says he pays her even more attention nowadays, and Mrs. Maxwell often urges me to keep an eye on my husband—she knows how I do!

These poor Maxwells are having some trouble getting used to their position after the one they used to have, and I'm afraid they may be even worse off, like the rest of us, before things get better. Dodo thinks I look too much on the dark side of things, and I certainly ask nothing better than that he should be right; but I've spent so much time listening to everyone talk about "hard times, *bad prospects, dark future,*" that I've got to the point where I no longer expect or believe in anything good, at least for a few years.

No doubt, and God be praised for it, we needn't be afraid of starving to death as long as the earth goes on yielding its fruits, but is it so wrong to want something more? We need more to live on, and it seems sad to see my husband working so hard without being able to expect much from his efforts. I don't think I ever spoke to you this way, dear Parents, and this topic isn't one of those I prefer. Nevertheless, we owe you these details, especially since we're living on your land, paid for with your money and belonging to you. We would so much like to see it flourishing and growing more valuable; this will surely happen when investment money returns to Minnesota—but when will that be? And besides, there's another thought that weighs on me more heavily than it should: I hope, dear Parents, that you don't think we are trying to arouse your pity with our complaints. You must understand that if we don't speak much about business it is partly because we don't want other people besides our closest relations to know all about our affairs.

Bella, in a very short letter I've had from her, tells me she is *"as well as can be expected,"* and from some other hints I gather that she is expecting a baby—I say "expecting" because I suppose she would be more explicit if it had arrived![5] Beyond that, she didn't take us into her confidence very much. Eliza, our dear sister, has delighted us with her little Marie.[6] It's odd that so far there is only one little boy in the family.[7] As for us, Theodore would prefer a boy and I'd prefer a girl, so that one of us will be satisfied—and for my part, God helping, I certainly hope that, however it turns out, the child will be strong and healthy. How I'd love to have you here with me, dear Mama! Don't you share my wish, even a little, if only out of pity for our isolation? Besides, I should be very happy to be so close to Mrs. Maxwell, who offered me her services as soon as I arrived here! That seemed amusing at the time, but I'll take her at her word and she will honor her pledge willingly.

Your most affectionate daughter
Sophie T. Bost

**Sophie to the elder Bosts**

Saturday, April 2, 1859

Dear Mother and Father:

If I weren't afraid of causing you a moment's fright, this letter would begin with the tragic words "I am a widow," and I am almost in that frame of mind as I write. Dodo left yesterday morning for St. Paul; I don't know just when to expect him back, and I miss him more than you'd believe possible—I can't think of anything else, especially in the evening, and tonight particularly because the wind is howling and it's snowing terribly hard. If you think I'm very foolish, it wouldn't surprise me much, because I've come to the same conclusion myself; and yet, you'll excuse me if I turn to you to occupy my thoughts.

Dear Mother, you wouldn't believe how empty the house is without Theodore. In the daytime I take his absence for granted and don't think about it in the midst of my housework, but his evenings belong to me and, except when he's reading, I can hold his hand and talk to him from time to time. Every evening comes to an end, and I still have him to myself a little while longer—the best time of the whole day—before we fall asleep. But this evening I can hardly make up my mind to go off to bed without a single kiss—and he's always so generous with them! What a baby I am! Oh, but I love to have my husband scold me for it! If the weather weren't so bad, I'd wait up for him a while tonight, even though he warned me that he might not get back before Monday or Tuesday, and I should even want him not to come back sooner because he intends to look for a cow and the delay proves that he has found one and is bringing it home slowly instead of returning by the riverboat.

Yesterday (to change the subject if I can) the weather was wonderful, but today there is a snowstorm worse than any we had last winter. The wind drives it through the cracks in the roof into our bedroom, where it falls down in a very agreeable way, and Marie and I laugh as we sweep out of the house a pile of snow that would frighten you. I suppose that at this very moment half of my bed is covered with it in spite of the sheet I nailed up under the slope of the roof at the beginning of the winter, so that if Dodo were here we would have to bring the bed downstairs and sleep on the floor, as we have sometimes done. Instead of doing that, I shall curl up in the corner that gets the most protection from the cloth and sleep all the time I'm not thinking of my absent darling. But don't feel too sorry for us, will you, dear Parents? In any event, you will see that I'll need some lessons before I'll know how to live all by myself again.

**Theodore to his parents**

Chanhassen
April 23, 1859

Here is a map of my claim that I've drawn:

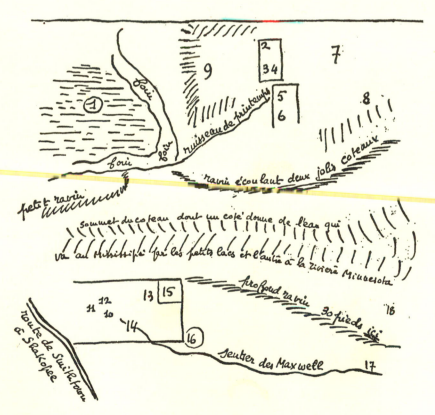

Sketch of my claim

## THE HONEYMOON

1. Marsh, but with good grass on the edges. A few *tamaracks* in the middle, and some *cranberries*, a bitter red berry.
2. The old house, which we're thinking of moving into this fall.
3. Garden.
4. Well.
5. Stable.
6. Future barnyard.
7. Field, cleared two years ago, but not yet broken.

6-7-8-9. Magnificent sloping field, almost level, but falling away steeply on the north side beyond the edge of Field 7-8 and bordering on a marsh outside the boundary of my claim. Field 9 slopes toward the west, a little to the north, and a good deal [more abruptly] toward the south. Field 7-8 slopes to the south to a ravine that drains away the rainwater.

10. Our present house.
11. Chicken coop.
12. Barnyard, with stable at southeast corner.
13. Field cleared and broken last year.
14. Field cleared and broken this year.
15. Small woodlot.
16. Small meadow.
17. The Maxwells' house.
18. The bee tree we found a year ago.

The northern third of the claim, except for a fringe on the northern boundary, is covered by brush and standing timber, but the trees are large, and two-thirds of the area is thickly wooded almost everywhere. The bee tree was in a small clearing. The eastern part of Field 14 cost me a great deal of hard work, being heavily wooded, but yesterday, April 22, I almost finished clearing it and set fire to several huge piles of *logs* which are now almost burned.

As you can see on the sketch, we intend to move out of this little house (10) in October or November and go to live in the larger one (2) to the north. This is partly to get more room and have our water supply closer to the house, also to have the advantage of a larger stable, but mainly so that I can work the land more profitably and use the best pieces of land. There I can roughly clear four acres in the time it takes me to clear one acre here, and I'll have a lot fewer stumps and richer soil. This fall I plan to sow these eight acres here in winter wheat after harvesting the corn, and I'll clear as much land as possible near the other house. Field 7 hasn't yet been plowed, but I've gotten rid of all the tree trunks and branches and need only to cut the brush again because in three years the bushes have grown up again with a speed that proves how rich the soil is.

**Chanhassen township**

[ **+**     My claim and house.

**-#**     Schoolhouse and church, one and a half miles at most [from my place].

**-##**     *Widow Maxwell*, a rich woman with two girls, one very pretty, so they say, and the other very likable, so I say. Two boys, sixteen to nineteen. Very good neighbors; a half mile from my house. Americans [Yankees] —Canadians.

**##**     *Hobson.* Pure-blooded Englishman. Very abrupt, but has a kind heart. Wife, three boys, one small girl. He's thinking of leaving. Has been a farmer all his life. A half mile away.

**###**     *Powers.* An excellent, handsome young man, got married last fall. [They are] Americans [from New England]. Always happy, good Christians, very nice and pleasant. He has been a schoolmaster. At most a mile away.

**#**     *Cleveland* [*sic*]. A tall, robust, hearty fellow. American [New Englander]. Has a good head on his shoulders. Represents our county in the legislature. Very polite, too. At least one and a half miles away. Large family.

**##**     *Fuller.* American [from New England]. Former schoolteacher. A well-bred gentleman. Very polite.

**###**     *Bingham.* An American [Yankee], music teacher. Also a gentleman. The wives of all these men have been schoolteachers.

**###**     *Lyman.* post office.

I am slightly acquainted with my neighbors to the north. They seldom come to church, where the congregation is rarely more than thirty or less than ten. On Sunday everyone wears silk dresses, satin vests, etc., etc. Then, during the week, people's clothes are in tatters on account of the brush.]

## THE HONEYMOON

Sunday, May 1

I would have liked to have sent this letter off to you earlier, but I am so busy that I have only my Sundays to rest and write letters. For two or three weeks now our weather has been splendid, and I work from sunrise until 8:30 in the evening—but the work is very tiring. It's very good to work hard and see the progress you're making when the weather is so good, when your land is so good, and when you have a wife who takes the housework off your hands and comes every afternoon to help gather up the branches and roots and make magnificent fires of them. Yesterday and the day before we planted almost all of our garden and our early potatoes. This is two weeks earlier than I've ever planted them (garden and potatoes) in Minnesota. I'm going to turn to fence building this next week, and will also sow my alfalfa and sainfoin, which I hope will grow well.

The business slump, dear Mother, has hurt us in several ways. Most of the money invested here came from New York and Boston, both of which withdrew all their capital from the West at the time of the Panic and have since kept it in their banks. Although the Panic ended a year ago, the money hasn't yet been able to flow back to the West; we are waiting until a good harvest this year forces this money to return to the pockets of the western farmers who, I hope, will profit by this lesson and will not immediately rush out and spend all their money on luxuries.

Another bad effect of the slump is that, with money so scarce, those who had bought land in order to resell it at a high price have been obliged to sell it for very little, and this has gone to the point where the Easterners, farmers as well as investors, have been discouraged from coming west, and hence they haven't brought us the industry and money we had expected.

But, dear Parents, I must thank you for writing us such a nice letter and also for the offers you made us. I was very much troubled to think that although at present I am working very hard, I couldn't see how I'd be able to send you any money this fall, not thinking that you would be insisting on it but rather because I wanted to do it. Now that you've written that you don't want me to send it, I am much more easy in my mind. By the way, the day I received your last letter (the one in which you told me not to buy a poor cow at a low price), I was in fact about to go out and do exactly that, and I would have done it if it hadn't been for the fact that the river was so high that the ferries couldn't cross it.

Incidentally, to explain why I spoke of "great rascals": my $27 loan to the *school district* for twenty-one months at 3 percent a month is nearly paid off, but I had two hours of wrangling about it with the *principal trustee*, one of the leading members of the church and also a businessman. This swine, having repaid me $10 on this note at one time, $13 another time, $10 at still another time, charged me 3 percent on all the money that had been paid without worrying about the interest that was due to me, thus making me pay 3 percent on $33 when I had only $27 drawing that rate of interest; by that reasoning, I would soon by paying him for having loaned him money. And in order to convince me of his good faith, he proposed that we should submit our dispute to the arbitration of another great rascal who had tried to play the same trick on me, who boasts of having done so, and who would have cheated me if I hadn't told him that if he charged me interest on the interest he had paid me from time to time, I would demand from him to be paid interest on the interest from the date of the loan. He told me that for the sake of peace he would allow me to keep the account in my own way, since this love of peace would have saved him two or three dollars. You have to be more on your guard with Christians than you do with other people, because the others don't go so far out of their way looking for subterfuges. As for my note on the *school district*, the trustee stormed out of the room three times during our interview, saying that he was not willing to pay me what I claimed, and finally I myself walked out too, saying that I meant to have what was coming to me, come what may. It was at the moment of my leaving that he admitted the justice of my demand.

I shall have, I think, 200 bushels of corn to sell and about 100 bushels of potatoes this year. Three or four years ago that would have brought me between $300 and $400. Besides this I have some beets, etc., which then would have sold for something but which now sell for such a low price that it isn't worth the trouble of taking them to market. But I have confidence in the future, and I believe that Soso is no longer as gloomy as she was a while ago.

Good-bye, dearest Parents, my fine oxen want to be watered, so I must go; and then I must get dressed up to go to church. Good-bye once again, and may God bless you and preserve you to us for a long time to come.

Your son,
Theodore Bost

# THE HONEYMOON

**Theodore to Madame Coutouly**

> Chanhassen, Carver County
> Minnesota, U.S.A.
> Saturday, May 21, 1859

Madame:

I should like to have been able to reply at greater length to your letter, but you will excuse a farmer if in the midst of his heavy springtime chores he cannot write for long at a time.

I find it extremely difficult to give clear answers to your questions, except for the first: I, as well as my wife, would be very willing to take in your son, but it is more difficult to fix the conditions because, not being at all acquainted with him, I do not know what he may be able to learn, nor what he can do, nor what he would like to do.

But before getting down to details, let me also say that this dream about South Africa also seems impracticable to me. Although I have never been there, I have seen enough of this sort of speculation to know that it would require not only a large amount of capital but also a complete knowledge of the country, of livestock, and of business in order to launch oneself into livestock speculation, whether it be sheep in Africa or cattle in North and South America.

Now, Madame, the lady who is our neighbor has a young boarder ten years old who is supposed to be studying (reading, writing, and arithmetic) but who helps them all the time with the household chores; for this she receives $3 a week, which is the price almost universally paid hereabouts for a man's room and board (laundry included). Foodstuffs being once more very expensive, one can only with great difficulty come out even at this rate. That would be the price I would ask if Edouard couldn't begin working right away or if I had to spend too much of my time to teach him the thousand and one things a farmer has to learn. If he learns easily and I see that he is producing enough by his work to repay me for my loss of time, I would no longer ask for anything after a few months—but I am bound to say that very few young fellows can do this by the end of a few months, all the more so because each month brings new tasks.

Considering this, you will see, Madame, that I cannot set a flat rate [*"prix fixe"*]. Twelve dollars would be the highest price, and *nothing* [word underlined in original French text] would be the lowest, the latter being possible but not probable. The young men who were with Henri Babut and me at the home of M. Vaucher in Bellevue paid quite a lot for their room and board, ate meals that were much poorer than what we have here, and still the hired help on the farm thought the arrangement was not a paying one for M. Vaucher because of the losses of time and the mistakes that were made. And besides, if Edouard should be tired out from the work, as every beginner is, it would be better for him and for me to know that he could rest. However, in this connection, I want him to come with the idea that he *should work* [words underlined in original French text] all the time and that you would have enough confidence in me to believe that I would know how to tell the difference between boredom with work and genuine fatigue, because at M. Vaucher's place I myself learned at first hand enough about those two things to be able to recognize them in others. Some of our most important and easiest tasks are also the most boring, and a beginner must pitch in with a willing disposition; afterward he will come to like them.

Another condition would have to do with tools, such as a hoe, a scythe, an ax, and so on, which almost every workman here owns; since these tools ought to last for a number of years, I should want him to buy them, and if he should leave before the year is out, he may take them with him; or, if he is to stay longer, I'll give him some new ones when he does leave. This rule is to make sure that I don't have more tools than I can make use of if he should leave, and also to teach him to take good care of farm equipment which deteriorates rapidly if one doesn't take good care of it.

As for bedding, let him bring a quilt if he possibly can; we can't get them around here, and the one my wife brought is invaluable for our cold winter nights. The other bedding would be as with the tools and wouldn't cost very much. All his clothes should be of strong material, even those for Sunday wear. As for everyday clothes, my wife tells me just now that he can buy heavy fabrics here and she will make them into shirts and trousers; all the farmers' wives around here know how to do this.

As for when he should come, I think it should be in the fall. It's true that in that event he'd have to pay his room and board during the winter because at that time of year the work to be done is such that he could give me very little help with it, and often whole weeks go by when no work can be done. But after making such a long journey, it would be better for him to get completely rested up, eat heartily, and get used to our way of life, instead of getting here in May, as I did, and being half dead from fatigue in August or September.

We intend to move out of this house in October and move back into the one my dear father calls one of my old barns, that is, a five-year-old house much larger than this one; Edouard could help me improve it if he came in October. Speaking of that, we would always treat Edouard as a young friend, taking his previous mode of life into account. But he must absolutely make up his mind that he won't enjoy all his former comforts in this part of the world. Out West here it is well recognized that one must expect small hardships, and one gets used to them quickly if one accepts them with a little goodwill. There are enough fine things and beautiful landscapes to please the most sentimental person alive, and enough opportunities to bring off big projects and put up with privations to satisfy even the craziest adventurers—me, for instance.

For you see, Madame, that although your son is only eighteen years old, he can carve out a place for himself in this region in a very short time: there are always people who get discouraged and leave the neighborhood, selling their land for a low price. It's true that almost all of them come back after having wasted two or three years hunting for better places to farm and not finding any, but anyhow they've sold out before going away; they spend their money vainly looking around, and finally return as hired workers and try to buy land hereabouts again. If, then, Edouard should acquire a taste for this kind of life, which is very probable, I'd like to know how much money you could let him have when he has had a chance to establish himself. It would be a pity to wait for years and years, while land gets dearer and dearer, before buying a farm, if he could buy one within a year at about half of what it's really worth. You must understand that I would give him no encouragement to buy if I saw that he had no real vocation for farming.

Fifty dollars would, I think, more than cover all the expenses of the trip here from New York, taking the New York Central, the Great Western Railroad, the Michigan Central, the Chicago and Dunleith, or [the line to] Prairie du Chien, or any other railroad terminal they may build along the Mississippi; then he takes the boat to St. Paul and another to Chaska, where he will find

French-speaking Swiss people to direct him here; or, if I know the day of his arrival in Chaska, I could go there and meet him. If he needs advice or directions in St. Paul, Prosper Fridayh (or Friday) will help him, I'm sure, since he is a Frenchman and an acquaintance of mine; he lives on the lower levee, near the wharves where the boats arrive in St. Paul.

I expect, of course, that he would respect the Sabbath and stay all week on the farm without seeking temptations elsewhere. Our surroundings are excellent: a schoolhouse and church are half a mile away; there are social gatherings in winter where men and youths hold discussions on all sorts of subjects. There is another at Excelsior where we often went last year on nice evenings for the same purpose. There aren't many places where he would find ways to spend money, unless he were to go to Shakopee, and I'm sure he wouldn't want to associate with that crowd of young rascals. To conclude, and to repeat: let him come with the realization that his work will not pay his expenses, that he must work with all his strength, such as it is; and if before the year is out he is dissatisfied, he can of course leave us on the conditions I stated above and I will do my best to help him find another place. As for my own part of the bargain, I will not force him to work harder unless I'm sure he is shirking out of laziness or discouragement.

So there, Madame, are the conditions that I consider fair. Awaiting your reply to this letter, you may be sure we shall be thinking of what is best for you and your Edouard.

Your very devoted
T. Bost

# VII

## The First Child

Along with their neighbors, Sophie and Theodore continued to suffer in 1859 and 1860 from the hard times that began with the panic of 1857. We have already seen some of the ways Minnesota was affected by the collapse of the land boom—the slump in farm prices, the scarcity of money and credit, the slowing of immigration, and the inability of many homesteaders to pay the government the preemption fees for their claims. The Bosts managed to hang on, but only by a slim margin; without stringent household economies and without loans from Theodore's parents they would have had no money to buy oxen or hire workmen to help clear their land; nor could they have bought farm implements and livestock. It is revealing that Theodore had to resort to barter deals on several occasions because his meager crops were selling for so little that it was scarcely worth his while to take them to market.

Theodore's poor health and lack of physical stamina continued to worry both him and Sophie. It seems probable that the pains in his left side of which he began to complain in 1860 were caused by a hernia, the result of attempting to do heavy stump pulling and "breaking"—tasks that were beyond his strength. No doubt he would have been glad to have had the help of young Edouard Coutouly who, in the end, chose not to come to Chanhassen, no doubt because Theodore's conditions—honest and realistic as they were—did not make the prospect seem very attractive. In a letter written to his parents in mid-June, 1859, Theodore regretted that he had been so conscientious; but he still hoped that "if it please God, . . . my family will still be enlarged by a boy or a girl—even, perhaps, by young Coutouly or, if not, by another young man."

This hope was never to be realized. Sophie and Theodore struggled on with the help of Marie and occasional help from neighbors and hired men. But the birth of their first child, a little girl whom they named for Sophie's sister, took their minds off their misfortunes and brought happiness to their log house.

**Theodore to his parents**

Chanhassen
August 21, 1859

Finally, dear Parents, and God be thanked, Soso has her little Julie Adèle by her side; they are both doing well. She began to feel her pains Friday the nineteenth at three o'clock in the morning, and she gave birth yesterday the twentieth at ten in the morning after a very painful childbirth. She didn't want to have the doctor for her delivery and, against my wishes, we sent for the midwife who lives near us; but at two-thirty yesterday morning I sent for the doctor who, when he heard what I had told them to tell him, thought quite rightly, as we saw later on, that it would be better to let nature take its course, so he didn't get here until ten o'clock. Nature alone wouldn't have done the job after he got here, and he had to cause Soso a great deal of pain until the arrival of little Missy a half-hour later. Soso behaved very bravely toward the end, and if she got very agitated in the middle of the process, that was certainly excusable after her ordeal of twenty to twenty-six hours.

I thought that Soso had really earned the right to give her child the names of her sister and of her friend. The next little girl we have will bear, I think, the name of her dear Aunt Marie and of her Grandma Bost. You see we're already thinking about the future! But for the moment, then, Soso and the baby are in the same bed, Soso recovering famously from her labor and the baby continuing to demonstrate that she has Bost lungs. We are so happy and quiet today, all by ourselves, getting along fairly well, the weather cool and moist, which keeps Soso cool at the same time that it does me good, both my body and my insides, which had been thrown out of kilter by two months of terrible heat and drought. So we are happy all around. The baby is very well shaped; she has black hair, blue eyes, a pretty little mouth; her head is a little out of shape, but it will gradually recover its proper form; we don't know how much it weighs. Mrs. Maxwell comes in two or three times a day to see how we're getting along, and I, though I don't feel well, am the nurse.

I plan to go and buy a pair of oxen tomorrow, and also the yoke, a sledge, two cows, and two oxen that were a year old last spring, five tons of hay, and perhaps some other things, getting the whole lot for $120; all this would have cost $260 two years ago, and just now it is even much cheaper than ordinarily because of the coming sale of two million acres in Minnesota. Everyone now living on these two million acres who doesn't have the money is obliged to sell land at half price to pay the government its $200 [a quarter-section]. Otherwise the land would fall into the hands of speculators or the *railroad men*. I could force him (this man) to sell to me more cheaply, but the price is already so low that I would consider it stealing to pay him less.[1] However, I'll wait and see, and if the animals are not all he claims, I'll make him reduce his price or else throw something else in on the deal.

But all this is of less importance than "the event that occupies our attention." All goes well for the moment. Excuse the shortness of this letter—I am not very well and need to rest. All my crops are flourishing.

Good-bye, dearest Father and Mother, brothers and sisters. Pray for my dear wife and our little daughter.

Your most devoted<br>Theodore Bost

## Sophie, then Theodore, to the elder Bosts

Chanhassen<br>September 18, 1859

Dearest Parents:

You already know about our great happiness, don't you? It is just four weeks since Theodore wrote to you to tell you of the happy arrival in this world and in our *log house* of a pretty baby-kins who turns out to be a delightful and much loved little girl! I was in a state of bliss while Theodore was writing his letter, and I'm even happier now that I've got my strength back; I feel completely well again and what an appetite! Just ask your son! He'll tell you I am ruining him with the flour bills I'm running up, not to mention the coffee, butter, potatoes, and ten etceteras. But this is because I'm eating for two: the baby, who is growing so fast that it will be worthwhile to feed her well, and also her Mama, whose cheeks need to be filled out again. I've lost so much weight I'm a joy to behold; I've never had such an interesting figure; but my daughter, by contrast, is fat and getting fatter every day. We admire her, naturally, with all our hearts; never has there been such a fine babykins, and never will there be another like her, at least for us, and that's all that counts. Poor little darling—she has a sadly inexperienced Mama; but fortunately mother-love makes up for my lack of experience, and everything is going beautifully.

For the first two weeks, I was constantly on tenterhooks and came running at her slightest cry; but Dodo soon got tired of seeing me always in the house and always doing something for the baby. By making me come outdoors he forced me to let her cry a little and let her sleep when she wanted to be babied, so things have been going much better since then. I have more time to myself; I go outside more; and I am no longer nervous, as I was already starting to be again. This isn't the first time my husband has shown more good sense than I have in a matter about which he should be a complete ignoramus; hence I have great confidence in his ideas— but I beg you not to tell him this: it would make him too conceited, and he would no longer allow me to oppose him, and then what would be the fun of being a woman?

I'm not altogether sure just how much Theodore has told you, although he read his letter to me. No doubt he will have told you that we were obliged to send to Shakopee for the doctor when our old ninny of a midwife admitted that she didn't know what to do next. The poor creature was very frightened and said she could no longer answer for my life or that of the baby. Mrs. Maxwell was also very nervous, and I wasn't in the pleasantest position imaginable. Poor Dodo—despite his anxiety, he was still the calmest of us all, but when it was all over, Mrs. Maxwell gave every appearance of being sicker than I was, though I'm happy to add that they recovered a little more quickly than I did. I have set the whole neighborhood in a tizzy at the scandal and horror of my going out for a walk in the dooryard on the ninth day, supported by Theodore. The bed was literally killing me; one more week and Theodore would have had nothing left of his Soso but a quavering, doddering old woman. Dodo was again the wisest of us all when he defied other people's opinions and allowed me to get up and go outdoors when I was dying of eagerness to do so. And so, here I am, fully recovered, God be praised, and nobody would know what has happened were it not for the occasional crying and screaming of a newborn baby in our *log house* (once so peaceful). But even so, what are heard much oftener are the singing and babbling of a silly mother who is always talking to a babykins who can't answer except by looking at her. What joy it gives us to have our little Julie in our midst: it will be delightful—and I can hardly wait—to teach her to say "Papa" and watch her run to meet him when he comes in from doing his chores. Everything in due time! For the next fifteen minutes we'll eat and sleep, we'll cry and make trouble and give lots of joy to Papa and Mama, just as all lucky little babies have always done.

Well, and don't you think I'm pretty wrapped up in our new treasure, dear Father and Mother? It's only that . . . but there I go again, and I've already been silly enough—especially when I remember that our melons aren't yet ripe, and I want so much to have a lot to eat all at one time . . . eat melons and kiss my baby girl—as far as I can see, that's about all I do. . . .

The garden has seen its best days. There's hardly anything left in it besides the cabbages from which I am soon going to make sauerkraut, and the green beans, but I didn't have enough of these to dry some as I wanted to. My flower garden is still very pretty, witness a beautiful bouquet that occupies the center of the table I am writing on where it goes very well with the goblet from M. Vaucher. But wait until next year, when I'll really have a garden that will amaze everybody—flowers, heaps of vegetables, and all tended, I hope, by a woman who can bend over! Three cows! The two new ones won't be here until the time comes when they can be shut up for the winter because, if we let them run free, they would always be running back to their former owner. Thus it won't be much before next spring that I'll start getting all the benefit from them, but then—what a lot of butter! And three calves besides, in all likelihood; and Dodo will have two yoke of oxen and his pair of young steers.

Don't you think we're getting off to a good start? Blessed be the Lord, and you too, dear Parents, for all the well-being that is going to reign in our household. Even if business stays in the doldrums, we'll be comfortable enough; and anyhow, I don't know why the money won't be coming back sometime or other. That's what I keep telling myself so as not to get discouraged all over again when I see all the different kinds of farm produce selling at such wretchedly low prices after all the work the poor farmers have put into them. Around here what you need is a knowledge of some trade to keep a few pennies coming in; that way, you can live on what you grow, along with a little barter. But we must be patient— everything can change, and as you told me once before, dear Mother, we aren't wedded for life to Minnesota (if it comes to that).

Well, I've come to the end of my paper and also, I think, of what I wanted to say to you. My baby has been wonderfully well behaved: she has slept for almost four hours without budging, which is really excellent. Give our very affectionate greetings to Samuel and his wife. Do I dare wish Sophie as pretty a baby (in reality) as mine is in my own eyes?[2] Good-bye, dear Mama and dear Father.

Your most affectionate daughter,
Sophie T. Bost

# THE FIRST CHILD

Dear Parents:

A frost on September 1 has killed an immense amount of corn and potatoes. The freeze came two days after a magnificent sunrise, but nothing on our claim was touched except for a few cucumber leaves. Still, my corn was planted very late, though it was not my fault, and for the past twenty days we've been having cold weather and the time of hard frosts is approaching. Of course, I've cut enough ripe, unspoiled grain to keep us supplied with flour and carry my livestock through the winter, but I'd like very much for the rest to ripen. The potatoes are doing very well and are growing fast—I think I'll be able to sell some next spring if the market is good. Powers says he is on the lookout for a steer to pay me back [for the one he allowed to die while he had it on loan]; he doesn't seem in any hurry to do it, and I don't like to threaten him with a lawsuit, though people say he never pays any of his debts unless he has that fear before his eyes.

The blackbirds have done a great deal of damage to the corn; flocks one or two miles long try to alight in the fields, and you'd die laughing to hear, at the same time, the mournful voices of Powers and his brother-in-law, Mrs. Maxwell, Anna, Bill, Mike, and Charley [Maxwell] shouting, beating on pots and pans, shooting off guns; also our Marie screaming and beating on a shovel, Soso shouting, me doing the same and pounding on a board; also Sarver, his wife, and their children hammering on a caldron and screaming at the top of their lungs—all on account of the same flock that circles around and gets too confused in the end to know where to come down. This is the way it has been for two weeks from 5:30 in the morning to six in the evening, more or less.

I've recovered my health and am getting along well again with my work. Soso and her baby, which she claims is mine, are in very good health, and both of them are as nice as can be—she says I'm a better papa than I give the impression of being. What a compliment! The maples have turned red, yellow, and orange; the oaks are a beautiful dark green, and the whole landscape is magnificent.

Good-bye, much-beloved parents.

Your most affectionate
Theodore Bost

# THE FIRST CHILD

**Sophie to the elder Bosts**

Sunday, October 16, 1859

Dearest Mother and Father:

. . . If you only knew how many times the joy of being a mother and holding my baby in my arms has kept me awake despite my weariness after a long day and my desire to fall asleep; then afterward I blame myself for my foolishness, which will cause me another day of nervousness. But after all, every rose has its thorns, and after I've gotten myself well pricked, it is to be hoped that I'll know how to put my fingers beside the thorns and pick the roses more calmly. Dodo, of course, is always prudent, so he gets pricked less often. I should add that in just a few weeks everything will go more easily for me. The autumn work being very urgent especially since we are going to change houses in two weeks or thereabouts), Theodore has Marie helping him as much as she can, and I would like very much to help him myself. So the housework rests almost entirely on my shoulders. You realize, dear Mother, that when you have a baby there is always washing or something else to do, so I keep very busy, especially indoors, whereas with my head the way it is, I ought to spend a lot of time outdoors. Soon we shall all be down in the dumps, and I am getting uneasy as much for Dodo as myself: indeed, I find his work as tiring as my own. I am always busy calculating how much he still has left to do and telling myself that it's more than he can finish without getting too tired; then, when I want to take some comfort thinking of how it will be in the winter, I have to admit that I look forward to having many, many things to do, all of them urgently necessary.

The house we are going to live in needs a lot of repairs to make it comfortable. Dodo has promised me various pieces of furniture which he says he can make and which I have difficulty getting along without. And on top of all that, he is determined to clear ten acres despite my objections and protests, and I am often afraid I'll have a husband who is worn out at the age of forty— you must admit that would be a real cause for worry! If my Dodo's constitution were really strong, the thought of all these additions we are planning would fill me with delight and I'd be very proud to have them all carried out, but you've seen his picture and you can judge whether or not he has the look of a man who can take on anything without wearing himself out right away.

Of course, he takes better care of himself than he used to, but the hardships he has undergone haven't done him any good. . . .

The doctor didn't use any instruments because, he said, I was strong enough to bear the pain. As for me, I think he was the one who was strong enough to torture me regardless; in any event, it was during the actual delivery that our darling's head got a little bit out of shape. Everyone says that will take care of itself; as for myself, I no longer notice it at all, and I think my little one is just as beautiful as I dreamed she would be; and she is really very pretty with her dear blue eyes which already laugh in such a fine and pleasing way, her adorable little mouth, and her cute nose—and besides, she has such lovely little hands and feet! Oh, how we love this little creature! Theodore, who, like me, has never had any special liking for very small children, is completely mad about his own, and it's wonderful to watch him play with the baby. He, too, is proud of her, and I don't think he was ever very much disappointed to have a girl, although he would be if, like one of our neighbors, I were to have five girls in a row.

. . . In general, the inhabitants of Shakopee don't have the best reputation in the world. Nevertheless, we have some good friends there, and I visited one of them for two days recently. I had gone with Dodo to Shakopee, and this lady—a friend of the Maxwells—persuaded me to stay overnight so I could visit a sort of agricultural fair the next day: flowers, articles made by women, etc. It was much better than I had expected, and next year we too are thinking of exhibiting something—perhaps some of my flowers if my garden turns out as well as I hope, and Dodo could put in various vegetables.

Good-bye, dear Parents. It's winter now, so we'll be writing more letters.

Your most affectionate daughter
Sophie T. Bost

**Sophie to Ami Bost**

Chanhassen
November 7, 1859

Dearest Father:

We received your letter of October 5 only yesterday afternoon, and, as you can see, we are losing no time in answering, as you asked. We are sorry you are in low spirits, and we were deeply moved by your premonition of your own death, described to us so affectionately. Indeed—oh, yes—you may be mistaken. It's more probable that you're mistaken, and I hope the Lord will preserve you a long time for your family and friends. . . . However, thank you, dear Father, for being completely open with us, and for regarding the sympathy of your children as some slight consolation. If that small growth is arrested, we shall be most happy and grateful; but if, on the contrary, it should take you away into the kingdom of glory—if, dear Father, our dearly beloved friend, you are to "pass away in your sleep"—we shall know how to seek you in the place where you're going . . . in the bosom of Jesus, reunited with the great family of the redeemed, and we shall rejoice all the more when it comes our turn to go. May God keep us from wanting to detain here below the souls of those He calls to Him! Especially when His children appear to have finished their tasks and are longing for repose. One of the most blessed hours of my life was spent beside the bed of my dying father, and I should like to have the great happiness of being at your side during the last years of your life and of closing your eyes with joy as well as sorrow. Last night I dreamed I saw you dead, but never had your face held for me such an appearance of life: I knew that your soul was not lost. Oh, may I only be as sure when the moment of the real test comes!

Your tenderly affectionate daughter
Sophie T. Bost

**Sophie to the elder Bosts**

Chaska, Minnesota
April, 1860

Dearest Parents:

We no longer have any idea whether we've written you or not since we got your last letters, nor even if it has been a long time. Not knowing, therefore, how long you've been without news from us, I will go back some time to pick up the thread, and will tell you that Theodore has finally received from Powers the ox we have so often spoken of, a replacement for our handsome Pete; this one is neither as good looking nor as strong, I believe, but he will do, and we are much relieved to get him. Our three cows all had calves last month, one unfortunately two months early, which leaves us with only two calves, but they are doing very well. One of the cows has been sick, and I really thought it was all up with her; but she's getting back on her feet again, and I am hoping to make a lot of butter this summer, selling enough to keep in clothing and groceries—but there are four of us, and, though our garments are simple, the bushes also wear them out a little faster than your fine asphalt roads.

If I had written you two or three weeks ago, it would have been a gloomy letter because we were then going through some bad times. Our stable, the barnyard fence, and all the hay had just been destroyed by a prairie fire. The cow was sick, our little darling too, and Dodo, my poor dear, was suffering a great deal from an inflammation of his stomach similar to the one he had last year. This illness didn't last long, God be praised, but the aftereffects have been fairly painful, and even now our Dodo is not as strong as he would like to be and needs to be for his heavy spring work. Add to all this the complete loss of nearly a whole month because of his illness and the weakness that followed it, and you will understand, dear Parents, why I still shudder when I think of that wretched time.

But we have reason to be very grateful, and in truth we are, both Dodo and I, because at last his health is nearly restored and because he can finally throw himself into his long-delayed labors. It was pitiful to see, a few weeks ago, how he would drag himself outdoors to work but would come in soon afterward, saying dejectedly, "It's no use, I can't do it!" That made me terribly sick at heart, and I was deeply concerned to see him always so thin and pale. Fortunately, he is better, and our life is getting back into its normal rhythm. For a few days we were very much afraid we'd have to give up all hope of clearing any new land this year, but Dodo is beginning to talk again of breaking his ten acres. This doesn't seem very wise to me, and I'd prefer it if, along with the field he cleared last year, he'd be content with four or five acres here. But he maintains he doesn't have enough, and, of course, he knows better than I do what he has to do. However, we've tried to hire a workman for this spring, but it was a little too late and all the available young men had already found jobs, so we shall simply press forward under God's protection.

I was telling you about how our stable burned. Although at the time we thought it a piece of bad luck, we have since realized that this one misfortune has spared us a much greater one. There was a man about two miles from here who set fire to a pile of weeds in his garden and then was unable to prevent the fire from spreading into the woods and marshes. Several of our neighbors had their fences burned up. Our fence, at the other house, was saved with difficulty, and, in all probability, if the first fire hadn't destroyed everything burnable round about us, everything on our place—stable, barnyard, and even the house itself—would have gone up in smoke. The fire was splendid to see as it swept through the woods and swamp, though it frightened me a little. As we looked out from the little house, where I had gone to join Theodore, we saw far, far away, long lines of fire or columns of flames spreading with a rapidity that a good, strong wind was helping only too well. If the unlucky wretch who did such a good job of burning his weeds had a penny to his name, he would lose it all in lawsuits, but he is a poor Methodist minister and there would be nothing to gain by suing him.

This year, unlike last year, has been very poor for [maple] sugar; we didn't even try to make any, which I regretted very much. Just think, dear Mother, what a pleasure it must be for a housewife to be able to dip into the sugar and molasses (molasses which has such a wonderful flavor!) without having to think of how much it costs! The idea is one that fills me with a special yearning, but it's one I'll have to put aside until my husband is able to imagine a springtime when he isn't breaking any new land. As for this year, of course, we haven't lost much because the [sugaring] season has been so short. If Dodo will kindly consent to make his wife very happy, and also make sure on innumerable delights for himself, he will figure out how to make two or three hundred pounds of sugar in '61 along with a large quantity of syrup. And then, and then! I can't comprehend how you would be able to resist the desire of coming to visit people so full of sweetness! Besides, when you have syrup you can make all your own vinegar and even beer—isn't that marvelous? All things considered, I almost envy the women whose husbands are not determined to break land, but in this matter it's a good thing Dodo is wiser than I am—though that fine gentleman has no trace of majestic scorn for the good things that can be made with sugar.

You ought to see the lovely summer wardrobe I've made for my daughter. Perhaps you'd think I am a little extravagant, dear Mother, to have sewn little bits of trimming and embroidery, on almost everything, but although I've never set much store by fine clothes for myself, I want very much for my daughter to be well turned out, and since embroidery costs nothing but the time, I wasn't stingy with it. So that's my confession, and Dodo doesn't at all believe that I've done wrong: Mimi [the baby's nickname] is so pretty in her little openwork stockings, embroidered petticoat, skirt and blouse likewise, etc., etc. With the fine smocks you gave me, dear Mother, I've made a long dress for this winter, a very pretty short one for this summer, and a little bonnet that isn't yet finished but will be very nice—hasn't this cloth worn well? Soon Mimi will be done with long dresses, which will be a great day. Also, I'm thinking of weaning her at the beginning of June, which I am a little uneasy about. What a chatterbox I am! Good-bye, dear Mother and dear, dear Father.

> Your affectionate daughter,
> Sophie

## Sophie to Elisée Bost

> Chaska, Carver County
> Minnesota
> April 7, 1860

That rascal Dodo has left me only a little bit of space, and the paper is so big and heavy that there is no chance of adding another sheet.[3] But there will be enough room, dear Elisée, to tell you that if you haven't forgotten us, as your letter assures us, for our part we often think of you with affection. I wish you lived near us here! If you can or if the opportunity arises, come and sample our mode of life! And then see whether you'd be able to give it up again for another one! In two or three years, when the hardest part of pioneering life will be behind us, our existence will, I think, be truly enviable, and I haven't the slightest doubt that any of our relations who comes to make us a visit would be enchanted by what he would see! Fields of corn, wheat, oats, and so on and so on; a magnificent garden with many vegetables that are unknown in Europe; orchards full of fruit trees and big groves of sugar maples—not at all to be sneezed at, my dear man, if you like sweet things! Promise any housewife such a store of goodies, and you will see her face light up!

I could tell you a great deal about the joys of being an American farmer. We have scarcely gotten any farther than the laborious existence of the pioneer, and I assure you that it takes strong arms and plenty of courage to tackle that job and bring it to a successful conclusion. Imagine to yourself a man in the middle of a dense forest which he has to clear. Tree after tree falls under his ax; some are used to build his house, and from others he splits rails to build his fences; most of them are put in piles to be burned and removed from the land; and then the new growth must be cut; then you gather up everything (branches, roots, and brush), make more piles, burn it all carefully—and then the soil is ready, though lots of stumps and roots remain! You go at it with the plow, drawn by two, three, or even four yoke of oxen—hard, hard work, my dear Elisée, which your brother was doing last week, coming in to me covered from head to foot with dirt—moist earth, turned furrows that often have to be laid in place, sometimes with your foot, sometimes with your hands, often by sitting down on them as hard as you can! One man leads the oxen and guides them along while a second man holds the plow, and this [second] man has the harder job, for he must be very strong to drive [the plowshare] in, hold back, jump over stumps, steer around tree trunks, and cut roots! But to the pioneer how beautiful is the sight of this land wrested from the forest, won by the sweat of his brow! In the evening, exhausted but happy, he shows his wife the most difficult spots, the richest soil, and the barren places—at least, this is what my husband does, and that's why I know a little bit about how it is done. So there you have your land broken; then you harrow it; then the first year you plant it to corn, potatoes, beets, or buckwheat; the second year you grow wheat; the third year it is prettier to look at: the stumps gradually rot, the small ones first, and then the larger ones disappear, and the pioneer grows rich with his fine fields and abundant harvests.

Now you understand why the first years are so hard! The husband has so much to do that he has almost no time to fix up the house or its surroundings—he doesn't even have time to think about making sugar in the spring or to plant fruit trees. No, he must clear land, he must break the soil, and even in the event that the first crops don't turn out particularly well, he has confidence—first of all in God, and then in the future, to reward him for his efforts. I've been telling you about the woodland, but there are also open prairies where there are no trees, hence no difficult clearing to be done, but by the same token no wood to burn in winter, no sugar, no shade, no shelter! I like the woods better, but then, I'm not the one who chops down the trees! When I came here two years ago, Theodore had already cleared a fair amount of land, but had broken very little. Last spring he broke seven acres, I think, and this spring he wants to break ten or twelve; but because he was too sick he has had to think better of that and will only do two. He wants to do the rest this summer and then clear something like fourteen acres next year. Wish him success, dear Brother—as for me, these ambitious plans make me a little afraid.

It seems to me that I have now ventured into a subject in which you must think I'm not very competent—but just come and see for yourself! Doesn't the sugar attract you? I hope that Theodore will be able to make two or three hundred pounds of it next year, and I promise that you shall have a small piece of it—whether brown or yellow, its flavor is wonderful.

Good-bye, dear Elisée. Send me a kiss, and I'll return it to you.

Your most affectionate sister,
Sophie Theodore

**Sophie to Ami Bost**

Chaska, Carver County
June, 1860

Dearest Father:

Although you suppose that our life is very eventful, it is actually quite unexciting, or at any rate we are so isolated that we depend on letters from you to be reassured that we still matter to someone in this world. When I say "isolated," I don't mean that we have too few neighbors! Far from it! But the neighbors, nice as they may be, don't take the place of family, especially, it seems to me, in this country where everyone has a friendly greeting for his neighbors, invites them in, and visits them on a footing of great intimacy, but at bottom has no more real feeling for them than if they were total strangers! It's only at the Maxwells' that I feel myself pretty much a part of the family—Mrs. Maxwell is so cheerful, open, generous, and youthful. It's true that she has all the defects of her qualities—sometimes she seems to me so frivolous, worldly, and almost vulgar that I think I don't want to see her anymore; but then she likes so much to borrow things and have company, which at times puts us out of sorts—but it's impossible to hold a grudge against her for whatever it may be! She has such a warm heart and knows so well how to make sure of getting a pleasant welcome. Mrs. Cleaveland is, I believe, the most estimable of all the women near here—pious, lively, enthusiastic, well educated, with attractive manners and a charming family of four well-behaved daughters and an excellent man for a husband—but she has so much work to do and her health is so poor that she can seldom get away from home. I go to visit her as often as I can; only it's quite far (two miles). The baby is heavy, and Dodo can't often take the time to come with me.

Yes, dear Father, June 5 is indeed our wedding anniversary—I'd have liked to have waited until the tenth [Ami's birthday], but considering the circumstances, Dodo couldn't have taken his fiancée home with him.[4] Anyhow, it was the tenth when we moved into our house, and this date brings back even happier memories than the fifth—all alone, as I was, so far from my own people, still so little acquainted with my husband, and just having come through such a long time of torment. . . . This year I shall wean my baby on that day, and so life goes!

It may be that the end of the slump is not far away and we shall soon see better days. In any event, it's out of the question to make butter that you can sell for only six cents [a pound]. We're going to try making cheese, and if that turns out well, it will pay us just as well or better, so people say. If it doesn't work out, I don't quite know what we'll do until the wheat, which is still young, can be sold—sing "five cents, five cents"[5] and laugh at our poverty, I suppose. In any event, everything is in God's hands, and this certainly brings us serenity every time our worries threaten to degenerate into discouragement or impatience.

We are having a day of rain so heavy that you can do nothing but reach for your blotting paper. No new books! Ah, that's the place where the shoe really pinches sometimes.

Your most affectionate daughter,
Sophie T. Bost

**Theodore to his mother**

Our Place
July 29, 1860

Dearest Mother:

You complain that we so seldom write, but I assure you that we—especially I—have little time for writing. We never have a light in the evening, and during the day we are extremely busy. Then on Sunday I'm so tired that I sleep while Soso and Marie straighten up the house and put on their best dresses. Today (Sunday) I am less tired than usual because yesterday I slept a little [longer] and worked a little less because of a fine shower that did us a great deal of good. Everything was suffering from a long drought.

Last Monday I began my haying and shall be at that until next Thursday, the day when I hope to start mowing my wheat, which promises a fairly good harvest, especially considering that this is only the second plowing after the land was broken and that the soil was virgin [forest] only fourteen months ago. Next year the crop will be even better if the weather is as favorable as this year. I've had to suspend work on breaking my big field owing to the heat, but I plan to resume it at the beginning of September. I want very much indeed to catch up with those neighbors who have made the most progress, but my health has been so poor this year that I haven't been able to finish all that I set out to do. Although I'm not in very good shape at present, I am in better condition to make my hay and harvest my grain than I've been in many years, perhaps because I haven't worked as hard as usual this spring.

I think I've told you that we've been hoping to see Minnesota recover this year from the slump we've been suffering from up to now. Our magnificent harvest will in fact, I think, pull us out of the morass, but our Democratic President, probably in order to pay us back because our state has just voted against his administration, is now resuming the [collection of money due the government for the] sale of land which had been postponed last year. This will remove something like a million dollars from the poor farmers' pockets; moreover, it will depress the prices of all foodstuffs until sometime in November, but from all indications there will then be a general recovery and the people of Minnesota who up to now have had nothing but disappointments will begin to see better days. We ourselves, though thanks to our parents we have not been in actual want, have still felt the pinch on many occasions.

People knew so little about this region that they often made unnecessary outlays and wasted an enormous amount of time on crops which, as is now evident, were not at all a paying proposition and require a tremendous amount of time which each of us could have used to clear practically twice as much land as we did. Oh well, we learn by experience.

Our neighborhood, which up to now has been spared any great tribulations, has just sustained a terrible loss. Mr. and Mrs.

## THE FIRST CHILD

Cleaveland went away with their four children on the Fourth of July to visit their sister and brother-in-law, who is a minister in Minneapolis.[6] On the fifth the two families went to bathe in a lovely lake famous for its rocky shore and gradually sloping bottom. The two older Cleaveland girls (ten and twelve years old) ran into the water, but all of a sudden one of them began to struggle and call for help; the second one went to give her a hand and also lost her footing. Their twelve-year-old cousin ran to rescue them and also got into deep water. Then Mr. Cleaveland threw himself into the water and his brother-in-law too, then his sister-in-law and everyone else. One after the other they sank without a word. Mrs. Cleaveland wanted to rush in after the others, but two men who came running up held her back while trying to save the drowning people, but one of them got tangled up in a shawl and his friend had a hard time rescuing him.

So there was poor Mrs. Cleaveland in a strange town, alone in a hotel with the dead bodies of her husband, her two oldest girls, her sister, her brother-in-law, and her nephew, with nobody to console her except two little girls of seven and four years of age and a nephew of two and a half. Twenty-five of us went to hoe her crops the other day, and we intend to do her harvesting for her if we can spare the time. The poor, dear woman! Her health is so feeble, and she bears up under this terrible affliction with so much resignation. Because none of the farmers hereabouts has offered to take her in, Soso and I have invited her to live with us for a while, perhaps spend the whole winter; but she says she has her cows and other animals to care for. I've told her to let her next-door neighbors attend to that while she stays with us. The very idea of leaving a sick woman all alone like that with her two small girls—and after what she has been through! Of course, she would be no burden to us. Her crops would enable her to repay anything we spent on her. And at least she wouldn't have to get up in the terrible cold to start a fire, living all by herself after having enjoyed such a happy family life. She has been the only one with a family of fine children brought up as they are in our old country, and she is the only neighbor of ours we would want to have living with us. She seemed to feel such a great sense of relief when we suggested the idea to her. We had thought that her close neighbors would have offered her shelter, since they are her friends, fellow-countrymen, and Christians, but we didn't want to wait till she was dead before we issued our invitation. Anyway, between now and winter a great many things can happen. Her relations may come from the East. But at least we shall have done what we thought was our duty, and the God of widows and orphans will not rebuke us when we appear before His throne.

But where is our dear Father and how is he? And you, dear Mother, how are you? I wish ever so much that I could be with you. I remember with so much pleasure those few months we spent together in Serrières, even though I was full of anxiety about my future. Who knows whether one of these days we may not all be together in Switzerland? If God blesses our labors, we hope to come back to live in Switzerland. Of course, that won't be for many more years, but we are young and you are not yet very old. Where are all my brothers and what are they doing? Several of them owe us letters, while we owe one to dear Ami [Junior] and Tim. But honestly, we are too busy just now.

By the way, Charles Boissonnas,[7] who has come back to America, has just written me that he would like to buy a farm near us and asks me for information. Which I have sent him. He hasn't yet given me any answer, and I think my letter must have gone astray.

Good-bye, good-bye, dear Mother and Father. My best to all my brothers and sisters, aunts and cousins, and also Mme. Vaucher.

Your most devoted and loving
Theodore Bost

## Sophie and Theodore to the elder Bosts (four letters)

September 22, 1860

Dearly Beloved Mother:

Your long, delightful letter got to us today; that is, Theodore brought it back from Chaska only two or three hours ago.

. . . Mrs. Cleaveland is not going to spend the winter with us, as I think we had told you earlier, dear Mother. She has decided to go back East to her family, who were insistent that she should return. So now the most delightful family around here has been lost and destroyed, but the noble woman bears her misfortune in a way that would be beyond me—so calm, sometimes even gay, active, stronger than she was before the tragedy, and making all her preparations to travel with wonderful energy. I'm afraid that once she gets home and the excitement is all over, she may sink, never to rise again. She herself almost seems to want that to happen. She kept the house all by herself, along with her husband, who helped her a great deal with the housework, and her two older daughters who were beginning to shoulder almost the whole responsibility for the household chores—the very ones who are dead! The eldest especially was very old for her age, almost too mature for a twelve-year-old, and so full of little attentions for her mother and so endearing to everybody! Poor Emma! My heart is often heavy when I remember the last time she came to our house with her sister Ella to spend the afternoon, both of them so well behaved, quiet, already such grown-up young ladies! The little nephew is with Mrs. Cleaveland, who is going to adopt him—he is a lovely child, very difficult,. self-willed and spoiled, but affectionate.

Since Mrs. Cl[eaveland] has been selling her furniture and so on, we have seized the opportunity to buy for not much money a lot of things we should otherwise have had to buy a few at a time—a lovely, solid dresser, a good sofa, a kitchen stove, a small worktable, and a number of other things, all of which we got for 150 fr. [$30], payable when we have the money, says she; next spring, say we. We've already had everything but the stove for a week, and you may well believe how much all that embellishes and improves our living room; now it is really a little *salon*, as clean as it is comfortable. On winter evenings I take great pleasure in sitting on the sofa close to our fine stove. Oh, if Dodo's health would improve! What a delightful winter we would have to look forward to!

But you don't know what a hospital this house has been! In the first place, Theodore has been complaining for a month of pains in his left side—I think I may already have told you about it, after the harvests, although then we were hoping it wasn't going to bother him any longer; but since then he caught whooping cough about two weeks ago from our little darling.

Yes, alas, our little darling has it too, and three weeks ago we thought the good Lord was surely going to take back our little treasure, and not just because of whooping cough; she had dysentery, a bad case of it, two or three teeth that were giving her a great deal of pain, and her mouth was full of aphthas.[8]

Finally, on Wednesday, the fifth of September, the doctor from Shakopee said she was very ill; on Thursday she was sinking lower; but on Friday God listened to our prayers and gave her back to us. Oh, what agonies we suffered all through those twelve days, when the poor little thing was asleep nearly the whole time, ate absolutely nothing, wouldn't look at anybody, and wanted only to drink and be quiet! But, by the same token, what joy when she began to show new signs of life, took a little food, and then fell asleep again, this time a very different kind of sleep—the sleep of the living! Never shall I forget either that torment or that delight! I would have been almost beside myself with joy if, just when the baby was recovering, my husband hadn't fallen sick. I hope, and I pray to the Lord, that this illness may be the last, and that after so many months of worries and sickness, our little family may enjoy good health again and get back to work with redoubled strength.

Mimi is not yet as strong as she was before this severe blow, and for a long time she hasn't wanted to smile or play games. Now she is doing both again with all her heart, and since yesterday she has been able to stand on her own feet, though not for long at a time. She is much thinner and had lost almost all her natural color. Her cough is still dragging her down, but I hope that once she gets over that, we'll see our darling making up for lost time. Mimi was one year old the twentieth of August, and she has begun to walk, holding onto chairs and walls, and she understands a great many things, lots more than the little Powers boy who is six weeks older than she is, a great big husky fellow and a beautiful child as well.

My garden has not turned out as well as it should have, at least not the flowers, because of the drought; my *reine-marguérites* [China asters] are nowhere near as beautiful as last year; I've had very lovely Chinese *oeillets* [carnations or marigolds] of all shapes and sizes; the double *oeillets*, the seeds of which I brought with me from Europe, haven't done well and neither have the *violiers* [an old-fashioned variety of red violet or gillyflower] and several others. If you have some flower seeds that can be sent in a letter, think of me, dear Mother, and I'll be very grateful to you for them. I love so much to care for my flowers, especially those that come from our old home!

But good-bye, dearest Mother. What a pity that I must close now.

Your loving daughter,
Sophie Theodore

Sophie Bonjour

Jenny Bost

Ami Bost

Theodore with the second Alice
on his lap, Julie ("Mimi"),
Alphonse, Theodore, Jr.
("Dodi"), and Sophie (1874)

Theodore, Jr. (around 1890)

Sophie and Theodore (about 1890)

The sixtieth wedding anniversary of Jenny and Ami Bost (1874)
Front row: Etienne, Jenny, Ami, John
Rear: Samuel, Paul, Timothée, Théophile, Augustin, Elisée

The New Frame House (1863)

Home in Pomona, California

Sophie Bost

Photographs probably taken around 1900

Theodore Bost

Theodore and Sophie in old age
(photo taken at their home in San Dimas, California)

# THE FIRST CHILD

Chaska, Carver County
September 22, 1860

Dearest Mama:

Having your letter here before me, I'll begin by answering your questions and by thanking you, as does Soso, for your so-welcome letter.

I can't remember anymore what I told Elisée about having to run after and bring home my oxen; I recall only that I had a very difficult time—too difficult—but I had to do it because once an animal knows it can get the better of you, it's almost impossible to reassert your control over it. Now, when one of my animals gets off course, I have only to yell and it immediately returns to its proper position—and eleven great oxen hitched nose to tail make a long line! All the same, it was just as well for me that I trained them to obey me last spring; otherwise I'd be obliged to let the beasts go where their whims lead them. The hardest thing around here is to make the animals from each farm stay together. All day long they are mixed up together, and when the lead cows separate, each of the other animals is supposed to follow its own bell. Almost every day this spring, one or two of my cows failed to follow my bell, so I had the great fun of grabbing their tails in one hand and a stick in the other, and after that it was pure pleasure to see us racing through the woods and swamps; time after time I was flat on my stomach in a very few minutes; on other occasions I caught up with the animal when it got bogged down, and then I would climb onto its back to encourage it by other means than gestures to get out (and take me out of the mud). But as I've said, I now almost never have to do anything but walk behind them, and sometimes I'd just as soon not go looking for them; only I've made a rule for myself never to let them spend the night away from home; I don't think I've broken the rule but once, and that was owing to a frightful storm.

By the way, we've had a tornado that smashed all the trees and flattened fences and crops along a strip six miles long and only 150 feet wide. I saw the cloud approaching by the flashes of lightning, and I went into the house without saying anything about it to Soso. Mimi was then almost at death's door and Soso was very much on edge, so I didn't want to scare her; I expected from one minute to the next to hear the roof being torn off and the trees crashing down, but when I went out again I saw the cloud moving past the Maxwells' and away toward the Americans'.[9] Haystacks, shocks of wheat, etc.—everything was swept away; the marsh grass, which had been flattened by the rain, was sucked up and left pointing in the direction in which the tornado had gone, so that it is possible to determine its width to within a foot.

Inasmuch as Sarver helped me to shock my wheat, I have helped him stack his hay, and the other evening, taking our two axes, he carrying a pair of mittens and each of us with a veil made of mosquito netting, candles, and pots for collecting the honey, we went by moonlight (?) [sic] to cut down our bee tree, which was three feet thick. We couldn't see our hands before our faces, so we just chopped away by guesswork, but the tree was of hard wood and so instead of continuing to chop after we heard it beginning to crack, we preferred to sit down[at a distance] and let the weight of the tree carry it down. Soon the little cracking sounds got much louder, the upper branches began to rub against nearby trees, still very softly and then—bang, bang, bang—the loud cracking began all of a sudden and—poof!—the tree was flat on the ground. We had felled it so that the hole where the honey was would be on top. We wrapped ourselves in our veils, lit our candles, and went to take a look. As luck would have it, a great number of large branches had fallen on top of the trunk. Sarver, who was holding the candle, was soon stung, which I think made him curse; I got busy stuffing rags into the holes which working in the brush always makes in our boots at the toe and on the sides; then I began to clear away the branches, but in a moment the bees were inside my boots and trousers and all over my body, which caused me to leap away a good distance from the tree and shout that I couldn't stand it any longer. Sarver himself could see no way to get the honey without destroying the bees. So I got some hay and we burned all the bees outside the hole; when there were no more of them on the trunk, I climbed up on it and with my ax made a hole about one foot by one and a half feet—no sign of honey, but a big hole on each side; we put in the candle very carefully so as not to set the tree afire, and saw the honey on the side toward the top of the tree. About then the bees came pouring out and began to sting us again, so we built up our fire again, I chopped for another half-hour, and then it was Sarver's turn to get to work. I stuck the candle into the split end of a long branch and gave him plenty of light with no danger to myself. Then with his bare hands he broke off the pieces of honey[comb] that were still stuck to the tree and afterward that which was mixed with the rotten wood in the hollow of the tree and scraped up with a spoon all that had run out after the tree fell. Then we went home. I gave him several pounds of honey for his trouble, and each of us wound up in his own bed around midnight. He didn't swell up at all, but my foot swelled badly.

And that's how the whole business went off, with nothing invented and nothing left out. The bees that survived are at work again in the deepest part of the hole.

I still hope I can establish a hive next year—I want to wait until cold weather sets in before I remove these bees from the tree and see whether they have enough honey to get through the winter.

Dear Father, we are sending this letter to Pau,[10] and we hope it will find you there in good health along with our dear Mama. I received yesterday your fine letter containing the 100 fr. from M. Perrot,[11] and I lost no time in buying a number of good things which we need so much, especially now that on top of everything else I've caught the whooping cough. Soso didn't know what to think when I came home with the extra money in my pocket, loaded down with a whole assortment of purchases and having, in addition, paid off a small debt.

Good-bye, dear Parents. Forgive me if this letter doesn't reply fully to all your questions—my head is all muddled by my coughing.

Good-bye to all the brothers.

Your devoted and loving
Theodore Bost

September 27, 1860

Dearest Father:

Very far from finding your "suggestion" a bad one, it has been a long time since we decided that it is a virtual necessity for Dodo to sleep alone so he will get more rest. During the worst part of our baby's illness I spread a straw mattress for myself on the floor, since it made no sense for me to lie wide awake in the bed while keeping poor Papa awake at the same time. I'd have liked to let things stay that way, but neither of us really felt warm enough, having to share the blankets, so for this winter at least we'll somehow have to manage sleeping together and even make up our minds to take the baby into bed with us. Anyway, she is very quiet now, and Theodore sleeps fairly well. You know what a disagreeable summer the poor dear has had. I'm not at all sure what is causing the pains in his side; I've worried about them a great deal and still do. Theodore has no confidence in any of the doctors around here and won't go to them despite the urging of everyone who knows him and worries about him. You know we are thinking about you, that we talk about you and pray for you. You do the same for us, and your prayers will sustain us when we are a little sad or discouraged, which doesn't happen unless Dodo is worse than usual.

Good-bye, dear Father. Thank you for sending the 100 fr. I'd like to thank M. Perrot directly, but without your permission I hesitate to write to somebody I don't know, no matter how much gratitude I owe him.

Many fond greetings to all our friends and relations, and lots of loving kisses to Mama Bost and yourself from your affectionate

Sophie Theodore

October 3, 1860

Dearest Parents:

. . . The [government's resumption of its] sale of land, which drained our part of the country of all its money, is forcing down the price of farm produce. Magnificent oxen, worth $180 in '57, are now offered for sale at $50; wheat has fallen by fifteen cents for sixty pounds [a bushel], but will soon rise again from all appearances. Speaking of wheat, we are quite annoyed with the threshers, who are neighbors of ours; they are so sure they'll get the job of threshing our grain that they spend all their time working three, four, or six miles from here so as to get the business away from threshers in other townships. Fortunately, these other threshers have come into our vicinity and are thus grabbing the wheat from under our neighbors' noses. The pigs (which the idiotic law allows to be turned out unconstitutionally to forage for themselves) have eaten up several bushels of my wheat, and I've had a quarrel with the Maxwells because I told them I would make them pay dearly if they didn't shut theirs up, but in any case, they've done it. Many shocks of grain have been ruined by the rains, which cause decay or sprouting; my shocks have suffered some damage, but not much.

From one of Tim's letters we learn that John is having good success in England and that the English, running true to form, "are giving to him to whom much has been given"—the Monthyon prize.[12] We are proud as can be and thank God that his work is thus crowned with success; we wish him ever-increasing success as he continues to do good. He works hard enough, to speak only in the human sense, to deserve a reward.

Good-bye to all.

Your son, Theodore Bost
Your Sophie

# VIII

# The Civil War Begins

By the late fall of 1860 Theodore is writing to his parents in a more confident tone. More land is being cleared and fenced, thanks to a temporary improvement in his health and to a deal he was able to make with a neighbor, the former Methodist minister Cheeseman, of whom we shall be hearing more. For the first time in nearly two years the Bosts were eating meat regularly. Farm prices were still very low, but with the coming of the Civil War the economic outlook for Minnesota farmers was about to become brighter. Theodore and Sophie are beginning to allow themselves a few rare comforts; they are still excited by the pleasures (and anxieties) of parenthood. They are thinking of buying more land or exchanging their thickly wooded farm for one that has been brought more fully under cultivation. The principal source of this new optimism was the fact that Theodore had been able to borrow substantial amounts of money from his father and mother, who had found themselves in easier circumstances thanks to Jenny Bost's legacy from her father. Sophie also had an inheritance to look forward to, but since the family property in Switzerland had first to be sold, it was to be some time before she actually received this.

Theodore still has many complaints. He objects to the callousness and dubious competence of the neighborhood doctor. Though an admirer of his minister, he is disgusted with the hypocrisy and cant that all too often pass for religious fervor among the members of his church. As an ardent Abolitionist he welcomes the outbreak of the Civil War, but is impatient with the North's military bungling and ambivalence toward slavery. Sophie, by contrast, though she is occasionally despondent, dwells on the cheerful news whenever there is any. She is especially pleased with her little girl, whom they have taken to calling "Mimi." With Theodore, she is absorbed in plans for a new frame house to replace their drafty log cabin. Her second confinement turned out to be an easy one, and on July 17 she can write to the elder Bosts that they have a new grandson, Alphonse.

**Theodore to the elder Bosts**

> Chaska, Carver County
> Minnesota
> December 9, 1860

Dearest Parents:

For two weeks now we have put off writing this letter, hoping for another one from you, but we've decided to send it off anyway. Since a few days ago we've had 100 pounds of splendid beef in our larder, the first time in twenty months that we've had any considerable amount in the house. So we are feasting, and my health has improved so much that I've already finished quite a long piece of fence. Cheeseman continues to split rails to pay for his cow;[1] he has already split 900. First he cuts down the trees, then splits them into two or four ten-foot lengths, depending on the diameter; I draw them with my oxen to the line of the fence; he splits them [into thinner pieces] and then I build the fence. By working at a moderate pace all winter, I'll have my whole *claim* fenced by next spring. He's going to split 2,000 more for me, and I'll pay him in grain if I can. Here the great thing is to pay for things with what you can produce on your own farm and sell [your crops] for cash.

Today we had an excellent sermon from our dear pastor. He is the first American I've ever heard preach in favor of fasting; he is extremely evangelical and a true model in everything; we love him as much for his human qualities as for his excellence as a minister.[2]

The other day we were visiting him, and he took us out behind his house where, after looking carefully in all directions to make sure we were unobserved, he gave us a glass of wine made from sugar and wild grapes; this made us double up with laughter.[3]

So good-bye, dear Parents. We are happier and happier all the time. We hope that you are too. May God be with you. Happy New Year to all, and particularly to you!

> Theodore Bost

**Theodore to his father**

Chaska

Beginning of January, 1861

Dearest Father:

You can't complain of getting too few letters from us lately, and I also know that I need not make excuses if I write to you again today. But this is more a business letter because it is written to tell you that I've received the $100 sent by the bank of Marcuard and Company on November 29. The duplicate sent December 6 had also been in Chaska for several days when I went down there December 31, which is doing pretty well for the winter mails. It's unnecessary to thank you again for this loan, which will allow me to hold onto my wheat to pay my workman in the spring instead of having to sell now at a rock-bottom price to pay our living expenses. Wheat has been selling very, very cheaply but is now starting to go up again despite the new crisis the crazy Southerners are expected to touch off. The newspapers have doubtless informed you already that the Southerners, who are dissatisfied with our future President, are rebelling and want to set up a new republic based wholly on slavery. From one point of view, we should let them go ahead, but for other reasons we shouldn't. It isn't known what Lincoln, the former rail splitter, now our President-elect, thinks about it. The leading Republicans are demanding that 100,000 soldiers be sent to pacify the South (a homeopathic treatment).[4]

. . . All the American religious journals contain reports about John's work and his prize. Since he doesn't write to us, we suppose he wouldn't have time to read our letters, so we'll content ourselves with wishing him success and with praying for his work and that of Samuel. How are all the other brothers?

But good-bye once again. A thousand kisses for the New Year to both of you and to all our relations. Believe in the affection of your most devoted and grateful son.

Theodore Bost

**Theodore to the elder Bosts**

Chaska, Carver County
Minnesota
January 11, 1861

Dear Parents:

Your letter of December 6 reached us four or five days ago; they [your letters] almost always take three weeks or less to get here. Each year the railroad gets a little closer to St. Paul.

You speak, dear Father, of loving one another while we are here below. That is true, and often I almost regret my various occupations which prevent me from thinking of you as much as I should like. Having been in bad health for so long, and not being able on that account to look ahead with confidence to the future, I had allowed myself to grow somewhat despondent. But now that I'm feeling better and am getting some help with my work, my mind is more at ease and I love everybody, especially my parents, more than ever. And I see more clearly that there is only one necessary thing, which is to leave the conduct of our lives in God's hands.

However, I again feel the need to explain some things that seem perfectly simple to me, an American, but seem to cause you uneasiness. To do this, I need to go into some detail.

My *claim* consists of 160 acres: about forty-five of these are easy to clear, costing only $5 or $6 (per acre) for the labor of removing trees and brush. There are about five acres of magnificent oaks which I could sell now for a good price, but not high enough, and besides, I don't have the strength to cut them this winter. Sixty acres are in dense woods which would cost too much to clear, would be very difficult to work for several years owing to the large number of stumps—and the wood has no market value. The rest consists of marshland, ravines, and steep slopes. If the money from [the sale of] "*Les Parcs*," at least $1,000, is paid to us,[5] I might clear this year the forty-five acres that are easy to bring under cultivation, and we'd have left over enough not only to buy a splendid farm already fully established (fields, stable, fine house), but also to buy horses and a wagon and still have about $200 to hire help on this new farm, which also consists of 160 acres, of which sixty to seventy (I think even as much as 100) would be easy (and hence cheap) to clear. This would be a great deal because $100 worth of help would clear as much on land where there are but few trees as $500 would clear in a more thickly wooded area. It's not just out of mere willfulness that I want to buy a different farm, and I don't think I'd buy a single additional foot if we should turn out to have less than $200 left over; but simply to hold onto the $1,000 without doing anything to the house when that money could do me so much good if invested in a farm — this would be false economy.

If, dear Father, I was so glad to accept your offer of $200 (that is, 1,000 fr), it was because I was convinced that it would not only pay me, but would put me in a position to repay you and even to send you a small amount every year if you should desire it. With thirty more acres cleared, this would be easy for me to do if God continues to grant us the same increase in prosperity we've enjoyed the last two years. So, dear Father, you can see that I may ask you (something I haven't done for five years) to lend me the remainder of those 1,000 fr. sometime this coming spring. When you promised them to me, I made arrangements and immediately undertook to have carried out a series of improvements for which the $100 you have sent me were not sufficient, and it is now too late for me to undo my agreements because the man I've hired, Cheeseman, has already gone to work in one corner [of my land] and cut down enough timber to make 1,000 rails which would be of no use to me unless I make a new field there. If, however, you can't do it, I will work things out with him somehow. If *"Les Parcs"* are sold this winter and they send us our share of the proceeds, then you will keep the rest of the 1,000 fr. since I'll have much more than I need.

If, dear Mother, I could sell my wheat for the price they get in Pau, I would hardly have any need to borrow money from you. Four cents[6] a pound would make us rich; but when, out of 150 bushels, we are obliged to keep fifty for flour and seed, sell another fifty at fifty cents [a bushel] to pay our debts, and then live for a year on the remaining fifty (which may sell for not more than sixty cents for sixty pounds), one can't really afford a hired man. But when, by way of contrast, a person has thirty acres in wheat, which [would, on the average, have] yielded 750 bushels this year, and when he has to pay only about $20 for hired help, then he can make money; but first he must have the fields, and for that he must have some money, or else cheat his workers, which many people around here do on principle—they say they'll pay them later.

The thick woods with which every *claim* in this region is more or less covered will in a few years yield not only the cash value of the timber, but even now it [lumbering] already employs thousands of people who get out *logs* and stack them along the river bank; even when you don't need the cleared land, it's still just as worthwhile [for the farmer] to make about $100 in this way every winter; then, after several years, the stumps are rotten and the plow is easier to handle than when you have to leave an uncultivated space around each stump because of the great number of live roots which the plow is unable to cut through.

Next Tuesday I plan to take Soso on the sled to St. Paul with Sarver's horse; I'm lending him my oxen in exchange. We'll leave, if it pleases God, on Tuesday and return Wednesday afternoon. Soso really deserves a nice little outing, and I think this will be one. It's a fine thing to be able to go in just a few hours to the capital of this state which promises so much and in so many different ways. We'll send you all the news about this trip.

**Theodore to his father**

> Chaska, Carver County
> Minnesota
> February 24, 1861

Dearest Father:

We've just now received the second installment of the money you're lending us, which we don't need at the moment, as we explained to you in our last letter. . . . I have therefore destroyed this last bank draft for 475 fr., which it is too dangerous to try to convert into cash in this part of the country. . . .

And indeed, dear Father, these 1,000 fr. will be a tremendous help to me, especially if my health is fully restored. This summer we plan to sleep separately, and I expect to sleep without worries if darling baby and Mama have enough blankets; and anyhow, Soso knows well enough how to pull them over to her side of the bed and leave my shoulders to keep themselves warm as best they can. Then I won't be awakened by the slightest movement of one or the other of them. At present, now that we are quite well equipped for farming and I have plows, a cart, oxen, etc., I can profitably hire one or two workers to help me clear land, and that will pay.

I explained to you in my last letter my reasons for buying another farm, and I repeat that we'll do it only if we have at least $200 free and clear to put aside to pay for having it cleared and plowed. As a general rule, it costs $10 to $15 an acre to clear, fence, and break a piece of land, which then brings in about $3 [a year] in net profits per acre; some land costs a great deal more to clear but also brings in more profit.

The American cent is just about equal in value to our *sou*; 100 to 95.

Yes, of course, we keep all the letters we get [from you] as well as those from our dear Mama Bost. We already have a fine stack.

Do not doubt, dear Father, that we have family worship morning and evening; in America they almost never have it except in the morning, but we prefer to have it twice.

We have a revival going on all around us, and nearly all our unconverted neighbors will be joining our church in a few weeks, we think. We have talked with many of our neighbors in particular and have attended prayer meetings and other gatherings, but in these assemblies we don't speak. I think, dear Father, that if you spoke it would have the effect of redeeming them, but it would have no effect if I did it. Allow me to tell you that these meetings, where everyone has to speak out in turn, aren't really suited to French religious ideas. I will gladly admit that American Christians are true Christians, but I can't behave with them as though they were my brothers; even our dear minister sometimes comes out with these American ideas according to which you judge a man not by his deeds but by his words—and only by the words he speaks in meetings at that.

Two years ago I went to Excelsior to fetch Dr. Snell for Mrs. Sarver, who was thought to be dying in childbirth. I urged him to hurry, even insulted him, telling him that if not as a doctor, then at least as a Christian he ought to come when called; but he said that a Christian shouldn't work when he isn't paid. I told him I had run this errand barefoot, in a thunderstorm, and in the dark of night for nothing and that he could very well go the same distance on horseback and that if Sarver didn't pay him, I would. But it was all to no avail—that miserly bandit went inside and sat down while I started back at eleven o'clock at night. Finally, along toward morning, Mrs. Sarver gave birth to one strangled baby and one live one. Six months ago it was the same story with another neighbor's wife—the same refusal and the same result; [but that time there were] two babies dead by his fault. Well, this animal (that's what he looks like, too) passes for being one of the most ardent Christians in this vicinity; he holds a high place in the church, and when I told Mr. Sheldon that his conduct was not Christian, he told me that Mr. Snell has a *prejudice* against the Chanhassen people, that he has already spoken to him about it, but that it's a *prejudice*; and likewise, *"He is a very good Christian,"* merely because he speaks during meetings.

The other day this Snell was presiding over a revival meeting. We met the unconverted father of those two [dead] babies going away from Excelsior and also the other father. Sarver, who was converted with difficulty, was forced to stay with us and worship under the leadership of the man who had murdered his child with his laziness and greed. And then, dear Father, one must listen at each meeting while the words "bear the cross of Jesus" are applied solely to the act of standing up in church when each Christian describes his "experience"—almost always in the same words: "I am happy to be able to say that I love God, that I'm a miserable sinner, and that I hope you'll all pray for me." All this is very fine, but it always makes me feel depressed and ill to hear fifty or a hundred people repeat it, always in a lugubrious tone of voice. Indeed, to hear adult Christians saying they consider it a cross to bear if they tell other Christians that they love their Savior, and then behave outside church in a manner indistinguishable from that of unbelievers—which happens a great deal oftener around here than in our old home country—is very disheartening; and it's even worse when the church takes such things for granted. I can't take part in these meetings, and this gives the false and painful impression that we are ashamed to bear the Cross. Nevertheless, I think I can say that in the presence of the unconverted I am less ashamed to bear the Cross than nine-tenths of our friends and brothers and that Soso's and my conduct toward the unconverted, as well as what we say to them, have done them more good than most of these "experiences."

Another thing that's probably good for the Americans, but painful for me to see, is the frenzy into which so many people throw themselves and the haste with which they force people to accept conversion or make themselves think they've been converted. They'll let years go by without talking to an unconverted man about God. All of a sudden the divine spirit seizes him, and then all the believers of whatever degree of piety or moral rectitude urge him on, harass him, and compel him to undergo conversion. That's the accepted way, and so I was surprised and delighted to hear a minister finding fault with this time-honored practice in our last ministers' conference in Excelsior. Our dear Mr. Sheldon told me afterward that the idea had never crossed his mind that you could do a person any harm by pushing him in this fashion, and he didn't seem to agree at all with my notion that Christians who behave badly ought never to speak as they do to unconverted people or in their presence. You realize, dear Father, that I don't believe in salvation through good works, but only that under "works" one should not include the act of standing up in church and telling Christians that one is a Christian. M. Fivaz[7] told me it's practically impossible in America to know for sure who is a Christian and who isn't. This is a result, I think, of the fact that church members constitute the basic stratum of America, and it is also a result of the absence of persecution.

Your turn, dear Mother. Wild birds are rare here in winter. They hide for weeks under the snow and only come out in the morning or evening of a day when there is a thaw; and when the snow is as deep and heavy as it is this winter, it's difficult to put salt on their tails. It's the same for deer, rabbits, and the like. In addition, the hares' fur turns white around the time of the first snowfall, so they are hard to see.

We haven't had any days as cold as it was last winter, but neither have we had very many fine days. That's the way it is with the weather. Cold, colder, very cold, less cold, etc.; almost melting, snowstorm, colder, colder, very cold, and so on and so on. Every week we've had one or two snowstorms. But no matter—this way I'm getting some rest, and I hope I can get back to work in about a month if it pleases God.

Thanks for the family news. Keep on sending it along to us— especially the doings of Auguste's family.

Good-bye, dear Father and Mother. Babykins is bringing me my slippers and is pulling the sock off my foot in her attempts to put them on me. She is teasing to go out for a ride with the oxen ("*boeufs, boeufs*"). But I'm taking them to a place where they can drink from a lake about half a mile from here. By the way, one of my little calves has died—he fell asleep near the door and got his head caught under a *log*; I found him half frozen, and he died a few days later. The other two and the rest of my livestock are doing very well. Good-bye, good-bye again to you all. I sent a letter to Tim a week ago.

Good-bye, *au revoir* for the time being.

Your most devoted and loving<br>
Theodore Bost

### Theodore, then Sophie, to the elder Bosts

Chaska, Carver County<br>
April 27, 1861

Dearest Parents:

I'm interrupting my work this afternoon to write to you because tomorrow, Sunday, I'll be too busy with visiting. Everybody is all excited and eager to start fighting[8]—even Powers, who is usually so peaceable. You have no doubt learned that at least 150,000 men are in arms in the North and that preparations are going forward in the Northern states to put 500,000 more men in the field in a few months' time. The report that our nation's capital was about to be attacked has begun to agitate the Yankees, who seem finally to be waking up. We in the North lack only one thing—a serious principle for which to fight. The only aim or principle at present seems to be "whether our government is good for something," that is, whether we can defeat the slave states. However, for people who are not warlike, this is a poor source of enthusiasm. If, on the contrary, we were told: "Fight for the abolition of slavery" (and not just for its nonextension), that would give us real dedication instead of mere excitement. Probably in a few months lots will be drawn to determine who goes off to war, and, although one is allowed to furnish a substitute, I think it is my duty to go in person after I have made provision for Soso's comfort while I'm away. We receive the news from New York and Washington the day after events take place there, and in St. Paul the other day we got a news bulletin only a few hours after the event, which added greatly to the excitement. From this you see that I've been in St. Paul, and, dear Father, it was to collect the $105 you sent me through [the] Marcuard [bank]. Like the other remittances, it was very welcome, and Soso was proud as could be to replenish our household supplies, especially now that we have two hired men, and Mimi finds her little wagon and her high chair both useful and enjoyable, especially now that a little American flag flies over both. I thought I was fulfilling the intent behind your sending this money by first giving Soso and Mimi what they want, while putting aside enough to pay my workmen.

If Ami [Jr.] will consult his may, he'll see that we're almost as close to New York as Chicago is when you consider the shipment of grain by water, and inasmuch as the building of the railroad from St. Paul to Lake Superior is being pushed forward vigorously, we count on being able in two or three years' time to sell our grain at the Chicago price. The Minnesota River has done a great deal of damage this year; a large number of settlements were more or less under water. At Chaska the current was so strong that people could hardly get into their houses. Warner [a local merchant] alone has lost 1,700 cords of wood and came very near losing his warehouse with several thousand bushels of wheat that are stored there. Why don't the brothers in Glasgow write to us any more? I sent them a letter not long ago.

Good-bye, dear Father and Mother. Think of

> Your most devoted son,
> T. Bost

Saturday, April 27 [1861]

Theodore has told you about the war—I hope you won't worry about it too much; around here nobody talks about anything else and that's all they think about, but I'm sick to death of hearing about it. As for anxiety, I haven't yet begun to feel very much. But it seems to me that Dodo's departure would be a mortal blow to me, and inasmuch as this prospect is too tragic, I find it easier not to believe for a single moment that he could be called up for service. Then, if it should really come to pass, God will provide as He has in so many other difficulties. What's certain is that the situation is critical and that so far as we're concerned I'd no longer be in favor of enlarging our property holdings, even if prices should become even more favorable than they are now. If all these goings-on had taken place last year, it would have been out of the question for Theodore to go off to war, considering his bad health, but this year he's so much better that he'd no longer have that excuse. Well, chins up! We'll soon know what's going to happen, and we'll write again soon no matter what! My conscience isn't entirely clear on that score, not having written to you for so long.

In the meantime, we are all better off in every way than we've been in quite a long time, and Dodo's health, if it remains as good as it is at present, is a fortune all by itself; as for myself, I'm getting bigger and spreading out like anything![9] Mimi is the most delightful child I've ever known, but I'm awaiting the next one with as much pleasure as can be.

Marie [Moseman] is getting more helpful all the time; just now, when I can't do very much work and we have two hired men living here for whom we have to wash clothes, I couldn't possibly manage all by myself, and as for hiring a girl from around here, they are as expensive as they are scarce and disagreeable. Marie is satisfied with everything we do for her and considers herself completely a member of the family. I hope with all my heart that she doesn't think about leaving us for a long time. We intend to pay her regular wages, and up to now nobody has shown any sign of wanting to lure her away. I won't give her up except to a man who can make her happier than we can.

Good-bye, dear Parents. It's time to go to church—I'll write to you again in a week or two.

Your Sophie

**Theodore, then Sophie, to the elder Bosts**

Chaska, Carver County
Minnesota
May 19, 1861

Dear Parents:

I think you read the newspapers enough to know how we're getting along with this war in which forts are taken and lost, arsenals, too, and even entire encampments without the loss of a single man. From time to time, "mobs" provoke a volley, but when soldiers fight with soldiers, it seems that they fire over each other's heads—perhaps this is why there are two or three hundred thousand men in the North ready to join up. In any case, everybody around here is anxious to avoid giving the Southerners additional grounds for resentment, but wants them to be given a good trouncing before we begin to really frighten them by taking them on in a good game of chess since it looks as though this is all our men are doing. Anyhow, our [Republican] party these past two weeks has paralyzed activity in the *Border Slave States* with its chess moves, for these states, though they had turned against the

North, are now letting their tongues hang out like oxen which, after trying to bolt, find themselves suddenly face to face with their driver! In our neighborhood we're trying to organize a *"home guard"* of local farmers, with recruits pledged not to resign except in case of absolute necessity. Twice a week we have military exercises.

As long as there are more people volunteering than can be accepted, I don't intend to join up, but if we are called to the colors to free the slaves and so put an end to these rebellions and if this should make our party weaker,[10] I'll make all necessary arrangements and volunteer. Have I ever told you I'm the only person hereabouts who wants to see slavery abolished? The Republicans want only its nonextension, but I want abolition, which is a different matter. But good-bye, dear Parents; this is only a brief letter, but if we get one from you, we'll reply right away.

Your most devoted son,
Theodore Bost

Dearest Father and Mother:
You, dear Papa, would not be able to recognize Marie, I think. Three years ago, she was only a child, but since then she has grown and her figure has filled out nicely, though she doesn't have a slim waist nor is she very light on her feet! She still gets along with us very well and has no thought of leaving us, I believe. I'm always complaining that she spoils the baby, but since I'm always there to watch out and put things to rights, I would rather she was indulgent than too harsh or negligent.

Has my mother [Mme. Bonjour] written to you recently? Or do you hear anything from Julie about how things are going with them? It seems that my poor dear mother is having difficulties with [selling] *"Les Parcs,"* and that weighs terribly on my mind. Until now she has been so little accustomed to dealing with land, sales, etc.; and now, just at the most vital moment, she has no disinterested person to help her! I hope that a serious buyer will turn up soon and that she'll be able to get rid of all these responsibilities. In this desire I am all the less selfish in that Mama has offered us—or rather has announced that she will be sending us—4,000 fr. toward our share of *"Les Parcs"* to buy some land Dodo has been offered for $800. But aside from the fact that 4,000 fr. make only $750—he tells me, though, that the man would have sold for that price or thereabouts—Theodore is not of a mind to buy a farm unless he has the wherewithal to launch the thing at once and set up our household properly either here or on the new place. So we hardly have any idea of buying this land I'm speaking of, at least for the time being. The future will show us which road to take. There is a farm adjacent to the one we have here, not so high-priced, but not so much improved, either, which we may try to buy—but everything is up in the air, and we're not at all worried or in a hurry. As long as business is bad, land will be selling at a low price, and that would be a good reason not to delay—[for] those like ourselves, I mean, who have confidence in Minnesota's future. But, on the other hand, this war with the South is a great stumbling block. If Theodore has to go, our farm would certainly be enough for me to take care of, almost more, I think, than I could arrange to have worked for me, since most of the available hired men live quite far from here. But we must keep our spirits up! Nothing venture, nothing gain! And although we shall not take too many risks, we won't be too timid either. I am terribly impatient to have this farm running really well and our affairs prospering briskly. Ami's notion that we can never do more than make ends meet makes me remember another remark he made before I left for America: "You'll find Theodore quite uncivilized and you'll have to domesticate him!" I am still savoring that one!!!

It's certain, and no one knows it better than we do, how much trouble, money, and time it takes to get a farm to the stage where it begins to be profitable! (Theodore himself had no idea of this when he first started out here.) Especially on new land and in such a recently settled part of the country. Especially, alas, with such unstable health as he has. The task is a heavier one than can even be imagined unless you've tried to do it yourself. It may very well turn out that we'll never succeed. If my husband's health worsens instead of improving, we'll probably not get ahead no matter how hard we try and in spite of all the help for which we are so grateful. It may even finally come about that this whole part of the country will turn out to be a failure, however impossible that may seem. But here we have all sorts of possibilities that weigh much more heavily on the good than on the bad side, so that I'm fully convinced that everything will soon take a turn for the better; railroads and steamboat lines are being established and will soon put us in rapid communication with the great commercial centers where our products are sold. As for those products themselves, wheat hasn't yet failed here for the seven or eight years it has been grown, whereas it fails once in every three or four years in the East. Besides, a great many sheep are being introduced in this region—Theodore intends to have three or four hundred as soon as possible—and that yields a very good profit, they say! So why worry? We're young and have time to wait . . . perhaps until our ship comes in, although neither of us sets any great store by riches, but in any case, I hope, until we are comfortably well off so we can raise our children well and do all the good that's in our power to do—which, in any event, we want to do now and from now on.

As for raising our children, Theodore is always saying that he'll buy me a piano just as soon as we have a good parlor to keep it in! This last clause postpones the carrying out of his intention to a hazy time in the dim future; but the haze can't last long, and I'm overjoyed to think that someday I'll see a piano again! But if it means waiting two or three years until we have a new house, how shall I find time to play? This is another grave question which Theodore, in the frivolous way men have, solves by saying that he'll see to it that I have time! Ah, Dodo! And what about the children running around dirty, with torn clothes, and what about the dinner burning in the kitchen, and your shirts that will be badly ironed! But the dear boy believes that I can look after everything and still play the piano too! Since I am really of the same opinion, we aren't going to fight about that.

All the same, I must admit that an American farmer's wife who has a family to care for has to keep extremely busy, even with a conscientious girl to help her! When you have to launder every week the clothing and bed linen for the whole family as well as for the workmen, mend all their clothes, the children's and the husband's, and attend to all the thousand and one etceteras of a household where you have no neighborhood baker nor anything else of that kind to depend on, and, above all, when you want to remain a lady in spite of all this, receive visitors, have an attractive living room and your children wearing clean, attractive clothes! To be sure, I'm still far from having learned all there is to know about my new and complex occupation, but I love it, which is a long stride toward perfection, and I'm not ashamed to learn from women who are more experienced in the art of *house keeping*, which is another advantage.

You have here, I think, the most completely inconsequential chitchat imaginable, but not having anything terribly important on my mind, I've just let myself go, writing in the informal style I like so much in a letter as in everyday life.

Good-bye, dearest Parents. I send you both many tender hugs and kisses!

Sophie

**Theodore to his parents**

Chaska, Carver County
Minnesota
July 17, 1861

Dearest Parents:

This is just a short note to let you know of the birth of Alphonse Ami Bost at one o'clock this morning.

Along toward midnight, Mimi fell out of bed for the first time and that woke me up. I picked her up and was falling asleep again when I heard Soso groaning downstairs. She thought it was only an upset stomach, but in a little while I went down. A few minutes after that she scolded me for not doing anything to help her, an unmistakable sign. Immediately I sent Marie to the Sarvers' to get him to go on horseback right away to fetch the doctor. She was still crossing our field when the baby was born, so I was obliged to do the midwife's job—and Soso is of the opinion that I managed very well. She had only two or three pains, and she feels fairly well now. We are very grateful that everything went off so easily. As soon as I had done what had to be done for the baby, she was insistent that I should run and tell Sarver not to go for the doctor. I went, but brought back his wife, an energetic, gentle, understanding woman, who stayed here until about seven this morning. Soso and the baby, therefore, are both doing as well as one could wish.

Good-bye, dear Parents, and God bless you.

Your most affectionate
Theodore Bost

The baby is a good big boy who, I think, looks a lot like you, dear Father.

**Sophie to Jenny Bost**

August 24, 1861

Dearest Mother:

I'm happy that our Mimi pleases you so much![11] I was afraid you might all be disappointed after having us tell you so many times that she's pretty! But she really is delicious enough to eat just now. She's bending over the middle of Marie's flower garden, picking portulaccas, petunias, and volubilis and filling her precious little basket which she takes with her everywhere. To me she seems the prettiest flower that ever grew in a garden! She likes her little brother very much, wants to hold him in her lap and let him suck her finger. The other day I laid the baby down beside her. Hearing a strange noise a moment afterward, I ran back and found the baby choking on his sister's finger, which she had thrust into his mouth as far as she could. I was so angry that I did the same thing to her by way of teaching her a lesson, but the funny face she made as she pretended to throw up made me burst out laughing! Another time she'll have a better idea of how to play with babies. She wants to stuff all kinds of things into her brother's mouth and is quite amazed when he doesn't want to eat raspberries and mulberries as she does. I'm very glad these two darling children play so well together, and they'll be playing together more and more if Alphonse keeps on the way he's going. You'd take him, and people have taken him, for a child of three months, he's so strong and seems so intelligent; he's been laughing now for a week, and furthermore he's sweet-tempered and easy to care for, hardly ever crying, sleeping three or four hours at a stretch, and playing blissfully when he feels like it. A baby like that is a delight, and I certainly don't begrudge the time I spend feeding and cooing at him. It's such fun to hold a little baby, to hug and kiss him to your heart's content, and to see him laugh a little more easily every day.

But that's enough about the small fry, though it's not the hundredth part of what I'd like to tell about my two treasures. I say "my" because Mister Theodore Bost isn't worthy of a son like mine! He doesn't admire him half enough, and can you believe that he thinks his son has a big nose, the wretch! And that he's still "very red"! The scoundrel! This Mister Theodore Bost is so filled with admiration, love, and tenderness for his daughter that he has nothing left over for his son! If I show him Alphonse in all the glory of a pretty embroidered dress, all sweet and clean, he just calls his daughter and tells her she is prettier, etc., etc. What do you say to such gross injustice? With a son like this? A son who hasn't given his Mummy a tenth of the pain that Mimi did! . . . Oh well, men will be men till the end of the world! But the worst thing is, I know very well that in a few months my husband will love his son just as much as he does his daughter, and that especially when Alphonse learns how to walk and talk he will desert his mother who fed and took care of him in infancy in order to run after this naughty father who made fun of him and his mother when he was completely dependent on her! Furthermore, they think I'm going to be satisfied to have children and raise them to the age of one or two years just so His Lordship can take them in hand and teach them to love him better than me! Wonderful! But never mind—I don't feel anywhere near as sorry for myself as you might think from all this. At least my little ones are always nice, so I can make them do just as I like, whereas at Mister Bost's age they begin to have minds of their own and aren't always willing to fall in with other people's ideas.

Theodore and I are still making drawings for our house from time to time. It's still a mystery when we'll be able to build it— perhaps next fall if things turn out well. Dodo was talking of selling his new yoke of oxen to buy lumber, for "cash" is as rare as ever hereabouts and it's almost impossible to sell anything for gold—a sad state of things, which this war with the South docs nothing at all to improve: tea, sugar, coffee, and all kinds of provisions have just gone way up in price; our direct [property] taxes are going to be higher than ever, and the wheat crop is very poor throughout this region, not half as abundant as last year. Theodore finished shocking his wheat last week; today he's helping the Insels to shock theirs. Both our crops[12]—are wretched compared with what we expected, and even then people say we won't be able to sell the little we have for money! Theodore says I'm mistaken and that wheat will sell for *cash*. Poor Minnesota! It is going through some very hard times! Happy are those who don't have to depend completely on what their farm produces for their food and clothing! We were calculating the other day that Theodore should buy himself at least $40 worth of winter clothes—he's almost destitute! I too need several little things, and it goes without saying that Mimi needs new clothes from head to foot. Fortunately we can afford to buy clothes for ourselves! And in that there's reason for not a little rejoicing. As for my son, he will be all right with the hand-me-downs from his sister and with what I sewed for him before his birth. Just the same, I'm busy embroidering some little shirts for him, because I can see that the ones Mimi had won't fit him much longer. Besides, it's important to me that he be well and handsomely dressed, so I'm going about it ahead of time. Soon I'll have enough sewing in hand to keep me out of mischief—sometimes I even have too much! But as for these children's dresses into which I'm putting such a lot of work, I've almost decided not to do any more embroidery for the children—with so many other things to do, it seems to me to be almost a blameworthy waste of time. But I suppose that I'll break this resolution the first time it's tested—how can I help myself?

You've known for quite some time that my baby was born much sooner than we had expected, on the seventeenth of July, and that I had a very easy time of it. I was so far from thinking of such things that I was gathering raspberries a mile away from here that afternoon. During the first part of the night I thought I'd eaten too many of them and gotten a case of colic. I often laugh when I think about it and about my perfect complacency when I felt the baby being born while I was all alone here with Dodo—except for Mimi, who had awakened and refused to quiet down unless she was allowed to sleep beside me on the sofa. Theodore must have told you, but I'm not sure whether, when he had taken care of the baby, he [did or] didn't run after Marie to tell our neighbor Sarver not to go for the doctor and to bring Mrs. S. to come and bathe my son. This one-two-three-go style of doing things has caused a lot of laughter at our expense in the neighborhood, but it was a lot more pleasant than my first confinement, which lasted such a long time and left me so weak. This time, however, I've recovered very quickly—the minute after giving birth I could have got up, and the next day it was hard for me to stay in bed. Since then, I've gone on getting stronger all the time except for when Mimi was sick, which was more exhausting for me than my delivery, and now I'm as lively and cheerful as a swallow in springtime! . . .

Sophie T. Bost

**Theodore, then Sophie, to the elder Bosts**

Chaska, Carver County
Minnesota
September 9, 1861

Dearest Father and Mother:

We're now answering the letter we received from you today, dear Father, even though Soso replied to one from Mama just a few days ago.

I'll turn first of all to the subject that has given us the most concern recently, though I've been putting this off since yesterday. For at least a month my health has gone steadily from bad to worse, though I can't say I've been really ill. [I have had] pains in my left side from the waist down, insomnia unless I've worked too hard, and much lassitude. Furthermore, the least excitement brings on palpitations. All this, along with this abominably conducted war, has almost made us decide to send me off to Europe for the winter, leaving my entire little family in the care of Old Mike[13] until next spring. But the expense would be too great, especially if I came back without being cured, and I think that this winter I'll take life very easy and get back on my feet that way. As for the doctors who practice in these parts, I'd never go near them. They always tell you there's something wrong with your lungs, your liver, or your kidneys, and it's a toss-up whether they or the illness will kill you first.

But speaking of the war, our Governor (of Minnesota) has just proposed to the President to recruit 3,000 men over and above the number we've already raised for the army. This will be impossible to do without the most burdensome kind of compulsory draft in this region where there are mostly young, poor families. If this war were in Switzerland and run by the Swiss, I'd be proud and happy to take part in it, but I feel more and more disgust at the thought of fighting for these infamous pigs and cowards, the Americans! Excuse this strong language, but when, at the sound of Southern bugles at Bull Run,[14] two or four American regiments, whose term of enlistment had expired that very morning, turned their backs on the enemy while Irish and German regiments, whose enlistments had also expired, remained to fight— this is enough to make a man furious; and when you hear (as I did two weeks ago) one of our fat Americans blaming Lincoln for not accepting the (imaginary) offer of Garibaldi and 20,000 liberal European nobles, arguing that these were only foreigners and that this would save the lives of 20,000 of their own people, it makes you wonder if such despicable egoists deserve to have anyone fight for them so that afterward they can spout about America's noble hospitality while refusing to give you the vote. And they insult you by calling you a Foreigner.

And then there's the cause of this war! They don't want to fight a war against slavery; instead, they want to force the Union on everybody. As for me, I want a war against slavery or immediate disunion. We're fighting for nothing, and the 250,000 men raised by the North don't really exist at all. The newspapers talk about 20,000 here, 20,000 there, of 50,000, of 90,000, etc., etc.; and then they say that there are no more than 55,000 Southern troops in Virginia but that these 55,000 are going to launch an attack and assume the offensive. If they'd form a regiment of Swiss, I'd be quite happy to join up with them, because the Swiss know how to fight and I don't like the idea of fighting alongside these cowardly and selfish Americans. I must say that a good part of the abolitionists, who are the most determined group of all, are not fighting in this war, at least as long as the troops [of the Union] are still sending slaves back to the South! Oh, Switzerland, Switzerland! You're a small country but how much more true feeling and real patriotism you have than there is in this country of blowhards and hypocrites! I hope this war will last long enough to teach American Christians how to behave like Christians.

Our Sonderbund War[15] was over in less time than this one needs to get started, and in 1857 Switzerland was all ready in a few days to fight against Prussia (at odds of two against fifteen) and would have won; whereas here they are nineteen against seven, and they are scared out of their wits. Yet the nineteen million are unanimous in trumpeting [their indignation] against Russell[16] because he wrote what all the Americans had already said, that the rout [at Bull Run] extended for fifteen miles to the rear and was one of the most disgusting that ever took place, especially when we know that the enemy was making no attempt to pursue them.

Hence there is no activity on our side because the people aren't responding to the appeals of Lincoln and the generals, while in the South there is great activity and decisiveness: armed robberies of banks, poisoning of wells and springs, blowing up of passenger trains, hanging of people by the feet, and other elegant things.[17]

Truly, the Americans are a great people.

I know that my sickly condition makes me see everything in the darkest possible colors, but all the same, this is a miserable war.

By the way, after that battle [Bull Run], the newspapers came out with exhortations to our troops, warning them that in the future they must not suppose that they have to do with mere Frenchmen or Englishmen, but rather with Americans who, like themselves, are brave, resolute, etc., etc.—it's pitiable!

Since writing these last words I've been expecting to be able to give you better news, but on the contrary everything seems to be getting worse. It's true there are more men who are signing up — but for what reasons! A soldier's pay has been raised from $11 to $13 a month, not including food, clothing, medical care, etc., plus $100 to be paid at the end of the war along with 160 acres of land. But the biggest joke is that it has been decided that Minnesota will furnish four regiments, three to serve against the South and one to guard our forts against the Indians. The first regiment left some time ago; the second has been trying to form for three months without succeeding; the third has a colonel, a lieutenant-colonel, and four or five soldiers; and the fourth, which won't see active combat and will have only to do guard duty in the forts, is almost fully enrolled even though it has been only two weeks since enlistments were opened.

Well, God knows what He is doing, but it seems to me that with this war He means to chastize the selfishness, frivolity, and hypocrisy of millions of Christians in the North who, after shouting so much against slavery, now want only to preserve the Union, slavery and all.

But, farewell, dearest Parents. I'll leave room for Soso and go out for a walk in the cold fresh air—we had out first frost this morning. Good-bye to all!

Your Theodore Bost

Chanhassen
September 29, 1861

Dearest Parents:

Why, in connection with my confinement, do you speak of our situation as "savage," dear Mother? Are there no country-dwellers in your part of the world who might have found themselves in the same circumstances? Especially if their baby was born two or three weeks sooner than expected. The Sarvers live a half-mile from here; it had been decided a long time ago that he would go on horseback to Shakopee to fetch the doctor while his wife would come over to be with me (since Dodo wanted nothing further to do with the midwife)—but no one imagined things would happen so quickly. In any case, I treasure a strangely sweet memory of the moment when, all alone with my husband, with Mimi asleep in my arms, her little arms around my neck, Theodore said, "It's a boy, Soso." I had fully expected it to be a boy, but we were so completely at peace, so happy, and I was feeling scarcely any pain and could tell Dodo where to find everything I needed—fortunately, I'd had everything all ready a long time in advance. Certainly if I am to have more children, I couldn't desire a nicer confinement than this one! It's true that God tempers the wind to the shorn lamb, and our isolation has never troubled us! It only makes us all the more appreciative of our neighbors' visits, which are always rather frequent, and as for myself—though I can always find some way of getting out of my shell—I have enough to do here to make me glad that I'm a little outside the center of things. Alphonse has been sleeping since lunchtime; Dodo is waiting for me to finish this letter and is curled up beside me on the sofa. I'll have to go quickly to get dressed up and then fix dinner, because at 2:30 the whole family is going to church together! Around here people take their babies to church—sometimes we have unplanned choirs!

Good-bye once more. Many greetings to Aunt Betsy, to all the brothers and sisters, to Concorde,[18] to Mme. Vaucher, and the rest.

Sophie

# IX

# The Lime Quarry

For a short time the dream of affluence, so strong in the minds of most pioneers, seemed about to come true for Sophie and Theodore in the form of a deposit of hydraulic lime that might have made their fortune had Theodore succeeded in buying the land in Northfield, Minnesota, on which it was located. Although we do not know exactly why the scheme never came to anything, we can guess that lack of ready money and excess of caution on Theodore's part were the reasons for his letting the opportunity slip.

The Civil War had begun to go better for the North, and as Northern opinion swung toward abolition, Theodore began to feel more enthusiasm for the Union cause. By June, 1862, he has stopped referring to "Americans" (his term for Yankees) as "they" and begins to write "we."

**Theodore to his father**

Chaska
October 29, 1861

Dearest Father:

There's no need for me to repeat how grateful we are to you for the "dispositions" you've made; to the very best of my ability I will go on paying to Mother the interest on these 200 frs. after your death, as I hope to keep on doing in your lifetime.[1] However, I should have scruples about accepting all you've sent us as a gift, because of my brothers, if I did not consider that I have earned nearly all my own living since I was fourteen years old and that since I've been in America I've had to work terribly hard to earn it, whereas most of my brothers continued their education beyond the age of twenty and they have all led a much easier life than I have; furthermore, this hard life was none of my choosing, although, through necessity, I have loved it on the principle that "if you don't have what you want, then you must want what you have." So I don't see that I am cheating my brothers in accepting the money you've given us. But there is one thing I'd like to ask of you, and that is to leave some particular thing to Sophie and me—one to each of us—as a souvenir of our very dear father—will you not do this? And yet I hope that we'll still have you with us for a long, long time. Like our dear Mama, you have finished your task and are waiting to be called on high, where there will neither be any more labor nor any weakness nor any want of faith. When it pleases God to recall us all to Himself, I don't think I shall be sorry to leave this earth—though it has fallen to my lot to enjoy a very happy life here.

At first we thought we wouldn't write to you immediately about a half-planned project we've had in mind for two weeks or so, but here are the details. You'll recall that last winter we hired a [former] Methodist minister [Cheeseman] to work here, an incredibly ugly man, completely lacking any talent for public speaking and very poor, but a sincere and honest Christian. Well, the other day Mr. Sheldon, speaking about a cistern, told me that Mr. Cheeseman knows of a deposit of hydraulic lime (lime that hardens in water) but that he refused to tell where it was. To have some fun with him about his lack of confidence in us, I teased him about it, not thinking it a matter of importance, but by his facial expression and his words I could tell that this poor dear man, a former stonemason, had taken this secret seriously. He revealed the whole thing to me under a pledge of secrecy. A mile and a quarter from one of our largest villages [Northfield][2] there is a rapid stream that can supply power for a mill; the bed of this brook has ordinary lime covering the hydraulic lime, which is similar in appearance to the other; without realizing this, the owner mixed the two kinds and roasted them, then put them in water, but, to use his words, *"The plaguy thing would not slack,"*[3] and he washed his hands of the whole thing.

Somebody told Cheeseman about it; he went and looked at it, tested it, and discovered that it was hydraulic lime. He said nothing about it to anyone, continued his studies, and found that the bed of the brook and the adjacent area included in the thirty acres that would go with the mill site consisted of the same prime quality lime. Being a stonemason, Cheeseman knows what he's talking about. He spoke of his discovery to the richest man of the vicinity [John Wesley North] under a pledge of secrecy, but this man had just tied up all his money.[4] Cheeseman proposed that the two of them should jointly buy this land: that is, North would buy the land and pay for building the mill; the running expenses would be shared equally; and Cheeseman would gradually repay half the cost of purchasing and equipping the quarry. But this man couldn't perform his part, having overextended himself, and Cheeseman was several times on the point of making his discovery public, especially once he saw that things are going so badly with him that he has hardly any chance of ever being able to buy [the property].

He offered to go into partnership with me on the same terms, and when I asked him if he was sure a man could make *good wages* at it, he replied with a rueful smile: *"Good wages! Why it is a fortune for the owner of such a quarry!"* There is only one good one in the whole United States, and that's in the state of New York; it would be impossible for this New York quarry to compete successfully with us at this distance when the costs of transportation would be against them and the low price of wood and the good location for a water-powered grinding mill would be in our favor. The property is, or was, for sale for $700, and I told him yesterday to write to the owner to find out if the place is still for sale. If it is, I'll go with him to look it over this fall, and if I find that there's a chance to get a good yearly wage out of it, I think I would like to make arrangements to buy it. I'm not anxious to make a fortune, but it would be more pleasant to oversee the workmen while living in comfort, working only as much as I'm able to, than to go on working like a horse without seeing the future get any brighter. The important thing would be to buy the property before anyone else discovers this deposit. Working the quarry could wait a while, though [an investment of] $300 or $400 ought to be enough to put the mill into operation. I'm going to write to Mama Bonjour to urge her to sell *"Les Parcs"* if possible; then, with the small amount that will still be coming to us out of Soso's portion, and that which we still have, we would buy this property. I know very well that the Americans are almost all rascals, but ever since I've known Cheeseman he has behaved like a perfectly honest man in contrast to all the others, and he must have the same opinion of me, or else he wouldn't have told me anything about this. The railroad is under construction only about thirty paces away from the quarry, which is a point well worth considering. But enough on this subject for this evening, dearest Father. When I began this letter I had no idea it would finish like

this, but my health and my nerves are so easily plunged into tur-
moil that I can't do anything nor even keep my mind on one thing
for long at a time.

Farewell, dearest Father and dearest Mother. What happiness
it would give me if I could have the means of letting you finish
your days in comfort!

Good-bye, and God bless you.

Your Theodore Bost

**Sophie to the elder Bosts**

November 29, 1861

Dearest Parents:

The doctor whom Th[eodore] has finally consulted tells him
to do no more hard work and to give up farming—which is a great
deal easier to prescribe than it is to carry out: The Dr. [sic] (the
one who attended me at my first confinement) says that Th[eo-
dore] has a partial ossification of the heart, which is what gives
him these pains in his left side on account of the too vigorous
beating of his heart—I'm afraid I don't understand much about it,
and Th[eodore] doesn't have a great deal of faith in the diagnosis
because he says "it has too big a name!" This Dr. [sic] has sol-
emnly assured me that there's no danger for the present and that
he thinks Th[eodore] is better than he was two years ago, that his
lungs are in better shape. He doesn't believe Th[eodore] will ever
be completely cured but that with a little care the trouble won't
get any worse.

That's all the good he has done us, but it's something at least
to have the opinion of an experienced Dr. [sic]. So you see, dear
Parents, that we are no better off, for it's completely impossible
for the time being to give up the farm and just about as difficult to
stay here without doing hard work.

In our last letter we told you, I think, about a mine of hydraulic lime, discovered by one of our neighbors, in which Dodo
could become a partner if he had the money. This is how matters
stand for the moment: Mr. Cheeseman has just written to learn
whether the property is even still for sale—sometime or other we
shall know what is to come of all this. Fortunately we are living on
our own place, and nobody will drive us away. In any case, we
mustn't think of selling this farm for several years: on every side
of us there are places for sale for $500 or $600 with as much or

almost as much cleared land as we have, and no buyer can be found for them. Before getting this doctor's advice we had been thinking of building a house and Theodore had already gotten almost all the boards sawed, but we gave up this idea right after that and we won't decide anything further on that score until we can tell what we have to look forward to in other respects.

You've doubtless read in the papers everything I could tell you about the war: it seems that the North may be getting the upper hand again. May God grant it, for surely we are in the right; I can hardly wait until it's all over. The thought of so many families in mourning wrings my heart. Here in our "Far West" we can't be too grateful for the tranquility we are enjoying in the midst of this tumult; and above all we ought not to complain if we are injured a little by the indirect effects of so many disasters, that is, by stagnation in business. Theodore is jubilant at the arrest of Slidell and Mason,[5] the Southern envoys to France and England; he even goes so far as to hope a little that John Bull will pick a fight and get his knuckles rapped. I hope, for my part, that nothing of the sort will happen and that once the South is pacified, we shall have peace. I am finishing this letter (Saturday the thirtieth) in a terrible to-do. Th[eodore] killed his old ox this morning: we had four men at the table for dinner, and at this very moment I have one here in the house cleaning fat out of the intestines! —it's delicious—but when at war you must be a good soldier! —we shall have about sixty pounds of tallow to sell for a very low price, because candles have gone out of fashion since they discovered those oil wells (*Kerosene Oil*) of which you've no doubt heard.

It's wonderful what progress civilization makes! As for me, my head is full of those pretty sewing machines that are being bought by so many families and are so delightful to have! Near here some people have been able to get these little fairies for between $10 and $60; a sewing table[6] I saw the other day cost $25 and was in perfect condition. The stiches it makes are so strong, so pretty, and so quick to make! I'm making Dodo's ears buzz, and he's promised me one of these machines when I have six children! Between now and then I'll have had plenty of time to wear out my eyes and fingers—don't you agree? And besides, there are washing machines, machines to wring out the laundry, even machines for kneading bread! Pretty soon we'll be able to get along without my hired girl. Speed the day! However, I have no wish to get along without my Marie—because she isn't an American girl.

It seems to me that I had a lot of other things to tell you, but in this confusion I forget what they were.

Good-bye, dearly beloved Parents.

Your tenderly loving daughter,
Sophie Theodore

**Theodore to his parents**

Chaska, Carver County
Minnesota
December 1, 1861

Dearest Parents:

Come back to stay in Europe? I'd do that only if I had no alternative, and as for working in John's establishment [at La Force], I wouldn't serve under his orders for anything in the world, and still less on an equal footing, seeing that it would be easier to take orders than to make my equal status respected by the owner of the domain. Mme. Bonjour was the first to bring up the idea of working with John, and we wrote back right away that she was to say nothing about it to any of the Bost family. I don't know exactly what it is that has always made trouble between me and John; we've never been able to get along with one another, and just now, when I have gained more independence than I've ever had before, I don't think we could possibly work together.

But this reminds me how pleasant I had found the idea of being with Ami again.[7] I was so discouraged, so lonely here in America, just as Alphonse Bonjour is at present in Australia. Therefore, I've been overjoyed to learn that he (Alphonse) would like to come and live with us here and be able again to enjoy family life. I have known what loneliness is.

The war goes on! Little by little, people's minds are turning against slavery, and this lends the war a higher moral meaning. Yet the slaves are not being freed, except as "property" of rebel owners and not as human beings. But before another year goes by I believe this will have changed. The Mason-Slidell affair has done me an immense amount of good. We were courting the goodwill of England, we were afraid of her, and all the time the Tories and the English High Episcopalians were hoping for the victory of slavery, though they had been trumpeting against it. And because our American navy is far superior to our army, and because in a war with England we'd at least know what we were fighting for, it wouldn't bother me at all if we had a little set-to. I am filled with disgust at these English Pharisees who, because they're deprived of their cotton, thunder against the impiety of a fratricidal war, whereas they are always waging some war for unjust or impious causes. I agree that this war isn't being fought directly against slavery on our side, but the other side is fighting for slavery and the African slave trade, in spite of anything Mr. *London Times* may say. Well, may God's will prevail! There is, indeed, a large number of sincere Christians in America, but they are overshadowed by the politicians—perhaps they're like the fire under the boiler in a steamboat in that nobody sees it, but it moves the whole great structure forward. Farewell, dear Parents, and thank you for all your sympathy.

Theodore Bost

**Theodore to the elder Bosts**

Chaska, Carver County
Minnesota
Sunday, December 15

Dearest Parents:

I was to have gone to see this quarry, but Cheeseman and I have to go to the mill and the roads are frozen too hard for wagons and there isn't enough snow for sleds, so we're waiting awhile. I don't know whether I've explained the thing fully to you. So I will repeat: Cheeseman is a practicing stonemason and has experimented with this lime, which he says is of superior quality. We're going to make further tests to be even more sure of this. The only quarry in the States that produces this lime sells it for a dollar a barrel, and of course makes money—otherwise they wouldn't work the quarry. Now at that price they are obliged to roast it with fuel (wood or coal) that costs more than it does here, and so they have to charge more per barrel. Here, however, since this lime has to be shipped 1,500 miles, it is worth $3.50, $4, or even $7 in the best times and $3.50 or $4 at present. Cheeseman says that every house in every village has a cistern for rainwater that requires one or two barrels [of lime] to make, and he can't imagine that the two of us could produce enough to glut the market. He says that two men can produce at least a hundred barrels a week. He has roasted another kind of lime a mile away from here; he knows how to build the ovens himself, so that from the start we could do everything our-selves. I already have a lot of the things we'd need, so we wouldn't have to buy them—a cart, a wagon, oxen, picks, shovels, etc.—and the only thing we'd need to buy is a grinding mill like the ones the Frillot people have and a building to cover the lime once it has been roasted and ground. I've told him very clearly that I had no desire to get involved in any speculative affair, and he told me the same is true of him, but that he saw the matter not as a speculative venture but as a "matter of fact." Neither of us wants to do any-thing but earn our daily bread, which I've hardly been able to do these last few years and won't be able to do unless my health im-proves greatly instead of continually going downhill.

Soso told you we weren't thinking of selling for another two or three years; however, I think that if the prospects for this quarry seem reliable, I'd sell this farm instead of renting it. The laws give so little protection to landlords here that tenant farmers can make a hopeless mess of the best farms and leave them in an unsalable condition. So it would be better to sell out at a low price than to rent and then have nothing to show for the money I've put into this farm, not to speak of my six years of work! You understand that I'm a little discouraged.

But good-bye, dear Parents—enough of my gossip.

Your most devoted son,
Theodore Bost

**Theodore to the elder Bosts**

Chaska, Carver County
Minnesota
February 15, 1862

Dearest Parents:

Soso tells me it's been a long time since I've written to you—is this true? It seems to me I wrote you a few days before I went to Northfield.

Our minister, Mr. Sheldon, is a prudent and discreet man; I spoke with him about it [the quarry] and at first he discouraged me, but then changed his mind before we'd finished talking. The day before, he had preached a sermon, and I gathered from the first words of our conversation that he believed I had taken his message to heart so that if I were to give up farming I'd become a minister—

something he and other people have often urged me to do. I think it was this little disappointment that made him want at first to talk me out of the Northfield idea.

Mr. Sheldon's opinion is that I should run the risk that others may discover the quarry rather than pay the price being asked. If someone else finds it, well, all right—it will be a sign from God; if not, the price of the property will come down and I can buy it. The place itself pleases me very much, situated as it is only a mile and a half from an attractive village where there are schools and churches and fine, upstanding people.

And what of the war? It is beginning to gather momentum, and the enormous patience of the Northern people is finally being rewarded. Instead of risking everything, like Napoleon, on a single throw of the dice, they saved Washington last April. Then, aside from fighting a few skirmishes, they enrolled 600,000 volunteers, made or purchased guns for them, procured cannon, etc., etc., and—wiser than I was—they waited patiently until they were ready. I must in justice say this for them: defeats and disasters have only added to their feelings of outrage. The people of this nation have a kind of confidence in their power that sustains them. No people ever felt such shame as they did at the defeat of Bull Run, even though their soldiers, who had marched thirty miles and were outnumbered four to one, who hadn't eaten or slept for thirty-six hours, had almost beaten the Southerners, and in fact it was only the arrival of 15,000 fresh Southern troops that overwhelmed them. On every occasion when the numbers of troops have been equal, the slave masters have taken to their heels before the men of the North; in several instances, they have fled without even pretending to fight, and I draw attention to the fact that in these latter instances the Southerners—unlike the Northerners—haven't had the courage to admit that they behaved like cowards, and claim they retreated in order to set up an ambush or that other generals failed to do their duty. And you must remember that the whole world, when this war began, talked of nothing else but the martial bearing and warlike ardor of the Southerners. The Northerners themselves, for the most part, expected to be beaten when the numbers engaged were equal. But we've seen that the Northern lumberjacks are as up-and-coming as the other side and much more persevering. The first two Minnesota regiments—our state has sent 5,000 volunteers so far—have the best reputation of any of the native American regiments, having been the first to fight and the last to run away at Bull Run. The second [Minnesota regiment], with the help of a German regiment, played the decisive part in the battle of Somerset.[8] Our young neighbor Bill Maxwell took part.

Write to us soon, and pray for

Your wholly devoted son,
Theodore Bost

## Sophie to the elder Bosts

Thursday, April 10, 1862

Dearest Parents:

I really think that this time you will have to be satisfied with a letter from me only. Theodore is so busy making [maple] sugar that he has no time for anything else, and to tell the truth, I'm just about able to say the same for myself. At this very moment, I am watching the kettles while the rest of the family sleeps—or at least pretends to sleep, for I think I hear Theodore tossing and groaning in his bed, which worries me greatly. The sugaring season has been very poor until yesterday, when the sap began to flow really well; that means we must take advantage of it as long as it continues. We've been boiling all day long, and tonight I've agreed to stay up until midnight; Marie will keep watch until 2:00 A.M., Theodore until four o'clock, and M. Boissonnas from four o'clock until breakfast-time. This week we have already made about ninety pounds, and by tomorrow night we hope to have made seventy to eighty pounds just in these last two days. You can see that it's well worth taking a little extra trouble for that! And besides, our sugar is so beautiful that one of the merchants in Chaska offered us 12½ *sous* [cents a pound] for it instead of 10, which is the current price; this pleases us, even though we don't think we'll have any to sell. Groceries of all kinds have become so expensive that we prefer to get along without tea, coffee, and several other things, falling back on substitutes that we can grow here on the farm. Instead of coffee and tea we use wheat or rye [kernels], roasted like coffee; the result is not quite as tasty, but I think it's just as wholesome, and it's certainly much cheaper! Theodore drinks a cup of chocolate once a day, which always does him good.

Well, now it's Friday. Everyone has done his nocturnal tasks and is off to begin the day's work. Theodore and M. Boissonnas have just brought in a large tub full of sap and have now gone to the marsh to bring home a load of hay; then they'll fetch wood for the stoves where the kettles are still boiling furiously (of course, we add cold sap from time to time). I've just finished tidying up a bedroom and I'm waiting for Marie to clear the breakfast table so I can start my ironing. Mimi is busy taking care of her doll while she tells it a great many things in a low voice; the baby is asleep; and, finally, Old Mike is clearing land with his oxen, finishing his last month of work for us. You can see that the Bost beehive is humming away full tilt as usual, and inasmuch as it's only 8:30 A.M., we all have a good, long day ahead of us. This afternoon we're going to *"sugar off,"* and I think the Powers and Mrs. Maxwell are coming over for a visit. They don't make any sugar, so they like to be here during the final stage, when they can eat the "taffy" [*tire*], that is, the molasses-like stage just before it turns to sugar, thick and firm enough to form pieces that you can draw out as far as you please. Theodore sent you some maple sugar from Canada, but ours is much finer, and when you grind it into powder it resembles the choicest quality *cassonnade* [unbleached, granulated cane sugar that has been refined only once] ; anyhow, I'd like very much to send you a pinch of it as a sample. And now *adieu,* dearest Father and Mother—my flatirons are hot and the baby is "all wide awake," says Mimi, so I'll have to get busy with all that.

Friday evening

Well, here I am, after a very busy and well-spent day, suffering from a toothache bad enough to keep me from either sleeping or taking my turn at the work we're doing tonight. I'm writing, you see, while our friend Boissonnas takes my place tending the fire under the big kettles. Theodore has gone to bed to sleep until three o'clock in the morning. He is tired out, although he slept well last night. Even so, how much better our dear Dodo is! Three months ago he couldn't possibly have worked a full day; but now he seems to be getting stronger in spite of his fatigue. I am still much concerned about the spring work, but God, who has sustained him thus far, may very well go on doing so—it is in Him alone that we trust. In any event, dear Parents, it would do your hearts good to see how our Theodore—though he works as hard as he can—is learning to pace himself better than in the past, how to stop before he's overtired. For me this is really a reason for joy and gratitude. He doesn't torture himself anymore, and as a result he accomplishes more rather than less.

But to get back to our sugarmaking: we've made seventy-six pounds today, not counting a gallon of syrup and what was eaten by our visitors. Tomorrow we hope to make about fifty pounds more, which would be a very good amount even if the season is over then. Unfortunately, our friend Boissonnas is leaving Sunday evening, and, aside from the pleasure of his company, we'll be losing a valuable helper. During the seven weeks of his stay with us he has done everything he could to be helpful to Theodore. He is a really nice young man—easygoing, cheerful, making the best of everything and no more trouble than if he had always lived with us, although we talk a lot about seeing one another next winter. You know, I think, that he has been farming for two years in Illinois. But in the winter there is nothing a person can do down there on the prairies, so he gets bored and the inactivity doesn't agree with his health. Since he feels free to come and go, he came to Minnesota to see his old friend from the Bellevue days and to work for the fun of it. He enjoys the sugaring, he works at it without letup, and after doing his level best to help us he says he's embarrassed because we're forcing him to take with him a few pounds of sugar that he helped make himself. Otherwise he is a little frightened of Minnesota; with all his love of work, he nonetheless thinks that up here a man has too much of it to do and is astonished that anyone can stick it out. Alas, I'm afraid he's completely right! But what can be done about it? And anyhow, neither Theodore nor I could bear to live on the prairies, and we'd have no complaints about anything if only business would pick up a little—and especially, *especially* [word underlined in original] if Theodore could enjoy good health. But all these things are in the hands of the Lord, and we bless Him every day for our daily bread which is so generously given us, and also for the fact that we're living comparatively happily and at ease during the terrible torments that are shaking this country.

No doubt you know as well as we do all that is happening. A few weeks ago people were expecting to see peace restored in two or three months; but then all of a sudden the people of the South seemed to decide to put up an even more stubborn and unyielding resistance. With all the horror we feel at seeing the war prolonged, we want the struggle to be carried on until the question of slavery is candidly faced and resolved! In any case, it seems very certain that the North will win, and that's the main thing. You must have read or heard about the *"iron clad"* ships. These are going to bring about a real revolution in the building of warships, they say. Oh how splendid it would be if peace were to be restored! It almost seems to me that this will never, never happen. And in truth, wars and rumors of war will last as long as this poor world lasts.

Good-bye, dearest Parents, dearest Mother, much-loved little Father. May the Lord bless and watch over you both. We often think of you, you may be sure.

Your most affectionate daughter,
Sophie T. Bost

## Sophie to the elder Bosts

Chaska, April 26, 1862

Dearest Father and Mother:

As for the Northfield business, I think we've already told you that the owner was to have written to our neighbor Cheeseman after coming to an agreement with a brother, to whom the land partly belongs, who is now in the army. This letter hasn't come, so everything else is held up, but, since we've never been anxious about the affair, we're not anxious now. In all this business, whatever happens will be by God's will, so we shall not try to force a decision or hurry matters—certainly not as long as we feel so well off here. Dodo's health has always been the main, indeed almost the only reason for our wanting to leave. The owner of this land says he's in no hurry to sell; he doesn't know he has any hydraulic lime, though everybody knows about the quarry of ordinary lime and the one that produces building stone. He has built a lime kiln where he took Dodo and Cheeseman, showing them those stones which, he said, won't dissolve in water! He asked Cheeseman (a former stonemason) if hydraulic lime didn't behave in exactly that way! The latter gave an ambiguous answer, but I have my doubts as to how long this secret can be kept! I fully expect to hear that this man is rubbing his hands for joy at not having sold out! Well, let us trust in the Lord! It will have been He that willed it so—isn't that so, dear Parents? And so long as we have food and some clothes to wear, that will suffice! I ask for nothing more, but for even this to be safeguarded, my dear husband's health must be on a firmer footing—and I hope it will be. There's one question I was forgetting: this property includes thirty acres of very good land, and the thing that gives it intrinsic value is the waterfall that can be adapted to many different types of machinery.

You ask about Charles Boissonnas? He has a farm in Illinois which he rents to a young couple and also works on it himself. I wrote to you, I think, the day he left here. We would miss him even more than we do if we didn't have Edmond Powers (our neighbor's son), the one who used to work for Th[eodore], whom we've hired for this summer.

It has been several days since our sugaring was finished. I'm not sure exactly how much we've made—in the neighborhood of 300 pounds together with a few gallons of molasses [syrup]; we'll see in the fall if we have any to sell, but we aren't going to stint ourselves the way we would if it were something bought and paid for. Theodore thinks as I do that one should not skimp and scrape when it comes to the household, and we economize too much in all other ways to be stingy in using what we produce ourselves. Besides, not having any wine or fruit, we (that is, the people in this vicinity) fall back on sugar. M. Boissonnas was absolutely astounded—he had thought we ate as simply as possible, and notwithstanding his preference for prairie farming, he often said that "you woodsmen certainly eat much better than we do." He likewise admired the ease with which I turn out *"cakes and pies"* and was impressed by how little trouble I took with them. It's true that I've made a lot of progress in this department, even though there's still room for much improvement!

But speaking of fruit. Did I tell you that Th[eodore] had ordered a whole collection of fruit trees from a nursery in Wisconsin? Twenty-five apple trees, two pear trees, two plum trees, and several others, and also some ornamental shrubs two lilacs, one seringa, and a number of other plants and flowers. They should arrive in a week or two, and we're very happy at the idea of starting a real orchard! I hope it will be a success. The nursery is in the same latitude and climate as we are and ships a great number of trees to Minnesota, where we count on having some fine orchards in a few years. Several of our neighbors have also sent away for trees. What, then, do you think of our *Far West*? In spite of the *"hard times,"* the war, and the bad crops, our region is getting ready for better times.

Good-bye, dearest Parents. May the Lord bless and keep you.

Your loving daughter,
Sophie T. Bost

By the way, Theodore has just been made justice of the peace for the township of Chanhassen.

More answers to your queries: Mimi speaks French and is beginning to speak English . . . thanks to our visitors, for when we're by ourselves we hardly ever speak anything but French. The religious periodicals we receive are: *La Feuille religieuse du canton de Vaud* [The Religious Paper of the Canton of Vaud], which my mother sends us, and (from here) *The Independent* published by the Rev. H[enry] W[ard] Beecher, which has religious news and a sermon, and also a *Tract Journal* and the *Bible Record,* which is sent to Theodore in his capacity as an agent for the Bible Society.

**Theodore to his parents**

Chaska, Carver County
Minnesota, June 6, 1862

Dear Parents:

This war, which began so badly for us in both the moral and the physical realms, has begun to take a turn for the better ever since the church, which had shamefully allowed itself to be led astray by false principles, has taken the lead and has set its face against slavery. Since the Christians have placed themselves in the front rank, I have taken my stand for the American cause against infamous England, which has become just what this country was four years ago — the champion of self-interest, money, and politics. The insolent blusterers have sent their *Warrior*[9] to attack us by shelling all our seaports and have smothered us with insults; and now, when the *Monitor* has demonstrated to them how far superior the Yankees are, they again talk of peace and compromise, all the while making prodigious efforts to make their navy stronger than ours by adopting our shipbuilding methods. But as one of our newspapers has said: "Go ahead and do it, and when you're through building them, we'll invent something that will annihilate you as our *Monitors* have annihilated you." When I look back over this past year, I can't help thinking that if God had not been on our side, we'd have been beaten. The American people needed to be taught a terrible lesson, both the North and the South, but especially the South, and we've been taught it, the South especially. After this will come England's turn, and in spite of their tortured arguments, they know very well that they have openly espoused the cause of slavery out of a desire for revenge and gain. As for France, she is no longer France—she is Napoleon;[10] therefore, America hasn't much to say to her. But England, after all her fine boasts, has turned her back on her duty in too flagrant a fashion for the world's sense of justice not to demand reparation. But after all, everything is in God's hands, and He always brings forth good from evil.

Your wholly devoted
Theodore Bost

# X

# The Indian Uprising

Although the letters of Theodore and Sophie do not bring to light any important new facts about the short but bloody Sioux war in the summer of 1862, they do provide a vivid picture of the consternation and terror that prevailed even as close to St. Paul and the protection of Fort Snelling as their neighborhood was. Theodore seems to have been one of the few settlers who kept his head in the midst of general panic and hysteria.

**Theodore, then Sophie, to the elder Bosts**

[On the envelope of this letter Theodore wrote:]
   The doctor is still uncertain but thinks he can get me a certificate of bad health next week.

Chaska, Carver County
Minnesota
August, 1862

Dearest Parents:
   Yesterday I sent a letter to Elisée that was written when we were completely distracted, especially the last words I wrote in Chaska. Tomorrow I plan to have myself examined by the Dr. [*sic*] appointed for that purpose, and if I am exempt I'll send you this letter right away to relieve you of all worry on my account. The Americans here who are Republicans advise me to seek an exemption so that the draft will fall on the young secessionists and Democrats of this locality, which sounds reasonable if somewhat cowardly. The political, or rather the military, news is better. The *Arkansas* blown up, our victory at Baton Rouge, Culpepp[er] C[ourt] House,[1] etc., etc., and if things are going better now that

211

we are outnumbered, how will it be when our 600,000 men have marched to the relief of our tired armies?

As for the Indians, the alarm was being sounded almost the whole night in Chaska while we were sleeping peacefully in our isolated house. You have no idea what a commotion there was. Everybody stopped harvesting crops; three out of four [had left] with their families, baggage, animals, etc.; many had left their wheat stacks half-finished outdoors—last night there were showers and today the rain continues—just what we need! And I am more certain than ever that it's only a riot by a few Indians one or two hundred miles from here.

I know, dear Mother, that I have to take it easy, but what's the use of knowing it when the work has to be done and when hired hands are scarce and almost impossible to find? I am teaching myself to be more patient; I can see how my land is improving: twenty-two acres broken in two years, and perhaps Alphonse will come and take over some of my heaviest work—that would be marvelous. The average yield in this region is eighteen bushels of wheat to the acre; the bushel weighs sixty pounds, and the acre is about half an *hectare*. This is about what my yield will be this year, maybe even twenty bushels an acre. Fortunately wheat promises to sell for a high enough price to allow me to build a new house, which we need very much, or at least to rebuild this one so that I won't have to move my bed every rainy night and so we can have doors and windows that close properly. When you have only a few acres that are broken, your living costs are enormous, whereas we can live very economically with respect to what we have to buy; you wear out a lot of clothing when you're clearing land, and as for boots and shoes, it is a real joy to see them fall apart—so you can see how it happens that those who have cleared a great deal of land are proud as can be to go barefoot in their new fields.

The orchard, strictly speaking, is no more than an eighth of an *hectare*, since I still have only twenty-seven trees, all quite small, but I see that my health will never be really top-notch, so I shall have to enlarge the orchard and the garden, especially the former. I find that trees interest me a great deal, and it's light work that suits me perfectly. Hence I am thinking that next year I shall strike out along this line, inasmuch as hardly anybody in Minnesota has planted any. Since orchards are very profitable everywhere and since, with our experience here in the North country, we now understand how to take care of trees, I feel pretty confident, with God's help, of turning a nice little profit on our fruit. When we get any, that is.

You speak, dear Mother, of saving up a little money to come back home [for a visit] one of these days. Yes, indeed, that's what we dream about, but up to now we have done nothing but *spend* money, and if I were to sell everything tomorrow, not only would I have nothing to show for my seven years of hard work, but I would even lose money, which is also true of every one of my neighbors. Thinking about this has helped undermine my health because I hate to feel I am throwing away my parents' money all the while I am working myself to death. But, God willing, the worst is over, and inasmuch as I shall have next year the harvest from ten acres that were broken this year, I think I can undoubtedly pay you some of your money soon. If this house could really shelter Soso and my children from the weather, I would even send you some money this year, but I think you would prefer that I provide them with shelter from the rain and the cold.

The strawberries and currant bushes occupy about an eighth of an acre this fall. That doesn't seem like much, but in reality it's a lot. Our vines have grown well but haven't produced any grapes. In winter we're obliged to bury the vine and cover it with manure to keep the freezes and thaws from killing the tendrils. As you'd expect, fruits grown in the north have less juice and sugar, but the juice is thicker and by adding maple syrup and water we can make excellent wine. So little by little, we expect to become as well off as your best [French] farmers, with our own wine, sugar, coffee (made from wheat!), beer, fruits of all kinds, . . . and magnificent taxes to pay.

Good-bye, dearest Father. Where will you be when you get this letter? May God bless you and all the rest of the family.

Your most devoted
Theodore Bost

Dearest Mother:

We are assured by all and sundry that Theodore will be rejected for military service on account of his poor health. This idea, though sad to think about from one angle, is very comforting from another. We'll know for sure about all that tomorrow if Dodo goes to Chaska for his [medical] examination as he expects.

And then there are these Indians! I would really like to know where they are after all the scare they've given us! I say "us," but that doesn't include Theodore because he has only laughed at the whole thing from the beginning. But that's not my state of mind. I dreamed night before last that my children were butchered before my eyes (probably because both of them were upset and I had taken them into my bed and was sleeping with an arm under each one, [as comfortable] as though I had been massacred myself. I confess that I didn't feel very easy in my mind, and it wasn't exactly reassuring to see all around me men and women rushing about, the former to fight and the latter to huddle together for safety. The previous morning I had gone with Theodore as far as the Powers' to visit Mrs. P who is recovering from childbirth, and she wasn't frightened, but soon Mrs. Cheeseman came in with her four children whom she hadn't waited to wash and comb. On the way home, I looked in at the Sarvers' and found the wife pale with fear and the children weeping, the father molding bullets for his musket and about to leave at top speed for Chaska, which is the assembly point. And then reports began to come in from all sides—the Indians were approaching through the forests in war parties of fifteen or twenty, destroying everything in their path; they were coming down the [Minnesota] river and would get to Chaska by evening. Then great numbers of neighbors piled what they could onto their wagons and departed; others were standing watch, ready to leave at a moment's notice, etc., etc., etc. In the afternoon I took the children and Marie to the Sarvers' because she [Mrs. Sarver] had sent word to me that she didn't want to be left alone and we were waiting for Dodo to come back—since he had gone away without his gun, he wouldn't be planning to stay [in Chaska]. We were all on the point of bundling up a few valuables and leaving for Fort Snelling where the garrison is (twenty miles from here)—many families had already gone to seek refuge there. Fortunately, we weren't foolish enough to do that because it wouldn't be at all nice to have to come back here today in the rain. I am impatient to learn what has really been happening, and I think we are going to have more occasions for enjoying a good laugh at the expense of those who were most easily panicked. Mrs. Maxwell was half out of her mind with terror. As soon as she heard the report (of a man galloping around the whole neighborhood calling on everyone to take up arms), she ran off to spread the news and got so exhausted that she was still white as a sheet that evening—and now the dear lady says she is very happy that she didn't make herself ridiculous!

Mrs. Cleaveland, the poor woman who has lost her husband, two children, a sister, a brother-in-law, and a nephew, all in a few moments, left for the East soon after the tragedy, with her two other children and her sister's little orphan boy. We still exchange letters—she is pious, resigned, and busy, giving lessons along with taking care of her children and her elderly parents. Her farm has been leased to our minister-mason Cheeseman because she couldn't sell it.

Good-bye, dearest Mother-in-law, I think you are very, very kind not to forget your children exiled in America.

> Your most affectionate,
> Sophie T. Bost

**Theodore to Elisée**

> August, 1862

Dear Elisée:

Early this morning I learned that the Yankton [Indians] and the Sioux were five miles from our home, killing and burning everyone and everything, and that I must go to Chaska to join the force being organized there. I didn't believe a word of it, but started off anyway. Along the way I heard even more wonderful news, and on my arrival here I saw about fifty families on the road, with horses, wagons, and people pouring in all the time. The reason I'm sending you this letter today is that I consider the whole thing another *humbug.* The more people come in, the farther away the Indians seem to be. The nearest they are known to be is eighty miles away, which is where they always are. In any event, I am going right home again because Soso is afraid. Still more wagons are coming in at this very moment. There are about a hundred Germans who are trying to practice military drill, but the officers prevent them from doing anything by giving conflicting orders. Another woman has just arrived with her skirts up to her knees—for what reason I don't know.

So you can see that we have no lack of pleasurable excitement; what with the Southerners, who take their pinches of snuff from Yankee skulls,[2] and the Indians, who strut around wearing our hair, we run the risk of losing our heads.

> Good-bye to all
> T. Bost

## Theodore, then Sophie, to Ami, Jr., and Timothée

> Chaska, Carver County
> Minnesota
> September 13, 1862

Dearest Ami:[3]

A note I sent to Tim will have told him about the war we're having with the Indians. They have wiped out several villages, among them one founded by the Hutchinsons[4] about forty-five miles from here. For two weeks the whole region was in a shocking condition. Many of our neighbors ran away, and for one day I kept the animals shut up in the stable, unable to decide whether to follow their example. Soso was nervous and urged me to take them to the Fort,[5] but in the end I told her I wasn't going to go until the Indians were actually visible and that if I did go, Minnesota would never lay eyes on me again. The idea of losing all the money I've put into this farm, along with my seven years of labor, was more than I could swallow. Besides me, there are only two other men who have stood firm and have encouraged others to stay on here because almost everybody had either left or had their oxen yoked to their loaded wagons. More recent reports kept arriving almost every hour.

Forts are now being built just about everywhere. The Excelsior people (four miles from here) are building one; they had all taken refuge in Minneapolis, but some of them have come back. The Indians commit the same atrocities as the Sepoys[6] because they're fighting for their liberty (which, like that of the Southerners, consisted of oppressing others); I believe England is going to take their side and heap insults on us because we treat savages, not in the English manner, but in such a way as to avoid being exterminated by them.

In any event, don't say anything about it to Palmerston or Russell,[7] who might say that it is already a foregone conclusion that the Indians will drive us out [of this region]. For the moment we have nearly 4,000 men fighting against them. We still don't know precisely how many of them there are, but it is thought that there may be 4,000 also, although so far there is nothing at all organized. It is feared that the Chippewas may join with the Sioux and Yanktons, etc., which would give us plenty to worry about. Whatever happens, once my wheat is threshed I'll ship it off as soon as possible and then if we have to leave—God will provide! But I think I'd never return to Minnesota. The direct [property] taxes will be enormous this year, on top of the high prices we have to pay for everything we buy and the low prices of everything we sell.[8]

Infamous and accursed England! Her day will come, and there will be a time when her hypocrisy will be punished! It was magnificent [before the Civil War] to hear the English praying for the success of the Republican party, the Christian party, the only party in which there are true Christians. Slavery was then an abomination, and the Americans were semi-savages. But the instant the South began to appeal to *"free trade,"* the savages all turned out to belong to the Northern side, and the abomination was now the attempt to force the South to belong to a country that had turned against slavery. Honestly, you have to be British to do such things, and you must only listen to Englishmen.

Excuse me, dear brothers, if I sound bitter. You may love liberty as much as I do; but in my heart I have a yearning for legitimate revenge, a feeling that would make me enjoy seeing the oppressors in the role of the oppressed, and I can't understand how anyone could come to their aid, helping them to maintain their oppression. Furthermore, the continual anxiety I feel (not, certainly, for myself, but for my dear family), the responsibility that weighs so heavily upon me of having to remain here on my farm while Soso is so worried—all this has very much irritated my nerves. In any event, the moment I know for sure that the Indians are within thirty miles of here, I shall take Soso to a safe place and come back alone to watch over my property until it becomes impossible to stay any longer.

September 14, 1862

Theodore's letter, dear brothers and sisters, tells you enough about the fix we're in. This Indian business troubles me terribly. I've always loved Minnesota and have cheerfully put up with the drawbacks of our existence here, but the idea of seeing our babies tortured by savages is quite enough to make a person disgusted with an even more beautiful region than this. When I felt so much sympathy for your difficulties five years ago [at the time of the Indian Mutiny], dear Bella, and for the anguish poor Tim had to undergo, I little imagined that some day I'd feel as great a fear on my own account, and especially for those little creatures who are more precious to me than life itself—but God may put an end to all danger even before you receive this letter, and I hope He will. Although the state of affairs weighs very heavily on our little family, and although we have the prospect of only just being able to survive for several years to come, we can at least live as happily as this land permits so long as our humble abode is secure. But if the Indians come and burn our house, I don't know what will become of us. Be very thankful, dear Bella, when you embrace your dear ones for me, that you need have no fear for the lives of those pretty little creatures! Never have I better appreciated the benefits of a civilized country or desired so much to live in one myself. So, with all my love of children, I am very happy that it is you and not I who have a new baby!

*Adieu, Bella darling and Bella's darlings.*

> Your most affectionate sister,
> Sophie

**Theodore, then Sophie, to the elder Bosts**

> Chaska, Carver County
> Minnesota
> November 21, 1862

Dearest Relatives in Pau:

Dear Father, I never thought I'd have to classify you, as you say, among those who reproach me about [my attitude toward] this war. I know you don't concern yourself much with politics. It's only that I'd have liked to feel that those members of our family who, because of Christian principles, do have political concerns were giving their sympathy to the Christian side.

Thank you, dear Ami, for Gladstone's speech[9] which, in any case, I had already read, and thanks particularly for your plain and simple admission that the British only see and only want to see [in the American Civil War] a political issue and want our destruction because we're getting too big for them. The North has insisted all along that this was what England desired and has always said that if only England would admit it, three-fourths of the animosity would disappear because one can respect a sincere egotist, but a lying, hypocritical egotist becomes intolerable. Let the British say they don't give a hang about the slavery issue and want only to enrich themselves without having to cope with an ambitious rival any longer—then everything would be fine and dandy; at least we'd know where we stand, and the Americans would only have to reply: "Go ahead; our turn will come." But when they sing the other tune—"You're not opposing slavery at all, and you don't want to oppose it; whereas we, while helping the South, will make terrifying faces at them until slavery disappears"—we feel that it's adding insult to injury and treating us as fools when they think we don't see what their game is.

If three-fourths of the army were not Republican (a fact that helped make the last elections more democratic); if ninety-nine out of a hundred church members weren't Republicans; if the rabble of British, Irish, Germans, etc., which is so numerous in America, very frequently deciding the elections, weren't 100 percent Democratic and pro-slavery; if the Democrats for the past eighteen months hadn't invariably sided with the South and resisted the draft; and if the whole Democratic party were not the only one in the North advocating peace with or without secession—a peace much more horrible and shameful than war—I would understand that one might hesitate to take sides for or against the South. But I can't view the matter in this way, seeing, as I have since 1850, the progress—religious, if not political—that the people of the North have made on the slavery issue. As was to be expected, it has been impossible to keep politics from getting entangled with this progress, which culminated in the election of Lincoln, an election which signified that slavery was *sectional* [emphasis in original], but liberty *national* [emphasis in original], that not only the Northern states but also the District of Columbia and the immense territories were and would remain free, and that slavery was a cancer that must be arrested by all means and destroyed if possible.

My appointment as Justice of the Peace pays me almost nothing, seeing that the Germans who get into fights with each other deal with their legal problems in Chaska where they can get liquor. I'm not at all inclined to share their tastes, and I hope I never have any dispute that will need to be settled in a law court. I have already prevented one bad one by taking a few hours to

work things out between the parties in friendly negotiations.
Good-bye, dear, dear Parents.

Dear Parents:

I am very, very annoyed with myself that we left you for such a long time without letters during those terrible times of fear during the uprising by the Indians, and I don't really understand just how it happened. In the first place, we had no idea that your newspapers would get so alarmed over this revolt, and besides, we were in such a troubled state of mind that we didn't really know what to believe or write. We can never be thankful enough for having been spared—isn't that true? And besides, I assure you, [we are thankful] that we didn't run away, leaving the few little possessions we have at the mercy of livestock or of marauders who took advantage of the panic to loot houses and steal people's crops.

By now life has resumed its normal flow around here, and we laugh when we talk about the sudden flight of all our neighbors and the many amusing incidents that took place in the neighborhood. But to the west of us all is desolation—prairie fires have mostly destroyed what the Indians didn't burn and the inhabitants had abandoned in their fright. And where the Indians have ravaged and burned, it goes without saying that everything is far worse: lots of farm animals were abandoned or stolen or have been lost or killed by soldiers—all this can be repaired in the course of time if the Indians are taken away to some place where they won't be able to do anybody any more harm.

At the moment, the savages are fleeing, except for 1,500 prisoners, of whom 300 have been condemned to death, but whose fate hasn't been finally decided because the government in Washington is opposed to executing them. Then there are three or four hundred at Fort Snelling who are said to be innocent and who will be kept there this winter. But it is believed that Little Crow, the Sioux leader, and Hole-in-the-Day, the chief of the Chippewas, have gone west toward [the] Missouri, making alliances with other tribes and looking to a great attack next spring. If they dare to make any trouble, I think they'll soon get more than they want. It was only the suddenness and unexpectedness of their attack that gave them the advantage this fall, and even then they were only successful in attacking isolated homesteads where the poor pioneers felt so sure they were completely safe that the majority didn't even have guns, and in villages that were just as poorly prepared to defend themselves, nearly all their men being away at war. They were driven off from all the forts, even though all of these were very poorly guarded—but the civilians who sought refuge in the forts were able to help the garrisons.

You may well believe that many horrible or exciting incidents occurred during those days of terror. The wife of a doctor, formerly of Shakopee, seized by blind fear, was determined to leave Fort Ridgeley. She went away with her two children and a young man to guide them—that was the day before the uprising, and nobody was expecting anything of the kind. She saw her guide killed beside her by an Indian; another one leaped into his seat on the wagon and took her as a prisoner to the savages' camp, where she was held until [General Pope] was able to rescue the majority of the female prisoners. Meanwhile she was continually threatened with death in every form, not to mention all the infamous outrages to which all these poor creatures were subjected. She herself has told Ms. [sic] Maxwell how the Indians, finding whiskey in stores [in the settlements], frequently came back to camp drunk, determined to kill all the captives, and how it was the squaws who hid them. Once the unfortunate woman of whom I'm speaking was hidden in a swamp for a whole night with her two children and, on another occasion, under a pile of hay where she had to smother her child, a little baby, so that its crying would not be heard by the Indians who were hunting for them on all sides—she thought it was dead, but it came back to life—no wonder this poor woman's hair has turned white! Another woman, also from Shakopee, gave birth to a dead child after reaching a safe place—many, they say, have given birth in wagons guarded by soldiers during their mad flight.

We have also witnessed a great many noble and devoted deeds. For example, there was a boy of fourteen whom his mother had hidden in the garden with his little brother, making him promise not to leave the child until he had taken it to some safe place in the event she herself should be carried off. Those were her last words after being taken captive—I'm not sure about this. Anyway, this fourteen-year-old, when the Indians had left, took his brother and headed for the nearest fort—Fort Ridgeley, some ninety miles away—and living on wild fruit and berries, often hiding during the day, traveling at night, and never letting himself lose hope no matter what happened, got there after a ten-day journey and was reunited with his mother who had escaped. They say this boy is to be educated at government expense. Another story: a young woman taken captive had been stripped naked, then turned over to the squaws [to guard] while two Indian braves argued over which one was to have her; one squaw, perhaps out of jealousy, warned her of what was in store for her and allowed her to run away—dressed (!!) just as she was. She walked about sixty miles, finding along the way six children who had hidden in the fields, woods, and swamps and taking them all with her to the fort. And there are a great many other stories.

But who can say how many poor little creatures lost on the prairies or in the woods have perished miserably—how many mothers whose hearts ache more bitterly than if they themselves had laid their children in the grave! And how many orphans! How many women whose husbands' throats have been cut before their eyes! Oh, it sends shivers up my spine! On the other hand, I don't forget that these Indians have been deceived and cheated by government agents. All that is certainly wicked, and I am astonished that we should have been living so unconcernedly while all these things were going on so close to us.

No news of Alphonse Bonjour.

Good-bye to all. Tender kisses to all and to each of you in particular.

### Sophie to the elder Bosts

Chaska
January 19, 1863

Dearest Parents:

You ask how we manage to protect ourselves from the snow and cold. As for the cold, we have two potbellied stoves, and we get them red-hot with pleasure or anger; that keeps us warm, and Th. isn't stingy with wood even though it's painful for him to cut it. As for the snow, it comes in through the roof, melts, drips onto the upstairs floor and then trickles down to the lower floor. It's awful, but what's to be done about it—the house isn't worth repairing. We had thought we would build a new one next year, or rather this spring, but we've just about given up the idea and it seems we must get along for a while as we are. You ask, dear Mother, whether Boissonnas is coming this winter, and here is a letter that just came from him in which he says that he'll "come to visit us when we have a habitable place where he can stay." "No one can understand better than I can what you have suffered, and yet I have never heard you complain." Then he urges us not to go back to Switzerland as, alas, my heart is always prompting me to do and as my mother and sister would like me to do.

Good-bye.

Your most affectionate daughter,
Sophie

**Sophie to the elder Bosts**

Chaska
March 7, 1863

Dearest Parents:

Just to amuse myself, and perhaps you too, I've just drawn up plans for our new house [showing it] as we hope to have it in actuality next fall, God willing. Theodore already has on hand a good part of the timbers for the frame, and you'd have a hard time believing how much good it does us to dream of living in a house that will be warmer, more spacious, and especially more comfortable and easier to keep clean than this one. For my own part, I don't yet believe in it, and I won't really believe in it for certain until the day we move into our new house and leave this one to the mice and bedbugs that are threatening to force us out of it. If I were to tell you how much damage the mice have done, it would make Mama Bost sick at heart, and, as for the bedbugs, it is impossible to get rid of them in log houses –they multiply so fast there, and even get inside the logs, and nobody has found a way to destroy them. I don't much like the idea of taking into a good new house wooden things and beds that are infested with this vermin, but with only a tenth of the trouble we take here we'll be entirely free of them in a short time.

I hope very much that you like our plan. I'll finally have a bedroom that can be closed off and a good place to keep linens and clothes, and also such a fine big pantry, which people have here in place of kitchen cupboards and buffets. The porch will make the children happy, and me too on hot days; we'll have all kinds of plants and flowers climbing on it, you may be sure! Theodore likes them so much, and so do we all. We intend to build a good [rainwater] cistern with a pump in the kitchen, especially for the laundry, just as soon as we have the wherewithal —everything has gotten so expensive recently that we've given up, for this year, what would be an immense convenience. As for the upstairs, it's very doubtful that we'll be able to finish it this year, but I'm not going to worry about that. If our friend Boissonnas comes to spend the winter here as he has promised, he'll be able to help Theodore do the main part of the job, and the plastering is not a big expense. All this is fun to plan and to dream about, but I say again that I still don't dare count on it, even though everything seems to be working out so well.

There are all sorts of things that frighten me—[especially] the Indians, who are said to be planning to make a new incursion in the spring. Not that there is any danger that they'll get as far as where we are, but all the menfolk will have to take up arms to drive them away. And then people are talking about a new levy of troops to fight against the South, and even though my Dodo has been exempted once, his health is better now, so I'm very much afraid he'll be taken by the draft. But God is still our protector just as He was last fall, and if it is for our good, Theodore will stay at home.

But in the meantime, all these thoughts make me a little downcast, and something that makes me even more so is the scarlet fever that's raging all around here and seems more virulent than ever. By tomorrow we shall have had three burials in a week in our little cemetery—all small children, and it's the same all over. One of our neighbors has lost two children in two days, and the last remaining one is in grave danger at the moment; another neighbor in Excelsior has lost his only two; our minister has three who are very ill; a lady who is visiting one of our neighbors buried one of her sons today, the other is at death's door, and the third child is very ill in the place where she left him, though the poor mother knows nothing about it. Isn't is terrible? Only two or three families have been spared. Ours is one of them, God be praised, but I tremble at the idea that from one day to the next our little darlings may catch it. Our only hope is that the disease has run its course and that, with spring coming on, the region will be able to throw off this plague. I assure you that all the faces you see are anxious or grief-stricken—so many children carried off all of a sudden is quite enough to sadden people's hearts. You know that Mimi has had scarlet fever, so there is less danger for her, and our Alphonse is so strong and vigorous that it seems impossible he should ever be sick. In contrast to all our neighbors, we let our children run and play outdoors just as usual, and our only precaution is that we don't take them visiting anywhere, and we also have them take preventive homeopathic medicines. With God's grace, that should suffice.

Good-bye, dearest Mother—in all your maternal cares, don't forget the exiles in America.

Good-bye, well-beloved little Father. I often miss the letters you used to write to me, and I remember with gratitude all the patience you had with me! It is so sad there is nothing I can do to show you my love—nothing at all, not even a daughter's tender kiss.

Your daughter,
Sophie T. Bost

**Theodore to his parents**

Chaska, Carver County
Minnesota
March 8, 1863

Dearest Parents

. . . Some time ago I sent Tim a St. Paul newspaper containing [an account of] the execution of thirty-nine Indians at Mankato, near Saint Peter. Have I told you that Dodd was killed by them at New Ulm? These Indians who were hanged were the worst of those who had surrendered, but the principal murderers are still out on the western prairies . . .

# XI

# The New House

After much hesitation, Theodore and Sophie finally made up their minds to keep the Chanhassen farm. The advice of Charles Boissonnas may have had something to do with this decision. The prospect of acquiring the Northfield property seems to have faded away. Sophie and Theodore continue to refer wistfully to the quarry from time to time, but without any realistic hope of being able to carry out their project; we do not know at precisely what date they decided to make no further attempt to buy the lime deposit. The purchase price no doubt continued to rise as the water-power sites along the Cannon River near Northfield were developed, particularly for flour milling.

The decision to stay in Chanhassen led directly to the building of the new frame house for which the Bosts had been making plans over a period of years. Theodore had accumulated a supply of lumber, had made an advantageous deal with a carpenter, and had received from Boissonnas a promise to come for the summer to lend a hand with the house. Finally, the old log house must have gotten more and more crowded as the children grew older and more active—and a third was on the way.

**Theodore to his parents**

April 11, 1863

Dear Parents:

For us the big thing is still the house. From time to time I work on the frame with a neighbor who is a carpenter; gradually the boards are being sawed, and my pine lumber is either at Excelsior or here; the doors are already made, so that if we should not build the house we could at any rate go in and out through a dozen doors—that's surely plenty! The carpenter has raised his prices to everybody except me because my job is a big one and because it was agreed that he would work for $1.25 [a day]; this is very good because we are having to pay much more for a great many things connected with the house; but I think we can build a good one from the materials we now have.

The American Christians are now having a difficult time. What with fighting against the South, against the cowards and good-for-nothings in the North—and probably also against the hypocritical English—we can count on having our hands full for some years to come. Most of us consider that we shall have to have things out with the South before going on to teach England what the word "neutrality" means. And it isn't hatred of "those English" that is leading to this war; the ship loaded with food for the poor of Lancashire should be only the first in this mission of charity.[1] The vast, rich West was prepared to send enormous quantities of grain and pork, the railroads were to carry everything without charge—and all this not in order to buy England's friendship, but to recompense the English poor for their attitude [of support] so far as our war is concerned. But there was deep indignation among all classes when, as we listened to England's complaints and jeremiads on the sufferings of the poor, we saw their Parliament vote enormous sums for their Prince, who already possessed so much wealth that the tenth part of it would feed all the poor of England for a year. And our farmers said to themselves that if the rich in England are getting fat at our expense by sending *Alabamas*[2] against us, we should certainly be foolish to go out of our way to feed the English poor when their own bloated rich people are helping to starve them because of their infamous sympathy with the slave masters. .

The more this war drags on, the more I see on one side the good-for-nothings, the slave masters, the ignorant, and the rich English, who have the reputation the whole world over for never being able to see Christianity anywhere except where they can make money; and on the other side the men of order and discipline, Christians almost without exception. I see that the former have nothing to appeal to but the argument: (1) that the masters have a right to their slaves, and (2) that England would make more money if the South were independent. And the latter [the abolitionists] say simply that the South was not oppressed, that God condemns slavery, and that the South shall not extend it in the direction of Mexico so as to surround the entire Gulf with slavery (by forcing Mexico to reinstate it).[3] Hence I can only take my stand with the party of liberty without worrying whether there may be egotists in the North or generous people in England or in the South. The question is not *"High born and noble-souled South against low, mean Yankees,"* but liberty against slavery. The

hypocritical notion advanced by some Englishmen that "the South would rid itself more quickly of slavery if it were free" is absurd.
Good-bye to one and all.

Your most devoted
Theodore Bost

## Sophie, then Theodore, to the elder Bosts

Excelsior, Hennepin County
Minnesota
Saturday, May 16, 1863

Dearest Parents:

The big news is that our friend Boissonnas is coming to spend the summer here, helping Theodore with the farming and with the house. This has already made us very happy, even though it is really too bad he couldn't get here in time for the plowing. Theodore has not been able to find a hired man at a reasonable price and is doing all the spring work by himself, apart from a little help (with sowing the wheat) from our neighbor Mike. It goes without saying that Th. is far behind with everything—I mean that everything should be in the ground within a week, but it won't be, and you won't be much surprised either to learn that he is very tired. But we cannot be too grateful that he isn't sick. For the first time in ever so long, my dear Dodo can eat right after he comes in from his work; previously he was so tired he had no appetite at all. This spring it has done my heart good to see him enjoy his meals, and he also seems happier and more vivacious than I've seen him in a long time.

As soon as he has finished planting, Theodore will be fully occupied with raising the house. He will have to bring most of the lumber from Excelsior, the sand for mortar and bricks for the chimney from Chaska, the lime from Shakopee, and then I suppose that if he can he will help the carpenter and do the farm chores. It will be very good to have help from Boissonnas—this will make everything easier and cheaper. And then no doubt we shall have this dear friend with us all winter.

Marie and I will also have a fair amount of work to do, having three men to look after the whole summer and sometimes more, but I shouldn't begrudge a little extra trouble if it means a fine new house—don't you agree? As for me, I have practically all my summer sewing in order, and just today I sewed so much that my hand is still all trembly, and with the children continually joggling my elbow, I am very much afraid that dear little Father may not be able to read this writing, though he is ever so familiar with it — isn't that right, little Father? Next week I'm going to give some help to a neighbor who doesn't have money enough to clothe her three oldest boys so that they can attend school. In return, I think her husband will make me a thing or two for the new house; he's a carpenter, although [mostly] he works on his farm, and as long ago as last year, when I took care of his wife during her confinement, he refused to accept any payment from Theodore for something he had done. They are some of the best neighbors we have, good Christians and honest people (!), well behaved and blessed with a splendid family of boys.

You still write about the Indians, dear Mother, and I believe that in fact they are going to cause "trouble" again, but I haven't tried to find out much about it, not wanting to upset myself, and even if Theodore knew all the bad news there is, I'd be no better off. All I know is that they are moving a large number of these Indians to the upper Missouri and that there can hardly be any danger from the others because preparations have been made for any possible attack and at all important places there are forts and soldiers. In any case, dear parents, we are quite far from the frontiers, and with all those soldiers stationed between us and the savages there is not much risk that we'll fall victim to any of their attacks. All I'm afraid of is that Theodore may be mustered into the militia and sent to fight them if they should get too troublesome. And then there is the big war and the great number of soldiers who are going to have served their two years and are due to be replaced by fresh conscripts—this worries me continually, but sufficient unto the day is the evil thereof, and it's completely useless to spoil one's peace of mind with fears of what may or may not happen. Besides, everything is in God's hands, and all things conspire to bring about the good of those who love Him; we take comfort in that both in good and in bad times.

Good-bye, dearest Parents, dearest Brothers and Sisters.

Your most affectionate daughter,
S.T.B.

Dearest Parents:

The cellar hole for our house has been dug out, and three-fourths of the boards have been hauled from the sawmill. The timbers are almost all finished—one more day with the carpenter and we'll have all the beams done.

Likewise, it takes an enormous investment to get a whole farm going. Quite a number of big, husky fellows near here have sunk three or four thousand dollars [into their farms], the proceeds of huge harvests for several years, and are no nearer to having a fully operating farm than I am; and besides, owing to my bad health, I haven't harvested half or even a quarter of the crops they have. This year the price of land has doubled on account of an influx of Dutch settlers, but there's hardly anybody except the Germans who can sell to them because the latter tell the newcomers to have nothing to do with the Americans. If another pack of Germans should move in, it's not impossible that I might sell out, not wanting to be stuck in the middle of such a bunch of ignorant Democrats. The pro-slavery party is losing strength steadily and will keep on getting weaker the longer the war goes on. The proof is this: an Irishman has just told me he thinks that if a Negro were treated from childhood as he ought to be, he might grow up to be almost as good as a white person! That's pretty good for an Irishman.

Your most devoted
Theodore Bost

**Theodore, then Sophie, to the elder Bosts**

Excelsior, Hennepin County
Minnesota
July 5, 1863

Dearest Parents:

This is only a very brief letter to give you our latest news. We haven't sold our place, and it seems we aren't going to sell because nobody has yet turned up who wants to buy. Immigration has abruptly come to a halt, and although the Dutch are beginning to come in once more, all the German and Swedish Protestants are trying to sell so they won't have to stay in a county governed more and more by bigoted Catholics and Democrats, and it's only natural that if so many people are selling, the price of land will go down, so I won't think of selling. I have again sent word to the carpenter to come and begin to build, and this week I intend to start work on the house.

Our friend Boissonnas has been here for three weeks and has already helped me a great deal. We've been helping a neighbor dig a well thirty feet deep; now this neighbor has come to help me dig one—we've gone down thirty-nine feet and still no water. For more than a year we've had no rain that penetrated more than six inches into the soil, and for four months no rain at all except for a few showers. The rain clouds form every week, but then they go away. Hence many fields sown to wheat won't be harvested, and the rest will yield only a quarter of the normal crop (except for winter wheat planted in black earth, where there will be monster harvests).

In spite of all these reasons for being downhearted, we went yesterday with two other families to the shore of a lovely lake eight miles from here, about four miles wide and four miles long, where we spent the Fourth of July. We all went in swimming, which is something I seldom do more than once a year. We had a very good time, although Soso and Boissonnas made a lot of indignant remarks about these wagons of ours which have no springs but go at a gallop over *grubs* (stumps) and *logs* and rocks.

July 5, 1863

Dearest Parents:

If Theodore hadn't already started to write you, I think I wouldn't have begun one of my own, but I don't like to send off such a tiny little scrap of a letter, so I'll add a few words even though I don't have anything very interesting to tell you. Dodo has told you how I complain about these wagons without springs and these bumpy roads, but a person has to have had the experience in order to dare describe it. This morning I am stiff as a board, and I ache from the tips of my toes to the top of my head! However, we had a very good time, and I'm not at all sorry we went; the children had a fine time playing in a pretty lake that gave me a twinge or two in my heart because it reminded me so much of our beautiful Switzerland. Then we had a nice meal on the sandy beach and even made some excellent tea on the spot, using a kettle we borrowed from some people who live nearby. It was all very picturesque, and we all enjoyed it very much, although friend Boissonnas, who speaks only a very little English, found himself somewhat at a loss in the company of our Americans. Incidentally, the pleasure turned out to be fairly expensive—you'd believe it if you saw the pile of dirty clothes that will have to be added to my regular wash tomorrow; the dust was terrible and it was extremely hot, so our light-colored summer dresses have taken on strange colors! As for the bathing, though it was just what we needed when we arrived at our destination, it would have been even more useful when we got home.

Marie stayed behind to keep watch over the house, so she's the only one who is really up to scratch this morning. Boissonnas is still asleep upstairs; Theodore is reading on the sofa; the children—both of them in a fairly bad temper—are playing and arguing about a heap of shells that I brought back for them; as for me, I've been dragging myself around, more dead than alive, tidying up the house a little, and I'm very happy to have been able to do that much. All last night I couldn't fall asleep; it seemed to me that I was always holding up the big lunch basket with one hand while trying with my other arm to prevent a child from being shaken up—with all this I became so feverish that I finally got up and went for a walk outside. You must admit that people have to be very determined to amuse themselves to obtain their pleasure at the cost of so much discomfort, but you can't stay home all the time, and a little fatigue will pass more quickly than the memory of such a nice outing.

Boissonnas, who has very good judgment, said he wouldn't be tired at all after three days of well digging, but I'm afraid the poor fellow is soon going to have had enough of that sort of entertainment, because if we don't find water at fifty feet, we'll just have to try again in another spot. A drought like this one is a very bad thing, and it's already too late to help the wheat crop even if we do get rain. Rather than having more than we can sell, we'll have to be thankful if we get enough to keep us in flour and provide seed for next year. . . . But what's to be done? We can't expect an unbroken succession of good years, and the Lord well knows why He is afflicting us. These threats of a bad harvest frequently make me feel so discouraged that I want to sell out and leave this region, but that too does not seem to figure in God's plans for us; may His will be done, even though we don't understand why we should always be tossed about by uncertainties. There is our house, which would already be well on the way to completion if this attempt to sell the farm hadn't gotten in the way, and now we don't even know whether we can get a carpenter, and anyhow it's going to mean that everything will be so late! Then there is a distinctly minor but also very real difficulty—almost no gardening has been done, and it's not going to be easy to have three or four men to feed for such a long time.

And in the middle of all this, Theodore says that I must let you know of the one pleasant event we have to look forward to— you'd laugh if you knew what he means! And yet Theodore is quite serious, but I wouldn't have spoken about it in exactly this way if I were the one to tell you about it first. Oh, if only we'd sold our place, if only I could be close to my mother and sister next winter! I don't speak about the help that is so easy to get in our own country—here a woman can go to great trouble to obtain it, but she will surely not find it anywhere! How different it might have been! However, forward march! I'm neither the first nor the last woman to go through it—that's some kind of consolation, I suppose; but my heart aches often enough for others so I can say that the prospect doesn't fill me with rejoicing for myself. And even so, I am better off than most of my neighbors because I have my good Marie to help me. What do the poor women do who are sick or at least in feeble health, but have to go on doing their ordinary work as if nothing unusual were happening? I don't understand how they can do it. I honestly believe that under the present circumstances if I had to cook all the meals, not only would I be unable to eat anything myself, but by the end of the month I'd either be dead or rid of my baby. That's what I think, and it may not be true, but I'm very glad not to have to put my idea to the test.

Good-bye, dearest Parents. I embrace you tenderly. Friendliest greeting to all the brothers and sisters.

Your daughter,
Sophie

**Theodore to the elder Bosts**

Excelsior, Hennepin County
Minnesota
Saturday, October 24, 1863

Dearest Parents:

It's been almost two weeks now since we ought to have written to you because it's been that long since we moved into this house here, and our excuse is always the same—too much to do. Our moving day was a Sunday, and it was raining. I didn't want to do it that day but, having bought (the day before) two black mares that stood shivering outside in the cold, we hauled our stove over here and made up our beds on the floor; then within an hour I had stabled and bedded down my two horses and tied up my other animals in our former parlor which we had been sitting in not two hours before. The only drawback with this stable is that the roof is too low and the doors don't close well—but these defects have existed right along.

Since then, life for me has been nothing but an uninterrupted succession of errands, the latest one being a trip to Minneapolis with Boissonnas, who is going back home to look after his own affairs just at the time when my season of heaviest work is nearly over. Then I also had to take some wheat there to be ground, the other mills being virtually shut down for lack of water.

So here we are now in a house where the doors can be closed and where a thunderstorm doesn't send rivulets streaming all through the rooms. How wonderful! And the children love to play on this new floor where they aren't always getting their little feet caught in cracks or losing their toys through the gaps. And Soso— but she will tell you herself what she thinks of it. As for myself, I enjoy it very much—the other place was weighing on my conscience—and the woodpile will last a lot longer.

Winter has arrived two weeks ahead of time, as if to make this splendid year complete. Drought, a frost in the middle of July, and another severe one in all the western states in mid-August, and then nothing but freezing weather since the nineteenth of October—which compels me to feed hay to my livestock at a time when everyone is short of it; as a result, you can't sell an animal for a good price. So it goes! But may God's will be done—it is He who sends us the rain and the sunshine!

Having had a great many trips to make and having had to let my work go in consequence, I am a little discouraged by thinking about the poor crops and the big expenses we've had, but I know that as soon as I can get back to my chores things will go better. In two weeks' time my big jobs will be cleared away, and I'll be free of worries. I mean to keep on trying to farm for one more year, and by then I shall know what to do. But my horses give me a lot of pleasure; the oxen were ruining my health and seemed to be tearing and jolting my body to pieces—but now my trips do me good instead of making me sick.

The elections this fall are going to be won mostly by the

Republicans, to the great confusion of the wicked, and the war is more and more revealing itself to be what it has really been all along—a war to deprive some men of the freedom to oppress other men—and if the South frees its Negroes (something I don't believe possible), it will simply be an admission that they've been in the wrong. In any event, it will only be done as a last resort, since they know they are going to be free anyway by virtue of the President's Proclamation.[4]

Good-bye, dearest Parents—may God bless you for all you've done for us. Good-bye, everyone.

Theodore Bost

**Theodore to the elder Bosts**

Excelsior, Hennepin County
November 22, 1863

Dearest Parents:

The war goes on demanding more and more men; 300,000 will be drafted in six weeks' time, and I have very little chance anymore of getting out of it. So many men have been exempted on account of illness that no more than 50,000 were accepted out of the 300,000 [examined], so this time they're going to be less choosy. I shall be glad to see that the draft is at last taking the proper proportion of rabble and Copperheads [covert supporters of the South] instead of filling the ranks with good Republicans and leaving—as in New York—the dregs of all nations to decide the elections.

But, dear Parents, you were enthusiastically in favor of the Italian war[5] (and so was I), even though that war was conducted by a Louis-Napoleon who had to do it to save himself—don't you understand that we have to be all the more tenacious in defense of a cause like ours? Maryland, Missouri, and Tennessee, three slave states loyal to the South . . . now want to free their slaves. . . . We have had to fight not only against pirate ships built and armed by the British, but also against the Copperheads in the North and in England. I'm sure you've read the addresses delivered in England by [the Rev. Henry Ward] Beecher; otherwise I'd send you copies of them. It has done all of us here in America a great deal of good to see that in spite of everything, his latest speech was greeted with so much enthusiasm. We don't like to see England altogether bereft of a few souls devoted to liberty and Christianity. It is really very odd to see how that nation has changed its attitudes as a result of this war; ten years ago, she was wholly absorbed in her egotistic preoccupation with money making, and you know I didn't spare them any of my reproaches. For the time being, she sees nothing in our struggle but a chance to remain mistress of the seas and of the world's trade! But God plans everything, and He has permitted the continuation of this war in order to raise the issue of emancipation in three or four slave states.

Happy New Year to all of you, dear Parents, and also to dear Ami and his family. May God sustain and bless them. Give our best wishes for a Happy New Year to all the other brothers. Why doesn't Etienne write to me anymore?

Good-bye, good-bye to all!

Theodore Bost

# XII

# "And the War Goes On"

The Civil War dragged on, though by the end of 1863 the prospects for a Union victory had brightened. To the farmers of Minnesota the war had brought many problems and uncertainties, and the Bosts were affected. Their letters continue to speak of poor crops, soaring prices, high taxes, and their fear that Theodore would be called up for military service. We learn also about Theodore's activities as a Republican local politician and officeholder. Sophie expresses envy of more prosperous neighbors who have sewing machines and mechanical clothes wringers. But the principal family news is the birth of a second daughter, Sophie Alice, with only Theodore and a neighbor in attendance, on February 12, 1864.

**Sophie to the elder Bosts**

January, 1864

Dearest Parents:

We hear that on all sides of us people have frozen to death, and I'm very curious to know how things have been going in Europe. Some of our neighbors have suffered very badly — among others Mrs. Maxwell who, not having any able-bodied men at home, can't have a snug, warm house. We've found her all dressed up as though she were going to pay visits, wearing a hood and covered with shawls, sitting hunched over the stove. It has often happened that for three or four days she has been in tears with her water bucket frozen solid beside the stove, etc., etc. Her health has been ruined. The poor woman! She is certainly to be pitied. The only son she has left at home is a drunkard, though she refuses to admit this to herself, and he doesn't show her much tenderness. I often feel very sorry for her.

If ever we are to have reason to appreciate our dear little house, it must be during this terrible cold spell. I have thought

237

many times how bad it would have been in our old garret, and I blessed the Lord for having given us shelter in such a timely fashion. It has given me so much pleasure to see my dear children running about and playing without realizing how cold it is [outside]. At night they sleep by the side of our bed so I can be sure they don't throw off their covers, and Marie has been sleeping on the living-room sofa because it has been very cold upstairs. Next year, if the crops are good, we can finish off and plaster the second story and then the whole house will be much warmer than it is now. I shall be very glad if Theodore can at least finish a [second] bedroom—the room directly over the parlor, which will have a fine big closet and a window. For the time being, since we have only a single bedroom, it is hard for us to put up even one [extra] person for the night. Dodo thinks he may do the whole job of finishing off this room—carpentry, plastering, and all—if he has the time, but in any case we couldn't have made any use of it this winter because we haven't any furniture for it.

Yes, dear Mother, we are well supplied with warm clothes for this winter—we all have four pairs of stockings. . . . I have made all our clothing as economically as possible, but it is of course important to be able to go outdoors without being cold—on nice days for the children, and all the time for Theodore. We'd like very much to make some sugar as soon as the season for it arrives, and we devoutly hope the weather will be favorable. Our supply will last until then, which proves how [frugal] we are, considering how many boarders we had last summer.

As for [wild] honey, Theodore hasn't found any for three years. He wants to buy a number of beehives so he can begin to keep bees as soon as possible. If we stay on—and it seems as though the Lord has decided to keep us here—Theodore will certainly have to try to earn money from something else besides corn and wheat; otherwise we'll be perpetually in want and fearful of the future. You know that he wants to set out some young vines. The ones we have now have done so well that we are very optimistic, and if it pleases God to bless him in this undertaking, it will be a source of profit, no doubt involving a great deal of work, but not strenuous.

All this often gives me more anxiety than I like to admit. Sometimes it seems almost unbearable to me to see my dear husband working harder than he is really able to do, while we go without little pleasures we have been used to, and all without our being able to see any more clearly what sort of future it's leading to. But I assure you, dear Parents, these moods don't last very long, and in the end I always think how fortunate I am that, thanks to our parents, we haven't suffered more than we have, and that, after all, our situation has improved so much since our marriage—almost every day we compare how we were then with how we are now. . . .

I have no idea what we'd do if somebody made us a good enough offer. Theodore is still thinking about that lime quarry. I would almost be inclined to put our money into U.S. government securities and, while we are waiting to see how things turn out, set ourselves up to give lessons in Minneapolis where people say that a French teacher would have enough students to keep him busy. We shall see. We'd have no desire to give up our farm if Theodore's bad health didn't oblige us to do so. It's a *home* we can leave to our children in addition to all the advantages it offers us. In any event, dear Dodo is feeling much better than he was two years ago, when he couldn't even cut enough wood for our household needs. Now that he has his horses, which give him so much pleasure and save him so much heavy toil, I hope he will find his work easier. May the Lord preserve us!

Your most affectionate daughter,
S. T. Bost

**Theodore to his parents**

Excelsior, Hennepin County
Minnesota
January 17, 1864

Dearest Parents:

Well, I am now over thirty! Yesterday we celebrated my birthday by inviting the Powers, the family we have the closest relations with, and we spent a very pleasant day together. A few days previously, we had been invited to their place where we met some young soldiers just back from an expedition into Indian territory in the wilderness some three hundred miles from here. They were on the march during that terrible cold spell that lasted from December 31 until January 6, struggling through the snow in country where there are no roads at all. In a number of places the mercury froze in the thermometer,[1] and we came within two or three degrees of it here for more than a week. Owing to the extreme cold, I broke my ax on the first day and had to go to Excelsior to buy another, and I assure you the trip was no fun. I don't know what would have become of us in the old house because I can't any longer jump out of bed and get dressed in an unheated room the way I used to do eight years ago. Our windows, which are only eight feet from our big red-hot stove, were covered with frost and ice from a quarter of an inch to an inch thick; this made the house very dark, but at least Soso and the children were good and warm inside the house, and so was I, but not outdoors, although I managed not to freeze anything.

Boissonnas is in Illinois, I think about four hundred miles from here—you can get there by boat for half the distance (when there is enough water in the Mississippi) and then the rest of the journey is by train. I don't know what he's doing this winter because he never tells us any of his business.

Boissonnas had the idea that we would be housed, dressed, and educated like his Democratic neighbors in Illinois. He was astonished to find that I still had good manners and persisted in behaving like a gentleman. He thinks Minnesota has a social tone far superior to that of Illinois, or at least to the Democratic area where he lives—and it's true. But I'm not sorry we went to the expense of adding a veranda; the children enjoy it as soon as the sun strikes it, and in summer we enjoy sitting there in the shade. If God would only give me better health, I think everything would be all right. If I were stronger I would always have plenty of chances to make money. Trust in Him! It seems that the Lord's will is that I remain here.

And the war goes on, though these last few weeks I think everybody is recuperating. In the meantime, all those impossibilities—declared to be such by the English because to them they seemed so—appear ever more possible to the Americans. But God is always on the side of His children when they fight for Christian principles.

Good-bye, dear Parents; warm greetings to all the brothers.

Your most devoted son,
T. Bost

**Theodore to his parents**

Excelsior, Hennepin County
February 14, 1864

Dearest Parents:

We have another little girl whom we've named Sophie Alice; we've named her Alice for Paul's wife.

The little one came to us at two o'clock in the morning on the twelfth, and she is in very good health. Once again Soso was too quick for the midwife, so a neighbor and I were all alone, letting nature take its course—it's almost a pity [we had so little to do].

Soso is doing very well, given the circumstances, and much better than in our old shanty. Marie manages very well, taking care of the new baby and doing the cooking; the house is clean and tidy, which was never possible in the other house at a time like this, much to Soso's annoyance.

We are awaiting the draft call of March 10 with impatience but without fear. I have sworn to uphold the Constitution of the United States, and I'm not going to turn tail just because a bunch of slave owners have attacked it. I don't see how anyone can be of two minds on this subject. The North has finally decided upon its course of action; the South knows this, and all its shouting and all its efforts can only postpone the day when the whole of this continent will be free. If the North is beaten again after our recent series of victories,[2] that will do nothing but bring down slavery and make even more certain the [eventual] triumph of the North, for our party seems to thrive only on defeat.

But good-bye, dear Parents—I still have a lot of writing to do, and as soon as Soso is better we'll write to you again.

Good-bye to all,
T. Bost

Very best greetings from Soso. Mimi is very proud that we let her hold little Alice in her arms, and she is so happy to be allowed to take care of her.

**Theodore to his parents**

[Added in margin:]
Boissonnas writes us that at the dedication of their French

church in Ottawa, they sang Papa's *Apocalypse*.[3] He says it was magnificent.

Excelsior, Hennepin [County]
Minnesota
March 17, 1864

Dearest Parents:

That expedition into Indian country was for the purpose of taking supplies to those who had been removed from Minnesota [to an area] five or six hundred miles to the west of here. Apart from that, the war against them goes on, and we have between 2,000 and 3,000 soldiers ready to march at the first thaw. A few of those who took part in the massacre of '61 [*sic*] and '62 are still being killed; their chief was shot last year by a farmer one evening when he had gone out to bring in his cattle—he saw two Indians, fired at one of them and killed him.

Sometimes I feel very disheartened. When we get a whole week of our terrible northwest winds and when I think that we have to live for at least six months [of the year] without seeing any flowers or even a blade of grass, it makes my heart heavy—but where in the world is there a place that has no disadvantages? Everything seems to indicate that we ought to stick it out here. Théophile may have written you that I am a little worried that somebody else may learn about that lime deposit, and I see that as my only hope for the future (in this life)—to be able to buy that property and live there without working myself to death and have income enough to be able to give help to other members of our family who need it. If this quarry is discovered [by someone else], it will be proof that God didn't want us to have it.

There is talk of a new draft of 200,000 more men, which would mean a total of 1,800,000 men mobilized to put an end to this farce—quite shocking in the nineteenth century—of a nation seeking to build an empire on slavery. But it must be said that the military authorities are very liberal and send home men who in Europe would be retained in the army. Furthermore, the above figure includes a large number of men who purchased exemption for $300. As for giving up on the war, nobody even considers it, although everybody wants to see the end of it. I believe the presidential election will decide everything. If Lincoln—or a better man, such as Butler or Frémont[4]—is elected, the South would be too discouraged to prolong for another four years a war that will be all the more pointless because all their slaves will be in our hands, laying the foundation for a free republic in place of a slave-holding aristocracy.

Boissonnas has probably enlisted by now—he's a true abolitionist and will make a good soldier.

Farewell, farewell to you all. May God be with you.

Th. Bost

**Sophie to the elder Bosts**

Sunday, March 20, 1864

Dearest Parents:

You are perfectly right, dear Mother, to say that Boissonnas is a bear—that's just what he is! I'd say so if only on account of his rude remarks about my little girl which I haven't yet forgiven him for; and as for his comment about Theodore's "fine manners," I suppose Boiss. was amazed to find that people hereabouts have too much self-respect to go about in rags as it seems his own neighbors do. He told us it is not unusual to find in the road garments so completely worn out that they had fallen off the backs of their owners. He wasn't able to understand how our neighbors and we ourselves could be less uncouth. But he is surrounded by Irishmen and low-class people, whereas we have Americans from the East who are well fed, educated, and ambitious to make as good an appearance as anyone anywhere. Our dear Boissonnas, therefore, thought I was spending much too much on the children's clothing because, even though I buy the least expensive materials, I try to find pretty fabrics and to make them as tastefully as I can, and because I keep the holes mended. All this was beyond his comprehension, and so was the fact that we insist on bringing the children up to have good manners, to eat properly, etc., etc. But he's an old bachelor. So let's make all necessary allowances for him—always excepting his treatment of my daughter, which aroused the indignation of everyone who witnessed it, even the carpenters. And besides, Boissonnas, old bachelor that he is, is very finicky about his own grooming and is very well dressed!

I think our church would surprise you. Almost every Sunday when the weather is good people come with horses and wagons—almost no oxen anymore—and although the church itself is only a rough little log building, some of our ladies come in silken dresses, cloaks of wool, velvet, silk, etc., and also satin hats with feathers, etc.; but among the congregation there are also many women who dress more simply in wool or muslin for the most part, or even calico [*indienne*] , and who don't feel the least bit humbled by the elaborate toilettes of the others. Hurrah for America and freedom, or at least hurrah for Minnesota. In the cities elegance is the watchword, and even in little Shakopee they say the ladies' fashions are extravagant. I myself have seen (four years ago) outside the gate of a small exposition of farm implements and other things a woman dressed in silk and velvet and all the trimmings; she went over and spoke to a man passing by who was dressed like a common laborer, and I was very much astonished to learn that he was her husband; she was tricked out in all her finery while he was hard at work. But all the most beautiful things our neighbors have are relics of their former lives in the East—several have brought their finest carpets, a few handsome pieces of furniture, some porcelain, etc.; and I hardly blame them for holding onto these things and enjoying them.

Incidentally, dear Mother, I was forgetting your question—do we have sewing machines? Oh, yes, and washing machines with mechanical wringers. A number of my neighbors who haven't been able to find hired help have bought washing machines or wringers; Mrs. Powers is going to have both, and that's a tremendous boon in a household like hers. We can easily get along without them, with two women in our home, but Theodore would give me at least a wringer if he could afford it—it is so much easier on the clothes—and the back!

Farewell, dearest Parents. Another time I'll try to make fewer demands on your eyesight and your patience.

Your very affectionate daughter,
S. T. Bost

**Theodore to his parents**

Excelsior, Hennepin County
Minnesota
July 4, 1864

Dear Parents:

At times, I'm afraid those noble allies—the South, the British aristocracy, and the Democrats in this country—may win the elections, and you must surely know that the Democrats have always favored the extension of slavery [into the territories] and will be ready to recognize the South in the hope that the pecuniary interests of the North-West [*sic*] will outweigh religious principles and cause all the western states [*le grand Ouest*] to join with the South, so that slavery will then be recognized as legal for the entire nation, the point which has been the source of dispute and division for thirty years, with the South wanting to legalize it and the North seeking to restrict it without being able to wipe it out legally. It's sad to see Christian people who fly in the face of ninety-nine out of a hundred Christians in this country and sympathize with the slaveowners merely because these slave masters, who live in luxury and idleness, have assumed a lot of piddling aristocratic airs that make you want to kick their behinds.

At last there is serious fighting, however, and that's what I've most desired. It is always more satisfying to see a general who is trying to accomplish something than one who is afraid [to try], and I hope the South will soon see that it has only one chance left—to surrender and give up slavery. This depends very much on Grant's succeeding in his campaign, because the elections could very well turn to the advantage of the South if we are beaten before Richmond[5]—not that the Republicans would lose heart, but many indifferent men who never vote would vote in that case in order to escape paying such high taxes. You know that in 1860 we thought we had done wonders in electing Lincoln to block the further extension of slavery. This year we're trying to elect him in order to root it out in all the states—which of course won't prevent people from telling us again that the South is fighting for freedom and we for slavery. Perhaps someday I can send you a picture of three slave children freed by our soldiers and one of a black man's back all crisscrossed with welts from the whips of those great friends of progress, liberty, civilization, and Christianity.

The latest issue of the *Independent* tells the story of a black man who tried one day to escape and take refuge with our troops; he was captured and given 200 strokes of the lash; then, though suffering from the effects, he escaped again the second day following and enlisted in the Union forces. Some people in the North may be cruel, but the fact that the laws prohibit slavery and the use of the whip in the North shows that the overwhelming majority in the North are opposed to them, whereas the contrary is true in the South.

My health has been better than it was last year. Anyhow, I am always fairly well when I don't have much heavy manual labor to do. My work as tax assessor for the township makes me work with my legs (or those of my horse) and with my head, but I can put up with that. Hence, if I still feel weak next year, I think I'll apply for a job as foreman of a work crew, but not a job as disagreeable as the one I had with Dodd.

Sunday, the seventeenth

Received this morning, dear Father, your brief letter of June 20, and I will hurry and finish this one.

I've just finished making my assessments, and if possible I'll rest a day or two before I start haying and harvesting.

There's a chance I may be nominated by our party for a rather good office. But precisely because it's so good, there will be opposition, both from the Democrats (who almost always win a majority) and from several lukewarm or cold Republicans who are interested in it and will work much harder than I'm willing to do to get elected. I've just been initiated into the party's inner councils, but I have no wish to be among those who hold high office; I'd rather be someone who compels them to make Christian laws even though the officeholders behave in private like rascals.

Farewell, farewell, dear Parents,

Your
T. Bost

**Theodore to his parents**

Excelsior, Hennepin County
Minnesota
Sunday, October 6, 1864

Dear Parents:

We are bound to render thanks to God that we are so well off despite the drought and the high prices. This is the first year we'll have had to depend entirely on my labor and the produce of our farm, and we're going to make ends meet. The [sale of our] colt, the hire of my horses, and a great many days' work for the town, etc., etc., have made up for the lack of crops—from this we see that God knows better than we do what is for our good.

As for that public office I was telling you about, I refused to compete [for the nomination], and my friend Powers is the candidate. Since the job calls for two people, he will take me on as his deputy if he wins, and I will then go to work in Chaska during the week, leaving the family here and coming back Sundays. Perhaps when the weather is good I'll go on horseback. [I hope] Father

Lincoln will be reelected to the great discomfiture of the slave-owners and all the Northern rabble. Five states, two in the East and three in the West, have just held elections in which the friends of liberty have beaten the supporters of slavery, and I assure you that this has given us all a great deal of encouragement. The great question at issue between the two candidates is: The Union with liberty or the Union with slavery, and the American people, who were proslavery twelve years ago, are almost all taking their stand against that infamous system.

All the same, it's amusing to hear England's horrified cries because we want to compel the South to obey a President who was opposed to the extension of slavery. She thinks it is criminal, etc., but *she* [emphasis in original] had the right to try to make America submit to unjust laws (in 1780) [*sic*] and to wage war against a Christian nation [Russia, in the Crimean War] to aid the Turks merely in order to protect their possessions in a country held in chains by England. It is instructive, too, to see how that country [England] insulted us continually when the South was dominant over the North, telling us we were nothing but slave masters, cutthroats, pirates, etc., interlarding these insults with a few words of praise for the Northern Christians who were working for the abolition of slavery; and now, when those same Christians are running the country and are trying to abolish slavery once and for all along with the system of butchery and piracy that has prevailed up until now, we learn that the South is a land of noble Christians who only want to part company with those infamous Northerners! Bah! It's too stupid. Maryland, Missouri, half of Virginia, and half of Tennessee are now opposed to slavery, having passed laws freeing their slaves, and [Kansas?] has gotten rid of its law permitting slavery—all this, of course, while England was explaining to us that slavery had nothing to do with this war and that we were just as much in favor of slavery as the South! All the offices in our county are held by Democrats and their company won't be pleasant, but our party needs men who aren't afraid to speak out loud and clear, and when I meet up with any Democrats, there is no lack of argument.

In Chaska there is a Moravian church that has just established an academy. So you see that we shall have good schools for our children if they grow up here.

The business about the lime quarry is marking time, dear Father, because I can only buy the quarry with ready money, and

I don't want to buy it unless I can earn it [the money] or else sell the place I have now, both of which are difficult to do. The man is still sitting on his quarry, no doubt continually astonished that his pesky lime refuses to be slaked. If Powers wins the election, I plan to go at once to Northfield to find out how much the man wants for his place and how much time he would give me to pay. What with the income from my office and my farm, I think I could pay off the amount in annual installments. . . .

We have been living very economically, but living quite well just the same.

Farewell, dearest Parents. May God bless you and grant you a happy old age.

Your most affectionate
T. Bost

**Theodore to his parents**

Excelsior, Hennepin County
Minnesota
November 13, 1864

Dearest Parents:

Do you know the song that goes:

The war has just been won by France
But I've three bullets in my back . . . ?

This is more or less the way it is with me. Lincoln has been reelected by a handsome majority in spite of all the lies, brandy, and money that were poured out so freely to defeat him, but Powers didn't get elected, which is not a disappointment for me because we have known for three weeks that there had been a mix-up in the soldiers' ballots we had been counting on. The Copperheads are all wearing long faces whenever I run into any of them; their newspapers are even saying that everybody (?) [sic] has an expression of despair on his face, that the country is going to the dogs, etc., and all because the party that stands for Christianity and freedom is again in power. I have often told you what elements the two parties consist of: the Catholics and the rabble are all Democrats here, and they are furious to have to recognize that we are their masters for the next four years. There are about as many honest and intelligent men among them as there are ignorant unbelievers on our side. The Protestant churches are almost entirely with us in the North, and even the English Christians I know in this region are enthusiastically for Lincoln. There are some intelligent Britishers who voted against him out of love for England, but it isn't loyal to swear fidelity to a government and then vote against it. I hope that like us you will have given thanks to God because Maryland has freed all its black people and abolished slavery—the same state that was the first to fire upon our soldiers as they were on their way to Washington; Missouri too is about to pass laws emancipating its slaves; and soon there will be no slavery [in the Union] outside Kentucky, the other slave states having been deprived of all their slaves by process of law. So we Republicans will come together on the day appointed by the President as a day of Thanksgiving,[6] and we'll be rejoicing that Lincoln has been reelected.

You are so far away you can scarcely imagine how bitterly this election has been contested. Six weeks ago, everything was going against us, both on the war fronts and in the political arena, and we saw that the lowest class of foreigners (especially low-class English and Irishmen, the Germans being much more polite and well behaved) was growing continually more insolent. Now they're having to drink the bitter dregs of decisive defeat in spite of their infamous frauds involving thousands of votes of soldiers already dead, their threats of conspiracy, and their appeals to the greed and cowardice of people. You couldn't go into a store owned by a Democrat without hearing the merchant tell some stupid German or Irishman that if Lincoln should be reelected the prices would all go up, etc., etc.—and the poor suckers believed them. We went to Chaska to hear a speech by our dear Governor Miller,[7] and I've seldom heard a speech so filled with eloquence, sarcasm, and jokes. He has been a Methodist minister, a general in our army, and now he is our Governor.

Farewell, dearest Parents. May God preserve you for all your children—this is the prayer of

Your most devoted
T. Bost


**Sophie to the elder Bosts**

Excelsior, Hennepin County
Minnesota
December 17, 1864

Dearest Parents:

You speak of "our cities," dear Mother. If you mean St. Paul and Minneapolis, they are fine cities, especially St. Paul, where there are magnificent buildings, a dozen churches, large hotels, streets that are very regularly aligned and made level despite the uneven terrain, and growing rapidly in all directions, pretty country houses in the outskirts with lovely gardens, ornamental trees, etc. Chaska and Shakopee, though small, are very nice towns, with 500 to 1,000 inhabitants in Shakopee, which is the bigger of the two, and several fine stores of which many larger places would not be ashamed.

Excelsior is only a small village that I think must consist of only twenty or thirty scattered houses. Each one is perched on top of a little hill . . . , has a vegetable garden and orchard, a few trees, a small field of potatoes or corn, perhaps a few beehives, etc.; [Excelsior has] a store, which is also the Post Office, where in winter the mail comes twice a week and often every day in the summer on account of the vacationers who come to Excelsior from long distances away to hunt, to fish in lovely Lake Minnetonka (Minnewashta is three-quarters of a mile from here and Minnetonka is four miles away), and to enjoy country living. Besides, you find a better class of people in Excelsior than in most small towns—they are almost all Christians, no liquor is sold there, and no form of vice is tolerated. Our dear Mr. Sheldon, who looks very much like Mr. Maxwell, has a very comfortable parsonage there, living in a large house which (with his eight children) he really needs—they range from age one to age seventeen—a fine barn, a big garden, lots of berry bushes, vines, fruit trees, and beehives—we hope very much he's settled there for life and we do our best to see that he wants for nothing in these times of scarcity.[8] Theodore, who up to now has subscribed $5 a year for his support, will henceforth give $10, which is almost more than we can afford, but is none too much for the minister. In addition to this, our taxes will amount to 250 frs. [$50] on account of the war.

We have already had some very cold weather with ice more than an inch thick in some places on our windows.

With Christmas and New Year's almost here, the children are very impatient to learn what presents they'll get—although Mimi has already told her father that she doesn't want him to overwork in order to buy her something. If ever I wished I were a little bit rich, it's when the time of year arrives for giving presents. It makes me very sad not to be able to offer a surprise gift to those I love, but who can tell whether one of these days the time may not come again? . . .

Farewell, dearest Parents. Lots of love to all the brothers and sisters. Heartfelt hugs and kisses.

Your daughter,
Sophie

## Theodore to his parents

Excelsior, Hennepin County
Minnesota
January 24, 1865

Dearest Parents:

Our last letter must have seemed rather gloomy. A number of small debts to pay and not much to sell, poor health—all this made us sad, but—thanks be to God—we are now more in the clear. I've been able to do some outdoor work with my horses, which pays very well. And then, if the Chanhassen people pay their taxes when they're legally due, I shall also collect my percentage as Treasurer and use it to pay my own taxes, but these are so high this year that people will put off paying as long as possible, with the result that a new Treasurer (tax collector) will be the one to receive them, since I don't expect to be reelected.

The almost universal prosperity of the North in the middle of this terrible war (which was supposed to ruin the country, a war that we couldn't endure for two years, while the South could bear it without difficulty, etc., etc.) shows us that God is on the side of those who fight for His principles. I still have copies of some Southern proclamations from before the war forbidding Northern ships to bring anyone but rich people into Southern ports because, foreseeing the war, "they didn't want to see the South inundated with paupers from the North who would be seeking refuge from famine by going South." And now the excuse they offer for killing by cold and hunger fifteen to thirty thousand Northern prisoners of war in three months is that they don't have enough food to spare for them![9] As for that, they're lying, as in everything they've said since the beginning of the war, but it shows how badly they've deceived themselves about the North as well as the South.

Mrs. Powers's brother has just been liberated by an exchange of prisoners from the mud hut where he was kept, and he was in such wasted condition when he arrived in the North that he didn't even have enough ambition to write to anyone for six weeks after he was exchanged, and one of his sisters had to do it for him. Think of the sufferings these poor men had to undergo in that place where, without tents or blankets, they were forced to live in pouring rain for twenty-two days at a time and in alternating sun and rain for six more months! When the most seriously ill were told they were going to die, they shouted with joy at the prospect of being delivered from their torment. And their executioners are those great "Christians" of the South who want to get free from the unbelievers of the North!!! Oh, dear Father, if you could see as many of the South's crimes as I do, you wouldn't be surprised that I can be so bitter against a nation [England] that—after praying for the abolition of slavery—now prays for the victory of the rebels who want to perpetuate it.

Tomorrow I'm going to Carver to work on "town" business in connection with the next drawing of lots [for the draft], and, although I'm exempt from this drawing, I shall try to get my name removed from the rolls for longer than just until next June—I'll write "yes" on the envelope of this letter before putting it in the mail [if I succeed]; if not, I won't write anything. Everything is going fine with our little family. Thanks be to God.

Good-bye, good-bye to all.

Your most devoted
T. Bost

**Sophie to the elder Bosts**

Excelsior, Hennepin County
Minnesota
February 11, 1865

Dearly beloved Parents:

There have been a great many accidents all around here, and some of them are really sad. Our neighbor Lyman has just left for the East with a young widow and a small child, and I fear very much that they'll have a painful journey because the trains are not running in many places. This Lyman sent his wife and two children East last spring, and we don't expect ever to see them again. Our neighbors are leaving this way, one after another, so that our circle of friends is getting smaller all the time. This is a source of unhappiness to us all, especially inasmuch as the Germans—all ignorant lower-class people—are becoming more numerous round about us, and I don't know anyone else who doesn't want to leave except the Powers and perhaps the Aspdens, an English family we don't visit very often. There is hardly anyone besides the Powers whom we consider real friends; we go there and they come here once or twice a week, and we get along very well together. Mr. Powers is a man of exemplary conduct in almost all respects, and Mrs. [Powers] is very nice. Besides, their children and ours are very fond of each other and visit each other a good deal. Their Freddy calls Alice his little wife and their Frank, the same age as Mimi, has taken a great liking to her which the little darling doesn't return very much. I must not omit Mrs. M[a]x[we]ll from the list of our friends; she often comes to see us, but I hardly ever go to their house.

Have we told you that we may take in boarders? The Congregationalist minister in Minneapolis to whom Theodore gave some lessons wants to come and spend a few weeks here with his wife and two children. If we aren't able to finish off another bedroom upstairs, I think we could let them have our bedroom and sleep in the upper story just as it is. There has been another "gold fever" this winter. Old Mike, who was supposed to work our fields, has caught the contagion and is about to leave for Lake Superior. I hope Theodore will be able to find somebody else; but in any case it's unthinkable that Theo should do it by himself—it would be risking his life to undertake these heavy spring jobs that lead on to hard summer work, and it's time he paid more attention to his health for the sake of his wife and children—don't you agree?

Good-bye, dearest Parents. Take life easy, dear Father, and look after your health for the love of us all. I embrace you with all my heart.

Your daughter,
Sophie

**Theodore to his parents**

Excelsior, Hennepin County
Minnesota
February 12, 1865

Dearest Parents:

Dear Tim has sent us £5 as a holiday gift, which is worth $50, and you know I was wanting to get hold of some money to buy some beehives, so this present came at just the right time. The main problem is to find the beehives. My bees did so well last year, with each hive producing three or four new swarms, that everybody now wants to keep bees. I've tried to get them from at least a hundred people, and it's possible I may have to order them from a long distance away. But if so, [I shall insist on] Italian bees of certified purity whose safe arrival is also guaranteed—maybe that would, after all, be the best solution. Since I've studied beekeeping, I believe I can take good care of them and make a profit out of them by using a patented hive that opens at the side and is designed for our cold winters. A large number of ordinary hives have frozen this winter with fifty to a hundred pounds of honey in the hive—the bees' breath froze solid onto the honeycombs, thus making it impossible for them to eat, and when it froze around the door it plugged it up and stifled them.

My good old steeds are still in good health and have never even shivered from the cold in our old house where I store my wheat and oats; the two mares, two cows, two small pigs, and twenty-five hens, all closed in together, keep each other warm. The grapes usually raised here are the most common varieties—Isabella and Catauba. The other, more delicate species are the Delaware and the Diana, still not very popular. During the winter weeks when I wasn't at home except (during the day) Sunday, I got up at five in the morning, started out after breakfast to draw wood to the schoolhouse or to Chaska, came back for dinner, and then left again right afterward, not getting home again as a rule until the children had gone to bed. When it's cold, my mares want to go at a gallop, and it's a great strain to drive them, even apart from the fact that the cold makes my whole body lethargic. Our vines have to be covered in winter, which is not such a hard job, and the grapes sell for a price that is all the higher because they are so difficult to obtain.

Good-bye, dearest Parents.

Your
T. Bost

**Theodore to his parents**

Chanhassen, Carver County
Minnesota
April 6, 1865

Dearest Parents:

Your last, very good letter reached us over three weeks ago at a time when we were quite sad and discouraged. Because the last draft was supposed to take the rest of the able-bodied men from twenty to forty-five in Chanhassen, we were virtually certain that we would see all our friends going off to war, leaving us alone with their Democratic and unbelieving enemies. Thanks be to God, Powers and Fuller have been rejected as unfit, and only Sarver was accepted. The last has been called up twice, and both times he has managed to get sent home by pretending to be sick. He has just sent his wife here asking me to get another man to take an oath that he, Sarver, injured his back two years ago, but that's something I can't do. So God has preserved our best friends to us and is punishing those who were the most eager to send us off to war.

But, dear Father, all our worries and anxieties about the war should give you some notion of the nervous state I'm often in when I write my letters. I should be quite vexed if you believed that I see only the nobler side of our government, and if you read our newspapers as Tim reads [extracts from] those of the South in the British press, you'd see that our Republican papers are the first to attack any failings for which our party may be to blame. But since I know that you rightly have a high opinion of Tim as well as of our dear Ami; and since it has seemed to me that you have been guided much more by their notions than by mine; and since I have considered as really infamous sins the attempts of the English to prove that our side (which from the first day of the war has fought against slavery and its defenders) was for slavery and the South for freedom, I have written to you about the general significance [of the war] and not about details. . . .

I had myself believed, as you did, that the sufferings of the prisoners had been exaggerated, but friends of ours who have actually been there [Andersonville] all say it was frightful. . . . They snatched up half-cooked beans that had been vomited up by other prisoners with weak stomachs, washed them, and recooked them to have something to eat, etc., etc. One of our neighbors, after months of suffering, finally gave in to the continual urging of the guards and enlisted in the Southern army to get better food; soon afterward he was recaptured by our troops in another battle; naturally he didn't put up much resistance before surrendering, and the government gave him a pardon as it has to thousands of other prisoners who let themselves be recruited by the South in order to escape the deprivations in the camps. And, as additional proof of the infamous character of their government, I see that their minister-plenipotentiary in England, not being able to deny the reality of their horrible sufferings, invented another lie—that we have deprived them of the means of feeding them [the prisoners] better! When the prison was surrounded by all their military depots and was hundreds of miles away from our troops! Thanks be to God, their infamous government is being defeated on all sides; even the English, realizing they are on the point of going under, no longer see in these rebellious slave masters the sterling qualities they found them to have when they expected to get all their cotton; . . . and our party recognizes more and more clearly that it was the sin of slavery that drew upon this country such terrible punishment. Besides which, our leading newspapers, even at the period when we were being accused of making compromises with slavery, said with all the northern Christians that this war would end only with the extinction of slavery.

But I see that your government bondholders are afraid that once our Civil War is over we may teach Napoleon [III] that we aren't fond enough of his company nor of that of an Austrian prince to want them as neighbors in Mexico.[10] I have no desire for a war with France, and I want still less to see a Catholic Mexico enter our Union; but the American principle—that Europe has no right to decide the destiny of America—is just, and if there should be a war (which I believe to be a certainty if Napoleon persists), let the chips fall where they may, and may God uphold those who are in the right!

Good-bye, dearest Father and Mother. Never doubt that despite the distance between us, your son will always love you very much.

Your
Theodore Bost

# XIII

# The Death of Alice

With the ending of the Civil War it must have seemed to Sophie and Theodore that some of their most worrisome problems were behind them. Theodore need no longer fear the draft; his health improved; the new house was more comfortable and easier to heat—which meant less wood chopping. The business cycle entered an upward phase, bringing better farm prices. His years of struggle with trees, stumps, roots, and bushes had finally enlarged his fields to the point where he could expect a modest surplus of corn and wheat to sell for cash. Sophie began to think that owning a piano and a sewing machine might soon be something more than a vague aspiration.

It was just at this moment that they suffered the cruelest blow of all— little Alice, the baby of the family, barely eighteen months old, fell victim to the epidemic of whooping cough that swept the nation in 1864-65.

**Theodore, then Sophie, to the elder Bosts**

> Excelsior, Hennepin County
> Minnesota
> August 22, 1865

Dearest Parents:

We had come to the conclusion that we should not expect that you would fully understand our reverses, so we had decided to say no more about them; but since the hand of the Eternal has once more been laid heavily upon us, I will dwell upon these losses only long enough to say that the reason we've been afflicted is that for the past three years our harvests have been no more than just barely sufficient to keep us alive; and on account of my poor health it has seemed to us that we should give up, and yet God kept us here. Neither of us has, even for one single moment, found fault with God's ways nor set our hearts on the things of this world, and we were concerned about our colts and our crops only

## THE DEATH OF ALICE

because these would have enabled us to pay our debts and taxes. By depriving us of both, God left us in ignorance as to what we ought to do—whether to go or stay. Therefore, since God has now afflicted us in a much deeper way, it was not that He wished to chastize us for our complaints, but rather to teach us always to look more above us where death can no longer prevail.

When you repeated to us, dear Father, the words of our dear little Mimi ("God could do something 'still more terrible' to us if He took away our children"), you cannot have expected that He would indeed be pleased to change one of our beloved little creatures into a little angel, just a few days after we had received your letter. Alice, our little jewel, our darling baby whom we loved the most on account of her mischievous gaiety and her great tenderness, got sick just ten days ago with a terrible case of dysentery; she was already ill with whooping cough and was cutting her eyeteeth. Ulcerations appeared at the same time in her mouth and on her stomach, and after treating her for twenty-four hours with patent medicines [*médecines allopathiques*], I couldn't bear to torment her with them any more and fell back on homeopathy. She had first shown signs of illness on a Sunday evening, and by the following Wednesday she refused to swallow any more patent medicine. She did take other medicines until the day of her death (yesterday evening), and her mind remained clear until yesterday morning, though she never spoke another word after Thursday when she called out to her mother in protest at being washed. Yesterday morning at three o'clock Soso awakened me. Alice, who had been having convulsions for six days, often for hours on end, seemed to be breathing her last; we were able to relieve her pain until six o'clock in the morning, but then she grew much worse and was suffering a great deal. So from then until evening we gave her sedatives and sleeping draughts, and in the afternoon she was calm, coughed vigorously, swallowed some liquids, and looked at us once or twice. Around four o'clock she seemed not to be suffering as much pain, and she died at half past eight. Her features took on an angelic expression during the last hours of her life. Our dearly beloved child! She had never caused us a moment's pain. She teased her brother and sister only to have the joy of rewarding them the next instant with hugs and kisses.

Our hired girl Marie has hardly stopped crying when she is by herself. Mimi has fits of weeping that come and go suddenly, but

Alphonse doesn't understand anything of what has happened. Soso and I, who have never thought we were raising these children just for our own sakes, have given her to God, though this has been a terrible blow for my dear Soso, who is in a very low state because of our trials. Our Christian friends in the neighborhood have shown us a great deal of sympathy—even before this happened. They have often said that if God did everything for the well-being of His children, it could be said that He is unjust in allowing everything we have attempted to come to grief while He blessed the works of our unbelieving neighbors' hands. Fuller is digging the grave. Powers will go to fetch the minister, will have the coffin prepared, and will conduct the ceremony. Mrs. Maxwell and Mrs. Langdon (this latter is an exemplary Christian who has been much afflicted) came and spent the night with us; the former is still here today. Our other worries are still with us, but God will provide. Good-bye, dear Parents—pray for us and write to us.

Theodore Bost

Dearly beloved Parents:

He is the Eternal: may He do that which seems good to Him! I have prayed a great deal for the life of my darling child. I don't know what my life will be like without her tender love. Oh Alice!—but God does all things for the best—isn't that true, dear Father? Oh, you mustn't believe that we have murmured against Him because of our losses! You can't possibly know how hard we've tried to keep our heads above water, nor can you know how we are tortured by the thought that we may not be able to hold out through this year. Oh, pray for us! Oh, our dear Alice—she was too sweet for this world. Mrs. Langdon told me this morning that, when she heard me say a few days ago that Lily [Alice] was "my sweetest treasure," she was afraid for me! Mimi is so loving now. And Theodore is more dear to me than ever. He is so full of sympathy and encouragement. Alphonse also has the whooping cough, but his case is milder thanks to the homeopathic treatments.

Send word of our affliction to our brothers and sisters. Good-bye, dearest Parents. I know that you will be praying for us. Our exile now seems so wretched! But our neighbors are very good people.

Sophie

# THE DEATH OF ALICE

## Theodore, then Sophie, to Jenny Bost

> Excelsior, Hennepin County
> Minnesota
> October 6, 1865

Dearest Mother:

Rather than delay writing for another week I'm sending you this sheet of paper on which one of the neighboring women has already started a letter. We and our neighbors are all very short of paper. Since the death of our darling Alice, we have been occupied with a great many things. She died during harvesting, and I had to do everything virtually alone. The wheat was beautiful to look at and the yield was good, but the oats were so flattened that you pulled them up by the roots while mowing, and I had to write off more than an acre of them; I offered what was there to a man if he would cut it and give me half, but inasmuch as someone had made him the same offer for a fine field of wheat, he preferred to mow the wheat. My horses, at least, are getting the benefit, and I'm building up their strength again by grazing them in that field. All this work, the death of our child, and our other troubles have nearly worn us out.

One night I heard a loud thud and guessed at once what had caused it. Alphonse—it was just a week after Alice's death—had gotten out of bed and while still sound asleep had walked to the end of the house where they never go in the daytime and had fallen from a height of nine feet onto his back or his head; I found him groaning and waving his hands. I picked him up and felt him all over, finding no bones broken. We couldn't get him to say anything, although he was clearly unwell. When morning came, he woke up as usual, complaining of a headache, and that was all. He still insists that he didn't take a tumble—that terrible fall didn't even awaken him. So we came off with nothing more serious than a good scare, but there are times when you would rather not be frightened. Of course we don't let him sleep upstairs any more—Marie is there, but she always sleeps too soundly to be aware of what the children are doing.

So dear Father is having a lot of trouble and pain in Geneva about his music.[1] It's sad to think that, having come to America in the hope of being able to help you, I am unable to do so. The same is true of nine-tenths of the young Swiss in America; it will take them many, many years to succeed. It takes energy and optimism [*gaieté*] and money, or else you must have an iron constitution and no tastes or needs [to spend money on] in this country. And for almost all the Swiss I know, the opposite is true: they feel alone, foreign, and depressed. Many of them start to drink and die of alcohol—I've known a great many to wind up that way. The rest vegetate and finally, after twenty years or so, get used to this country, their children grow up, and they get fat and comfortable. Things work out differently with young men who find relatives or friends here when they arrive, for they can profit from the advice and help of those who have been living here for years.

We feel that our dear little Alice has left a great emptiness in our lives—I would never have believed that a child of that age could leave so deep an impression behind her. She was so playful and so loving! The homeopathic doctor in Minneapolis told me that from the start of her illness there was nothing we could have done, that the brain had been attacked by the fever that comes with the whooping cough, the sores, and the dysentery. It was this, he said, that made her throat turn black. Dear little Alice! We hope to find her again soon up there where there will be no more suffering. Good-bye, dear Mother—give our warm greetings to our dear Father in Geneva. Pray for us who, in our exile, have suffered still another great loss—one of our children. Good-bye until we meet again! [*Adieu et au revoir.*]

Theodore Bost

## Theodore, then Sophie, to Ami Bost

Excelsior, Hennepin County
Minnesota
October 15, 1865

Dearest Father:

Your two remittances reached us at a time when nearly everybody here had piles of money and was spending it on clothes. Our old stonemason, a Methodist minister, who has been in abject poverty for four years and was confined to his bed for three months this summer, has received a few hundred dollars, and when I told him how pleased I was to learn the news, all he could say to me was: "*I feel good!*" The Powers have just returned from selling a lot of livestock. . . . Good old Mike,[2] who has just sold his farm, making a profit of $500 in three months on the sale, has paid my taxes for me and has also paid Alice's funeral expenses—he told me not to be in any hurry to repay him, and that it wouldn't kill him even if I never paid him. From the sale of my wheat I have bought a complete new wardrobe, literally, so I can teach in Minneapolis, and we've sold enough to provide the whole family with good clothing. Another creditor has told me he'll wait another year, and still another [creditor], though he was at first impatient, realized that it would not pay him to be in too great a hurry, so he is still waiting. Our debts (big ones for us) amounted to only $100, but when you have to go out and clothe a family and pay living expenses for a year, lacking even a single penny to pay the debts that are weighing on you, and when the future is not at all bright, it gives you gloomy thoughts, even when you have no other troubles. But, in spite of all this, we've never thought that God was punishing us in excess of what our sins merited, although, as good Christians, we've been astonished at the prosperity of people who, in our opinion, did not deserve it.

You know that one of my mares that I almost lost has more or less recovered, but I've sold her to Powers at only a slight loss; besides, I've had the use of her for two years. I couldn't afford to take the risk that she'd have another attack, and Powers could afford it. With the money she brought, I've bought ten beehives with the knowledge of my creditors, who in this country have neither the power nor even the atrocious idea of crushing and vilifying a man if he goes bankrupt. Since I must be away in Minneapolis, I don't want in any case to leave Marie with more than one horse to feed and take care of; and in this way, too, I'll save a whole winter's feed bills. I'll hire a horse in the spring, and I'll rent one of my fields to someone. If God wills it, my beehives will soon bring me the wherewithal to buy another horse if I need one. So with this money[3] I have more than enough to pay all my debts, and even if I find that I'm not doing well in Minneapolis, I can come back here and manage to get along. The Congregationalist minister in Minneapolis has offered to help me, has arranged for an article about me to appear in the local newspaper, and has given me a good start, which I badly needed.

So I now have twelve beehives, and I needed anyhow to go to Minneapolis to have some boards sawn for another fifty or so hives. I'll be able to work on them in the intervals between lessons.

Dear Father, we think of you often, of all the troubles you

are having when at your age a person ought not to have anything but Heaven to think about. How much I hope you may live long enough to see all your children not only treading the right path (which I know you believe to be the only important thing), but also happy and at their ease on this earth. As for us, we are young and should expect to have losses and trials. If our sorrow was great at the death of our much-beloved Alice, we can fall back on our youthful resilience, and besides we know she is happy. Our little darling! We were speaking this morning of her joy at being able to close a door when she found one open, and about how hard she would work bringing wood into the house with the other children. She was so strong and seemed so full of vitality! Her nice plump cheeks were sunken after only three days of illness, although even after that she twice jumped out of bed and ran into another room without being fully conscious of what she was doing. The thing I found hardest to do was to measure her body in feet and inches in order to have her coffin made. But that's all over now, and we know that up in Heaven she can have nothing but loving thoughts about us. It will give you pleasure to know that we're going to buy a few toys for our two children. Alphonse has never had any, and Mimi only a very few.

Next year our farm should be lovely. My apple trees have grown tall; the cherry trees and the plum trees should start blossoming. We also hope to have a fine flower garden, and if we have good weather in July I should have about forty hives full of bees. Our new arbor has given us a great deal of pleasure, and our good neighbors have been able to share the grapes with us. Now our debts will be paid and the future looks clearer, so that we have hopes of still enjoying some good times here below, cherishing happy memories of our child who has gone on before us. . . .

In three weeks' time we are going to decide whether Negroes are to have the vote in Minnesota. As for me, I say yes, but the decision may go against us because last year our party took a clear stand on the principle that a man who can neither read nor write should not be allowed to vote. The purpose was to exclude a larger number of Democrats, but now it seems it would look very awkward to admit all the ignorant Negroes as new voters just because they'd vote for us. Anyhow, the immense gain we've made is that there are no more slaves.

Farewell
Your Theodore Bost

## THE DEATH OF ALICE

Dearest Father and Mother:

     After spending most of the night talking about your good letters, and thinking about them and about how to reply from my heart and even in my dreams—now that I sit down to write, all the words have flown away. Dear Father and Mother--your sympathy and your kindness are a precious balm in our affliction, and I thank you both, and I thank God for giving us such loving parents. Having already accepted 100 frs. from my dear Mother, my first thought (and Dodo's too) was to decline your too-generous remittance, dear Father; but after talking it all over last night with my dear husband, I see more clearly than I had previously how much anxiety these debts had caused him, contributing this past summer to undermine his health and sap his strength, so I've urged him to accept your gift rather than wait, as we had at first intended, until he had earned the money in Minneapolis (which is doubtful). I wrote to my mother the day before I left for Minneapolis with Theodore (and I'd have much preferred to stay here), but this outing has done me a great deal of good from a mental standpoint, although physically I was extremely weary when I got home again: the change of scene and the new faces that I had dreaded seem to have done a little to raise my spirits, and I feel more like myself than I did all last summer.

     Mimi weeps for her little sister almost every day, and yet she has such a cheerful disposition, without any trace of melancholy; we take so much pleasure in this child—she wins the hearts of all those who get to know her even a little bit. And as for our son, I sometimes fear that I may be getting too proud of him, he is so handsome and carries himself so well, is so intelligent, etc. Both of them ask me continually why God doesn't send us a new little baby in place of Alice. Alphonse wanted to know the other day whether I couldn't lay an egg and hatch it like a hen so as to have a little chick! And Mimi laughed and laughed with pleasure at this idea. Poor dears, they miss their little sister very much and speak of her in such a loving way! Dear Alice—our hearts will never cease to mourn your loss; my great consolation is that everything God does is well done, and besides that, our precious little one has never known the sorrows of this life and the bitterness of death—but none of this can prevent our hearts from being filled with selfish regrets.

     As for having more children, may the Lord's will be done. Dodo and I love these little things so dearly, and our house seems so empty since Alice has left us that we would be grateful to be expecting another one; and yet Theodore's health is not good enough to make us desire a large family to bring up.

Good-bye, dearest Parents. May the Lord bless you and keep you in good health.

Your loving daughter,
S. T. Bost

**Theodore to his parents**

Minneapolis, Minnesota
December 10, 1865

Dearest Parents:

Your last letter from Geneva, dear Father, has reached us, along with the one from Mother—they both came the day I returned to Chanhassen to spend Thanksgiving day with my dear little family. Consequently we had many reasons to be thankful that day. The death of our child, which must be proof of God's love for us, still leaves us full of sadness, and yet it is from that time on that everything has begun to go better with us. Poor Soso! She is having a great deal of trouble in reconciling herself to Alice's death. Almost every night she wakes up from having dreamed about her and goes on crying for hours—it's for this reason that after New Year's I intend to stay at home, since I'm not making enough here (in Minneapolis) to make it worthwhile to give up farming when, in addition, my wife wants me there with her. And besides, with my debts all paid and with a little money left over just now, thanks to our dear parents and friends, I've gotten back into the swing of things. Here, more than anywhere else, money makes everything easier.

Our little Mimi is a most delightful child, and much inclined to prayer and other Christian observances. She often says to me when the church service is over: "Oh! I like so much to hear people praying!" The other evening after saying her little prayer she said to me: "How I love to pray! When I've finished saying my prayers, I always want to say them all over again." And yet she is a nuisance on account of her determination to make her brother's life miserable. It's true that she has a very nervous temperament.

As for our dear Alphonse, his nature is solid gold, always begging us not to punish his sister for picking on him. Because he is too much of a crybaby, I had to punish him severely once when I was at home on a visit; he had gotten into the habit of crying the moment he failed to get his own way; so I whipped him until he finally understood that the more he cried, the more he would be punished, and in fact this cured him completely—at least for as long as I'm there. But after that whipping the dear boy didn't want to come near me, realizing as he did how naughty he had been; but wherever I went he followed me with his eyes, and his expression was so loving that I took him in my arms, and for a long time he just clasped his arms [me serra le cou] around my neck without being able to speak a word. Unlike Mimi, he drops off to sleep right after supper and wakes up around half-past five in the morning and talks to himself in his bed until his sister wakes up. He doesn't take much interest in religious life; about all he thinks about is tying strings onto everything and driving his horses. His health is excellent.

I'm not going to accept any more public appointments.[4] The pay is no more than what a common laborer earns, and you make enemies and trouble for yourself. In many parts of this country people make it a practice to defy the authorities who ordinarily— not wanting to incur the enmity of their close neighbors—let them get away with it. Cutting timber on government land, working on Sunday, refusing to pay dog license fees, and so forth, were becoming more and more common, and I put a stop to it in spite of several people's threats: I had several dogs killed. This threw a scare into the dog owners, and at present all goes well. The odd thing is that all these people are glad to see me when they meet me during my visits home.

I assure you that it gives me a great deal of pleasure to find that I'm being so well received in Minneapolis. If I were not so reserved, I'd have made a lot more friends. Furthermore, I can listen to music, which is something we don't have at home. Just as soon as we can afford it we're going to buy a melodium,[5] as much for ourselves as for the sake of the children. The latter have been having a marvelous time—they came here with Soso to have their pictures taken, and they saw the falls of the Mississippi, the woolen mills, the sawmills, the bridge made of wire cables, etc., etc. Since we have friends here and drive our own horse and buggy, the expense amounted to nothing but the loss of time coming into town, which is very good.

As for myself, I had come both to give lessons and to run the agency for my patented beehive; but seeing that those who were to have furnished me the means of going ahead are abominably slow, I've decided not to wait for them any longer, so I'll give up the few pupils I have; I get very bored in my spare time, not being able to find suitable work, considering my health. . . .

I plan to leave tomorrow morning (Saturday, the sixteenth) to see how my family is getting along, so I will end my letter here.

Theodore Bost

# XIV

# Trees and Bees

Forced to recognize that heavy farm work was beyond his strength, yet unwilling to give up the farmer's way of life which he loved, Theodore kept trying to find some rural occupation that would bring in enough money to support his growing family without bringing on lengthy spells of physical exhaustion. For a while he had thought that the lime quarry might allow him to combine light farming with managing a business. He was able to earn a little money by working for the town as a tax assessor and by giving French lessons in Minneapolis. But beekeeping and the complementary occupations of fruit-grower and nurseryman turned out to be the most successful of his various sidelines. Since his early adventures as a gatherer of wild honey, he had been interested in bees. The reader will recall that after cutting down his first "bee tree," he had wanted to domesticate what remained of the swarm. We do not know whether he ever carried out this plan—probably not, because for the next several years there is no mention of bees in the Bosts' correspondence. But, as we have already seen, Theodore learned in 1865 of a greatly improved patented beehive, and was soon busy selling "rights" to make these new hives to his neighbors, at the same time using the enforced leisure of the Minnesota winter to build large numbers of them for his own use. The income from these activities was to prove a lifesaver in years of crop failure (particularly during the grasshopper plagues of the 1870s), and yielded many welcome "extras" in normal years.

**Theodore to his parents**

Excelsior, Hennepin County
Minnesota
March 18, 1866

Dearest Parents:

You know that we had debts of $100 and that the cost of living in this country is so high that we couldn't see how we were going to survive, considering our bad crops. Well, right now our debts are paid, and I am about to plant $33 worth of trees. I've made

268

$200 worth of beehives for my own use, and I think I'll be able to make enough more of them to enable us to live well this summer and, if it pleases God, to put a little money into machines to make the hives. Everybody wants to keep bees, but few people invest enough to get good hives, and as a result the bees do nothing but multiply without ever making much honey; and the same people lose their bees in the wintertime because they have no way of opening the hives to inspect them. Hence we have good hopes, although this year we don't yet have enough bees to make the business really efficient.

The agency I have, dear Mother, amounts to this: you understand that patented articles cannot, as a rule, be made or imitated by anybody. But things made of wood, which are heavy and bulky, cost too much to ship from a factory, so the owners [of the patent] sell the right to make and use their patented articles. Thus the proprietors of my hive sell to any individual the right to make and use their hive for $5; the buyer can then make hundreds of them for his own use. This is called an *Individual Right.*" At present, King, the owner of the hive, in order to make money more quickly, sells to whomever he wishes the right to such and such a town, county, or state, and whoever buys this concession has an exclusive privilege of selling rights to individuals [in his area]. Since I was the first person in Minnesota to buy a *county right*, I was able to get it for $10, and if a hundred people want to copy my hives, that will bring me $500. Up to now, I've sold only five or six ($30), not having tried very hard to do so because I want to get a good start with my own bees before other people get ahead of me. Now, in addition to Carver County, which cost me $10, I act as King's agent, selling [rights to] towns or counties for him, giving him 40 percent of the proceeds and keeping 60 percent for my pains. I had found a buyer for Hennepin County for $70, of which $42 was my own share; but then I decided to keep that county because it would cost me only $28, so I now own the right to sell the hives in Carver and Hennepin counties, and I think the first [individual] right I sell in Hennepin will be to a marble cutter so as to get a stone to put on the grave of our dear child. So it is that on this earth everything is mixed—the right to build houses for bees is linked with a monument to mark the house of the dead.

I think I'd rather be in France, and yet it seems impossible as things now stand for us to leave Chanhassen. Part of our hearts would always remain here.

I will end this letter by telling you that in two weeks we are to have another election and that I shall refuse to accept any office. It would bring me nothing but trouble with a lot of low Germans who in Europe would speak most respectfully to a magistrate, but who don't want any law at all [in this country]. The salary, incidentally, is the same as the wage of someone hired to load manure, and I would prefer to do the latter.

Good-bye, may God bless you. Greetings to all the brothers, relatives, and friends.

Your Theodore Bost

**Theodore to his parents**

April 20, 1866

Dearest Parents:

Our bees, smelling the spring air, were making a fine uproar in the cellar. So we took them outdoors last Saturday evening, and on Sunday we watched all of them leave their hives, where they had stayed since the first of November. A day or two before that, Soso and I had driven the bees out of one hive, cut off all the shelves of honeycomb, which we put into frames, and then we put these frames into one of our new hives. This spring we intend to put all of them into our good hives so as to have no more difficulties with hives that can't be opened for inspection.

I didn't lose a single one of my hives this past winter, although everyone else lost a great many. This fact doesn't prove that I have a lot of skill, but it does encourage me with respect to the future; and since my new hives will allow me to know what's going on inside, I hope I won't lose any bees.

For two weeks, I haven't been feeling very well, which I attribute to getting my feet wet all the time after having been able to keep them dry for seven months; on top of that, the false accusations and the unpleasantness I've had in connection with our township's buiness have caused a recurrence of my headaches. As for these accusations, Powers and I have convened a meeting of the whole township at which the man who falsely accused us has promised to make a complete retraction. In the meantime, this has caused a big stir in all the villages around here, and it is all very disagreeable, especially because our neighbors are more than happy to hear bad things said about Christian Republicans. If it were not essential for me to complete my term of office in order to protect the interests of our Republican party, I'd have resigned my [township] office last spring, but then all the German scum would have elected a man who has no principles in my place. They have beaten us 60 to 12, but next week we think we'll beat them, and in any case we'll give a few of them a good trouncing. The whole thing started because I insisted on enforcing a law, which is something the chief officers of other townships in this county didn't dare do. Since I did this, the other towns in our county began to do the same. All these are nothing but petty annoyances, but a person doesn't like to be accused of being a forger, a thief, etc., when he was only trying to do his duty. My Democratic neighbors are paying no attention to party lines in this matter, and they'll support me and vote for our party on this occasion. If it were not for the great principle that one can only raise the masses and the dregs [*la masse et la crasse*] of society to a higher level by teaching them through experience to govern themselves, a great many people in this state would favor excluding the dregs of the old country from voting in this one where ignorant foreigners make up nine-tenths of the support for slavery and Catholicism in the North.

We were very sorry to learn of John's illness. What an iron constitution he must have! May God preserve him, for his "Family"[1] must have great need of him, though of course God knows what is for the best.

Everyone here greatly admires Eugénie [John Bost's wife], that is, they admire her photograph.

But it's time to go to church, so I will close this letter and give it to our minister to mail in Excelsior. You know that our great struggle against slavery goes on in Washington "by civil means" ["*civilement*"], no longer with guns and knives. May God protect the right! Good-bye, dear Parents. God bless you.

Theodore Bost

## Sophie, then Theodore, to the elder Bosts

July 1, 1866

Dearest Father and dear Mother:

Our letters have crossed in the mail. . . . We wrote to you, I think, just after we'd gotten our first swarm of bees, and since then I believe we've received a dozen. There are twenty-seven in all and we still expect several more. The bees keep up a continual buzzing, and I very much enjoy watching them at their work; being scarcely able to work myself, it should make me ashamed to see all these little creatures so busy, but sooner or later I hope I'll get a little more of my strength back and in the meantime I'm very thankful that I've always been fairly well. Dodo was so sick—but now it's my turn to drag myself around, and they are all telling me to be patient and careful, two qualities that aren't part of my nature.

But I really wanted to talk about the bees, and about Theodore, who takes more and more pleasure in doing whatever has to be done for them. He was just getting ready to go to Minneapolis when the mare got sick, so he wasn't able to go until last week, but he has managed to sell a few hives and to earn a little something as agent, and the dear boy has set almost all his earnings aside to insure his life in his wife's favor (for $1,000—that is, 5,000 fr.). I almost scolded him for it, and the next day in Chaska he bought me a little machine for wringing out the wash—something I didn't scold him for, because wringing clothes is becoming almost impossible for me to do,[2] and these machines pay for themselves in a year by saving wear and tear on clothing.

So you see, dear Parents, that we've done a lot this year: we've planted 140 [fruit] trees, . . . made all these fine beehives, and so on.

You won't find this a very good photograph [of the new house], considered as a work of art, but you can get a good idea of what the house is like, and that's the main thing. You have to be a little patient to see all the details—and the beehives, one of which can be seen quite well; Theodore and Mimi [are] right behind the hives; [you see] the horse and buggy with a man by the horse's head, and Alphonse (looking like a little monkey) on the seat, Marie with her curly locks standing in the kitchen door, and Soso, all dark, sitting on the porch; the old house is partly visible at the left and also part of the two big oaks that give us shade on the west side. As a whole it gives a reasonably good idea of our little abode and will give you as much pleasure to receive as we have in sending it.

With many loving kisses,
Your daughter Sophie

Dearest Parents:

Here is a picture of our beautiful new house. We didn't want to miss the opportunity of having it taken at a third of what it would have cost us if we'd had it made by one of the local photographers, and since we seem to be prospering, we view this expense almost as an obligation, thinking that when so many of our brothers and our parents have made sacrifices for us, they would be very pleased to see how well we're doing.

Three days ago I sold the first honey of the season at thirty cents a pound: fourteen pounds of honey from a swarm only six weeks old that had already filled its hive, that box, and half of another. They don't all do as well as that, but we see that we're going to be able to buy the new clothes we need and more lumber for next year. We've just had the rain gutters installed all around the house, had the cistern rebuilt, built (by yours truly) a kitchen, all of these being outlays one doesn't have to make every year. And then in one hour of work [on beehives] I made enough money to pay the premium on a life insurance policy for $1,000.

We succeeded quite easily in refuting the accusations that had been made against us for our conduct of public affairs, and those who now hold our offices are very sorry to be where they are, all the more so because we give them very little help and keep the point of the sword at their backs so as to teach them to be more careful about making such accusations against us.

Good-bye, dearest Parents. May God be with you.

Your
Theodore Bost

**Theodore to his parents**

T. Bost
Excelsior, Hennepin County
Minnesota
Easter, April 21, 1867

Well, dear Parents, here it is Easter Sunday, but still no grass and no flowers to hide eggs in, no jonquils, no hyacinths or narcissus, nothing but mud and, in a few specially favored spots, ice and snow.

Everything is very late this year. The willows have only just started to flower, which is a setback for us because their blossoms provide a lot of honey for our bees.

Now to answer your questions. Our twenty-two best swarms were completely covered up and out of sight according to the best recommended practice, but that doesn't seem to work here. In an ordinary year they do very well when the autumn is dry, but this year they sustained a great deal of damage, though nowhere near as much as those I had left outdoors. We'll begin again with twenty-five to twenty-seven hives, almost twice as many as we had last year, and this time the bees are all in our own good hives. We sell almost all our honey in boxes (very pretty) and haven't had to touch our reserve honey for our own use; instead, we've taken honey from inside the hives for the family. If we have a good year, I think we shall find a good market for our honey, seeing that so many people in this part of the country have lost their bees.

I never owned but 160 acres, that is, a square of land half a mile on each side, which makes one-quarter of a square mile; of that I sold forty acres three or four years ago, but I hope that this fall I can buy another forty acres which will be of more use to me than the land I sold.

We are at a good, safe distance from New Ulm,[3] where they may have had a small Revival, but there are so few good Christian souls that no one goes there. That nest of infidels burned our Savior in effigy a few years ago, expelled from the public schools teachers and pupils who believed in the Bible, etc., etc., and for those very actions, we say, the place was burned and the people massacred by the Indians. Last Christmas two Americans were murdered[4] for no reason at all, hanged and then thrown into the river underneath the ice by the whole population of the village, inspired, as they claimed to be, by their divine inner light. The surrounding American villages were arming themselves in order to wipe them out, but were pacified by promises to the effect that the law would punish the murderers; the trial was begun and it was found that 150 people were directly implicated in the business, but the prosecuting attorney couldn't see any way of getting them convicted because the whole population was guilty, so the matter was allowed to drop. Facts like these do more than dissertations to prove the efficacity of this inner light. The Redskins are, like these unbelievers, at a very agreeable distance from us; it's true there is much talk of a war against them, but there is always more or less fighting going on with one or another of the various tribes.

In my last letter I was telling you about the things that are worrying me. The principal one was the accusations against me and Powers, including thefts and embezzlement of public money, etc., etc., which our accusers said they could prove from the town record books, then no longer in our possession. Not being a businessman, I thought perhaps I might have made some mistakes in our complicated bookkeeping, but after fifteen months we grew weary of these accusations, which were now taking the form of legal proceedings, so we demanded an [impartial] examination of the books which yielded some results that were not at all pleasant for our enemies. For the eight years when we were "in power," it has proved possible to find only trivial errors (totaling forty cents) in accounts running into thousands of dollars, whereas just in the past year that our enemies have been keeping the books it has transpired that at least $40 have been taken which they will have to pay back. All our neighbors, both Democrats and Republicans, took our side, and we have all contributed to make up a fund of 140 frs. [$28] to defend Powers in a trial which will not take place now that the books have shown which side committed the fraud. The upshot is that this attempt to harm us has, in the end, helped us; but for the past fifteen months a number of people have been looking at me askance. Powers and the county officers have all been my strong defenders, and those who were so delighted to see us in difficulties now look rather foolish.

Greetings to all the brothers and sisters, also to Concorde,[5] Mme. Vaucher, and the rest.

Your son,
Theodore Bost

**Theodore to his parents**

May 31, 1867

Dearest Parents:
Yesterday, May 30, at half past three in the afternoon, Soso gave birth to a beautiful (?) [*sic*] big boy. She is now resting quietly in bed, not having suffered much, though more than she usually does. She had been complaining these past few days of indigestion and back pains, but if it pleases God all these will pass. We're calling this boy Theodore Charles.

It's another one of those [late] springs. True, we've had two days in a row without rain, but here comes another downpour.

The apple trees aren't yet in bloom. The wild plum trees are just beginning. Almost all the apple trees had their roots frozen this last winter and are consequently dead. I've lost several that had at first put out new leaves (the branches being still alive), but they soon withered because there were no roots.

Good-bye, dear Parents. I've just written to Tim. Tell the other brothers [the news about the birth] when you write to them, seeing that I don't have the time just now. When it rains I work on my hives upstairs, and in good weather I work outdoors. I've planted over two acres of corn, about half an acre of potatoes, an acre or so of oats, about half an acre of orchard, and I'm about to sow about three and a half acres to buckwheat.

The weather is very bad for the bees, but God will provide! This discourages a lot of people, though, from buying their own bees, so I'll find it easier to sell my honey.

The children are well. Forgive my writing in such haste—I have a lot of correspondence to attend to.

T. Bost

## Theodore, then Sophie, to the elder Bosts

June 10, 1867

Dearest Parents:

We weren't going to send you this letter for another ten days, but dear Mother's fine letter with the few words added by you, dear Father, made us decide to send it next Sunday. Remember, dear Father, that we no longer expect you to write us letters and that we are completely satisfied with a few words that show you are thinking about us. Be very careful not to go running any more errands in hot weather—we want to have you with us for many more June tenths to come![6]

Our last letter may have caused you some pain, but the bad state of business all over the country and the cold, rainy weather had put all of us somewhat down in the dumps. Recently, though, we've had nearly a week of hot weather which has made everything start to grow and has partly made up for lost time. Some of the oats I had sowed and harrowed by noon on June 4, Wednesday, had already come up in almost all parts of the field by Sunday the eighth, which is only four days, and these same hot days have brought out the blossoms on the plum trees and currant bushes—in June!—and are making almost all the flowers wilt. Another thing that had caused us much sorrow—I'm not yet entirely reconciled to it—was the loss of half of the fine apple trees I planted five years ago. Besides, the bees had suffered a good deal, and in addition the money and credit in our part of the country were in a very bad state; that had an effect on my own business, and it is difficult to acknowledge that God has the right to make the wicked prosper when so many of His children can't make ends meet.

Mother, dear, we did have the books examined just as soon as that could be done; it was necessary for the annual town meeting to decide whether it would be done or not. Those who had falsely accused us now claim that the committee did not do its work as it should have, and they are trying to make trouble for Powers, who is a good Christian and won't defend himself except when he is pressed too hard, never attacking the others. Good old Powers is very lucky that he has a few loyal friends to support him.

The newspapers are having a prodigious amount of fun with the purchase of Russian America.[7]

A law has been enacted which provides that the New Ulm murderers are to be brought to trial in another county. These people have petitioned to be tried in New Ulm, but they've been told "No." I suppose the good Christians, although in a minority there, are more numerous elsewhere. But good-bye, dear Father and Mother.

Your son,
Theodore Bost

## Sophie to the elder Bosts

June 16, 1867

Dearest Parents:

Perhaps it would surprise you to hear me say that all these accusations and lies directed against Theodore have scarcely worried me at all and only to the extent that they got under his skin. To see a lot of rascals attacking a worthy man is pitiable and nothing more. Those honest people who let themselves be taken in will sooner or later come to their senses, and as for the others, they'll go on as before and it doesn't matter much. *"Leave it down"* [Drop it!] [8] is the only thing to do; Theo and our estimable friend Powers will live to see themselves honored by all those whose good opinion is worth having; however, I hope that neither of them will ever again accept a public office, and I think I can be sure that

Theo won't do so because his health isn't good enough to enable him to cope with more troubles than he already has in his own business. It has done him harm to try to do more than that, as we have realized too late. I'm almost afraid to say that Theo is a lot better since his illness last winter, because every time I say something good about his health he loses it. Today he is very tired from his two days of plowing, yet very pleased to have done it, for all our land is now planted to crops; I had expected that a few acres would have to be left fallow, but Old Mike sowed them to oats, and if Theo can in addition clear some land, that will be another little piece we'll have gained. He has arranged things so that he won't have to cut the hay in the marsh, which relieves me of some serious worries because that job has always brought on one of his illnesses and, two years ago, came near to giving him a fatal sunstroke.

Good-bye, dearest Parents, Theo is telling me I must hurry up. Good-bye, little Father, I'm sorry to have to leave you for now. Had I known I never would be able to see you again, I don't know if you'd have succeeded in sending me so far away from you!

Greetings to all the brothers and sisters.

Your most affectionate daughter,
Sophie T. Bost

**Sophie to the elder Bosts**

Excelsior, Hennepin County
Minnesota
Sunday, July 21, 1867

Dearest Parents:

I wasn't the one who was taking my time about giving you this beautiful (?) [sic] big boy;[9] it was he who was in no hurry, for I was all ready and beginning to get impatient two or three weeks before he arrived. But at last he is here, and the pleasure he gives us is difficult to describe! And anyhow, you may remove the "(?)" from in front of [sic] "beautiful boy"! Because in fact he is growing very beautiful—"*a noble boy*," as Mrs. Powers told me the other day. I must admit that he was quite ugly right after he was born. I had been so afraid he might be deformed that I sat up in bed just as Mrs. Maxwell was taking him from the midwife; I saw him and wasn't exactly flattered but was very grateful just the same that he had a human face. Like Mimi, he had got his head squeezed during the delivery; with a good doctor that wouldn't happen, but all the same I should be grateful that I've come through the childbirth in such good shape, apart from that, and that I'm recovering my strength so well even without the care a nurse would be able to give me. My health is excellent, and my beautiful (!) boy is so plump that he is a credit to his Mama. He weighed sixteen pounds at six weeks, and his flesh is good and firm and white and has been that way for several days; he already smiles nicely and makes pretty cooing sounds and funny faces; I'm already looking forward to all the good times we'll have with him next winter.

The other two children were away from home the day I gave birth and were quite surprised when they came home in the evening to find this dear little treasure. Mimi's first response when she found her voice was to shout: "Oh, Mama! Is it a sister?" and Alphonse, after giving me a long, hard look, burst out sobbing that "he'd always known that if this baby came, Mama would be ill!" But soon he and his sister were both equally delighted, and now I don't know what they'd do without this little brother. Theodore has also concluded that his son shows good promise for intelligence and beauty, and as for myself, this child makes my heart warm again and gives back to me a little of the joy that little Alice took away with her, even though during the first few days after his birth it seemed to me that this new baby was more likely to reopen the old wound.

We are very glad to have some slightly more cheerful news about dear Father's health; we've worried a great deal since getting your latest letters. We know, dear Father, that it's really selfish of us to want to keep you here with us on earth, but our hearts don't know how to reason and the thought of losing you is terribly painful. In spite of being far away from you, as long as you remain here below we'll always feel less lonely in our exile.

Theodore has told you something about his health. It's very hard to bear when a person has to try harder and harder to convince himself that he can't trust in his own strength and that a few days' work will put him flat on his back once again . . . but in this as in all things the Lord knows better than we do what is good for us: perhaps He doesn't want us to succeed according to the ways of this world until after we've given up wanting to.

You may well say, dear Mother, that Theodore doesn't let himself get discouraged easily! I think he's sublime! I think if it had been me I'd have pulled up all the rest of the vines; but he just goes quietly to work replacing the dead ones [that had frozen]. I do very much regret the loss of those well-grown apple trees that everyone admired so much, and as for myself I don't have much confidence in the half that have survived—the disappointment is only postponed to some later time! But the crab apples do seem to be trying to survive; the apples are small, but they have a good flavor and the trees bear enormous quantities of fruit while still quite young—in a few years we should have a lot to sell. Theo is trying to make the most out of the land he has, and he also wants to get more income from those things that don't require too much hard labor—orchards and beekeeping are less exhausting than wheat and corn, which my poor husband is not up to growing, at least not enough to sell, for a long time to come.

We have to go now and have our Sunday "lunch," and then get the children ready for Sunday School and church: we have a very fine day for it, the second time this summer that we've had good weather on a Sunday. Theodore isn't feeling well enough to go, and I'll have to stay home on account of the baby; besides, it's necessary for someone to stay here to look after the bees—as soon as they've finished swarming, I plan to take Dodi [the new baby, Theodore, also called Doddy] to church, which is the custom here.

**Theodore to his parents**

> Excelsior, Hennepin County
> Minnesota
> September 15, 1867

Dearest Parents:

I'll answer the questions Mother asked that apply to me, and Soso will answer the others.

We have fifty-seven hives, including the four I am going to trade for a horse. I'm thinking of selling two more, and there will be a few that I'll break up, taking their honey and distributing the bees to other hives that are short of bees. We've produced more than 900 pounds of honey, a very good harvest, considering that in the spring all the hives I had were weak. The hives are almost all full of honey. Since I sold almost all of it for thirty cents [a pound] (in our paper money; the equivalent of twenty-two *sous* in yours), you can see that, thanks be to God, we've done very well for ourselves this year. But it takes a lot of money to put into the business and to make both ends meet, and we are always very happy when we can make a profit and improve the house and provide everyone with warm clothing. During the basswood [flowering] season, the beehives yielded a fourteen-pound box every ten days, and if I had put out larger boxes, they would have done still better, but we've done very well anyhow. My hive has attracted a lot of interest this year, and I'm counting on selling many "rights" in the next few months. The basswood honey is beautiful as can be, nearly as clear as crystal. Incidentally, since we were unable— as we had so much wanted to do—to send you a box of this honey, I've filled one of the honey boxes with a large number of pictures of Minnesota—views of Minneapolis, the Mississippi in winter and summer, pine forests with lumberjacks, the falls of Minnehaha— six of each, and if any of you finds he has a double, you can exchange. You'll see that there isn't anything exceptionally beautiful, except for the falls of the Mississippi, which are very striking this year because of the high water. This spring there were such cloudbursts that the banks beside the falls were carried away, so the falls receded some seventy feet as a result of this washing. Fifty million [board] feet of pine went over the falls instead of being held back by the "booms," which is a big loss for the Minneapolis people.

We have painted the hives in four or five different colors so that the bees can tell them apart. . . . we have Italian bees, which have three yellow stripes on their abdomens; they are said to be better than the other varieties, but up to now they've cost me more than I've gotten out of them. We'll find out next year what they can do. I'm going to put all my hives in the cellar; there they'll be warm and I can keep an eye on them; I have no way of making a [special] cellar for them this year; that will be something to do next year if God pleases to preserve them for us.

When I said that in the wintertime people here [do little except] keep warm and visit the neighbors, I meant that in addition to taking care of the animals, cutting and splitting wood (which is no small matter), selling one's grain, making trips to the mill, etc., etc., one finds a little time to go visiting. The agricultural papers recommend more and more that one should work hard when there is a lot to do, and then exchange visits when there is time. Remember that all American farmers live a half-mile (more or less) away from each other and that they have only a few opportunities of exchanging and comparing their experiences. Besides, we have two months when the weather is so cold that one becomes utterly exhausted working outside.

Today I finished putting everything in order upstairs so as to get to work again making beehives. Since there are about sixty different sorts of boards, nails, pieces of glass, etc., in a hive, it's necessary to keep your workshop in the most perfect order possible, and everything upstairs is now very pretty to look at. I still have to make about seventy-five hives for myself in addition to "keeping ourselves warm and exchanging visits."

For the last two weeks the bees have stopped working inside their boxes and have even removed a part of what they had put into some of them; if we don't have any more warm weather, I'll put them all indoors in a day or two.

# XV

# Alphonse Bonjour

Despite several recurrences of his back trouble and complaints of pain in his left side—probably caused by his hernia although diagnosed by a local doctor as "ossification of the heart"—Theodore seems to have enjoyed better health in the late 1860s. We find him taking time off from his farm chores to attend fairs, at first as an exhibitor and promoter of his patented beehive, then as an organizer and official of the Carver County Agricultural Society. His bees continued to prosper, and he began to realize some profit on his orchards and on the sale of nursery stock. In close alliance with his close neighbor and good friend George M. Powers, Theodore became active in local politics as a Radical Republican, holding minor offices and working for the election of Grant. He was also a strong supporter of Ignatius Donnelly, that stormy petrel of Minnesota politics, as we know from a letter dated September 7, 1869,[1] in which Theodore promised Donnelly his support while regretting very much his inability to attend the forthcoming State Convention—". . . . but I am hard up and have to stay at home."

But the family's affairs were changed more dramatically by the sudden arrival of Sophie's brother, Alphonse Bonjour, recently back from nearly twenty years in Australia. Minnesota appealed to him, and while looking around for a place of his own he willingly took over much of the heavy farm work.

**Theodore to his parents**

Excelsior, Hennepin County
Minnesota
October 25, 1868

Dearest Parents:

By the time this letter reaches you our elections will have taken place, and, God willing, our next President will be Grant and our Vice President will be Colfax, a strong Christian. The previous elections show that the current has been setting in their direction.

It always surprises me to find myself on the same side as the majority. I believe the majority has come over to my side.

But I was forgetting to tell you that I've been to the Minnesota State Fair, held in Minneapolis, and that I won the prize for the best beehives and another for the best honey. My apples, though they didn't win a prize, were much admired. I took them afterward to the Carver County Fair, and there they took second prize. I received many favorable comments in the newspapers for my other farm products, which made me happy on your account. People are beginning to pay a little attention to T. Bost, but as soon as a person emerges from the crowd he arouses jealousy, and if ever you see me in such a position you may be sure that someone else has put me there and that I did not put myself forward.

Furthermore, I don't want to get involved with anything but farming. I am Vice President of the Agricultural Society of Carver County. In another year we'll have a splendid fair in our county. This year was the first one we've ever had, so nothing was well organized and the officials weren't at all popular. The prizes I won in Minneapolis were $5 and $2, besides which I received a certificate with the first prize. The two children were with me all four days of the fair, and Alphonse slept one night on a haystack outdoors and two nights in a barn in all his clothes. They had a wonderful time. So did I, although I had to spend a lot of time talking with people who came up to look at my beehives or my apples. I had a ticket that allowed me to go out and come in again without paying, thanks to a highly placed friend. We saw a large number of very valuable animals that have been imported by a prominent politician who is spending for our benefit as well as his own the money he has stolen from us. Although I'm keeping only a few animals, I intend to have nothing but good ones, and when I'm in a position to buy some I know now where to find them.

Soon the bees will be going into the cellar. I've lost a lot this fall, and not many hives have any honey to spare; many haven't even made quite enough [to carry the bees through the winter]. But God may well give His protection to the few that I have, and if even half of them are still alive next spring it will still be a great many more than we had last year when we did so well.

Taking everything into account, we are more encouraged than otherwise, and we hope to have more of everything to sell next year. It's amazing how we've been able to get along on so little this year.

**Theodore to his parents**

T. Bost
Excelsior, Hennepin County
Minnesota
November 21, 1868

Dearest Parents:

I think I've told you I won a first prize at the Minneapolis Fair. Right now I'm competing for another prize: an essay contest on bees for which there is a rather large prize. I have no idea how many contestants there will be, and I don't really expect to win, but I am better at writing than I am at cutting cordwood, especially in the evening. Since no rules have been published, I don't know how to meet whatever conditions there may be, but we shall see. At least it doesn't cost me anything to try.

Yesterday I put forty-one hives in the cellar. I still have thirty outside which I'll bring in tomorrow. They are all light, and four or five are very light [compared with their normal weight]. However, I hope to winter all of them. The main thing will be not to set the house afire: the contents of the cellar alone are worth nearly as much as the house itself. The trip to the fair was good for me in that it gave me some enthusiasm and the desire to have some really good livestock. And this experience of having won some prizes has also given me the idea of branching out into other high-quality products.

We subscribe to a political paper that costs a dollar a year; we also get an excellent farmer's journal that comes every month and costs another dollar; and we are thinking of taking a literary magazine (*Harper's Monthly*). Instead of eating the few bunches of grapes we grew, we sold them to subscribe to this magazine, but we're getting low on cash. Still, we must have something to read during our long winters when we have to go for two or three months without seeing one another [that is, our neighbors].

Dear Sister Julie is sending us the religious paper published in Neuchâtel, and this gives us much pleasure, though we often fail to receive the current issue.

Six miles from here we now have a railroad that will soon connect with the Central Pacific Railroad, and nine miles north of us there is the Minneapolis line which extends westward toward the Pacific but has been finished for only sixty miles west of Minneapolis. They are talking of building one from Chaska to

Minneapolis and another one running through Chaska to the southwest.

Greetings to all the brothers.

Theodore Bost

**Theodore to his parents**

St. Paul
February 3, 1869

Dearest Parents:

I have only a few minutes in which to tell you that I've come to St. Paul to attend the meeting of this Agricultural Society. They've awarded me the prize for my essay on bees ($25), but they aren't going to pay me until next August, and inasmuch as the other money that was owing to me was sent (so they tell me) last Saturday and I haven't received any mail since then, I find myself with almost no money in my pocket. But Mr. Rochat, a jeweler, is putting me up at his house, and I'll go home tomorrow as I came here, by the train to Chaska. The trip will have been well worth what it's costing me. I've made the acquaintance of a large number of people, and the trip has given me a lot of pleasure.

We've just had a three-day snowstorm, but the weather is clear and not cold.

The hotel where I had planned to sleep yesterday caught fire and burned down last night; it was a huge building valued at more than $200,000 and was full of guests. It is believed that no lives were lost.

Your
Theodore Bost

**Theodore to his parents**

[Added in margin:]

Although [in our last letter] we didn't mention Papa's birthday on June 10, we never forget to keep a place for him in our hearts.

Sunday, June 6, 1869

Dearest Parents:

It was just eleven years ago yesterday that we were married in St. Paul, and on a Saturday too. Just think of all that has happened since then! And how much our lot has improved! I told myself then that I would willingly work very hard for ten years if I could enjoy an easier life for the rest of my days, and everything seems to indicate that the years to come will be less hard. With fruit trees of all kinds, a garden in good order (we even have asparagus!), enough grapevines for our own use, plum trees so fine that tree nurserymen have been asking me for cuttings, an excellent house, an even better wife, delightful children, and about sixty hives full of bees—who wouldn't be happy? And I can say that I am even happier than I deserve to be. There are only two things I still desire: one is a visit to all my relatives, especially the old people, and the other is better health.

Our excellent and well-loved minister, Mr. Sheldon, preaches [in Chanhassen] only every second week, though he continues to attend to his duties as minister. He is about to begin a series of talks against rationalism, unitarianism, spiritualism, and all the other "isms" that agree in rejecting the Bible and—here as well as in Europe—have no other effect than to lead weak souls into worldliness and indifference. The treacherous and hypocritical manner that is typical of ninety-nine out of a hundred of those people ought to be enough to open everyone's eyes if men did not have a natural preference for darkness over light. A minister in Excelsior, who claims to belong to our church, who held an important post in our schools for two years and officiated as one of our number, confessed when he was almost at death's door that he was a rationalist, a spiritualist, etc., etc. Another (a Methodist) wrote a pamphlet about his dismissal from the ministry, expressing indignation that he had been removed when he had never preached against our Methodist doctrines but had only spoken as an individual—I thought his protests were ridiculous. But something I don't understand is the enthusiasm so many people still have for books like Renan's *Life of Jesus* and those very new ones (as if there were any such thing) that give all sorts of reasons for not believing in the Bible and in Jesus! As if the Jews in Jesus's own lifetime hadn't brought forward all these very same objections.

But all these doubts and all these underhanded books and conversations, although in the first instance they only cause harm, really do nothing [in the end] but make more fully apparent the beauty and truth of the Bible. And the fact, which is every day more evident, that those who turn away from the Bible soon abandon also every Christian principle and go off in pursuit of worldly things and the service of Mammon, proves to all well-intentioned people that there is a fundamental error in their reasoning, however estimable may be some of those who are advancing such arguments. A certain confirmed rationalist whom we all know[2] has written to me after recovering from a grave illness, but he has convinced himself that his ideas are so splendid and so much better than ours that he'll never condescend to give them up in favor of simple faith in Christ, and I won't write to him anymore because it would be useless. His son has been writing for a Red newspaper in France and has had to go into exile for political reasons; he has died in the army. I feel sorry for the poor old man—his last letter didn't give the impression of a person who is happy.

In closing, my heartfelt love. Best greetings to John and his wife.[3] And likewise to all the brothers and sisters-in-law.

Your very devoted
Theodore Bost

## Theodore, then Sophie, to the elder Bosts

T. Bost
Excelsior, Hennepin County
Minnesota
August, 1869

Dearest Parents:

Since our last letter we've all been very busy; first, there were the grapes to be picked (thirty-two buckets full) and taken to market; then—hoe, hoe, hoe. Then this gentleman from Alsace[4] decided it would be pleasanter for him and his wife to come and live with us, so we had to go and fetch them and look after them, and in this way the time has passed very quickly. I've gone fishing with him several times, which provided us with a supply of cheap fish and gave me more recreation than I've had for three years. He and his wife are true friends to us and came to us (partly, at least) because they saw we were in greater need of money than the Langdons. He has just gone back to St. Louis, leaving his wife and two children with us for another two months. He and I have had innumerable discussions of religion. He used to be a thoroughgoing rationalist but has since come back to principles that are far more Christian; still, I couldn't restrain myself from telling him that his outlook couldn't bring him happiness. These last few days we didn't do much discussing because it had become pointless. But he is a charming fellow, and we're very happy to have made his acquaintance.

The bees haven't made enough honey for us to have any to sell, which is a hard blow to us, seeing that we have a lot of plans in the works. The most likely thing is that M. Goepp will find me a position in St. Louis as a French teacher. I must earn some money, and I must give my body some rest. If I had a little something in reserve, I'd stay here, but since I don't have enough, this fact, taken together with the state of my health, will lead me to decide to go to St. Louis if I can find a good position with good pay. These bees—or rather the weather—have played a nasty trick on us: though the basswoods were covered with flowers, these had no smell, so I was afraid the bees wouldn't be able to find enough honey to carry them through the winter. Fortunately, the hot, humid weather we've been having for the last month has enabled them to find plenty in the buckwheat, and their hives are now quite full of honey, but their boxes are still empty and the nights are getting colder.

The other plan would be to stay here and work to build up my [beehive] agency and sell fruit trees for other people. If I can put aside about $100 in the next month (and I may be able to do it since I have a few little business matters pending), I'd prefer to stay here. Yesterday I made an agreement with a nurseryman according to which I'll furnish branches and he'll graft them onto the root stock, and at the end of a year he'll give me half of those that have taken; by a year from now this should give me at least a hundred trees to plant; in addition, I am trading cherry seedlings for good apple trees, and with these I can fill in the gaps in my orchard. This afternoon we began gathering our little apples (crabs) which we hope to sell for a dollar a bucket; people use them to make preserves. We expect to have twenty to thirty buckets to sell. Doesn't it do you great honor to have a son who has become so distinguished (!!) in America? In a few years one will hardly be able to sell these apples at such a high price, but then the trees will be yielding more heavily and in addition I hope to improve these trees by grafting onto them other varieties which we are able to obtain each year in our state.

You may be sure, dear Parents, that I won't do anything in haste. But when you pray to God to show you the path, and when He sends you a friend, as He has sent me this M. Goepp who has offered to try to find me a good teaching position, it seems to me that He shows His hand in that.

I'm very busy this evening so I'll close by sending you love from the bottom of my heart.

Theodore Bost

## Sophie to the elder Bosts

Excelsior, Hennepin County
Minnesota
October 23, 1869

Dearest Parents:

I almost forgot to answer your questions. M. Goepp was paying us $14 a week for himself, his wife, and two little girls, and $8 when he's not here. [He pays] in paper money, which isn't worth as much as gold, but it's a good price just the same for room and board. I'd be happy to have Madame and the two children again next summer; as for him, though he was very nice, he was a little demanding and he annoyed Theodore by borrowing his horse and gun and then not taking good care of them. Madame didn't help me at all with the housekeeping, but Marie and I have managed very well. In June and July it would be more difficult because I would have so much to do in the garden and with the bees, but if everything seems promising I'll do the best I can. M. Goepp was talking about sending us his family again during the ten-week [summer] vacation when he wants to travel, perhaps going out to visit California.

You probably know by now that he didn't find a position for Theodore, and although it seemed to us that we ought to accept his offer to look around for one, I am almost thankful to God for having left me my husband. Winter frightens me enough without being left to get through it all alone. M. Goepp's idea was that if Theodore could get a good position in St. Louis, we'd sell our place here and go and settle near St. Louis where I, too, would find some pupils to teach. He was continually telling us, just as many others have, that this was not the right kind of life for us and that it was a pity for us and our children to go on gathering moss here; but then he detests country life (so far as the work goes), and we like it, which makes a great deal of difference.

We are located some two hundred leagues from St. Louis. The steamboats make the trip up to St. Paul in four to five days (the fare is $20). Minnesota is very popular in summer with people from the South trying to get away from the heat, and they come up here on account of our clean air and pretty lakes. A boarding house in Excelsior has had twenty to thirty people for two months or more.

Oh, yes, we make our own candles, but not so many now that we are burning kerosene, and we also make most of our own soap—you have to learn all sorts of trades in this country, and it works out very well too. [You learn] the dyer's trade, for example, and a number of others. This fall, with the help of Mrs. Powers and her sewing machine, I made a suit for Theo; for quite some time I had been making him vests and trousers. I'll be very pleased when I have a machine of my own because that will save me the trouble of having to knit for Mrs. Powers so she can sew for me whatever doesn't have to be done by hand.

Good-bye, dear Parents, and especially my dear little Father. I send you lots of tender hugs and kisses.

Warm greetings to all the brothers and sisters.

Sophie

**Sophie to the elder Bosts**

Excelsior, Hennepin County
Minnesota
February 27, 1870

Dearest Parents:

Inasmuch as Theo has buried himself in his newspaper, I will unceremoniously help myself to some of his letter paper and write for a few minutes while my poor little Albert is asleep. Theo says I'm going to tell you all of his heart-rending story, dear Parents, but [by now] you should have read the letter we just sent to dear Samuel and his wife, so you know that our friend Mrs. Powers has died in childbirth, leaving, besides her five children ranging from three to twelve years old, the little [newborn] triplets who are thus thrown into the world without a mother's care in their infancy. The poor father could surely find people who, for money, would take in these little orphans [*sic*], but that would be a greater expense than he is able to bear, despite his splendid, prosperous farm and all the effort he puts into it.

Anyway, it's some consolation for him that he can place his children with friends; hence we were the first who offered to take one. At first there was some question whether we would leave the care of little Albert to Mrs. Powers's young sister until my health should be somewhat mended since my last illness, but she had to adopt the second of the three babies (who we had at first believed was going to live with another neighboring family). So on the day of his poor mother's funeral we brought home our little adopted son. The poor father was very anxious that we should be the ones to take him, and every morning he sends us a bottle of milk from a cow that has just freshened, and the dear little fellow is doing well even though he has already had one serious illness since we've had him. The loss of Mrs. Powers is a very painful one for us, witnesses as we were to her suffering, her death, and the agonizing scenes that followed. I was deeply affected by the whole thing and at first it made me ill, but I am fast getting back on my feet and I hope that springtime will find me as well as ever and able to take care of my family. The children are naturally delighted with this new acquisition, and when Julie stops going to school, which will be in three weeks, she will take over a lot of the child's care.

I don't know whether dear Mother may not think I'm at fault for taking on another child in this way. My only fear was that he might be a burden to Theo, but I will do my best to lighten it. As for sleeping accommodations, Theo decided right away that he'd sleep upstairs, which will allow him to get a good night's rest and relieve me of the worry that the baby might keep him awake.

Dear Mother, what would our lives be without your long letters? They are like manna in the desert! You were especially good to write when you weren't feeling very well.

Loving hugs and kisses from your daughter,

Sophie

## Theodore, then Sophie, to the elder Bosts

T. Bost
Excelsior, Hennepin County
Minnesota
May 1, 1870

Dearest Parents:

This time we have a real piece of news to give you—the arrival of Alphonse Bonjour nearly four weeks ago. This took us a little bit by surprise, but we're very glad to have him with us. He's a fine big fellow, a very hard worker with lots of experience at most types of farm chores; he shows in his style of working that he's been working hard for the entire fifteen years he has spent in Australia, the last ten years tending grapevines and breaking horses. For the past two years he has been the boss of a big crew of workmen. Naturally he's happy to be with his sister, and although the first days of his visit here the weather was atrocious for someone who had just come from the tropics, he seems to be enjoying himself, finding the neighbors so much more agreeable, polite, and kind than the Australians. He is very nice with Sophie and the children, and there's no end to his consideration for me—he always takes on the hardest part of the work. After his arrival all my plans were upset, and for several days I worked a little too hard; then, having caught a cold, I found myself flat on my back, or rather my side, for three days. Now I spare myself and intend to go on doing so. As for his faults, he hasn't shown any yet. They are hard drinkers in Australia, but he says he cares nothing for strong liquor except when he's in the company of those who use it, and so, since neither we nor our neighbors drink any, he isn't tempted. He doesn't even think about it, and up to now I'm very glad to have him here. He likes this country so well he wants to settle down near us.

We've planted about a hundred trees this spring. All my trees are doing well, but since they yielded too much last year there are only a few that will be loaded with fruit.

Alphonse thinks it would be too bad to sell out now, just when I've succeeded in establishing such a fine plantation of fruit trees on my farm. I have to say, too, that our place is delightful now. All the young trees I planted four, six, and eight years ago seem very healthy. Some of them are over ten feet high, and since each one is sixteen feet from the next one, the effect is very pleasing, especially near the house where there are shrubs among the fruit trees. But enough about that.

Soso has plenty to keep her busy, what with the baby, who often gives us more music than pleasure, and, since Marie is away at the Powers' house, she has to do all her own housework and has much too much to do. Her brother's visit—especially since he has just been with her mother and [her sister] Julie—is doing her a great deal of good. The children are happy as can be to have a real uncle in the house.

My friend César Pronier has been named a delegate from Geneva to the Evangelical Alliance [congress] in New York.[5] I'd be extremely happy if he came and paid us a visit so we could talk about the people we knew at the Vauchers', on the way to America, and at the Fivaz'.

Well, dear Father, you were thinking of writing us a little something, weren't you? You know how much it would mean to us, but don't go and tire yourself out with it. May God sustain and bless you both, dearly beloved Parents, and give you good health until the time when He calls you home to Him. Good-bye and fondest greetings to all.

> Your most devoted
> Theodore Bost

Dearest Parents:

Everything is so pretty all around here, it's a treat for the eyes and the nostrils! In the evening we sit on the piazza until around eight o'clock, resting and talking. Then the children are put to bed, and my two men read by lamplight or talk while I get everything ready for the night and take care of dear baby. The truth is that we've leaped from winter to summer with an interlude of only four or five wretched days. My brother is very happy to be here, seeing that Theodore needed exactly the kind of help he can give him. He came from Berne where he was very bored, not yet knowing whether he'd go to Australia, California, or America, and I'm delighted that he decided to come first to make us a visit; we'd like to think he might be able to settle near us, and our Julie especially is very anxious not to lose her uncle again.

> Good-bye to everybody,
> Your Sophie

**Theodore, then Sophie, to Jenny Bost**

> T. Bost
> Excelsior, Hennepin County
> Minnesota
> August, 1870

Dearest Mother:

I have only a few minutes in which to reply to your good letter of August 8 and 9, having decided to take the two oldest children for a cruise on Lake Minnetonka on a steamboat operated by an excellent Christian.[6] He charges five cents per child for a trip from one end of the lake to the other (six miles) and back again, a special rate for those who attend Sunday school. This will be the first time our children have ever been on a boat or train, and if I am to go away, I want to give them this good time. This trip to Europe which has seemed for so long an impractical dream will now apparently take place after all! Shall I then have the joy of seeing and embracing you again? There's no question I'd much prefer to make the trip with Soso and the children, but that's out of the question for the time being. We shall have to live out our lives here, according to all indications, and we can be quite happy living here. As for the trip, I think it would be best to come this fall as soon as I've been able to put everything in order and attend our local fairs—you know that I'm an officer of two agricultural societies, and my duties are heaviest during the fall fairs from September 15 to 25.

Hastily, then, dear Mother (and dear Father too if you read him this letter), may God grant that we shall see one another once again.

Theodore Bost


Dearest Mother:

You are really kind and generous, dear Mother, more than we had any right [to ask] or any thought of expecting, and if Theo accepts your offer (which he still hesitates to do), it will only be because he believes it his duty to do everything he can to regain his health. When we received your last gift, we did indeed tell one another that "this is all Mama can do or ought to do for us," and we thought, as you know, that we would put the money to one side to see if there might not be some way we could put some of our own with it. But since we wrote that letter, the bees have produced hardly anything at all, our crops (except the corn) have been worse than miserable, the rain came much too late for the wheat and especially for the oats, so that we had made up our minds to give no further thought to Theo's making a trip to Europe. He was going to go the following week to St. Paul to see whether he could arrange for enough lessons—and besides, I thought that with your deplorable war, the details of which we have followed with interest and anxiety, you might not find that this was a very opportune time.[7] Fortunately, you are far away from the frontier, and I hope Theodore will bring you some consolation too. For the moment, six months are the most our Mimi will agree to, and even that is doubtful—she burst into tears at the first word about his going, and I'm afraid we shall have some more of these emotional scenes right up to the moment of his departure. So it goes! God will provide. I still can't fully realize that this immense change is going to take place in our lives which have been so quiet up to now. I can't let my thoughts dwell from an instant on my desire to accompany my husband, or else I'd be incapable of thinking about anything else. Good-bye, dearly beloved Mother. May the Lord bless you and give you back in happiness all you have done for your children!

Your tenderly affectionate and grateful daughter,
Sophie Bost

# XVI

# Theodore in Europe

Theodore's back pains and headaches seem to have taken a turn for the worse in 1870. Writing on July 8 to his parents and Timothée, he speaks of "several relapses." Having no confidence in the local doctors, he had written to his friend Goepp in St. Louis, who in turn had consulted medical men, including a leading specialist, there. "After several letters asking about my symptoms, they decided their first impression was correct—it's an inflammation of one of the membranes in the spinal column, which causes secondary disorders, including these fierce headaches. They say the whole trouble is due to my getting too exhausted and that I must quit work altogether and, if possible, take a sea voyage. [I must] let the nervous system recover, not bend over to do anything that would produce fatigue. But the good people have forgotten to send me the money to pay for this voyage. . . . [Letter of July 8, 1870, to his parents and his brother Timothée.]

Jenny Bost decided that somehow the money must be found to bring Theodore to Europe for further medical consultations and treatment. She dipped into her own savings and persuaded Timothée (whose iron and steel business in Glasgow had made him a fairly wealthy man) to put up the rest. Alphonse Bonjour urged Theodore to go, and agreed to carry on the heavy farm work in his absence. It was arranged that Theodore would pay him the going rate of wages when he was able. And Sophie undertook to look out for the bees.

**Theodore to his parents**

Glasgow
Friday, October 28, 1870

Dearest Parents:

I'd have written as soon as I arrived here if Tim hadn't done so, but you can easily understand how tired I was. May God be thanked for His protection during this voyage and also for the great pleasure of seeing Tim and Mary again, and later . . . the rest of the family. Do you know that it was only by mistake that I fixed upon the tenth rather than the third for my departure? Once the date had been set, I didn't want to change it—but if I had left a week earlier, on the third, I would have been on the boat that went down with the loss of all on board except for one sailor. When I heard this news, we were still on the high seas, and I was filled with terror at the thought of what might have happened to my dear little family if they had lost me and with gratitude to God for having protected me in this way. But my first emotion was one of deep regret at having caused my wife and children to run such a risk.

Still, how happy I am to be with my brothers, sisters, nephews, and nieces, and especially to be able to see you again, dear Father and Mother!

But now that I'm here, I'm not very sure just how to go about getting to where you are, and I don't know how I'll be able to reach a decision. On the one hand, I'd like to hurry immediately to your home and spend several months there resting; on the other hand, I'd like to see my brothers and say hello to them first, then go to you to get back on my feet, stay until I'm feeling really well, and then leave to go directly back to my family in the West.

And from still another point of view, I was delighted to be able to go and spend two or three weeks gallivanting around Switzerland. In America every time I thought about doing that it made the blood run faster in my veins.

I have just about decided with Tim's help that perhaps the best thing would be to go to Le Havre and from there to travel by train, swinging around through western France, just what I had already thought of doing if it hadn't been for the difficulty of being arrested as a Frenchman or a spy.[1] If God wills it, therefore, I may be with you in about two weeks.

I still have a lot of letters to write to other people, so for the present, dearest relatives in La Force, I must send you my love through the mail.

Your son and brother,
Th. Bost

## THEODORE IN EUROPE

**Sophie to Jenny Bost**

December 28, 1870

Dearest Mother:

I can't bring myself to realize that my husband is under your roof! It seems so strange! From time to time I do really grasp it, and tears of happiness fill my eyes: my poor husband whom I love so much, who has wanted so badly to see you again—there he is, face to face with his mother and father. He has seen so many of his brothers again, he has revisited Switzerland, my family, my friends. Everywhere his arrival has been a festive occasion; everyone loves him so much. From all sides they write things about him that please me so much, and everywhere they are so kind and generous to him and to us here. And then I hear from everyone how lovingly he speaks of his wife and children. Watch out—here come the tears again. Nevertheless, Theo knows how rarely I cry, but since yesterday evening I've been doing hardly anything else; my nerves are jangled; I have a terrible headache. And so, dear Mother, be indulgent as you so well know how to be; take my poor head on your maternal lap and let me cry—it sometimes does a person good, you know.

Well, Christmas has come and gone. Dear Mother, how did you spend the day? And how will you begin this new year that will so soon be upon us? Will there be no glimmer of hope in the dark skies that hang over France? Will you not at last have peace? It seems to me it is certainly high time. Oh! may the good Lord bring about a lasting peace and grant that poor France may rise again from her sufferings more quickly than can be expected from our human standpoint. Oh, may He give us the peace of mind that nothing can take away. This is what I ask of Him for myself, to let me place myself entirely in His hands with complete submission, to accept all He sends me as coming from a Father who chastizes His children in love and not in anger. This is such a consoling thought that it gives me the strength to go forward with renewed courage. He is tender and good in all His ways, don't you think so, dear Mother? And your confidence has never been disappointed. And yet you have had many pains and sorrows! But you are so strong, dear Mother; the Lord gave you so much power over yourself and others! And besides, our lives are all fleeting, and the end draws near. Then we shall all know peace. I know that the Lord will gather me in, though I am but a weak member of the flock, for love of His son.

People have often told me that I'm strong and brave. You now see the opposite qualities in me, dearest Mother, because I can't shake off the melancholy that lies heavy on my heart: hence I can't write you a pleasant, jolly letter to thank you for all your kindness. . . . But just wait till the next one. . . . My head will be feeling better, God willing, and I'll try to say something lively to relieve your loneliness.

But why am I talking about [your] loneliness? You have your son Theo, and not only your son, dear Mother, but my husband, whom I love so much, the dearest person I have in all the world. He's the one I shall tell to cheer you up in my place for this once; another time I'll take on the job myself. He is so good at teasing people and making them laugh—that is, when he feels like it. Get him to tell you some things about our Dodi, that rascal. My brother, who at one time didn't care much for him, has completely changed his attitude and treats him very well, though he doesn't always do as well by my Alphonse, and sometimes it's quite painful for me to have to interfere to get him to take a different tone with the little fellow; and yet I do it, knowing very well that Theo wouldn't want, any more than I would, to have the child's nature soured by unfair criticism or by harsh language to which he isn't accustomed. You can be sure that the dear boy will be happy to have his daddy back in charge of things here! He is shy and a little afraid of his uncle, so he needs his mother to stand up for him once in a while (even though his Mama is not exactly a doting one).

In the evening

Good-bye, dearest Mother. I'll write to you again on New Year's Day, God willing. May the Lord bless and keep you. Goodbye, my dearest Theodore. No one but your wife could send you as much love as I do. Fondest greetings to John and his family. But I beg of you not to show this letter to anyone.

Your Sophie

**Sophie to Jenny Bost**

February 4, 1871

Dear, kind Mother:

I've just written such a long letter to your son Theodore, and it's so late at night, that I have hardly any time or space left over for you, but nevertheless this letter shall not go on its way without a few lines for my mother-in-law. Well, at long last our dear traveler must have reached his destination. I hope he's sound asleep at this moment behind your closed shutters. Soon it will be Sunday, and I'll follow you both to church. Oh dear Mother, forgive me if I speak to you only about my darling! It's just that here I miss him so much, especially at night when everyone is in bed and I feel so lonely—I don't say this to complain or to grumble, but that's the way things are. Oh yes, I must really have loved him to let him go away like this, but then . . . Enough of that. It is sufficient to say I'm very happy to know that my Theo has finally got to your house. How full of joy you must be these days to be reunited with him, a reunion which I hope will go on giving you happiness right up to the last day. And after that, kind Mother, you must let him go away again without too much regret. You've learned to live without him, but there are people here who couldn't learn how to do that. It seems to me that I've been waiting a terribly long time for Theodore to write me a letter from La Force. I've always expected that he would benefit most from his stay there. Oh, may the Lord grant our prayers for his recovery!

I am also very impatient to learn whether your cruel war has finally ended,[2] whether your poor soldiers will be coming home, and all sorts of other matters connected with the war.

Good-bye, dear Mother. Embrace that son of yours who is the dearest being I have in the whole world.

Your loving daughter,<br>Sophie Bost

**Sophie to Jenny Bost**

Saturday, March 25

Dearest Mother:

At last another letter from you. It's something of a novelty, but I don't hold it against you at all for neglecting me a little bit because you are spending so much time on my husband. Once he's no longer there, you'll write to me more often, won't you? We can sympathize with one another then about the need we both have for him, can't we? For I am quite sure, dear Mother, that Theo's coming departure will leave you with a great feeling of emptiness. Isn't it true that there is no ignoring his presence and that he is able to fill a whole house with it? Consequently, how empty our *home* is without him! Everybody we know praises me for my courage in letting my husband go away, and sometimes I feel I'm a silly goose for being so impatient to have him back, thinking of all the reasons I had for wanting him to make the trip. And may God be praised for bringing it about that, despite all the unfavorable or painful things that have happened, his trip should have succeeded so well and that, most important of all, his precious health should have improved noticeably (it *is* improving, isn't it?), that all our brothers and sisters have been so kind and so happy to see Theodore again, and finally, dear, kind Mother, that you are having this fine visit from your son. Twenty years' separation! And you don't think his nature has changed for the worse, do you? When he's no longer with you, you must tell me a little about what you think of him, and whether you can understand how and why his wife loves him so much. Can you love such a man, whom you call a miserable wretch because he wants to chase you away![3] If he comes back here and tries to do that to me, what will become of me? I'll surely accuse you of having spoiled my man after I've had so much trouble bringing him up properly!

Well, however it turns out, we'll be very glad to open ranks and give him back his place in the family. Oh, dear Mother, what a blessing it will be to get him back again! You do understand that, I'm sure. And how grateful we shall be if his health has permanently improved! You must preach Theo a lot of sermons on the necessity of not undertaking any more strenuous tasks. I am so much afraid that when he returns with his strength back, thanks to the good rest he's had, he'll want to use it without any sense of moderation and will cause new injury to his poor back. Am I not right that you would favor our leaving Minnesota? If I weren't so timid, I would certainly say the same, but I think it's possible even here to arrange things in such a way that we can have a somewhat easier life. Anyway, we shall see!

My brother thinks the [fruit] trees are going to be well covered with blossoms, especially the *Fall Stripes* [apples] that suffered some damage last summer. We must hope this isn't its last effort [before giving up the ghost]. I can hardly wait for spring to come, although from another point of view I worry a little: the time will pass more quickly, but there will be more doubts and difficulties. However, since my Theo promises he'll be satisfied whatever happens, I'm not going to torment myself once I've done the best I can. I am so happy Theo isn't distracted by worries about the farm. He does miss his wife and children a little, doesn't he? For that, dear Mother, I wouldn't find any fault with him at all; I'd even give myself a pat on the shoulder with egoistic satisfaction. So let him be easy in his mind about leaving his affairs in my brother's hands and in mine—this pleases both of us.

Good-bye, dear, kind Mother. Give Theo a big hug for his wife and let him give you one for your daughter. My very affectionate greetings to our dear sister Eugénie and her dear husband [John]. Tender kisses to those three delightful children whom Theo loves so much.

Good-bye, dear Father—it's so strange not to be able to write to him anymore. I was deeply touched to learn that he hasn't entirely forgotten me, even though he confuses me with others. And, dear Mother, watch out for my interests when some pretty woman comes to call on you! Here there are quite a few who have the impertinence to await my husband's return with impatience! At least I shall be there to make sure their joy doesn't turn our poor traveler's head!

Your daughter Sophie Bost

## Sophie to Jenny Bost

May 13, 1871

Dear, kind Mother:

I haven't written a word to anybody, not even to my husband—it has been so hot that I'm tired out. But at least it's good to know we've gotten a lot accomplished and that I helped as much as I could. I've even done a number of things my lord and master wouldn't approve of, and for that reason I did them a little reluctantly; but I haven't damaged my health in any way, and it's such a great satisfaction to do all I can so that my Theo will be pleased by everything when he gets here. For that to be so, I should be finishing the last flowerbed at this very moment, a bed of dahlias, and maybe another one for climbing plants, but I'm so tired from painting the dining-room floor that I decided to allow myself an hour's respite before getting our late-afternoon snack. Oh that floor! For a long time now it has been an eyesore to me— the paint all worn off in spots gave it such a piebald look—but now it's beautiful as can be and will be easy to keep clean. I've had so much fun this spring spending lots of small sums of money to make things pretty to look at. So I repainted that floor, something that ought to be done every year, but hadn't been done for three years, and I've also put on some very pretty (cheap) wallpaper in our bedroom and had a rug woven from all the rags that had been saved up for the last two years; I also made some pretty white and rose curtains, a few small decorations that are homemade but came out well, two tables made by my brother which I've covered with white and rose draperies—all this has made me such a lovely little nest that I scarcely recognize it as my own. I've also bought some varnish that I'm going to use to restore the shine to several pieces of furniture—that will make them bright as can be. Haven't I done well, dear Mother? And don't you think that Theo will not be displeased by these things when he gets home?

The more important matters, materially speaking, also seem to be getting ready to welcome him by going well. All the fruit trees are so loaded with blossoms that unless there is some unlikely accident we can expect a large crop. Nothing can be said about the bees until the honey season, as we learned to our cost two years ago, but at the moment they must be rejoicing at the flowering of the fruit trees—in any event, every apple tree is covered with bees, and as soon as the clover blossoms open I'll give them boxes to fill if they please. Then comes the swarming, and this is the time I've been worrying about ever since Theo's departure because it is a very exhausting time, frequently made very complicated by various other tasks—we'll have a large quantity of gooseberries to gather, ten bushels I suppose, and while I'm altogether delighted with this wealth, I'm a little bit afraid that the bees' swarming will interrupt everything and take up all our time. But if God gives us health and strength, all that will be put in good order. My brother is full of goodwill and helps as much as he can with all these little things, but it goes without saying that I don't like to steal his time away from chores that are more important to the farm. . . . But the children will help and I hope very much that with everyone working together we shall be able to do what has to be done. These large green gooseberries ordinarily sell quite well, likewise the currants, and I have an ambition to get all these things out of the way before Theo's return and to pay last year's taxes with the proceeds. That will be a great comfort to him, I'm sure. Our bees will be doing well if they pay Marie's and my brother's wages and give us something to live on this coming year.

Speaking of what we pay Marie, you know that we've never paid her a regular, stated wage, and for this reason I have often managed to get along without her, since I don't presume to have the right to keep her here when she could be well paid for her time elsewhere. But this spring she has had several offers and I fully expected we would lose her, which gave me a real fright, so I asked her to stay on with me and offered to pay her whatever anyone else might offer her. She is perfectly content to stay, and would even stay for nothing, which wouldn't be just; but in any event my mind is at ease so far as she's concerned. As soon as the great springtime rush is over, I shall leave her free to go out and work for other people for a few months, something that always raises her spirits—unless we are fortunate enough to be able to take in some boarders for a while. I'm so eager to earn enough to buy a sewing machine, and you may well believe I need it, since I do all the sewing for the whole family. I don't even speak of buying a musical instrument, which still hovers before my eyes in a far distant future—but for this year I can hardly even dream about anything like that. . . .

Well, my hour's rest is over, and the sandwiches are ready. Good-bye, dearest Mother. What a joy it will be, dear Mama, to get Theo talking about you and all those around you! How impatient I am to listen to his long stories and to get better acquainted with so many of your friends. I know what he'll tell me about poor Father will be really painful to hear. Alas! It's terrible to realize how much he has changed for the worse! But once again I've run out of paper before I've run out of chatter!

Good-bye, dearest Mother. Your daughter sends you lots of affectionate hugs and kisses.

Sophie T. Bost

May 20

I just found a letter from Theo. He's going to stay in Switzerland two more weeks than I had expected, and that doesn't suit me at all. The weight on my shoulders is getting very heavy, and I am impatient to have the master back home again. And on top of everything, the bees! I'm terribly afraid I may lose a large number during these two weeks that are perhaps the most important of the whole year. In short, I'm completely discouraged and depressed. A bad storm forced me to stay in Excelsior overnight. I shall go home on foot, as I came. Good-bye, dear Mother. I'll never let my husband leave home again!

## Sophie to Jenny Bost

June 15, 1871

Dearest Mother:

We're so impatient to have him back here again after these nine months of separation. In my mind an acute anxiety is mingled with the joy of anticipation—from his most recent letters it seems that Theo hasn't benefited from the trip as much as we had hoped. He wasn't able to see Dr. Krieger, which is a great disappointment to me, his back is "still there," and he speaks of just learning to put up with it; once again, he took no more pleasure in the things he was seeing and was full of longing to be home again. All that talk has made my heart sink into my boots. I know only too well how things will work out: after the first few weeks, or maybe months, after his return, the dismal old story of his bad health will begin all over again. But then, "God's will be done!" You and I, dear Mother, so many of our dear brothers, and my Theo himself have done all that was within our power to strengthen the one that's so dear to us. I shall be eternally grateful that my husband has had the privilege of revisiting his family, homeland, and friends! I know the memory of all this will be a great joy to him all the rest of his life, whether it be long or short, and that it will encourage and sustain him for a long time to come. Beyond that—trust in Him who knows better than we do what we need. I fortify myself in all my worries with the thought that the Lord has helped and sustained us all up to this point and that He will do so until the end of our lives.

In the evenings all sorts of thoughts jostle one another in my mind while my three carefree little ones run and play outdoors. And I haven't said a single word to cast a shadow on their joy. The two older ones, Mimi especially, are already too much inclined to be fearful and anxious, and I want this homecoming to be unalloyed happiness. Oh what bliss—to be all together again, to bear all our sorrows and joys together! Living as we have in isolation, I think we depend more on one another than is ordinarily the case. In any event, I know that I can't live any longer without my husband and that he misses me a great deal too. It's even a genuine pleasure to know this, especially now that we expect to resume in the near future all our sweet habits of intimacy. And how I rejoice not to have on my shoulders any longer the full responsibil-

ity for all our affairs, great and small. If I had it to do for a long
time, I'd change a lot of things that I don't want to alter now that
the master is returning, but it's time the master was here to exercise his recognized and indispensable authority. You must surely
understand this, and also how delicate and difficult I've found my
task—isn't that true, dear Mother? I haven't wanted to spoil
Theo's last days in Europe by telling him about all the household
annoyances; and yet I feel that I must beg him not to prolong his
stay abroad any longer than he had originally planned. Otherwise
he would blame me later for having kept him in ignorance of the
need I have for him.

Well, then, here I am in the midst of the bees' swarming; if
Theo were here, he'd surely know far better than I do what needs
to be done. Taking care of seventy beehives is certainly quite
another matter than letting a few hives take care of themselves. I
know enough about it to do pretty much whatever there is to do
for the bees, but quite often I don't know precisely what needs
to be done. So I open the hives and move things around without
difficulty, but that's all mechanical—the true science is more difficult, and that is what Theo understands to a greater degree than
I do; so if I were working under his direction I'd have full confidence that everything would be all right—assuming, naturally, that
it was a good year. Up to now I don't think I have made any major
blunders because I do everything very cautiously, though our tiny
bees have presented me with a fair number of problems. The season has been favorable up to now, all the hives are in good condition, and if we could only get some rain, I would hope for an
abundant crop to gladden Theo's heart and relieve us of worries
about money.

Another "plague of Egypt" has attacked our gooseberries and
currants; the caterpillars have eaten all the leaves off the gooseberries without my being able to do much about it—the bushes are
so thick and so prickly! We've had to pick and sell the berries
while they were still small, so they didn't sell as well as usual. I've
saved the currants by continually picking off the caterpillars; for
several days I did almost nothing else but that, and I had night-
mares about the filthy little beasts. Now the only ones left are in
coccoons and will soon turn into butterflies that will lay their eggs
underground in preparation for next spring. But we'll be there
too! And I've been told about one or two countermeasures that
we're going to try, because it would be too bad to lose all of our

little berry patch. Theo will be happy to see all the vines and apple trees so heavily loaded. The house's surroundings are getting more and more attractive, so I'm not afraid Theo will see anything he can find fault with; and my brother has gone to a lot of trouble to make sure everything looks well cared for. Since a few days ago we've had a pretty little heifer, half Jersey, which Dodo calls his little cow, and I hope the other calf will also be a heifer and that we can raise both of them. Our beautiful big sow, if she has her litter in August, will have all the sour milk she wants because we will finally have two cows again and even three if the bees earn us enough money to buy another.

I was forgetting to tell you something that may interest you, dear Mother: we have eighty-two beehives, and if things continue at this rate there will be over a hundred when Theo gets here — enough to make a whole village, don't you think? If they all were to give us some surplus honey this year, we'd be able to stop living from hand to mouth!!

Don't make fun of me, dear Mama; I'm in such a fever of impatience that it's not very nice any more — a real fever, so bad that I can hardly sleep or eat. I suppose part of it is due to worry about the bees and various other things, some anxiety about Theo, etc. In four weeks, if God pleases, all of this will be over.

Your loving daughter,
S. Bost

## Sophie to Jenny Bost

July 13, 1871

Dearest Mother:

Do you realize that I'm expecting my husband a week from now? More than half a fortnight to languish for him! After all, that's still quite a long time, and it seems to me that the blessed day of our reunion won't ever come. . . . But I tremble with joy when I think that this letter will only be finished after his return. Oh, may God grant that our reunion will be a happy one; we're looking forward to it with so much joy on both sides. . . . For several days I've been unable to eat or sleep on account of nervous fatigue, so I was afraid I wouldn't be able to keep going, but, God be praised, I feel quite well even though my body is very tired; however, that will soon pass despite the fact that my twentieth birthday is so far in the past! Theo will perhaps find me very thin; to my great mortification, everyone tells me I look exhausted, but since my health hasn't suffered, my husband will just have to resign himself to having grown younger all by himself. Oh, let him just come home in better health, and everything will be all right!

Monday, July 17

This is the birthday (ten years old) of our eldest son and more than two, three, or four days until the return of his dear Papa. So time is passing, and today we have put the whole house in beautiful order in anticipation of that great day! If I weren't determined not to let anything spoil this occasion, we would nevertheless be very sad today, dear Mother, for God has judged it good to destroy in a few minutes the work of a whole summer by sending us two days ago, during the night from Saturday to Sunday, a terrible hailstorm that has reduced everything to shreds in a swath a mile wide and I don't know how long. Our farm was at one end of the storm's path, so we didn't suffer as much damage as some others, according to what people tell me. I haven't had the courage to go anywhere to see the destruction, but several neighbors were here yesterday, Mr. and [the elder] Mrs. Powers among others, who have lost all their crops, absolutely all—wheat, oats, corn—all so promising to look at the previous day—and not a particle left. What are they going to do with eight small children! It's beyond my understanding, but they are very calm and resigned, even cheerful. My heart was full of pity for them because I know how long a time it will be before there will be another crop, and when you think that in the meantime they'll have to buy everything! Seed for next year and food for this! Oh, it's terrible! And I was deeply moved by their thoughtfulness in coming to see me as well as by their saying how sorry they were that after all the trouble we've taken to make everything look prosperous for Theo's return a disaster like this should have happened. Yes, I was really downcast too, and yesterday I was very discouraged and worried—nothing for our animals to eat, nor for us . . . and what about our bees who perhaps are not going to be able to find anything from which to make honey. . . .

But this feeling has passed! God will provide for everything! My beloved one will be here, and he must not find low spirits as well as ravaged fields. I have begun to believe that the bees will be at least a partial success since I've seen them working so busily today—something they weren't doing yesterday—and I've also found that the buckwheat, on which they depend in the fall, hasn't suffered as much damage as the rest: it was right on the edge of the hailstorm, and it will be retarded (which is bad enough) but not lost. Our beautiful apple trees have suffered a great deal, less than lots of other people's trees because they still have a good number of apples left on them, while those belonging to our nearest neighbors, the Sarvers—who have lost all their crops—have been so badly injured that they may well die. Just imagine—at the foot of a little slope in our field, hailstones were halfway up to Mimi's knees at nine o'clock in the morning, though the storm, which lasted only ten minutes, had ended at three o'clock. By ten in the morning there was still enough left to fill several wheelbarrows.

Well, now I've told you all about this sad business. I didn't have the courage to do it yesterday because all my strength had been drained away, and the two older children couldn't stop looking on the dark side of things, worrying that we'll all die of hunger next winter. Today, seeing how I go about my household chores, they've recovered their normal liveliness. We still have much to be thankful for, don't you think? We're all still alive and in good health to welcome home our beloved Papa. It really breaks my heart to think how he'll feel when he gets here and sees his fields, etc., in such a terrible state, but there's no help for it, dear Mother. We must be happy just the same, mustn't we? And we shall be, I think. Just let my Theo come back to me safe and sound, and we'll be happy enough just to be with one another. There'll be time enough later on to worry about "What are we going to do?"! Maybe he'll go and teach, or maybe the bees will produce enough for us to live on! Oh, may the Lord just preserve his precious life and grant that we may be quickly reunited!

I'll take leave of you, dear Mother, on this note of hope and will let you know in a few days, God willing, that our Theodore is back home again and that all the tribulations of the outer world will not prevent us from being very happy in our own house! May God grant it! And again, may God grant it!

**Theodore, then Sophie, to the elder Bosts**

July 21, 1871

Dearest Parents:

You see that I've finally arrived at my destination safe and sound, very happy to be back with my dear wife and children after so long an absence. It was the day before yesterday (the nineteenth) that I got here, having spent four days on the journey from New York, including, however, a stopover of twelve hours in Detroit and twenty-four hours in Chicago. I didn't feel very tired at all after this long trip, which shows that my physical strength has improved a good deal.

I had so much hoped and intended to write you a good jolly letter, and I *should* write you one because I've found my whole little family in good health; Soso is a little too thin, but the children are big and plump. However, in Minneapolis I learned that a terrible hailstorm had destroyed all the crops in this neighborhood, that the apples and the apple trees had been destroyed. That was a horrible shock and almost made me want to throw in the sponge, but I finally decided I shouldn't allow myself to be too downcast and instead should let the children, who are already sad enough, see their father with a cheerful look on his face. However, I found my oats cut to pieces; likewise the corn, but still standing though the leaves are in shreds; the potatoes are also in tatters, as is the rest of the vegetable garden, but the apple trees weren't killed although half the apples have been knocked off and the other half have been pretty well spoiled, especially on the young trees. Wasn't it a disappointment to find things in such a state? But it is God's will, and we must learn to submit. Besides, a few hours after I got here, my trunks arrived and I assure you there were shouts of joy and astonishment that would have done your heart good. You see, I had two big trunks filled with presents, and it took quite a while to sort everything out!

I am busy cutting oats so as to have at least a little green straw. I'm leaving the corn as it is to see if perhaps it will recover, but I don't think it will; the only chance is that it may put out a few more leaves and thus provide me with a little more fodder for my animals.

Alphonse is talking of going away to Australia as soon as possible, that is, as soon as he can earn enough money. He thinks he can hire out as a worker in a nursery. With my crops ruined, I have no means of paying him as I ought to.

The bees have had a severe setback in that this storm has stopped the production of honey, but we think we'll be able to carry them over [the winter] all right. I shall probably go to work teaching this winter. But good-bye, dear Parents, and especially you, dear Mother. How happy I am to have seen you again and to have made the acquaintance of so many members of the family I had never seen before.

Good-bye to all my dear friends in La Force, good-bye to all my brothers—I'll write to them soon, but for the moment I must get back to my work. Everything seems to have been so well cared for during my absence, the crops clear of weeds, etc., and then this wretched hail came along and ruined everything!!

Good-bye. Your most devoted and grateful

Theodore Bost

Dearest Mother:

I have only a few minutes, but we'll write to you again soon. Since Theo's arrival, my heart has been so happy and grateful that I almost feel guilty for not being worried about the future. But how can I torment myself when I have my husband back, when God has preserved him from all dangers during his journey, and when I find him looking so much better than when he left? Oh, how good it is to be a family again, to see the father in charge of everything, relieving me of that burden of responsibility.

And what a tremendous number of presents! What an avalanche of joys! How generous you have all been! Dear Mother, I can never find words to tell you how much pleasure this gives us and how useful many of these gifts will be—so many things I'd never think of buying, especially just at present, that have come to us all at one time! Oh, if the hailstorm hadn't come, how light our hearts would be! I suppose you'll say that in this country there will always be something like this! Yes, I've thought that often enough these past few days! But wouldn't it be pretty much the same anywhere? In any case, here we are, so what can be done about it? It's terribly hard to know. All that's certain is that so long as we can't sell we're obliged to stay! As I write I am looking at your beautiful embroidered cushion, dear Mother. What delicate work, so well done and with such nice shadings of color. It's really amazing that at your age you have retained all your sureness of taste, of vision, and of touch. And I am so delighted with it, dear Mother. Theo talks so much about you! And you know with how much love and admiration, not to mention gratitude. It already seems so natural to have him here in the house that I never stop having an instinctive reaction of surprise because he knows so much about you and your doings.

But we must take leave, dear Mother. I don't know what I've written, but you may be sure my heart has been deeply moved by all your kindness.

Good-bye. Lots of tender, warm kisses.

Your loving daughter,
Sophie Bost

# XVII

# Another Alice

During the year 1872 the farm was carried on with indifferent success. There was bad weather, another plague of grasshoppers, a fire, and all sorts of other problems. The situation continued to be aggravated by Theodore's ill health. Only the income from the orchard and the bees enabled the Bosts to make ends meet. They sold 1,000 pounds of honey produced by ninety hives.

One plan after another was tried to bring in more income, including the sale of music boxes sent from Switzerland and of cloth sent from Belgium by Théophile. There was talk of selling the farm and moving to the city where Theodore might be able to earn a living by giving French lessons. But none of these ideas came to anything.

To make matters worse, relations between Theodore and Alphonse Bonjour became strained, so the latter went to live in Excelsior.

As the year 1873 began in this atmosphere of gloom, Sophie knew that another baby was on the way.

Theodore to Jenny Bost

March 15, 1873

Dearest Mother:

It has been only a week since we sent a letter off to you, but I'm writing to say that Soso is ill, and I'm starting this letter now so I can add whatever news there may be as it occurs.

Do you remember the Powers baby that Soso was caring for? We've just heard that he has died, at midnight. This was a hard blow to Sophie, who had gotten very attached to the child, and the effect was to stop her [labor] pains, but she's calmer now. After a beautiful day yesterday, last night was atrocious. It was still snowing hard this morning, and there's a strong northwest wind. Not exactly the thing to cheer a person up.

Yesterday I put my bees outdoors. There aren't many hives that are healthy and at full strength, and all the hives have lost more bees than is normal. I'm not dissatisfied, though, because I wanted to reduce the number of my hives. Apparently a great many have been lost in this part of the country, which will keep the price of honey high enough to make it pay.

We've sent Julie to school. She knows what's going on and had grown so nervous that she couldn't stop crying and was doing more harm than good. Alphonse has the horse all harnessed and hitched up in case someone has to go for the doctor. For the time being, we have a sort of midwife and another neighbor. We had hoped to have Mrs. Powers, but she can't come.

Sunday morning

The baby was born yesterday at eight o'clock in the evening. It's a pretty little girl who's doing well, and Sophie now feels quite well after having been ill for so many months, more than she usually is [during pregnancy]. Her confinements have been quite painful—though few of them are easy! Visitors are beginning to arrive; it's the custom here for people to make a lot of calls on women who have just given birth.

I'm going to write Tim and have just written to Berne. Yesterday we had a letter from Mama Bonjour and dear sister Julie from Berne.

Good-bye, dearest Mother. I'll write again soon, in a couple of weeks, I think, although my existence is very full these days. Warm greetings to John and his family.

Theodore Bost

**Theodore, Sophie, and again Theodore to Jenny Bost**

T. Bost
Excelsior, Hennepin County
Minnesota
April 13, 1873

Dearest Mama:

I promised two weeks ago I'd write you a letter, but one thing or another has prevented me. This last week I've been very busy in Chaska. I was a member of the grand jury, and inasmuch as the judge appointed me foreman of that jury and we had a number of important cases, I'm quite wrought up and exhausted.

It would have pleased John and Elisée to see how severe I was with the German Catholics. You'll recall that I've been complaining that we're under the domination of lawless Germans. For ten years they've refused to prosecute the hundred or so saloonkeepers who sell beer and brandy without being licensed to do so. This time, even though we were opposed by the prosecuting attorney, all the lawyers, all the civil officers of the county, and all the Germans and saloonkeepers, we've spent three days drawing up indictments against several who will have to stand trial, or else they will all have to pay for licenses. All this was supposed to be secret, but the Germans on the jury, for one thing, revealed what was going on, and we could have started proceedings against those people. They knew we were out for their scalps. As for myself, I didn't exactly sit with folded arms, so I'm quite popular in the saloons. Our whole effort may fall by the wayside, but everybody agrees that it will force the saloonkeepers to take out licenses, and that's the most I dared hope for in a county of German Catholics. The next [grand] jury will have our example, and also the rough treatment we've received, to guide them, and I've given the Germans fair warning that I'm going to work for their defeat.

All the same, it's odd to have to fight here against an all-powerful Catholic majority in this county, though not in the state as a whole. The vote [on the grand jury], though there were no religious issues, was exactly split between the Protestants and Catholics, with one Swiss, three Englishmen, two Americans, six Swedes, and two German Protestants against eight German Catholics. It has been a great victory for us. Nobody up to now had dared to attempt it or had had the persistence to stick it out to the end.

I was forgetting to tell you that Charles Boissonnas turned up here a few days after the baby was born. He is much better-behaved than the previous times, willing to do anything, gentle with the children, and, on our part, since he may never come again, we want him to have good memories of us. He is going back to Europe, and his relatives may induce him to stay there.

I've also been very busy with the little chores involved in taking care of the lambs. We have fourteen, and several of the mothers have only a little milk, so we have to nurse their babies until the grass begins to grow. It's delightful to see the little fellows gamboling about, and we all have a lot of fun watching them go about their business in the barnyard.

The bees have suffered a lot this past winter, and all over the neighborhood there has been a strange series of accidents. Mr.

Sheldon has had ten hives drowned in his cellar; Stone had ten burned; Howe lost twelve the same way; and Murray lost thirty-eight out of forty. Then there is a lady who is quite famous in this respect—her house burned down last winter with a loss of 200 hives; and another man had seventy-five hives burned. I count on beginning the new season (in about a month) with sixty hives—we're down to as few as that.

Our cow has had a calf, but then the cow died of an incurable disease—her insides were in a horrible state. I'm planning on buying a young cow because the lambs need milk and so do the children. The latter have just finished going to school, and at the moment they're busy playing ball with "Uncle" Charles. I'm going to join in the game—my brain is tired. Good-bye, dear Mother, lots of love to dear Father and to all the members of John's family and their friends.

Your son,<br>Theodore

Dearest Mother:

Well, I missed your birthday on March 10, but five days later I gave you a lovely baby granddaughter. I'm sure you would love her very much, though I can't say she's the best-behaved baby that ever was. My two girls, Marie and Julie both, do everything they can to spoil her; but she's a precious treasure whom we all love very much, even Mr. Dodi, who apologizes for not having loved this baby right away by saying that he didn't know she'd turn out to be so pretty! How happy and thankful I am that it's over and that I've got my health and strength back in spite of a few aches and pains that still keep me off my feet a little. It's delightful to have a little girl who reminds us of our first Alice and even has her name—we all loved her so much! Just the same, we would have liked to name our little girl Eugénie, but in English they would pronounce it Joudginie, which would ruin it! So we'll just call her that within the family. The baby seems to be in excellent health; you can almost see her growing, and she's beginning to smile at us; we're eagerly looking forward to the time when she'll recognize us and be able to sit up a little—it will be easier then to hold her in our laps. It's been so long since I've had a baby around the place that it throws me off my stride to have to interrupt my household work so often; thus I had had my heart set on making some progress with my sewing, but I've hardly touched the machine[1] since my confinement, and when Marie leaves me, the housekeeping will take all my time. Since M. Boissonnas has been here I haven't thought of working in my garden except for pleasure and to get a little exercise. As for the bees, I'm very much afraid they aren't going to produce very much this year.

If God pleases, we'll have enough hives left to get well started again, and beyond that the Lord will provide. For my part, I recall one dismal year when everything seemed to be going against us—the death of our two fine colts and then of their mother, the weather very unfavorable for the crops; Theo ill, etc. I was so discouraged I couldn't seem to care much about anything, but when our dear little Alice died that fall, I saw in it a judgment of God and resolved never again to let myself sink into such despondency.

Because so many bees have died, we shall have to do a lot of very unpleasant work—empty many of the hives and clean out everything. If you could only see our living room! Pails full of quite good-looking honey—but not salable. Three small casks of diluted honey to make vinegar, a kettle full of spoiled honey to be made into vinegar, and outside a barrelful of old honeycombs to be melted down into wax, and that's not all, because upstairs there are still some hives we haven't inspected. In the cellar there are about thirty hives full of honeycombs and all ready for the new swarms. . . . If we have any swarms! We have been working at this for two days, and there is still the wax to melt. But Marie is bringing Miss Baby who is calling for her Mama. I must close now, dear Mother.

Good-bye, dear Mother. Tender hugs and kisses to you and Papa.

Your Sophie

Sunday, the twenty-first

Just a few more words, dear Mother, before we send off this letter which has already been delayed so long. Soso has told you how many bees we've lost. It doesn't make me any richer to say that all the others have suffered more than I have, but that shows there was no negligence on my part. I can't understand what went wrong—the hives were all in good order; the queens, the eggs, plenty of honey—all mysteriously gone. And I had made such detailed plans for next winter—lining my cellar with brick so the rats can't make holes anymore!

Good-bye dearest Mother, dear Father, and all the dear ones

at the house called Meynard.[2] Shall we ever see each other again on this earth?

Good-bye to all the brothers and friends.

Theodore Bost

## Theodore, then Sophie, to Jenny Bost

T. Bost
Excelsior, Hennepin County
Minnesota
October 19, 1873

Dearest Mother:

It's only owing to the strangest accident that I'm writing you on a working day. For the last month on rainy days I've been working to line my cellar with brick, but this afternoon there was such a downpour that it ran through the outside door and turned the place where I was working into a mudhole. So I quit, cleaned myself up, and sat down to write to you. Your letter of September 27 took sixteen days to get here, which is quite fast for that French line.

Since Boissonnas left, we've been snowed under with work. When I began this cellar job, I had no idea how much work it would involve—carefully leveling and smoothing the floor and sides, mixing my mortar and laying the bricks, which I had never done before, nor even had a good chance to observe close-up. In addition, I've had to make about twenty-five trips to Chaska to get materials. But I don't regret going to all this trouble or the labor I'll have next winter getting out cordwood to pay for the bricks. It looks so good everywhere it is finished and promises to be warm and comfortable, even if the rats should still get in a little bit this winter on account of my not being able to cement the floor for lack of money. Naturally all the farm work had to be done; there was the buckwheat to cut, wheat and oats to thresh, corn to cut, a trip to the mill and one to Minneapolis, three days for our fair, where I won enough prizes to pay for my newspapers and magazines, and as an additional prize sixty trees, apple trees of rare varieties which up to now have come through all the winters successfully. Hence, together with some other varieties which I propagated this past year, I'll have another hundred trees to plant next spring. People hardly know what it is to be completely discouraged in this country. It will take a number of years to replace my fine trees, but, God willing, this will be done unless we get some more winters even more severe than the last one, which is possible but not probable.

Fortunately, I am physically almost in good enough shape to keep up with all my work, having felt fairly well this fall aside from one cold and some rheumatism that affects my arms and shoulders—the result of working in the cellar and of handling wet, cold bricks.

Alphonse has run almost all the errands in Chaska to fetch bricks and sand; this keeps him busy from 5:30 [A.M.?] until 7:30 [P.M.?], and he often makes two trips a day. He's very proud of this, and when he saw me leaving for the mill the other day he came and walked all around the wagon, looking at the springs, bolts, etc., and in the end he pulled a ball of string from his pocket, saying, "Here, take this—you may find it'll come in handy in case the harness should break somewhere." It's true that our hills, tree trunks, and rocks are hard on both horses and harness.

Dearest Mother:

The [meeting of the] Evangelical Alliance has just been held in New York—we've seen something about it in the papers. There have been several meetings in Minneapolis, some relating to missions, for example, which we would very much have liked to attend, all the more so because the city had extended hospitality to all visitors, but Theo didn't want to go without me, and how could I go with a small baby in my arms? So we have to be content with the crumbs, that is, with what we can read about in the newspapers or learn from friends.

Good-bye—may the Lord bless you and keep you.

Your daughter,
Sophie Bost

# XVIII

# Storekeeper in Excelsior

With the year 1874 came several important changes in the lives of Sophie, Theodore, and their family. Indeed, we may say that with the decision to exchange the rugged existence of a pioneer farmer for that of a small-town merchant, Theodore was responding—even if unwittingly—to the fact that the first cycle of settlement and economic development of their region was drawing to a close. Railroads had displaced oxcarts and steamboats. A market economy was replacing the self-sufficiency of pioneer households which, as they often said, had meant "living from inside their fences." Farming was beginning to be mechanized, and farmers (the more successful ones) were relying more and more on large-scale production of cash crops. Mainly because his health was fragile, Theodore had not been able to move in this direction, and his valiant efforts to develop specialties like beekeeping and fruit growing had been largely defeated by bad luck and the harsh Minnesota winter climate.

The year 1874 marks a turning point in another sense. Both Ami and Jenny Bost died soon after celebrating their diamond wedding anniversary. Jenny's monthly letters no longer arrived at the Excelsior post office (housed in the general store of "Jones & Bost"). By the same token, fewer letters went in the opposite direction as family ties with Europe loosened. Sophie—more and more plagued with "rheumatism" (probably arthritis)—seems to have left letter writing to Theodore. He kept up a sporadic correspondence with his younger brother Elisée, as we shall see; but from this time on we no longer have a continuous account.

**Theodore to Jenny Bost**

T. Bost
Excelsior, Hennepin County
Minnesota
March 1, 1874

Dearest Mother:

This letter won't get to you by the tenth, but it was only this afternoon at teatime that we suddenly realized your birthday was coming on the tenth and we want to make up for the omission as soon as possible. And the worst of it is that I'm not sure whether it's the seventy-eighth, seventy-ninth, or eightieth birthday[1] you're about to have—you see I was rather young when you were born, so it has slipped my mind.

In my last letter I told you I had written to Tim to find out if he would advance us some money so I can buy a partnership in this store. Dear brother that he is, he wanted to telegraph me right away to draw what I needed on a banker, but not finding any telegraph office [listed] in Excelsior, he decided it would be fast enough to write offering right away the amount I had asked him for. Since the business was urgent, the price of lumber was going up, and cartage rates are much higher in summer than in winter, Jones and I immediately ordered the necessary lumber, about 20,000 feet, which we'll pay for as soon as dear Tim's money arrives. Although they've opened another store this year that will compete with us, Jones has sold a lot more goods than in other years. But his store looks very run-down, and it's old, damp, and unhealthy. They have threatened to take the post office away from him, and that brings in a large number of customers in a place where everybody calls for the mail and makes some purchases at the same time. Right now he has decided that he should have put up a new building and that people are attracted by the very idea of a new building. So far everyone in Excelsior seems very pleased that I'm going into the business, and my neighbors think it's high time I gave up heavy labor.

All this fuss and furor has upset me a great deal. You don't give up a style of life you love without feeling some pain, and I love farming. But I'm becoming a storekeeper because I don't know what else to do, my health and strength are on the wane, and this small store certainly promises to allow us to live better than we could by farming. I think Tim would have preferred for me to set myself up in some town on the railroad or in Minneapolis, but in towns that have a bright future the taxes are always enormous and a person needs a lot of experience or a great deal of capital to get started there, and like as not you wouldn't have any idea of what you were getting into, whereas here in Excelsior we know what to expect. We have many, many friends here, and it isn't every day that a merchant who is a good Christian and also a good businessman offers to take you in as an equal partner, even putting more of his own capital into the business. And besides, in Excelsior one has a chance to do all sorts of things—take in boarders, do gardening, grow fruit trees, and so on. There are lots of people who would like to go into business here, and that's something that annoys and worries me. I'll have to sell this place and take my family to Excelsior to live, and I can't, especially in winter, let them live outdoors. I think I'll wind up buying a place near the store if I can get a loan to pay for it with, which Jones thinks is likely, until I've sold the farm. We'll have to reach a decision this week or next. We're thinking of a pretty little cottage, smaller than our house here, with forty *ares* (not acres)[2] of land in fruit trees, well cultivated and well fenced. All this is a pesky nuisance, but don't worry, dear Mother—I won't do anything without getting good advice and carefully weighing the pros and cons.

I'll close in a hurry because I want to take this letter to Chaska tomorrow when I go there to deliver a load or two of cordwood. The snow is melting fast these spring days, and the roads are less and less good for sledding. Good-bye, dearest Parents and friends.

Your most devoted son,
Theodore Bost

**Theodore to Jenny Bost**

T. Bost
Excelsior, Hennepin County
Minnesota
April 10, 1874

Dearest Mother:

My dear little Alphonse brought me this letter [to you] from Soso this morning, and I'll send it off right away [with this one of mine]. At the store I have hardly any time to write because people are talking to me all the time and I have to interrupt what I'm doing. This is a crazy life I'm living—having my farm and family five miles away, having to take care of the horses, keep my books, and sell all kinds of goods—but my health is much better. I have a lot more energy, and my head feels better than it has ever felt. The new store is rapidly approaching completion and will bring us customers that the old store was causing us to lose, and besides, I couldn't stand the old place any more.

Easter has come and gone, and instead of hiding eggs in the grass we could have hidden them in heaps of old snow. The roads are in a bad state, what with melting snowbanks and holes full of frozen mud, so we are having our goods brought to Wayzata, six miles north of Excelsior, straight across Lake Minnetonka from us. The warehouse is on the edge of the lake; one can take huge loads on a sled that runs easily over mirror-smooth ice thirty inches thick. This is cheaper for us than to make trips to Minneapolis with a wagon or sled. I do this hauling two or three times a week, and it does me good to get outdoors. As soon as the roads are good or at least passable, I'll be indoors all the time. This year the spring is late and cold—it's unusual to see the ice so solid so late in the season, and to see such large piles of snow.

Up to now business has been very slow because the roads are so bad, but I'm doing better than on the farm and I feel better.

Your most devoted son,
Theodore Bost

**Theodore to Jenny Bost**

T. Bost
Excelsior, Hennepin County
Minnesota
June 1874

Dearest Mother:

Jones and I continue to be very busy, quite aside from the store, with the new building. Much of the time we both work at it, leaving the clerk to wait on customers. He [Jones] is painting the new building and is putting cellar walls under the structure—we built in the winter and were thus able to place only a few stones at the corners, so the thaw has caused some settling. I draw water, paint, fetch sand and stone with the horses, make mortar, and run errands to Minneapolis. Then in the evening I must keep the books and wait on customers, who are more numerous between six and nine or ten in the evening than during all the rest of the day, Saturday night especially, so it's not until after ten in the evening that I can go home on Saturday over roads that resemble those near Asnières; hence I'm often tired on Sunday.

I don't know if I told you in my last letter that I was thinking of buying a little house with about an acre of land just a short walk from the store; the whole property [is] well fenced and planted to vines and fruit trees. I've closed the deal, arranging to pay the price in several installments. I really needed a place to live near the store, but I couldn't and wouldn't cram myself in opposite the store, as Jones wanted me to do, in order to recover in this way some money that was owed to him. We wouldn't have had a real home there; we'd have practically lived right on the street without a garden and with no view; and I'd have been roused up at all hours of the night. The children are overjoyed at the idea of having a garden, a nice house (although not as good as the one we have here), and a delightful view of this pretty lake.

When you told me about the approaching reunion of almost the entire Bost family, the news made my heart ache;[3] but after all, I've had my turn, and a splendid turn it was, so I'm not inclined to complain, only it would have been very enjoyable for me if I could have been there. How happy I shall be to be thinking of all my dear brothers reunited with you two dear old parents. How I wish that Papa might really be able to take part in the reunion!

Your most devoted son,
Theodore Bost

## Theodore to Timothée

T. Bost
Excelsior, Hennepin County
Minnesota
June 16, 1874

I don't know what you must have thought of my most recent letters. The truth is that I had had so many difficulties of all kinds and was so weary in mind and body from working sixteen hours every day at work to which I'm quite unaccustomed—and all this during a very *dull*[4] season—that I was almost sorry I had gotten into this business—or rather, I didn't know which foot to dance on. But by now the worst is over. My partner's family—his wife, his son by his second wife, and others—had made up their minds that I was to be kept in a subordinate position and that they could help themselves, as senior partners, to whatever they wanted from the store; they saw I was determined not to quarrel with Jones—all this had reached a point where my patience was just about worn out. Jones was afraid to quarrel with his Xanthippe,[5] who had pressed him to hire her son as clerk. After praying for guidance, I took the bull by the horns and in a few words I ticked them all off. Jones himself had to admit that he was in the wrong without even putting up an argument, and since then the skies have cleared. I am the boss in the store, and Jones's thieving son keeps his distance, which astonishes everybody, accustomed as people are to see him lording it over Jones, and thank God I think everything is going to work out fine. Business is slow, so we think it's high time to dispense with the clerk, whose wages are a big expense for the store. Although I'm thinner than I was a few months ago, people say my color is better, and thank God I feel better, though I'm often tired; but I think the work will be less tiring now that my position is clear. In a store like this, where you have to be an expert on all the articles of so many different kinds, it takes time to memorize the prices, and these, moreover, are always changing. The summer boarders are beginning to arrive, which gives us another class of customer at the same time that it allows our hotel and boardinghouses to pay us several big bills they owe us.

It's 9:30 P.M., and I've been on my feet since 5:00 [A.M.] without interruption except to bolt my meals, so it's possible that this letter will seem distracted. These eighteen-mile trips over country roads are very scenic but rather tiring in very hot weather, so I'm going to bed after stepping out for a breath of air.

Once again, dear Tim, thank you for all you've done for me. My life is less of a burden to me, and the future seems much brighter than before, both for me and for my family. Be sure to give my love to all our family and friends when you see them and lots of love to your own family.

Your brother,<br>Theodore Bost

**Theodore to his family**

Minneapolis<br>July 8, 1874

Just a few hasty words in the hope that you'll all be together when this letter reaches you.

We just had a fine letter from dear Eugénie, received yesterday, with a message added by Mama who tells us you will all be getting together July 23—we'd thought it was going to be in August.

We've been in the new store for several days now, and the rich tycoons are arriving from the south to rest from their labors. This brings an entirely different sort of trade—silk goods, ribbons, and lace, along with which you always have to sell small quantities of kerosene, lard, hooks, glass articles, mosquito netting, cigars, and paint. This keeps us steadily on the go from five in the morning to ten-thirty at night. Business is quite brisk, but with all the outlays we've had these last two months we don't know exactly where we are in terms of profit and loss.

Good-bye, my dear ones, may God be with you. I know you are thinking of us. There's something that makes the tip of my nose itch every time I think about your reunion, and this brings tears to my eyes, but I had my celebration four years ago.

In much haste,
Theodore Bost

### Theodore and Sophie to Elisée and Clémy

T. Bost
Excelsior, Hennepin County
Minnesota
September 20, 1874

Dearest Brother and Sister:

It's high time we wrote to the only brother who has written to us giving any details on that great and splendid family reunion about which we had worked up so much enthusiasm. It seemed to us that if we couldn't be there, we would at least get a lot of joyful letters. Instead of that, we've received your letter which has made us rejoice for all of you on account of that, or rather those celebrations; then two long weeks went by. We were expecting from day to day to get those promised letters, especially those from Mama and Eugénie, when all of a sudden came Tim's letter announcing Mama's death [August 24]. You can imagine what a blow that was to us. We had never expected anything but letters that would bring us lots of pleasant details and happy news. We wanted to enter into all your meals, your comings and going, your conversation, etc. But instead of that, to get this news! It was a long time before I could take it in; it seemed to us that this mother who had written to me so regularly every month for twenty-three years should still have had a good number of years to live. She was a mother to me more than to any of you during all these years of exile because she was almost the only one who corresponded with us, and her letters were all the more precious to us because we knew that it tired her to write us such long ones in order to keep us informed about what our brothers were doing.

By now I have accepted this loss. She could not have died at a more happy moment or have left a better memory of herself, and it is with thankfulness to God that I remember how it was given to me to see her once more, to her to see me again and to have all her happy children gathered around her, and to see them not only one after the other, as she did four or five years ago, but all together and with the majority of their wives and families. How fortunate also that our father, who for a number of years hasn't seemed to be able to hold his ideas together, did get more and more coherent. And then, what good fortune that she had such a short final illness, that she died with all her faculties intact, and that she died in comfort after so many, many years of poverty. I so much hope that poor Paul, about whom you've told me scarcely a single word, didn't cause her any suffering. Poor Mother! She was worried that he might not make the celebration a happy one, though she still hoped for the best, and our poor, dear Paul, face to face with our two dear old parents, will, I believe, have forgotten his *"fancied grievances."*

Thus your letter, dear Elisée, has been the only one we expected that has given us joy; the others, when they arrive, if they do arrive, will carry the aura of this sudden loss and will not be what we were expecting.

But what happiness it must have been for all of you and for our dear old parents. We imagined that we were with you, dear brothers and sisters, and we seemed to hear your laughter and puns. I could see Mother watching each and every one of you with that same happy expression she had thirty-five years ago in Geneva when on a winter evening her youngest son came home and she said: "Well, at last we're all here." What patience she must have had with all those little Holophernes![6]

Dear Clémy, I am so happy about the good news you've had about your brother.[7] It always makes me sick at heart to think about all the young men who leave their home and country. I've seen so many of them go stagnant and die of boredom or strong drink that I would never advise anyone to emigrate from Europe, except good-for-nothings who may still be able to reform.

But good-bye, my dear ones, and a thousand kisses to the children.

Theodore Bost

# XIX

# Back to the Land

From this time on, the letters become more and more infrequent. Ami Bost died at La Force December 24, 1874, four months after Jenny's death, but we have no letters from Sophie and Theodore that mention his death. There is only one extant letter for the years 1878-82, a period when there was, however, much family news of both sides of the Atlantic. In America, Sophie gave birth to her sixth and last child, Edward, on November 17, 1875, making five children in the home. Theodore sold his farm, but storekeeping didn't suit him, so on January 29, 1877, he sold his share in "Jones & Bost" to L. F. Sampson and acquired a new farm about four miles from the old one. In Europe, Paul died in 1876, Etienne in 1882; John opened his ninth asylum at La Force in 1881.

On June 5, 1883, Sophie and Theodore celebrated their silver wedding anniversary and the marriage of their eldest daughter, Julie, who was twenty-four years old, to Lucius T. Bishop.

The remainder of the letters in this collection are addressed to Theodore's younger brother Elisée, pastor at Le Pouzin (Ardèche), and his family, with whom Theodore continued to correspond.

**Theodore to Elisée and Clémy**

Excelsior, Minnesota
December 11, 1883

Dearest Brother and Sister:

This past year and just recently, you've both—and you especially, dear Clémy—had a great deal to try you.[1] It's something that everybody has to go through, but ordinarily it's gradual and the repeated blows are more difficult to bear. But what a consolation for you to have so many children [six at this time] and to have them of an age when they don't cause you a lot of moral anguish, when you are still in control of their spare time, the company they keep, and so on. Let's hope they will remain under your

329

roof and will have enough confidence in you to follow your guidance and bring you nothing but happiness

For us, fortunately, the worst is over. Our children (the two older boys) have caused us some fairly serious worries because in this country the parents are pretty well under the thumb of their children but for the time being, though it sometimes goes against their grain, they're staying at home instead of going to dances and staying out until two in the morning, frequently in quite bad company and almost always with lower-class people, able to find amusement only in card playing, billiards, and cigar smoking. Alphonse is taking singing lessons, often in the evening, and I've taught the two boys to play chess; they're proud of being good players, better than their friends who play other games.

As for our Julie, she has never given us any worries at all, aside from her health; she has a very strongly Christian character, is good natured, full of seriousness and enthusiasm, very much like our sister Marie. The two younger ones promise to be very well behaved, and besides, we've had more time to attend to their needs and pleasures than we did for the older children.

Well, it has been twelve or thirteen years since I turned up at your house during a very bad time. It was a wretched winter for you, my dears, what with the cold, your illness, and the Prussians. Oh, that reminds me that you French are going off to fight the Chinese![2] Here the prevailing sentiment is more or less against the French, almost entirely because they seem to be picking quarrels nearly everywhere on account of those Jesuit missionaries. Poor Godless France!

It's winter here, very cold at first, then three weeks with no snow and thawing every day. Since yesterday it has been 14° Réaumur [63.5°F.],[3] but we're well sheltered and have our animals and fodder under cover. To appreciate our present state you would have to have spent twenty years when everything was just the opposite. Our crops have been very poor, and our New Year will be an extremely modest affair, but we shall all be together—the Bishops will come and spend the day with us, and we'll be as happy as kings even if money is scarce.

I'll end this letter without saying much about my dear Soso, who I hope is going to write to you, but just before Christmas she has a great deal to do, and she's having trouble with rheumatism in her hands and arms.

Your most devoted
Theodore Bost

[P.S.] A thousand hugs and kisses to your whole crowd from all of us.

## Theodore to Elisée and Clémy

T. Bost
Excelsior, Minnesota
February 27, 1884

Dearest Elisée and Clémy:

We've reached that point in the year when the money is flowing out on all sides and very little is coming in. Taxes to pay, subscriptions to newspapers and magazines, feed to buy for the livestock, clothing, mittens, schools, etc., everything goes out the window And when you've had poor crops, that's nothing to joke about. Our pledge for the support of our minister is 225 frs. [about $45], and that's no more than friends who are in similar circumstances have agreed to give. In addition to that, there are always a number of good causes to be supported; and then we must build a parsonage; and then people are talking of building an "academy" (a school equivalent to the seventh, sixth, fifth, and fourth classes of our secondary schools, except that the students are older than in Europe),[4] and all our friends are paying their share even if they have to borrow the money, which is something I very much dislike doing and haven't done yet—you have to draw the line somewhere. When it comes to money, Americans are very generous, even those who will cheat you with the most complete cold-bloodedness—but in any case, you don't have to have very warm blood to be a good cheater.

On top of all this, we're at the most discouraging time of the year—snow on the ground for three months, very cold weather for four months, and continual heavy freezes. It's very stimulating at the beginning to see the thermometer falling to the freezing point of mercury, but after three months when it varies between 10 and 40, around 20 most of the time,[5] [when you're] always wearing many layers of clothing and heavy shoes and mittens—in the end you feel crushed and stifled, and you yearn for warmer weather. Well, it will come sometime—too bad this is leap year, which makes February a day longer.

Our minister[6] is very enterprising; dissatisfied with our choir, he has gone to work to teach music to about a hundred of our young people. Our two older boys, who are very shy, didn't want to go. For one reason or another, we hadn't been able to give them music lessons though they both have good voices. Our minister promised them that after three lessons they would know not only all the elementary principles, but also all the scales, being able to find the *do* in each and every key and to read hymns at sight! Well, that's how the Americans are—they have incredible self-confidence and great facility when it comes to learning anything. I can't say they have very much true musical feeling; however artistic their music may be, it's always very cold and dry—brilliant but without any soul. So our boys are learning, and that takes up a lot of afternoons and evenings. They have "musical conventions," they sing cantatas, and so forth. A choir of twenty-five set out last Sunday to sing a piece in rapid tempo, and it was horrible enough to give you a nervous collapse. Yet a more difficult piece was carried off very well. But nothing discourages these people, and it's always somebody else's fault if things turn out badly. I often think of those beautiful voices in the asylums at La Force and wish we could hear something as fine as that in our church.

Good-bye, dear children—Lonlon, Tonton, tirelarila, etc.

Your most devoted brother and uncle,
Theo. Bost

# XX

# The Pioneers in Old Age

For twelve years, from 1884 to 1896, there are no letters. And yet, great changes took place in the lives of Theodore and Sophie. In September, 1887, they left Minnesota for good and moved to California, settling in the little village of Pomona, then about thirty miles east of Los Angeles, which was quite a small town at that time. The reason for their leaving Minnesota is not known, but it may have had to do with the attraction of a milder climate and also with hopes for new economic opportunities. Perhaps, too, they had stayed in touch with their former minister, Rev. Charles Sheldon, who had moved to California in 1883; he may have persuaded them to move or helped them get established there.

They took with them their oldest daughter, Julie (Mimi) Bishop, her husband, and the three younger children: Theodore (Dodi), who was twenty years old at that time, Alice, who was fourteen, and Edward, who was only twelve.

Dodi did not stay in Pomona, but went in 1888 to Tacoma, Washington, and then back to Excelsior where he worked for a Democratic newspaper, the *St. Paul Globe*. What must his father, a fierce Republican, have thought of that? Dodi later developed tuberculosis and came back to live with his parents in Pomona, dying there in 1899 at the age of thirty-two. Alice was engaged in 1893 to Ernest Pratt, but he was accidentally killed. In 1902 she married William Johnstone. Edward became a carpenter.

Marie Moseman — "Little Mary" — followed the family to Pomona and died there, probably around 1890.

The two Alphonses (uncle and nephew) stayed in Excelsior. Theodore's oldest son married Lula Seamans and carried on the farm that had belonged to his parents, building up a nursery which was not very successful. Alphonse Bonjour eventually went to Pomona, where he died in 1898.

On the European side of the family, Samuel died in 1888, Augustin in 1890. But there were many, many marriages and births.

In Pomona, Theodore had a farm and specialized in fruit growing. He never enjoyed much prosperity and tried to make ends meet with various supplementary occupations.

**Theodore to Elisée and Clémy**

Pomona
January 8, 1896

Dearest Brother and Sister:

We Americans move from one end of the United States to the other, but we feel at home wherever we go.

And yet, going from the interminable winters of Minnesota to the winters of Southern California (not to be confused with Lower California) is like going from Russia or Siberia to Italy. Here, you realize, we're proud of our mild, unchanging climate; yet every four years we have terrible sandstorms that do a great deal of damage. We've just had one, not much stronger than an everyday Geneva breeze and lasting only seven or eight hours; but it has destroyed a lot of oranges and even entire citrus groves, whipping the loaded branches into a frenzy, and then came a rather heavy frost (4°R.).[1] The sand, the electricity [?], the great dryness of the air—everything worked together to ruin our fruit, flowers, and lawn. You know, of course, that the only rain we get here falls during the winter. Twelve (American) inches are sufficient, but this year we've had only two inches so far, and everybody is worrying, but there's still time enough to have some splendid cloudbursts, and besides, it's not for us to decide how that's going to be, so we must have faith.

You are probably aware that this part of California was inhabited by thousands of Mexicans before the [American] annexation in '48. These people are still here, many of them pureblooded Spaniards of the lower class, the rest either of mixed blood or Negroes.

The California Indians aren't like the ones I've known in the East [that is, east of the Rockies] —Chippewas, Sioux, Winnebagos, and the rest; the local ones are of average height and work well if somewhat slowly; they have large, bony hands and feet, whereas those we were familiar with in the East were slim, agile, lightly built, with small hands and feet—and mischievous, cruel, and treacherous in the bargain.

The Mexicans don't mingle very much with the American race; they are Catholics, drunkards, lazy, and ignorant, and they usually live on the lower slopes, having gradually sold the better locations to the Americans.

We also have some Basques who intermix with the Mexicans, and I have a hard time telling them apart on account of their dark coppery color. These Basques, and some people from Béarn, are sheepherders, an occupation that paid well before we got this Democratic administration, thanks to which they've changed their political allegiance. The seven counties in the southern part of California are collectively known as Southern California, though they do not form a separate state, and any two of them are as big as Switzerland. Our population is better than that of Northern California, having more recently arrived from the East, whereas the northern part of California was for the most part composed of adventurers, forgers, and the gold hunters of '49, and their descendants still bear the traces. In most of our villages around here and to the south everything is quiet on Sunday, and in almost all the houses one can hear children playing the organ or the piano and singing hymns for recreation.

Many fond hugs and kisses for everybody from

Your American brother and uncle,
Theodore

**Theodore to Elisée and Clémy**

July 4, 1899

Dear Elisée and Clémy:

After six months of magnificent weather, we've suddenly had a terrible heat wave, with temperatures rising almost every day to 100° and 101°F. (31° to 32°R., I think).[2] And I assure you that picking up apricots off the ground in a sandy orchard with a burning sun on your back, or loading a lot of seventy-pound boxes, you have no reason to complain of the cold. And yet, as I sat yesterday with a breeze blowing upon my weary back, soaked with sweat, I picked up a bad backache that keeps me from working; otherwise I'd have worked all day today in spite of its being the glorious Fourth of July. Everywhere else in this region all work has stopped, but here the apricots compel us to work harder than ever every year. These extreme hot spells actually cook them as they hang on the trees. Do you know how we pick them? By hand if they are going into preserves, but if they are to be dried, we stretch big pieces of cloth on the ground, someone climbs the tree and shakes the branches, and then we knock down the rest with sticks. We belong to an association that takes care of the drying and marketing, and they employ a couple of hundred women, girls, and boys to cut them in two while about fifty men look after the fruit. They're often obliged to work night and day, including Sundays. Our association receives between forty and fifty tons per day, and there are two others in Pomona. This [the harvest] lasts from two to three weeks; after that come the peaches and then the plums, but by that time things are not so hectic. With the apricots, though, you have to hurry.

And so now you are having to look at the more somber side of life—eldest sons falling sick, but also with a promise of grandchildren—we do have to live through a strange mixture of emotions. The recent death of Dodi still weighs on us like a very heavy burden, especially for me—I've never felt really close to him, and now I've had to watch him die without getting to know him as a father should know his son. Alphonse and his wife, who took care of him for so many months without suspecting that he had consumption, are having a hard time recovering from the pain of his death. It's the same with Edward here with us, though he never speaks about it. As for this boy, his fiancée [Olivia Wigton] came over and spent a few hours talking with complete candor to Sophie. She is a delightful young woman.

Yes, I certainly am interested in the Dreyfus Affair,[3] and you will be shocked to learn that I'm the only Frenchman (?) [sic] here who defends him; all the others, Catholics as well as Protestants, are supporting the army!! It seems as though the Latin race were sinking into decay, losing its moral integrity along with its virility. But a person hardly knows how much to believe of what he reads in the newspapers. For years they've been calling Dreyfus a Jew, but I came across an article that claims Dreyfus makes himself out to be the son of Protestant parents. Isn't the Dreyfus family of Mulhouse Protestant? It is also said that his judges come from the Ecole Polytechnique—is this a good or a bad omen for him? It's a very strange business from start to finish and it seems impossible that it should not be cleared up because, after all, there are many fine qualities in the French national character. I see that he's back in France and that his health is better. But I'd like it better if the French could comprehend how much other nations despise their methods of maintaining an army. To destroy an innocent man so that certain officers should not be found guilty! Well!

In this country we've also had some misdeeds in high places

owing to our Secretary of War [Russell A.] Alger, and McKinley is coming in for a lot of blame for keeping him in his cabinet. The public is wholly opposed to Alger, but he has political allies in Michigan, where he comes from, and McKinley is afraid that, if he fires him, the coming elections in Michigan may go against the Republican party. This Alger has done us [the Republican party] a great deal of harm here in Southern California.

I certainly would like to make another tour of Europe and meet again, or rather meet for the first time, all these young people. It's been almost thirty years since my last visit—that's a long, long time!

Well, then, give my affectionate greetings to all those dear nephews and nieces, as well as to your dear Clémy and to yourself from all the members of our little tribe.

Your brother,
Theodore

**Theodore to Elisée**

December, 1900

You speak of the Boers—like you, I sympathize with them. It's magnificent the way that little handful of people has held its ground against a great nation that boasts of ruling 300,000,000 souls.[4] And it's a crying injustice that they're being conquered. In any case, I've always maintained that nobody has a right to own more land than he can cultivate himself; nothing belongs to us, everything is loaned to us, and when a race like the [American] Indians doesn't want to work or raise any crops, it's right that they should disappear. That's what happened to them in the Spaniards' part of America. And the Spanish themselves, doing nothing but herd cows and sheep, have had to make way for the Americans who transform the deserts into orchards and allow a thousand people to live where the Spanish had the means of supporting only one. We see this every day. There remain a few huge farms which still belong to Spaniards (Mexicans), houses built of unfired brick, no trees around them, and almost always two or three saddle horses tied up outside, showing that the young men are visiting the girls; and no more than half a mile from there, marvelously beautiful orchards, artesian wells, and everybody hard at work.

Therefore! Oh yes—where were we? Therefore, the Boers

stand for the patriarchal system which is superior to the Indian way and better than nothing at all, but when they pass laws and persist in discouraging everything that would tend to increase the population, it is necessary that they should lose out, even if each individual Boer is a better man than most of the soldiers who are harassing him. The earth has to be populated, and woe to those who obstruct this law. I've seen the British at work in Canada, and I've seen the Americans from one end of the United States to the other. I've seen plenty of crying injustices, plenty of weaklings crushed by the strong, but when all is said and done, good wins out over evil, well-being triumphs over poverty, and education over ignorance.

And so I console myself over the Boers' defeats. These last two years, with the two deaths we've had [of Alphonse Bonjour and Dodi] and all my trials with this prolonged dry spell that threatened to ruin us and has damaged our orchards, forcing me to work twice as hard though my advancing age makes it urgent for me to have some relief—these two years, I say, have aged me a great deal, and I look forward with satisfaction to the time when all this will be at an end.

Well, that's that! A thousand good wishes for all of you, and may God help us all and grant that we may love Him.

Your brother,
Theodore

Affectionate greetings, naturally, from Sophie, who remembers you very well.

## Theodore to Elisée

January, 1906

Dear little brother and all the tribe:

It's been quite a long time since we've exchanged letters, and very often I've wanted to overcome my laziness, or rather the difficulty of writing. My poor old head is heavy and tires easily.

Just think—in four days I'll be seventy-two years old! And you yourself can't be far from seventy either. What a lot of things have happened in our two lives! Trials and joys, joys and trials. At times, life seems very hard to bear, but at other times one sees a good many reasons to be thankful. With you, as with us, it's the children above everything else that bring us the most happiness.

We're separated by several thousand kilometers from our Alphonse [and his wife], but they write to us every week and keep us posted on their doings. His second wife is more robust than his dear Lula,[5] and she's so full of life and energy that Alphonse too has taken on new life and energy. Their children, too, are very well.

By the way, the letter that came from him today tells us that he is in the process of filling several icehouses; on the last day, being short of help, they loaded their sled with blocks of ice, and little Leon drove the horses home all by himself for somebody else to unload. I'll bet you don't have a six-year-old lad who could do that! Their children have a great liking for music, singing solos and duets (is that good French?) with voices that are sweet and pure. It's rare to hear sweet voices in this country; pure, yes, but only about as sweet as a military band. Anyhow, modern sacred music, or damned modern music [*la musique sacrée moderne ou sacrée musique moderne*] is very different in this respect from the kind we used to know. At our house, at least when we were children, Christians felt they were of little account, and their hymns were often almost lugubrious. At John's home in '70, I heard good healthy children singing "Yes, I wish to die." I felt like telling them: "Blockhead [*Ganache*], go do some work first!" Here the music is full of spirit — this whole country with its 80,000,000 people mostly sees itself as being swept forward by progress instead of being trampled upon by the pope and the Catholic clergy. Our laws are getting better all the time, and the people are rising up against the rich swindlers. There are still many evils to be set right, but a person can be certain that this will be done.

Incidentally, what is your position on the separation of church and state?[6] Dear Samuel, seeing how weak the French Protestants are, wanted [provision to be made for] at least one Protestant minister in each *département*. How will the ministers be paid [henceforth] in those places where [the Protestants] are so few in number? As for me, I'm only too happy to welcome this separation, and I've always had a pure and wholesome hatred for the Catholic system, though I freely admit that there are good and ardent Christians among them

Well, then, good-bye to my very dear Brother and all his tribe, and *au revoir* for the time being.

Sophie wants me to tell you that she sends to you and yours her warmest friendly greetings. That goes without saying.

Theodore

**Theodore to Elisée**

Pomona, California
May 31, 1908

Dearest Brother:

First of all, thank you very much for your letter and also for the fine photos and that good book about François Coillard.[7] Your letter [is] so full of warm feeling; the charming portrait [of Clémy] . . . is such a good likeness, though her expression is sadder than any I've ever seen on her face—perhaps it's due to her long bouts of illness—while you look younger than you are now, like all the other members of the older generation. If you sent us all this for our silver wedding anniversary, it's a pity it took twenty-five years to get here, but never mind, it will do just as well for our fiftieth! It's our Julie now who's celebrating her silver anniversary, and we're having a big get-together at their house—a hundred guests, just from three to five-thirty in the afternoon, refreshments, lemonade, three kinds of cake, coffee, and ice cream—next Friday, with the party in the afternoon for the guests and supper in the evening for the family—seventeen in all—plus three friends who are coming from Los Angeles.

I've skimmed through the book about Coillard and enjoyed it very much. I noticed what I feel sure is a mistake—it was (he thinks) the first time Papa had heard the *Gloria* and the *Magnificat* sung by a full choir. If my childhood memories, which are still vivid, are not deceiving me, I was in the balcony of the Oratory, [a church] in Geneva singing one or the other of those beautiful hymns along with a large choir and, with the sublime presumptuousness of a nine-year-old child, telling the director Samon (?) [sic] that such-and-such a line must be sung exactly "the way Father had told me." The thing I remember is that we all had a good laugh over the incident.

Our best greetings and good wishes. Sophie, *of course*, joins me in sending you our thanks.

Your brother,
Theodore

During the year 1909, Theodore and Sophie, then seventy-five and seventy-four years of age, agreed to give up their farm, which they sold, and moved so as to be close to their Johnstone children who were living in San Dimas, six miles northwest of Pomona.

The same year, Alphonse left Minnesota and moved to Texas to grow cotton, settling in Robstown, not far from Corpus Christi.

In Europe, Sophie, wife of Samuel, had just died (1909); Théophile died in July, 1910, and Bella, Timothée's wife, in December, 1912. Only a few letters remain from these years.

**Theodore to Elisée**

San Dimas, California
May 21, 1910

Dearest Brother:

I'm not sure this *card* will arrive in time for your anniversary. I wish I could send you a letter, but it's too much for me. I must tell you that for six months now I've been having trouble with my eyes. Things are all right now that they've removed one, but the other is very weak and my brain even more so. But I feel I must not fail to send you a sign of friendship for the fourth.[8] Here we're celebrating on the fifth (our wedding anniversary), either here or in Pomona with a few of the family. Not having a horse, we hardly ever get to see them  What a different life we and our children are leading, compared with your life in Europe. Alphonse, though he's 1,500 miles to the east of here, is really farther west than we are: everything [where he is] has to be built up from nothing, and the surroundings are much less civilized. Everyone is well. Again, a thousand affectionate greetings.

Your brother,
Theodore

**Theodore to Elisée**

Beginning of August, 1911

Dear Elisée:

Thank you for your letter. I had been wondering time and again why we've been writing so little! The world is full of "reasons why." And behold, here is a fine letter from you with lots of news, and so welcome to the whole family. I'd like to be able to show all these Americans, who always seem to believe that the French have neither homes nor families, what you and the Cadiers can do in this respect.[9] Having lived sixty years in America, I'm convinced that there is more devotion to the family among us than there is here. When Margaret (Tim's daughter) [Margaret Turner] was here I asked her, "When you get back to Europe, what will you tell them about us?" She replied, "I'll tell them you have a very united family."

It's been at least twenty-three years now that Alphonse has been living far away from us, and he has never failed to write to us once a week. And his children—whom we've never seen—are all the time begging us to go and visit them. But I think it's 2,000 miles from here and would cost more money than we can afford to spend. When we sold our place almost two years ago, we set aside a certain amount of money to make the trip, but my eye trouble and later the operation swallowed up everything and more, so we were obliged to stay here in our pretty little house.

For their part, Alphonse's family would like very much to come here, but they have so much building to do—house, barn, cabins for workers, a well 200-400 feet deep to be made. They're busy drilling it at this very moment; at 114 feet they found a plentiful source of water, but very salty and brackish, so they've had to go deeper, no one knows how far, to try to find drinkable water that will also be usable for irrigation. Being fifteen miles from the sea, on land that probably was once submerged, there is some doubt whether they'll find any that's better. What a lot of things people have to undertake in this country—so many problems—and when you think you've done everything, millions of insects come and destroy your crops. Once again, what a lot of "whys" in this world!

What a strange thing memory is! After fifty years I find myself singing a tune from [our days in] Melun: "Azor, my darling, my love, be adorable and ravishing, etc." Do you recall it? One night I woke up with just two notes in my mind—not very much, for there are lots of melodies that begin that way. It tormented me all day long. The second night a third note appeared, which tormented me even more. I made no effort to remember more of it, but my brain continued its work and one day I found that I had the first line, with the rest coming soon afterward. This happened last year, and then I forgot all about it. And just recently I've been hearing (inside my head) the evening concert of the military band in Melun—the thing had gone completely out of my mind, but it will come back. What has become of those tunes, and where will they finally come to roost?

Protestants. It must be difficult to keep up with the church expenses. Speaking of that—the amounts people from around here spend to support the churches are enormous. Pomona is growing all the time and has perhaps 15,000 inhabitants, so these past two years it has had to enlarge, or rather build, three or four churches. Our Congregationalist church will cost $100,000, of which one-third will be covered by the sale of the old church. The Baptists have built two for the same amount. The Methodists and the Presbyterians have each spent about $60,000. Some other little churches are on a more modest scale. People speak of "rivalry," and there is some of this, but the churches get built, and almost all of them are out of debt. Where does all this money come from? We don't have any millionaires.

Ministers [here] ordinarily have a [yearly] salary of between $1,200 and $1,800, which is more, I think (?) [*sic*], than you are paid in France; but on the other hand they have heavier expenses.

So there it is—is this enough gossip for you? Thousands and thousands of loving greetings to all your family, if you can remember them all, from my wife and me.

Your aging brother,
Theodore

# XXI

# Echoes of War

# (1914-18)

Curiously enough, the war years brought more and longer letters from Theodore to his brother Elisée. No doubt the news headlines and his natural concern for the European members of his family go far to explain this renewal of interest in the affairs of the old homeland. Theodore, like the majority of Americans, took a rather moderate pro-Allied (especially pro-French) attitude at the beginning of the war, refusing to believe the early atrocity stories about the Germans. Then, as time went on and Allied propaganda grew more effective, he became increasingly impassioned in his denunciation of the Kaiser's wickedness. His uncompromising Republican partisanship comes out in his denunciation of Wilson's conduct of the peace negotiations, and in general he becomes less liberal and his ethnocentric prejudices grow more vehement with advancing age.

**Theodore to Elisée**

San Dimas, California
February 11, 1915

Dearest Brother (and all the tribe):

Let's have no fixing of blame nor making of excuses. We all know what keeps us from writing letters, and we both know that this in no way interferes with our feelings for one another!

Day after day we follow the news of this unprecedented war, however contradictory the reports must necessarily be: along so vast a front there are bound to be victories and defeats for one side or the other. In any event, the Germans have missed their chance at several points: they haven't taken Paris, nor have they reached the English Channel nor overrun Russia, and we very much hope they will have to withdraw from poor Belgium and the north of France. How fortunate that our dear Switzerland has been able to remain aloof from these chaotic events—the reason, I suppose, is that with her 300,000 men on a war footing, no enemy wants to attack.

I don't believe, dear Brother, in all these atrocity stories we're told about the Germans—it isn't at all compatible with the discipline they showed in [the Franco-Prussian war of] 1870, according to all that Samuel told me in Versailles, and it doesn't agree with the findings of several very neutral committees that have investigated a thousand reports from both sides. The Germans have done enough bad things, but they shouldn't be accused of crimes they haven't committed. They may say what they will—their behavior toward Belgium is enough to condemn them for all time to come: they've broken their promises, torn up treaties, devastated and crushed that poor country which asked nothing better than to remain neutral—all this is inexcusable, and I certainly hope the Allies won't make peace without insisting on a financial indemnity. As for making reparation for all the human beings who have been killed or injured, we must leave the settlement of all that to One who knows what must be done and *when*.

What a horrible thing war is—to decimate a population, kill the best citizens (physically speaking), squandering the money that ought to be used to accomplish good ends—all this is abominable.

Almost everyone here sympathizes with the Allies, but a strong body of dissidents exists in the form of 12,000,000 Germans and their direct descendants who compel our government to be more neutral than we wish it to be. During the first few months of hostilities all types of economic activity were harmed: our crops, wheat and cotton, could only be sold at quite low prices. At present business is picking up again, especially munitions production, automobiles, bicycles, millions of garments, sets of harness, saddles, etc., which go almost entirely to the Allies; the British navy would seize anything that was shipped to the Germans.

*Adieu*, Love, *Good Courage* [as in original]!

Theodore


**Theodore to Elisée**

San Dimas, California
June 25, 1915

Dearest Brother:

I have been expecting a letter from you from one day to another about the death of our dear Tim, but I don't want to wait any longer. I had received the news of his first operation with details that seemed to indicate that he would soon die. Then came a second letter from Mag [Margaret Turner] which didn't refer to his death [May 18, 1915] but spoke only of his funeral. I had kept up closer relations with this good brother than with any other member of the family since the death of our dear mother, and we are going to miss his letters a great deal. Since Bella's death, Sophie and I are the only couple in our family with both members still alive.

And, as for you and me, which of us will outlive the other? Only God knows. Very likely it will be you, not only because I'm two years older than you, but because I feel fairly certain that I'm more worn out than you. Having only one eye would mean nothing if the other one were strong, which it is not, but my head, which has tormented me all my life, is getting much weaker. Yet who can tell?

And at present things are quite different, and sometimes I despair of continuing the struggle. And then, false news every day adds to my anxiety. It seems impossible that a nation that is so horribly in the wrong should triumph, and I do not give up hope, but the strength and prowess of the Germans are prodigious; they are united and much more patriotic than the British, who are making no more of an effort than they absolutely have to.

Let's write to one another more often. We must tighten the bonds between us. A thousand thousand loving greetings to the whole family.

> Your devoted brother,
> Theodore

**Theodore to Elisée**

> San Dimas
> Los Angeles, California
> August (?), 1917

My dear, my only, my posthumous[1] brother:

Everybody on our side is magnificently brave. The British have had the hardest part of the job up to now, but the others are going to get their turn. Our men from around here are eager to go and join up with their friends in France and Belgium, and we are told that great reinforcements in men and munitions are on their way. May God protect them from the submarines.

It has done our hearts good to see the Allies take it upon themselves to grab the Dutch navy without asking the Germans whether they might do it or not and without waiting for the Germans to take it first. Poor Russia should have made her experiments a year or two ago so she could be of some help to us instead of making such a hash of things now. As far as I'm concerned, I'd have told the Japanese and Chinese[2] to press forward with their 200,000 soldiers and then find fault with their decision later on if the occasion should arise, but the Americans have mistrusted all that is not Anglo-Saxon, except for the French, since this war started.

And what has been happening in your family or families? It seems to me that, all things considered, they have gotten off rather easily. Two of our boys have been called up but haven't yet reached the front. One of them, Donald Bishop, is busy all the time repairing trucks and autos, but he isn't in the trenches. The other, Harold Bost (Alphonse's son), has passed the examination, but it appears that for the moment he is to be left on the farm because his ailing father cannot carry it on all by himself; but from one day to the next he could be called up. There is also a second son who is of the right age to be included in the next contingent to be sent off. It seems very strange to go off to fight a war so far from home. *Well*, all the boys are ready to go off to war with enthusiasm. Let's hope they'll come back again after they've helped put that wicked Kaiser in his place—how does he dare to speak of God as his partner?

As for us oldsters, we stay at home. Sophie and Alice are both working nearly full time for the Red Cross, but, as for myself, I can't even help grow food in the fields, gardens, etc. I've had a nasty shock which has taught me that one may be "called up" without being mobilized for war. Although I'm still walking around and able to go on foot as far as the center of town, I can't work any more. In the first place, my old head torments me, and then my hernia gets worse all the time, and [I have] other failings. The long and short of it is that I'm getting old.

*Both here* and in Texas a long drought has discouraged the farmers, but here a couple of weeks of rain have filled the underground reservoirs. At Alphonse's place they're still hoping for rain. And there's absolutely nothing that can be done about it, so they've come to the point of saying, like the official to our father when he said he depended on God to pay the church expenses: "Ah! That's risky." Delightful ignorance!

Well, then, dear brother and all your families—be of good heart, God is with us and He is *not* risky. Let us do the best we can, however feeble it may be, to crush this oh-so-powerful enemy.

So, good-bye to you all. My wife joins me in sending all good wishes.

> Your loving brother and uncle,
> Theodore Bost

### Theodore to Elisée

> San Dimas, California
> Day of the Escalade,[3] 1917

Dearest Brother:

We'd be very happy to have more news from you. We have plenty of news furnished wholesale by our newspapers, often very good news, but at other times not good.

Before this war the Anglo-Saxons boasted a lot about their great superiority over the Latin race, and that angered me. But now it's not at all the same state of affairs, and our American troops are doing justice to the French and are proud to be [fighting] alongside French veterans; and these Yankees are pretty good at learning anything there is to be learned.

And now Jerusalem has been taken, despite the Germans' promises to the Mohammedans, and Paris has *not* been taken.

Here are a few family items. Sophie has just observed her eighty-second birthday; she's getting old, but is still spry and enjoys good health; she keeps very busy all the time—the Red Cross, other societies, including one for the French; also sewing and knitting and so forth. She has rheumatism in her knees. As for myself—36,000 causes for complaint, getting more deaf, my good eye is getting weaker, and I have to go easy on it; it's very hard to see things at a distance, but I can still read very well without glasses, and so can Sophie.

Well, there you are. Best greetings to all of you from us, and a thousand good wishes for the New Year.

> Your brother,
> Theodore Bost
> and Sophie

### Theodore to Elisée

> San Dimas, California
> May 2, 1918

Dearest Brother:

Many things remind us that we're at war, apart from the draft, or rather the appeals for volunteers. There's no end to the list of good causes for which people are taking up collections. In the first place, [there have been] three great campaigns to sell war bonds: number one, an appeal for $1 billion; followed by another for 2 billion (*dollars, of course*); followed by another for a minimum of 3 billion or, if possible, 5 billion. When I came to America, and right up to the war of 1860, our country was in debt to Europe for millions of dollars, and we've been completely unaware of the repayment of these debts, which weighed on our industries. Everything came from Europe, and we had nothing with which to pay for it except our cotton and wheat.

And now these few millions have been paid off ages ago. We are self-sufficient in the commodities we need. We can skim off billions of dollars to pay for this war and lend a billion (more or less) to our various allies. It's a mystery where all this money comes from, considering that during the same time we've had to build everything up from nothing. Out here we had to build Los Angeles and its seaport, San Pedro, wharves, dikes, etc., and bring in thousands of workers, build housing for them, cut down the forests 500 miles from here, open up huge quarries of hydraulic lime, bring in from Pennsylvania and the East—even, I believe, from England—all sorts of materials to build fleets of ships to replace those the Germans have sunk.

Very well, these ships are being built. One of the biggest of them, the *Los Angeles*, has just been launched. No sooner was it afloat than the senior captain suggested that for its first voyage it should be sent to France filled with supplies and clothing of all kinds for the poor people of Belgium and Northern France who have had to suffer so much these last four years from those devilish Germans. It seemed impossible to me that such a large ship could be filled [with gifts]—but these Americans! The suggestion was accepted with enthusiasm, and from all directions there poured in a flood of foodstuffs, about forty tons of beans, and on the same scale came clothing, etc., and the ship's hold was filled while the ship was still being completed; in about two weeks they plan to send it off, and if it gets there after running the gauntlet of submarines, it will be up to you to unload it.

While this was being done, $1 million had to be collected for the Red Cross. No sooner was that collected than another campaign for $1 million was started. They think it will be fully subscribed by the end of this week. The more people give, the more they are asked to give, and nobody protests except those who don't like baker's bread!!! I'm one of these latter. I've been ill for several weeks, as you can tell from my scribbling, and I don't like to have my habits disturbed. But to win this war I'd sacrifice more than that. When you get this letter, that great [German] offensive aimed at Ypres and Amiens will have taken place,[4] and we hope and believe that the right will have triumphed, despite the best efforts of the devil and his son, the Kaiser. Those millions and billions I was speaking of—that has only to do with California; the other states are giving their quotas too.

But where does all this money come from??? From the sale of munitions in part, but our whole region is in the midst of a building boom. In 1887, Los Angeles had 20,000 inhabitants; now there are more than a million. Instead of a swamp near the seacoast, we have a port that will be better than San Francisco's. I thought I was writing to our dear brother Tim, to whom I used to tell everything about subjects that interested him, but, by God's grace, he is far away from this world of clay and if he's interested, it's only to say "Thy kingdom come." It's up to us to help with our puny strength to bring this to pass.

I feel I'm getting very old; Sophie has aged much less than I, but she has rheumatism which I don't have. She is always at work on something; there's always an opportunity to do some work: *Belgian Relief, Red Cross work*, and the housekeeping besides, knitting and crocheting and taking care of me when I take a notion to stay in bed.

## Theodore to Elisée

San Dimas, California
December 8, 1918

My very dear, only, and unique Brother:

A lot of things have happened since [I wrote] my last letter which was, I think, not long before the end of the war. What a splendid finish to an atrocious war because, even though some fighting is still going on, there are no longer any of those great battles with heaps of dead and wounded. We're getting to the point of understanding how to wind it up properly. There's no use trying to determine who has done the most [to win the war]. We say that we ended it with our fresh troops who replaced the Allies who had suffered so much for more than four years. Each nation boasts of having done its best and is willing to agree that everyone else has done the same.

It remains now to finish things off properly, and I hope that the outcome of the [peace] conference at Versailles will satisfy the Allies, if not the Germans, who have no right to be satisfied, though they too did the best they could. This question of reparations, these millions that they'll have to pay, doesn't seem to bother them, according to the newspapers, which say this debt will be all paid off in twenty-six years. They'll need to work pretty hard to be able to do it, but in the last fifty years they've built up a lot of financial power, and I'm very glad that on this score our people haven't shown them any indulgence. These payments should suffice to rebuild Belgium and France, replacing what was destroyed, but they won't begin to pay for the suffering, the deaths, the invalids, the loss of time, and the exhaustion of minerals that God had deposited in these countries so that a good use might be made of them, whereas human beings (?) [sic] have misused them to destroy the world. And the Germans, who were so sure that Wilson didn't want [an end to the] war that would humiliate them—what arrogance!

Speaking of Wilson—you have been surprised that people here don't admire as much as you do what he has done or not done. We give him credit for a great many things, but for a long time I've been wondering how long he'd be allowed to set himself up as a Kaiser in this country, which is full of good minds; and when he took it into his head to decide how we should manage our elections, he got rapped on the knuckles. In the first place, he's a rabid Democrat, elected in large measure by the whole pro-slavery party and by the dregs of the cities at a time when our Republican party was divided between the so-called Progressives [and the regular Republicans], and Wilson did his level best to crush the party of Lincoln and of Lincoln's successors. Indeed, a year ago the Republican party was almost snuffed out, but as an eminent man said, you can't destroy a party whose members are so much higher in quality than the others, and our elections have certainly proved him right. We had lost the House and the Senate, but now we have a strong majority in the House and also [have made gains] in the Senate, though it will take years to change the latter, and among our delegates at Versailles we have several excellent minds, although we also have a President who, in spite of the protests of the country, appoints himself (the sort of thing he is always doing) the chief of our delegation. All our Republican Presidents have appoint Democrats to certain offices which they could have filled [with Republicans], but this fellow completely ignores all those who aren't Democrats and is continually imposing himself on the country although there are many, many old Republicans who are his superiors from every point of view, men whom the country had wanted to have appointed as delegates to Versailles. Our party has given him its support all through this war while his own party was voting against him, and for these reasons we're indignant. Well, that's enough on that subject.

A thousand affectionate greetings and best wishes for the holidays.

Your devoted, loving, and only brother,<br>Theodore Bost

## Theodore to Elisée

San Dimas, Los Angeles County<br>June 4, 1919

My very dear, still unique, and posthumous Brother:

Oh! This war! All sorts of things make me sick to my stomach. For four years, as I awoke in the morning, I asked myself what horrors I'd find in the newspaper; then came the Armistice with all its promise, and day after day I'd keep asking myself how things were going. One forgets that, after all, the Germans have been chased out of France, and even if the compensation for the damage they've done isn't what it ought to be, it seems to me it should be enough to get France back on her feet again. I'm much more eager to see the cities and villages rebuilt properly than to have enormous cathedrals. Each to his own taste. As you go from Asnières to Bourges, you see the great church (the cathedral) which towers over the thousands of wretched houses around it; Papa didn't admire it at all, and would have preferred to see greater equality and well-being.

How good it is not to be in daily expectation of more deaths in our families [from military action]. We are awaiting Edward Bishop from one day to the next. He hasn't been involved in any of the great battles. His assignment was in the camps, leading the young athletes, etc., football. Donald Bishop has been occupied the whole time in repairing machines and has earned good money all the while. I've been riveted here for months and couldn't go to see our boy Edward; but he came here to get us last Friday, and we've stayed four days [with him].

This property of about 150 *hectares* [330 acres] goes under the name of Bost and Johnstone, but the latter has put in more than half the value because it was necessary to invest enormous amounts in building and developing everything, and we still have to build a fine house that will do us justice, miles of cement pipe, huge barns, concrete silos, drill a deep well that will give about *200 inches*[5] *of water* with a powerful *engine*, buy all kinds of machines. Right now they have about a hundred cows, about a hundred young stock two to three years old, a hundred yearlings, about twenty horses, about forty pigs; and the little girls have around fifty rabbits and two hundred chickens. Just think of the work: 200 acres in wheat, barley, alfalfa (*légumes*) [*sic*]. They expect to harvest 1,000 tons of grain and hay and sell 1,500 to 2,000 pounds of milk per day. But the expenses! All the same, they are beginning to show a profit. They are a wonderful family. He and his wife make a fine couple, and they have four daughters between ten and sixteen or seventeen years old. Everybody has work to do, and there are no servants in the house, but they employ ten to thirty workers when the workload is at its peak: building projects, ditching, threshing grain, etc. It takes a pretty good head to keep track of everything.

Theodore

# XXII

# "All Flesh Is Grass"

These last two letters complete the pilgrimage of Theodore and Sophie Bost and close a seventy-year record. They require no further comment.

**Theodore to Charles Bost, son of Elisée**

> San Dimas
> Los Angeles, California
> April 23, 1920

My dear Nephew:

We received your letter of February 27 at the same time as the one from Hélène Cadier which also told us the sad news of my dear brother's death, the last (except for me) of our fine big family of ten boys.[1]

He was the one I spent the most time with up to 1848 and even beyond that up to the time we lived in Neuchâtel, where I left him until my return in '70 to Le Pouzin where I came so close to making your acquaintance on the first day of your life. During all our school days we were very close, and I took it upon myself to be his protector on several occasions, an attitude I've never outgrown. So far as age goes, we were only two and a half years apart, but we've always been very close, notwithstanding the fact that our lives have been so different. With the exception of my brother Tim, he was the brother with whom I corresponded most, and I accept your offer to be my correspondent in his place.

What happiness to be almost finished with this war, if it can indeed be said that we're done with it. We don't any longer have such vast numbers of dead and wounded and threats of famine. In your country they blame a certain party, the party of Lincoln,

354

Roosevelt, McKinley, the Protestant party, the party whose leaders have always been cherished and venerated, but who have been replaced by the pro-slavery party, friendly to the Catholic masses although the President is a Presbyterian. It's no use trying to explain how all this has come about. Plenty of defects in our system of government have become apparent, though our party has loyally respected the rights of the man who, legally speaking, was our chief of state. But this has been an uphill job, and we'll all be happy when we again have a leader who will respect the rights of other people. The great majority are for the League of Nations and will ratify it in the end. Meanwhile we have chaos, revolts, and revolutions; but God reigns above, and let us never forget that.

I must finish, then, with a thousand good wishes and expressions of sympathy for all of you, dear cousins of both sexes and other relatives.

Let's write frequently.

Your most devoted
Theodore Bost

**Sophie to Charles Bost**

San Dimas, Los Angeles County
California
June 26, 1920

My dear Nephew:

Your good letter of June 9 reached me yesterday, and I hasten to reply, even though the news is not good. When you wrote, our family here was in great sorrow and distress on account of your Uncle Theodore's illness. It started with a malign erysipelas which quickly developed into blood poisoning. It could only end in one way, and on the nineteenth my dear husband expired peacefully. May God be thanked that He has recalled His child to Him, for the doctor feared he would lose his mind completely; the delirium, which lasted three weeks, was the most agonizing part for all of us; and our poor invalid's sufferings were greater than any of us could imagine. There is no use going into all these details, which are so painful that they leave cruel memories. He couldn't recognize us any longer; he thought he was being neglected all the time we were surrounding him with the most devoted attentions; and there was even a danger that the sick-nurse might refuse to go on with her duties. No, dear Charles, I really cannot go into any further detail. Be grateful that your dear father and your family have been spared [what we went through].

All our friends in San Dimas and Pomona have sustained us with their prayers and sympathy. Your uncle had many friends, and very few of them were aware of what was going on at our place. The funeral was held Monday, June 22. The casket was covered with flowers, so many that they spilled over onto the floor. It goes without saying that our dear children were completely devoted and did everything they could do for their father and me. I was able to sit with him night and day, for which I thank God with all my heart.

And now I shall try to recover from these weeks of agony.

If you can find time to write to your old Aunt Sophie, I hope she'll be able to answer you in a little more reasonable manner. I know very little about your immediate family, now that our dear Elisée is no longer able to answer the roll call. He always wrote us such fine letters. But now, this is the last of the ten brothers who have gone to be with their elders. There remain only two sisters— Effie in Versailles and I in San Dimas. Soon you, who were the youngsters, will be the old people.

With affection,
Your old Aunt Sophie

This is the last letter. Sophie died at the age of eighty-seven on November 6, 1922, two and a half years after Theodore. Their graves are in Pomona, California.

# Postscript

From 1859 to 1973, there were born fifty-three descendants of Sophie and Theodore bearing the name of Bost: six children, nine grandchildren, fourteen great-grandchildren, and twenty-four in succeeding generations. In addition there were eight grandchildren named Bishop or Johnstone, twenty-nine great-grandchildren named Bishop, Benner, Montgomery, Hand, McKeeman, Rimpau, Thomas, Schaefer, Patton, Westlake, Mitchell, and many others belonging to younger generations. All are American citizens.

No one has been able to find a single scrap of writing received by Theodore and Sophie from Europe—all these old letters have completely disappeared.

# NOTES

# Notes

## Introduction

1. Ami Bost attended the Moravian institute in Neuwied, near Coblentz, from 1798 to 1802, that is, from age eight to age twelve. He then returned to Geneva to study theology. During his student years, like many young Romantics of Protestant background, he was strongly attracted to Roman Catholicism; for a while he considered taking monastic vows, and he read extensively in the literature of Christian mysticism.

2. Ami Bost, *Mémoires pour servir à l'histoire du Reveil religieux des églises protestantes de la Suisse et de la France* (2 vols.), 1854; supplementary vol., 1855. Vol. II, p. 434.

3. The elder Bosts came into a substantial inheritance from Jenny's father at his death. Otherwise, we know that Timothée, a successful businessman, was persuaded to lend or give money to Theodore at various times. In particular, Timothée joined with Jenny to pay for Theodore's trip to Europe in 1870-71, and he sent Theodore a telegraphic money order in 1874 to enable him to buy a partnership in a general store in Excelsior. So far as we know, none of this money was ever repaid, though Theodore made interest payments when he could.

4. Ami Bost, *Mémoires,* vol. I, p. 211.

5. *Ibid.*, vol. II, p 243.

6. Soon after his arrival in America, at a time when he had been eating well and doing light work, he reported that his weight was 154 pounds. Theodore was five feet nine inches tall, hence rather scrawny.

7. The baptismal name of M. Vaucher (as all members of the Bost family invariably refer to him) is not known.

8. Letter from Theodore to his brother Paul, dated "Bellevue, 29 Octobre 1848."

9. Letter from Theodore to his father, January 1849. Ami Bost had just lost his chaplaincy in Melun; he and Jenny had then gone to stay briefly with friends in Versailles. In the spring of 1849 they came to stay with the Vauchers and went on from there to Neuchâtel.

10. Ami Bost, *Mémoires*, vol. II, p. 425.

11. Her father, without categorically opposing the marriage, was reluctant to agree to Sophie's departure for the wilds of America, and her final acceptance came only after her father's death. From her letters it may be inferred that she had been attracted to another man, at least briefly; the ending of this relationship may finally have cleared the way for her acceptance.

### I. Off to America

1. The word was coined in 1827 by the German physician Samuel Hahnemann, inventor of the system in which sick people are treated by giving them extremely small doses of a substance (for example, quinine) capable of producing in a healthy person the symptoms (for example, fever) of the illness (malaria). The word "allopathy," meaning traditional medicine, was introduced in 1843; it was used by Hahnemann's followers to mean "overmedication," whereas they insisted that most drugs were harmful and that the doctor's role was to allow Nature to bring about the cure.

2. Not far from Neuchâtel.

3. Jules Roussel and César Pronier. We hear nothing further about the former, but Pronier had been with Theodore on the Vaucher farm and they remained in touch for many years. After farming for a short time, Pronier returned to Switzerland in 1853 to study theology and enter the ministry. In 1870 Theodore learned that his old friend was planning to attend the New York meeting of the Evangelical Alliance in 1873. Theodore apparently did not meet Pronier in 1870-71, though he spent some time in Switzerland, nor did the two friends see each other in 1873 when Pronier was in America. Pronier died on his way back to Europe when the *Ville du Havre*, on which he was a passenger, was lost at sea.

### II. A Wanderer in the New World

1. St.-Jean d'Iberville, Quebec.

2. The term "piastre" was used as a synonym for "dollar" at this period.

3. Theodore had never been in Ireland, so he presumably means "back to Europe to settle in Ireland." His brother Tim was living there and had suggested that Theodore might manage a farm or do farm work for him.

4. The *arpent*, used in France before the introduction of the metric system, was a little smaller than the English acre. A thousand *arpents* would be the equivalent of 499 *hectares*, or 928.4 acres.

5. In December, 1853, Theodore had been baptized by total immersion in a pond during a week's visit to his old friends at Grande Ligne; a hole had to be chopped through the ice.

6. The reference is to the Crimean War, which had just broken out.

7. Theodore is actually referring to the terms of the Missouri Compromise of 1820.

8. This was the celebrated Anthony Burns. Money was collected with which to purchase his freedom, and he ended his days as a Baptist minister in Canada.

9. Theodore means the Catholic population of Quebec. Savoy, then part of the Italian kingdom of Piedmont, was also Catholic.

10. Theodore had a Réaumur thermometer in Minnesota. On the Réaumur scale, 0° is the freezing point and 80° the boiling point of water.

11. By J. Wesley Bond. The book was a piece of "booster" literature.

12. Meaning that mournful expressions are out of place.

### III. Westward to Minnesota

1. The point of Theodore's joke is not clear. Presumably he is alluding to the pound sterling, a "hard" currency, and the contrast between it and the American paper dollar whose value was highly uncertain at this period.

2. See below, p. 35. As with other immigrant groups, the Swiss who were already established here tried to help newcomers get a start in the New World. The reader will have noticed how often this "Swiss Connection" has already worked to Theodore's advantage, and this was by no means the last time he was helped out of a tough spot by compatriots.

3. That is to say, from French-speaking Switzerland. Lausanne is the principal city of the canton of Vaud. This was not, strictly speaking, Theodore's own *pays*, which was the country around Geneva, with secondary attachments to the Neuchâtel area just north of the Vaudois region.

4. Captain William B. Dodd played a considerable part in the opening of the Minnesota River valley to settlement in the 1850s, but not much seems to be known in detail about his activities. His road, begun in 1853, originated at the Lower Landing in St. Paul and had reached the settlements at Rock Bend (now part of St. Peter) and Traverse des Sioux by the time (midsummer, 1853) a surveying team headed by Captain Jesse Lee Reno (for whom Reno, Nevada, was later named) had made its way there from the junction of the Big Sioux and Missouri Rivers (now Sioux City, Iowa). Reno's route then followed Dodd's road to the Mississippi. Dodd was probably financially interested in the St. Peter settlements; his early clearing and bridge-building work was paid for in part by contributions which he solicited in 1852 from settlers in the Minnesota River valley who had flocked there by the thousands after the Indian Treaties of Traverse des Sioux and Mendota were signed in 1851. Captain Reno recommended in his report to Congress that Dodd be paid $3,270 for the work his crew had done in 1853, but Dodd had to wait for his reimbursement until Congress finally appropriated the money in 1862. Dodd continued to build his road westward along Reno's trace in the following years; contracts were let in May, 1855 (the date of Theodore's arrival in St. Paul) for the Mendota-Mankato sections, and, as we learn from Theodore, construction resumed that summer south and west of St. Peter. Funds voted by Congress were depleted by 1858, by which time the road had been built (though only very sketchily in some stretches) to a point about seven miles west of the Blue Earth River. Dodd himself was killed at New Ulm by Indians during the Sioux uprising of 1862. (See Grover Singley, *Tracing Minnesota's Old Government Roads*, Chapter VI, "The Mendota-Big Sioux River Road" [St. Paul: Minnesota Historical Society, 1974], pp. 39-52.) Theodore's first-hand account brings out some of Dodd's less endearing traits and gives an idea of his business methods; much of this material will be new to historians.

5. Philippe Suchard, founder of the well-known chocolate firm. He came to the United States in 1824 and published an account of his travels in German and later in French.

6. Actually only a few miles south of the center of St. Paul on the Mississippi opposite Fort Snelling and the mouth of the Minnesota River. Since Mendota was never much more than a trading post maintained by the American Fur Company, it probably would not have appeared on maps obtainable in Europe, and Theodore would have had no occasion to go there during his brief stay in St. Paul. As the ensuing discussion reveals, moreover, his grasp of Minnesota geography was rather weak at this time.

7. An obvious slip of the pen: he means that the *weather* has been dry.

8. Perhaps Theodore had meant to write "years," meaning the time since his arrival in America; but his memory was at fault if he really meant that he had been in Minnesota five months. When he wrote this, he had been there only three months—no doubt it *seemed* longer.

9. All these are places in Switzerland and France where Theodore had lived while growing up. It is difficult to know how literally to take his statement that during all those years he had been thinking of coming to America. No doubt America had had a romantic interest for him even as a child, but his memory may not be reliable as to the time when he first began to think seriously of emigrating.

10. Theodore's comparison is puzzling. Perhaps he is thinking of the twisted wax candle or taper used in religious ceremonies; or he may have had in mind a candle that has been softened by heat.

11. Literally: "by taking three homeopathic doses in one." See note on homeopathy, p. 362. What medicine he took is not specified, but the chances are that it was a patent medicine containing either alcohol or laudanum.

12. A play on the French word *cousin* (mosquito or daddy-long-legs in popular parlance) which he had used in his preceding sentence.

13. "In advance" may mean "in advance of the date when I would ordinarily be writing to you" or "in advance of receiving your reply to my last letter."

14. Large, handsome public gardens on the south bank of the Rhône in the center of Geneva.

15. His parents' address at that time.

16. Elisée was Theodore's younger brother. Whether the piece of red cedar had any symbolic significance is impossible to determine.

17. The second oldest daughter of Ami Bost, Jr., died in May, 1855.

18. Etienne, an older brother, had married Sophie Vivien June 26, 1855.

19. The lake of Bienne is in Switzerland, just east of the lake of Neuchâtel. It is not clear to which "Saint-Pierre" Theodore is referring; probably he means St. Peter, Minnesota, from which this letter is dated.

20. A piece of inspirational literature written by Maria Susanna Cummins; it enjoyed very wide distribution following its publication in 1854.

21. The expression *revenir à mes moutons* (literally, "to come back to my sheep") is idiomatic in French and means "to return to my subject," "to get back to what I was talking about." Theodore is also making a play on words here; he means "to get back to my true vocation of farming."

22. A mission northeast of Montreal where Theodore spent some time regaining his health in September, 1854.

23. Marie had been a governess, a teacher, and a lady's companion in well-to-do families.

24. By Solon Robinson (1803-80), published in 1854.

25. Carver's Cave, named for the eighteenth-century explorer Jonathan Carver, adjacent to Indian Mounds Park in the limestone bluff at the edge of the Mississippi in St. Paul.

26. The Know-Nothing Party grew out of the anti-Catholic and anti-immigrant agitation of the 1840s. It was revived in all parts of the nation after the election of 1852, and by 1854 it had become a major force, reflecting the breakup of the Whigs and Democrats over the slavery question. Officially named the American Party, the movement was popularly known as the Know-Nothing party because it consisted of secret lodges whose password was "I know nothing." By 1856 internal dissension over slavery led to the rapid disruption of the party, and many of its former members switched over to the new Republican Party.

27. There was and is no Fort Atkinson in Minnesota. Theodore may have read about

a George Flower, who was a member of a British settlement in Albion, Illinois. Fort Atkinson was an early frontier post in Nebraska.

28. *Nicht ferschté [versteh']:* Swiss-German for "I don't understand."

29. Theodore who, as a Baptist, wanted to show that he disapproved of this form of baptism, uses the hybrid word *sprinkla,* the English word "sprinkle" with the ending "-a" of a first-conjugation French verb in the simple past tense.

30. In April, 1853, about seventy-five settlers from central Massachusetts (the Northampton Colony) had come to St. Paul. A short time later four families—the Cleavelands, Powers, Lymans, and Moores—consisting of people who were mostly if not all Congregationalists, went to live in the place that was to become Chanhassen, just east of the southern tip of Lake Minnewashta where Theodore's claim was located. His quarter-section was adjacent to and south of the eastern part of what is now the University of Minnesota Landscape Arboretum. At about the same time, a second group, also heavily Congregationalist, the Excelsior Pioneer Association, came from New York state to found the town of Excelsior, about five miles to the north on the southern edge of Lake Minnetonka.

### IV. Alone on the Claim

1. Louis XIV (reigned 1643-1715) is supposed to have said, *"L'Etat, c'est moi"* ("I am the State").

2. Sebastopol, fortified by the Russians, was besieged and finally stormed by the French and British forces, thus ending the Crimean War (1854-56). The city actually fell in September, 1855.

3. Marie Narbel was Theodore's first cousin since she was the daughter of one of Ami Bost's sisters.

4. These are the words of a hymn from *The Pilgrim's Progress* as translated and set to music by Theodore's father.

5. The question mark is in Theodore's original letter. He had apparently just decided to grow one, and the results were not yet very impressive.

6. The brother in question is Timothée in Glasgow. Theodore and later Sophie frequently routed their letters to the elder Bosts by way of Glasgow, where Ami Bost, Junior, also lived; the letters were then readdressed and sent on to France. This arrangement had the advantage of saving postage while keeping the Glasgow relations up to date. It did, however, sometimes make it hard to tell to whom this or that remark was addressed—the effect is more or less the same as listening in on a "conference call."

7. As in Theodore's original. The meaning seems clear; the boat went every third day, or twice a week.

8. From the father of Isabella ("Bella") Lennox, the Scottish girl Timothée was courting. They were married in October, 1857, two years and one month after Timothée's proposal, to which Bella's father long refused to agree.

9. Sophie was almost exactly a year younger than Theodore, having celebrated her twentieth birthday on December 7, 1855. At this time, Julie was taking care of children in an institution in Hofwyl—Hofwil in present-day spelling—in the canton of Berne. Sophie was teaching school and working as a governess in England and Scotland where, in the fall of 1856, she made the acquaintance of Theodore's two brothers Timothée and Ami.

10. Theodore, who had formed a low opinion of the Irish during his work with

Captain Dodd's road-building crew, presumably is not certain whether the mailman is or is not an Irishman, only that his carefree ways are typical of the Irish.

11. The word should be written: Chan-has-san. It means "the tree with sweet sap," "the sugar tree." The name seems to have been chosen by Mrs. Clarissa Cleaveland or her brother-in-law, the Rev. Henry Martyn Nichols, who at this time was living in St. Anthony. The Cleavelands were among the earliest residents of the village. Their name was frequently misspelled "Cleveland" in the local press and even in official records. Theodore and Sophie also sometimes use this incorrect spelling. The correct form is used hereafter.

12. Although the clarity of this description leaves something to be desired, the general layout of Theodore's two-room cabin was apparently the following: there was a larger cabin, twenty-three feet by thirteen feet, which he calls his living room, floored with split oak logs and with a cellar; it had a peaked roof loosely covered with shingles. This was the newer cabin, but it proved to be too hard to heat, so he moved into the original claim shanty, a lean-to about eight feet by eight feet, with a floor of split basswood logs and a very leaky roof, probably unshingled. Between the two was a connecting door, which he calls the east door of his living room—that is, of the large cabin—so it must have been the *west* door of his bedroom (the smaller lean-to). Because the two cabins were so poorly joined, it was possible to see the sun and the moon at the same time through the open spaces around the doorframe.

13. Etienne, who held a pastorate in Wanquetin, near Arras, had married Sophie Vivien on June 26, 1855.

14. The hero of James Fennimore Cooper's novel of that name.

15. In southern France, where Theodore's father and mother were then living.

## V. Waiting for Sophie

1. At this time, Sophie was employed as a governess at Philiphaugh Castle in Scotland.

2. For whom Jacob had to wait fourteen years.

3. The Minnesota land boom of the mid-1850s was approaching its height. Within a year, owing to the financial panic of 1857, the bottom was to drop out of the market for farm products, forcing many settlers into bankruptcy and ushering in a period of hard times and depressed land values that did not really end until after the Civil War.

4. Theodore was technically only a squatter on his land, waiting, as were his neighbors, for the government survey of his area to be completed. At that time he would be obliged to "preempt" his claim by paying for it in cash at the rate of $1.25 an acre—a total of $200 for his 160-acre claim. The money he had already paid the previous settler was only to indemnify the latter for his "squatter's right"—an unofficial title to the land that was dependable only because of the determination of all the settlers to take drastic common action against anyone who attempted to "jump" an occupied claim—action that might include anything from a bloody nose to a lynching.

5. See note 30, chapter III. These neighbors were New England Congregationalists who had settled near Lake Minnewashta in the spring in 1852; most of them came from Northampton, Massachusetts, or from the nearby towns of Williamsburg, Belchertown, South Hadley Falls, and Easthampton. H. M. Lyman of Northampton was Chanhassen's first postmaster. We shall hear a great deal more about George M. Powers of Belchertown, who was a former schoolteacher; he became a particularly close friend of Theodore's; the Powers and Bost families were often in each other's houses, and the men were firm allies in the new Republican party. The Adams referred to is probably the surveyor Andrew W. Adams, who named Lake Hazeltine for Susan Hazeltine, the young school-

teacher (Chanhassen's first) whom he subsequently married. Theodore accompanied Adams and acted as his interpreter in negotiations for land which Adams bought from German and Swiss settlers (see pp. 100-102). (See Charles W. Nichols, "The Northampton Colony and Chanhassen," *Minnesota History*, 20 [1939]: 140-45.)

6. Théophile's wife was an English girl, Eliza Baker. He had met her while he was a theology student at Montauban and she was studying French in a boarding school there.

7. Timothée had great difficulty obtaining the consent of Isabella Lennox's father to their marriage, and Sophie Bonjour's father, while not saying "No," was proving most reluctant to see her accept Theodore's proposal.

8. See note 11, chapter IV. Arba Cleaveland and his wife, whose maiden name was Clarissa Sikes, came from Belchertown, Massachusetts, in April 1852, with the Northampton Colony. Mrs. Cleaveland was a sister of Nancy Sikes Nichols, the wife of Rev. Henry Martyn Nichols, leader of the colony. We shall hear a great deal about the Cleaveland family, who lived just over a mile away from the Bosts, attended the same church, and shared with them strong interests in antislavery (later Republican) politics and temperance. The settlers from the Connecticut Valley of Massachusetts are the subject of three articles by Charles W. Nichols, the grandson of Rev. Henry Martyn Nichols, in *Minnesota History* (19 [June, 1938]: 129-46; 20 [June, 1939]: 140-45; 21 [June, 1940]: 169-73); these are based on the Nichols Papers in The Minnesota Historical Society and on articles in the *Northampton* (Mass.) *Courier.*

9. Théophile was living in Paris and teacher at the Duplessis-Mornay Institute. Batignolles is (or was then) a suburb of Paris.

10. These temperature figures are not easy to make sense of. On Theodore's Réaumur thermometer, 0° was the freezing point and 80° the boiling point of water. It is the editor's guess that the first figure given in this paragraph should be -12° R. [5° F.], though Theodore did not use a minus sign in front of the figure 12. However, +12° R. would be 59° F., which would not exactly have deserved his adjective "chilly." The following sentence seems to deal with very cold weather, hence with *minus* degrees R. (below freezing). The most reasonable interpretation is that Theodore wrote "warmer" when he meant to write "colder" or that he was being ironic. A temperature of -20° R. equals -13° F.; -30° R. equals -35.5° F.; -4° R. equals 23° F.; -5° R. equals 20.75° F.; and -10° R. equals 9.5° F. His meaning probably is that Minnesota weather seems less cold than European weather because of the sunshine and low humidity in winter.

11. We do not know exactly what M. Bonjour said, but from other indications in the correspondence we can infer that he had told Ami Bost he would not stand in the way of Sophie's marriage to Theodore if she herself were wholeheartedly in favor of it.

12. The Selkirk settlement was founded and promoted by Lord Selkirk, a Scottish nobleman, who sent over the first body of mainly Scottish and English pioneers in 1812. They established a colony in and around Pembina in the valley of the Red River of the North on land granted by the Hudson's Bay Company. After the international boundary was surveyed, this Red River settlement was found to be on American territory, whereupon some colonists withdrew to Canada. In 1825, 1826, and 1827 great damage was caused by the record floods of those years; the majority of the Selkirk colony then moved farther north and settled in the vicinity of Winnipeg, while other refugees from the Pembina colony (including several Swiss families) moved to lands adjoining Fort Snelling.

13. Theodore means 36° 30' N. Lat. This was the northern boundary of slavery fixed by the Missouri Compromise of 1820.

14. By the Kansas-Nebraska Act (1854).

15. Sophie Laguerre, wife of Theodore's older brother Samuel. Ami and Jenny Bost were living with them in Salies-de-Béarn.

16. About three acres.

17. See note 4, p. 366.

18. A reference to Aesop's fable "The Man, the Boy, and the Donkey." Attempting to please everyone they met in their journey, they at first mounted the father on the donkey, then the son in his place, then both together. Finally, because each of these arrangements met with someone's displeasure, they both got off and walked. Moral: In trying to please everyone you will please no one.

19. Anna (Fanny) Maxwell was married soon after this time, but whether or not her husband was the "young Irishman" Theodore disliked so much is not known.

20. Minnesota entered the Union as a free state together with Oregon in 1858.

21. Samuel's wife was expecting a baby.

22. One can only assume that Mrs. Maxwell had said "sovereignly good."

## VI. The Honeymoon

1. Marie had died on August 3, 1858, in Salies-de-Béarn. The news had apparently not reached Chanhassen by early December when this letter was written. As with several other letters from or to Theodore and Sophie, the letter may have gone astray in the mails or may even have been lost in a shipwreck.

2. At this time New York was in the throes of a sensational religious revival which had begun with a meeting held in the old Dutch Reformed Church building on Fulton Street. The principal preacher was Charles G. Finney, an eloquent speaker who had evangelized both in Europe and in the United States. In 1835 he wrote *Discourses on Religious Revivals,* part of which was translated into French by Ami Bost. At the height of the revival in New York, there were as many as 50,000 conversions a week.

3. Mrs. Sheldon's husband was the Rev. Charles B. Sheldon, who had come to Excelsior in 1855.

4. The Sarvers were Easterners: they lived next door to the Bosts and were the people Theodore and Sophie called on in emergencies such as the birth of a child.

5. While this letter was crossing the Atlantic, a son, Ashton, was born to Bella and Timothée on February 15, 1859.

6. Eliza and Théophile had had a daughter, Marie, September 5, 1858.

7. Sophie was mistaken. Actually there were seven granddaughters and three grandsons.

## VII. The First Child

1. Theodore seems to have been a better Christian than businessman. He repeatedly complains that his Yankee neighbors drove hard bargains with him. They no doubt expected he would do the same when he held the advantage, but as in this case he could not do so. This probably helps account for his continual money problems and the recurring need for help from his family in Europe.

2. One of the other Sophies in the Bost family, Samuel's wife, was expecting a baby.

3. Adding an extra sheet would mean paying another five cents in postage. Details like this bring home to us how scarce money was on the Bost farm and what strict economy they practiced.

4. Sophie, in one of her rare allusions to her wedding, means that she and Theodore were obliged to get married immediately on her arrival in St. Paul because it would not have been possible for them to live in his cabin as an engaged couple even for a few days—no doubt because so many of the neighbors were strict New England Congregationalists—and they didn't have the money to live separately.

5. Words from a popular song or nursery rhyme.

6. Mrs. Cleaveland's sister was the wife of the Rev. Henry Martyn Nichols, who had a church in Minneapolis. The tragic multiple drowning described below took place at Lake Calhoun, west of Minneapolis, and was widely reported in the press.

7. An old friend of Theodore's. They had been together in Bellevue (near Neuchâtel) working for the Vaucher family, and they crossed the Atlantic together. Boissonnas, still a bachelor, acquired a farm in Illinois and sometimes came to help Theodore during the winter, beginning in 1861-62. He came in the summer of 1863 to help build the new frame house (see chapter XI, below).

8. Sophie seems to be describing the symptoms of thrush, a children's disease common at this period; the *aphtes,* or aphthas, are whitish pimples that appear inside the mouth. The disease is usually associated with malnutrition.

9. Probably the reference is to the Powers family, occupants of the quarter-section just to the east of the Maxwells, who had the quarter-section adjoining Theodore's on the south.

10. City in southeastern France where Ami and Jenny Bost were then living.

11. We know nothing of M. Perrot except that in the next letter Sophie refers to him as "somebody I don't know and hence could not write to thank" without Ami Bost's permission. Perrot was presumably a friend of the Bost family who sent the 100 frs. as a gift.

12. This valuable prize, awarded by the French Academy, had just been given to Theodore's brother John in recognition of his philanthropic endeavors. John was touring England to collect money with which to build more asylums. He had already founded three: one for orphans and two for the mentally retarded.

## VIII. The Civil War Begins

1. Cheeseman may have been the same Methodist preacher who set a prairie fire while burning a pile of weeds (see pp. 156-57 above). He was a neighboring farmer at this time, having given up the ministry, and he and Theodore had made a barter deal whereby Cheeseman split rails for fences in return for one of Theodore's cows. Later they were both interested in acquiring a lime quarry.

2. Probably the Rev. Charles B. Sheldon, who came to Excelsior in 1855 to take over the ministerial duties of the Rev. Charles Galpin, who thenceforth busied himself with a variety of business enterprises. Sheldon lived in Excelsior but preached also in the little log church in Chanhassen. Sophie and Theodore were devoted to him. In January, 1883, the Sheldons moved to California, and the Bosts moved there soon afterward.

3. "Rev. Sheldon was a strong advocate of temperance and fought saloons out of his village [Excelsior]," according to a memoir by Rev. Edwin Sidney Williams annexed to the Minutes of the Fifty-First Annual Meeting of the General Congregational Association of Minnesota (Minneapolis, 1906), p. 41.

4. Theodore, an ardent abolitionist, means that 100,000 men would be a drop in the

bucket, as, indeed, the future was to show. South Carolina had already passed its Ordinance of Secession on December 20, 1860.

5. The reference is to the sale of the Bonjour family property near Neuchâtel, of which he estimates that Sophie's share was $1,000.

6. Theodore wrote *sous,* a word he uses interchangeably with "cents," though, as he notes below, the French *sou* (one-twentieth of a franc) was actually worth .95 of a cent if one compares the gold dollar with the gold franc. For practical purposes, the French franc was worth twenty American cents through most of the nineteenth century except for several years during the Civil War when the dollar (the greenback) suffered from severe inflation in terms of gold. Theodore also uses the expression "sixty *livres*"—about sixty pounds avoirdupois—to mean a bushel; one bushel of wheat would, in fact, weigh about sixty pounds.

7. The former Swiss pastor with whom Theodore stayed for a while immediately after his arrival in America. See above, pp. 5-7.

8. On April 14 the Civil War began with firing on Fort Sumter.

9. Sophie was over five months pregnant with her second child, Alphonse, who was to be born July 17.

10. If the Republicans should lose support as a result of coming out squarely for the abolition of slavery.

11. Evidently a photograph had been taken and sent to the grandparents. It has not survived.

12. Corn and wheat were their two main crops at this time.

13. "Old Mike"—last name unknown—was a neighbor who worked for Theodore at various times and helped the family in a number of emergencies.

14. The first battle of Bull Run, fought just south of Washington on July 20, 1861, ended in the rout of the Federal troops.

15. Fought between the seven Catholic cantons and the rest of the Swiss Confederation. It broke out in 1847 and lasted three weeks. The dispute referred to a few lines below took place over the Prussian claim to the district of Neuchâtel, and war was just barely avoided.

16. William Howard Russell was the war correspondent of the *London Times*. He had simply reported what the American press had already correctly printed: the Northern troops had run away.

17. It is obvious here that Theodore had been reading the lurid atrocity stories in the Republican newspapers he subscribed to and was carried away by his indignation.

18. Concorde Bein was an old family retainer. She came from Strasbourg and was a minister's daughter. For twenty years she lived with Ami and Jenny Bost as a household helper. She never married and always refused to accept any pay other than her room and board.

## IX. The Lime Quarry

1. Probably a reference to Ami Bost's will made in 1861. It may be inferred that Theodore's father intended to provide for the cancellation of his son's debts to him. In addition, each surviving child was to receive a legacy of 5,521 frs.

2. Northfield, Minnesota—on the Cannon River, about forty miles southeast of Chanhassen. It has not been possible to determine the exact location of Cheeseman's find. There are many small, abandoned quarries along the bluffs of the Cannon and Little Cannon Rivers and of Prairie Creek. Dating mainly from the late nineteenth century, these

were worked for building stone and agricultural lime. However, there seems to be no record of a naturally occuring deposit of hydraulic lime in the bed of a "rapid stream" within a mile or two of Northfield. Of course, there is always the possibility that Cheeseman was mistaken about the qualities of his limestone, which would account for the apparent failure to exploit the deposit he described.

3. Ordinary lime dissolves in water, but hydraulic lime, after being baked or roasted in a kiln, hardens when mixed with water. It is used for lining cisterns and in making mortar for laying bricks.

4. A shrewd, hard-driving businessman, civic improver, visionary idealist, and emissary of Yankee culture, J. W. North (1815-90) came from an old New England Methodist family. In the early 1850s he practiced law in St. Anthony where he was in close touch with pioneering Congregationalist ministers like H. M. Nichols, Charles Galpin, and Charles B. Sheldon of Excelsior. Some members of Nichols's Northampton Colony had gone in 1852 to settle near Faribault, on the Cannon River, and in January, 1855, North visited the neighborhood of what is now Northfield in search of mill sites. During the next few years he built sawmills and gristmills, platted the townsite of Northfield, and opened a hotel there. He was the president and chief stockholder of the Minnesota and Cedar Valley Railroad, mortgaging his real estate holdings to raise capital. The railroad project was hard hit by the aftermath of the panic of 1857, however, and the company was virtually bankrupt by the fall of 1859; North lost his fortune and moved on westward after the outbreak of the Civil War. He was well known as an antislavery lecturer, temperance advocate, supporter of women's suffrage, and Republican politician. Besides Northfield (named both for himself and for Northfield, Massachusetts), he founded five communities in Minnesota and Nevada. When he told Cheeseman that his funds were "tied up," he was evidently referring to his unlucky railroading venture. (See *Continuum: Threads in the Community Fabric of Northfield, Minnesota* [Northfield: Bicentennial Commission, City of Northfield, Minnesota, 1976], pp. 23-43 *passim;* see also M. Stonehouse, *John Wesley North and the Reform Frontier* [Minneapolis: University of Minnesota Press, 1965].)

5. John Slidell, the Confederate envoy to Paris, and his companion James Murray Mason, who was on his way to represent the South at the Court of St. James, were seized from a British ship, the *Trent,* November 7, 1861. News of this high-handed action by a Union warship gave rise to war fever in Britian, and a declaration of war on the United States was narrowly avoided by the release of the Confederate commissioners December 26.

6. Either a sewing machine with an attached table or a sewing machine to be used on the tabletop.

7. A reference to the suggestion made by his brother Ami, Junior, soon after Theodore's arrival in America, that he go to Ireland to farm some land belonging to the family of Ami's wife.

8. Theodore probably means the battle of Mill Springs, fought some ten miles west of Somerset, Kentucky; it was a Union victory.

9. The *Warrior* was a British ironclad, the first English warship to be built entirely of iron. The *Monitor,* a Union ironclad, was built to fight the Confederate *Merrimack,* a wooden ship whose armor consisted of steel rails mounted vertically and close to one another on the vessel's sloping sides.

10. Napoleon III, who greatly offended Union supporters like Theodore by supporting the Confederacy and by sending a military expedition to put Maximilian of Habsburg on the throne of a short-lived Mexican Empire.

## X. The Indian Uprising

1. The *Arkansas* was a Confederate gunboat that had been armored with iron rails. It was run aground and blown up by its own crew to keep it from being captured during the Union attack on Baton Rouge. Culpepper Court House is a town in the Shenandoah Valley of Virginia.

2. Another atrocity story that had been making the rounds; Theodore himself seems skeptical, as he is about the immediacy of the Indian danger.

3. Ami, Junior, had just retired from business on account of bad health. At this time he had moved with his family from Glasgow to Tours. His brother and former business partner Timothée was contributing to his support.

4. The famous "Singing Hutchinsons," who came to the Minnesota Valley around 1855.

5. Fort Snelling, about twenty miles from Theodore's farm.

6. The Sepoys were native troops that rebelled against British rule in India in 1857. Timothée's wife and her parents—her father was an officer in the Indian Army—barely escaped from the massacre of Cawnpore.

7. Viscount Palmerston was Prime Minister and Lord John Russell was Foreign Minister of Great Britain at this time. The British incurred a great deal of blame from Northern sympathizers like Theodore by covertly recognizing the belligerency of the Confederacy and building commerce raiders like the *Alabama* for the South.

8. Theodore fell into arrears with his taxes in 1863 *The Valley Herald*, Chaska, April 16, 1863, p. 2). His property that year was assessed at $300, and his tax liability was $9.30. The Maxwells' taxes were also past due, as were those of some forty other Chanhassen families.

9. William Ewart Gladstone, a strong advocate of free trade, was Chancellor of the Exchequer in the Palmerston ministry.

## XI. The New House

1. There had been discussion in the Northern press about sending a ship loaded with food and other supplies for the British factory workers who had been thrown out of work in large numbers because the Union blockade of Southern ports prevented cotton from being exported. The textile workers of Lancashire nevertheless supported the antislavery cause, whereas most upper-class opinion in Britain supported the South's struggle for independence. Apparently no "relief ship" was ever actually sent.

2. The *Alabama* was a Confederate commerce raider built in Britain. Its operations gave rise to great indignation among Union supporters like Theodore, and the United States not only protested strongly during the war but presented a claim for damages afterward; a compromise settlement was eventually reached.

3. Slavery had been abolished in Mexico in 1829.

4. President Lincoln issued the Emancipation Proclamation January 1, 1863, freeing all slaves in rebel-held territory.

5. Waged by the Emperor Napoleon III in alliance with the Kingdom of Piedmont for the expulsion of the Austrians from northern Italy in 1859. After the bloody battles of Magenta and Solferino, France made a separate peace, annexing Nice and Savoy but leaving its Italian allies in the lurch.

## XII. "And the War Goes On"

1. Mercury becomes a solid at approximately -38° F.

2. The year 1863 had brought several important successes for the North: Gettysburg (July 1-3), the surrender of Vicksburg (July 4), the battle of Chattanooga (November 23-25). The Union had gained control of the Mississippi and cut the Confederacy in two, and the way was opened for Sherman's invasion of Georgia.

3. This was a piece of choral music composed by Ami Bost in 1829.

4. Like many radical abolitionists, Theodore considered Lincoln too moderate on the slavery issue. His favorite candidates were Gen. Benjamin Franklin Butler, the Federal commander in New Orleans, and Gen. John Charles Frémont, the explorer, who was in command of the Union forces in Missouri.

5. The Union's Army of the Potomac, commanded by Gen. U. S. Grant, was then (May, 1864) fighting its way around the northern and eastern approaches to Richmond; in this heavily wooded region — "The Wilderness" — both sides sustained terrible casualties in bloody hand-to-hand combat. Grant was the victor, inasmuch as Lee failed to prevent him from occupying positions south of the city from which it was later taken.

6. November 24, 1863, had been designated as a special day of thanksgiving by presidential proclamation. It had long been observed in New England and elsewhere in the North and became a national holiday from this time on.

7. The Rev. Stephen Miller had led a regiment of Minnesota troops against the Indians in 1862. Promoted from Colonel to Brigadier-General in 1863, he served as Governor of Minnesota in 1864-65.

8. The Rev. Charles B. Sheldon had come to Excelsior in 1855 (see note 2, p. 369). At one time, Mr. Sheldon hoped to persuade Theodore to enter the ministry.

9. Theodore is referring to the notorious Confederate prison camp at Andersonville, Georgia, where as many as 35,000 Union troops were held under atrocious conditions.

10. John Slidell, the Confederate commissioner in Paris, had offered to give Southern military aid to Napoleon III in Mexico once the South had won its independence. In the meantime, France would recognize Southern belligerency and would give material and diplomatic support to the Confederacy. Though sympathetic to the Confederate cause, the Emperor recognized after Gettysburg that a Union victory was all but inevitable and cut off French aid to the South.

## XIII. The Death of Alice

1. Ami Bost was in the process of republishing his musical works.

2. See note 13, p. 370.

3. A remittance from Ami and Jenny Bost, who had come into a rather substantial inheritance on the death of her father.

4. Theodore had been appointed Justice of the Peace for the Chanhassen district. Before this he had worked as tax assessor and as tax collector.

5. A parlor organ.

## XIV. Trees and Bees

1. "La Famille" was the name of one of the asylums built by Theodore's brother John at La Force in southwestern France. In addition to a church, a parsonage, and a

school, he had built three big hospitals for the insane, the mentally retarded, epileptics, and chronic invalids, these were named Bethesda, Siloe, and Eben-Hezer. When he became ill he was supervising the construction of still another, to be called Bethel.

2. Sophie had begun to suffer from "rheumatism"—probably arthritis—in her hands and as the years went by her elbows and knee joints were also affected.

3. New Ulm, in the Minnesota River valley about sixty miles southwest of Chanhassen, was founded in the mid-1850s by a German colonization society, the Turner Land Association, which traced its origins to the War of Liberation (1813-15) against Napoleon. Forced to emigrate to America after the failure of the liberal revolutionary movement of 1848, the "Turners" (members of the *Turnverein,* or Gymnastic League) had adopted socialistic principles and were also strongly anticlerical; many were freethinkers. In 1858, their newspaper, the *New Ulm Pioneer,* declared: "Many want all church humbug banished, others believe [that] to strike out the church is necessary. We are absolutely inclined to the latter opinion." Further, "the Bible, a mixture of moral truth, moral falsehood, and natural-scientific lies . . . is absolutely unfit for scholastic instruction." (Translation by Mrs. William Durbahr, cited in Noel Iverson, *Germania, U.S.A.: Social Change in New Ulm, Minnesota* [Minneapolis: University of Minnesota Press, 1966], p. 66, note 40.)

4. Theodore here describes, with some inaccuracies, the sensational "Christmas Murders" in New Ulm at the end of 1866. The victims were two Yankee trappers from Mankato, Alexander Campbell, twenty-seven, and George Liscom, twenty-five. Anti-Indian feeling was still very strong in New Ulm, where the worst massacre of the 1862 Sioux war had occurred. The two trappers, dressed in woodsmen's clothes that resembled Indian dress, may have been mistaken for half-breeds; at any rate, they made some remarks that were taken as slurs by a crowd of tipsy Germans celebrating the holiday in the National Saloon and went on to stage a realistic Sioux war dance. In the ensuing brawl, a German ex-soldier, John Spenner, nearly killed Liscom with an ax and in turn received from Campbell a knife wound from which he died a few hours later. Handcuffed and jailed by the local sheriff, Campbell and Liscom were dragged out during the night by a crowd of drunken Germans; both were stabbed, bludgeoned, and hanged; the bodies were then further mutilated and crammed under the ice of the Minnesota River. The leader of the mob, John Gut, an A.W.O.L. soldier from the Tenth Minnesota Regiment, was finally brought to trial and convicted after crowds from Mankato had threatened to destroy New Ulm; twelve others indicted with him jumped bail and were never caught. After his case had been unsuccessfully appealed to the U. S. Supreme Court, Gut's death sentence was commuted to life imprisonment (and later reduced to ten years) by Gov. Horace Austin who, as trial judge two years earlier, had condemned Gut to be hanged. Theodore doubtless read about the murders in the St. Paul newspapers to which he subscribed. (See Walter N. Trennery, *Murder in Minnesota. A Collection of True Cases* [St. Paul: Minnesota Historical Society, 1962], pp. 44-52.)

5. See note 18, p. 370.

6. June 10 was Ami Bost's birthday.

7. Alaska, purchased from Russia for $7 million in March, 1867.

8. Sophie's command of English was generally excellent, but once in a while her ear for idiomatic expressions was not accurate.

9. This is an indignant reference to the question mark Theodore had placed after "beautiful" in his letter announcing the birth of Alphonse. Theodore thought, or liked to pretend, that his children were all very ugly at birth, something that annoyed Sophie—he may, in fact, have said it only to tease her.

## XV. Alphonse Bonjour

1. Minnesota Historical Society Manuscripts Division, M138, roll 41, frames 457-58.

2. This is a reference to the Mr. Rochat mentioned in Theodore's previous letter. His first name is not known. He was a jeweler and came originally from Locle in French Switzerland. He had known the Bost family before coming to America, and he extended hospitality to Theodore when the latter had to be in St. Paul overnight.

3. Ami and Jenny Bost had moved to La Force, where they were to spend the last years of their lives in the home of their son John and his wife, Eugénie.

4. M. Goepp and his family had been staying as paying guests of the Langdons, prosperous New Englanders who lived near Theodore and Sophie.

5. The Evangelical Alliance, founded in London in August, 1846 — Ami Bost had taken part as a delegate from the Reformed Church of France — brought together some fifty denominations and went on to hold great international meetings in Paris, Geneva, and elsewhere. Its 1873 meeting was held in New York.

6. Charles Galpin, Excelsior's first minister, who had given up full-time preaching in 1855 to become a jack-of-all-trades: dentist, carter, blacksmith, schoolteacher, steamboat owner, captain, and no doubt others on occasion.

7. The Franco-Prussian War had begun on July 19, 1870.

## XVI. Theodore in Europe

1. At this moment, the Prussians had encircled Rouen and were advancing toward Bolbec and Le Havre. It seems unlikely, therefore, that Theodore could have gone by way of Le Havre. Although we do not know his actual itinerary, he could have crossed the Channel west of the mouth of the Seine, perhaps landing at Cherbourg or St. Malo; he could then have traveled south to La Force without crossing German-held territory.

2. The armistice was signed January 28, 1871; the revolt of the people of Paris (the Paris Commune) began two months later.

3. Jenny had apparently reported in one of her letters that Theodore had jokingly threatened to put his mother out of the house, perhaps to prevent her from overworking.

## XVII. Another Alice

1. This is the first mention of Sophie's sewing machine, which must have been bought almost a year earlier, perhaps with some of the proceeds of the good honey harvest of 1872.

2. The name of the large house in La Force where John's family lived.

## XVIII. Storekeeper in Excelsior

1. It was in fact her seventy-ninth birthday.

2. Four-tenths of an *hectare*, or about nine-tenths of an acre.

3. The family reunion, set for the summer of 1874, was to celebrate the sixtieth or diamond wedding anniversary of Ami and Jenny Bost.

4. Theodore means "gloomy," and goes on to explain why he was feeling that way.

5. A reference to the wife of Socrates, who had a sharp tongue.

6. In the Old Testament Holophernes, the general in command of Nebuchadnezzar's army, was killed by Judith. The name Holophernes means "the terror of all nations." This is no doubt what Jenny meant.

7. Clémy's brother, Adrien Siefert, had emigrated to Chile some five years earlier, going from there to Tahiti. He died two years after this, soon after his return to France.

## XIX. Back to the Land

1. In 1877, Clémy had lost her brother and sister, in 1879 her mother had died, and her father had died September 3, 1883.

2. France was in the process of occupying Indochina and had just taken control of Tonkin.

3. It seems likely that Theodore meant to write -14° R., which would be +0.5° F. At a temperature of 63.5° F., the weather would hardly be described as "very cold," nor would farm animals need to be kept indoors.

4. Theodore contributed $350 to put up the building and was one of nine members of the Board of Trustees. The school was "Christian but not sectarian."

5. Again, it seems probable that these are below-freezing temperatures on Theodore's Réaumur thermometer. A temperature of -10° R. is 9.5° F.; -40° R. is -58° F.; and 20° R. is -13° F. These are more or less plausible mid-winter temperatures for Minnesota, except, perhaps, for the low end of Theodore's range, but it should be remembered that the mercury would have frozen in the thermometer at approximately -38° F., or -31° R., so anything below that would be a guess. The readings given *could* be in Fahrenheit degrees, except that they would then be too high; moreover, Theodore specified Réaumur degrees in his previous letter and is unlikely to have changed thermometers in the meantime.

6. The new minister was the Rev. Isaac L. Cory, who replaced the Rev. Charles Sheldon in June, 1883. Mr. Sheldon had moved to California after twenty-eight years in Excelsior.

## XX. The Pioneers in Old Age

1. It seems obvious that Theodore is speaking here of four Réaumur degrees *of frost*, that is a thermometer reading of -4° R., which equals 23° F. This would correspond to his expression "a rather heavy frost" and would be cold enough to do serious damage to an orange grove.

2. A temperature of 31° R. equals 101.75° F.; 32° R. equals 104° F.

3. Captain Alfred Dreyfus was a Jewish army officer who had been falsely accused of espionage and convicted in 1894 on evidence deliberately fabricated by high-ranking officers in the French army. Anti-Semitism among conservatives opposed to the Third Republic played a part in his condemnation. France was bitterly divided for ten years over the issue of Dreyfus's guilt. He was vindicated in 1906 after his defenders succeeded in showing that perjury and forged documents had been used to convict him.

4. The Boer War between England the Dutch settlers of South Africa had broken out in 1899. British speculators and prospectors were seeking to gain control of the Transvaal, having already driven the Boers from Cape Colony. The Boers had forbidden alien immigration in an effort to remain independent.

5. Alphonse's first wife had died in July, 1902, leaving him with two children. In 1904 he married Hattie Brisbin Sampson, a widow with two children. He stayed in Excelsior until 1909, when he sold out and moved to Texas.

6. In France the law providing for the separation of church and state had been voted on December 9, 1905. This meant that the clergy, including Protestant pastors and Jewish

rabbis, were no longer salaried public servants but had to be supported by the faithful through voluntary contributions.

7. In 1908, Edouard Faure published a book on François Coillard (1834-61), a Protestant missionary in Africa, who had known the Bost family at Asnières-lès-Bourges, his birthplace, and had a great deal to say about them in his book. He tells how in 1844 at Christmastime, Marie Bost had led the children of the parish in singing the *Gloria* and the *Magnificat* composed by Ami Bost, "who had never heard them sung until then."

8. The fourth of June was Elisée's birthday.

9. Hélène Bost, one of the daughters of Ami, Junior, had married Alfred Cadier, a Protestant minister in the south of France. They had a large family. Taking their sons and sons-in-law together with those of Elisée and Clémy, there were among them: seven ministers and missionaries, two military officers, two engineers, one lawyer, one doctor, and one professor.

## XXI. Echoes of War (1914-18)

1. Theodore's meaning is that Elisée has outlived him, or at least that he is likely to do so. In fact, it was to be the other way around.

2. Theodore seems to be referring to China's declaration of war on Germany and Austria-Hungary (August 14, 1917). Japan had already done so (August 23, 1914) and had proceeded to seek annexation of German colonial holdings in China.

3. Geneva annually commemorates the preservation of the city's independence when soldiers of the Duke of Savoy tried to scale the city walls on the night of December 11-12, 1602, and were repelled.

4. The German "Peace Offensive," planned and executed by Gen. Erich von Ludendorff, was launched in March, 1918. It was halted in the northern sector around Amiens, but made alarming gains in the direction of Paris until the tide was turned by French resistance and the arrival of fresh American troops.

5. It is not clear whether Theodore means 200 inches per acre, or 200 inches of water pressure at the wellhead.

## XXII. "All Flesh Is Grass"

1. Elisée had died February 16, 1920.

# INDEX

# Index

Abolition: Minn. Republicans favor, 110

Abolitionists: press hostile to, 59;
Boissonnas agrees with, 243

Adams, Andrew W.: as delegate to
Republican state convention, 99; goes
with T. to Clear Water Lake, 100-102;
T. visits, 105; identification of, 366n5

Aesop's Fables: allusion to, 119, 368n18

*Alabama* (Confederate raider), 227, 372n7

Alaska: purchase of, 277, 374n7

Alger, Russell A. (Sec. of the Interior):
involved in scandal, 337

America, economic growth of, 349-50

Americans, traits and attitudes of: their
coolness, 54-55; their combativeness,
55; their disrespect for law, 62, their
obsession with money, 66-67

Andersonville, Georgia (prison camp),
255-56, 373n9

*Apocalypse, The* (cantata by Ami Bost):
sung in Ottawa, Ill., 241 Ashland,
N. Y., Heddings Institute of: T.
teaches in, 22, 27-29, T. leaves, 26

Aspden family (neighbors of Bosts), 252

Australia: T. not attracted to, 10; A.
Bonjour in, 200, 293-94; A. Bonjour
thinks of returning to, 311-12

Babut, Henri: with T. at Vaucher farm,
144

Ball family, 9

Baptism: T. baptized at La Grande Ligne,
15-16, 362n5; T.'s views on, 68,
365n29

Baptists, 58, 343

Basques: in So. Calif., 335

Baton Rouge, La. (Battle of), 212

Beecher, Henry Ward: gives address in
England, 235

Beekeeping: T. wants to buy hives, 238,
253-54; T. learns of new patented hive,
254; T. buys hives, 262, 271-72; T.
acquires agency for, 266-67; T. explains how agency works, 269; T.
makes hives, 269, 282; bees winter
well, 270; mixed results in *1866-67*,
274, 276; T. has fifty-seven hives,
280; T. sells honey, 280-81; T.
describes hive, 281; T. loses bees,
284, 314-15, 318; T. writes essay
on bees, 285; T. puts hives in cellar,
285; S. tends bees during T.'s absence
abroad, 304, 307-08; accidents to
hives, 317; S. describes cleaning of
hives, 318

Bees: T. finds "honey tree," 131; T. and
Sarver cut down wild bee tree, 168-69.
*See also* Beekeeping

Bein, Concorde (family retainer), 194,
370n18

Bellevue, Switzerland: T. homesick for,
39, 59; T. recalls life with Vaucher
family, 144

Big Woods: T. describes an outing in, 86-87

Bingham (neighbor of Bosts), 101

Bishop, Donald (grandson of S. and T.):
service in World War I, 352-53

Bishop, Edward (grandson of S. and T.):

service in World War I, 352

Bishop, Lucius T.: marries Julie Bost, 329; moves to Calif., 333

Black suffrage in Minn.: to be voted on, 263

Boarders: S. and T. take in, 253, 288-90

Boer War: T. comments on, 337-38; origin of, 376n4no.2

Boissonnas, Charles: comes to America, 164; helps make maple sugar, 204-06, 208; returns to Ill., 208; expected, 222-23, 224, 228; speaks little English, 231; helps Bosts build new house, 231-32, 369n7; his impressions of Minn., 240; reports performance of *Apocalypse* (q.v.), 241; S. annoyed with, 243; an abolitionist, 243; last visit to Bosts in *1872*, 316-19; ties with T., 369n7

Bond, J. Wesley: T. reads his *Minnesota and Its Resources,* 23

Bonjour, Alphonse (S.'s brother), xii, xix-xx: comes to Minn., 283, 292-93; helps T., 294; helps S. run farm, 297; thinks of returning to Australia, 311-12; quarrels with T. and moves to Excelsior, 314; dies, 333

Bonjour, Julie (S.'s sister), xii, xix: T. confuses her with S., 80-81; Jenny Bost prefers her to S. as wife for T., 85; opposed to S.'s going to America, 127

Bonjour parents (S.'s father and mother): M. Bonjour's reply cheers T., 104-05; Mme. Bonjour sends S. and T. a Swiss religious paper, 209

Borel, Julie (S.'s cousin): will go with S. to Minn., 126; her father withdraws his consent, 130

Bost, Alice (Sophie Alice, the first Alice): dies of whooping cough, xxi, 257ff.; S. pregnant with, 233; born, 237, 241; Mimi fond of, 241; plays with the older children, 253; funeral arrangements for, 259, 261-62; sad memories of, 261, 263; Mimi weeps for, 264; S. continues to mourn for, 265

Bost, Alice Eugénie (the second Alice): her birth, 317, 326

Bost, Alice (Trew): marries T.'s brother Paul, xxiii

Bost, Alphonse Ami (eldest son of S. and T.): born, 187; punished for crying, 266

Bost, Ami (T.'s father): his music, xiii, 105, 241, 260, 373n3no.1, 340; translates *The Pilgrim's Progress,* xiii-xiv; his career summarized, xiii-xvi; grief at T.'s departure for America, xv-xvi; relations with T. and other children, xvii; Pastor Fivaz writes to, 3, 5-7; bids T. goodbye, 7-8; T. cites his opinions, 9-11, 63; T. sends him violets, 40, 92; sends message to Baron de Freudenreich, 49; offers to lend T. money, 50-51, 176; arranges T.'s marriage to S., 80ff., 96-97, 104, 108, 120-24; receives word of S.'s acceptance, 124-27; T. answers his questions, 109-10, 222; S. and T. concerned about health, 133, 155, 276 279; moves with Jenny to Pau, 169; suggests T. sleep alone because of insomnia, 169-70; sends T. money, 174, 177, 181, 261, 264; his will, 195-96; differs with T. on Civil War, 218; stops writing letters, 225, 246, 276; favored Italian wars of unification, 235; gets photo of new house, 272-73; no longer understands letters, 303; his death, 329

Bost, Ami, Jr. (T.'s brother), xxi; marries Mary Cave, xxii

Bost, Auguste or Augustin (T.'s brother), xxi-xxii

Bost, Charles (son of Elisée Bost), xxiv

Bost, Charles-Marc (grandson of Elisée Bost): publishes *Les Derniers puritains,* xxiv

Bost, Elisée (T.'s youngest brother): born, xxi; receives letters from T. and S., *1874-1920,* 329ff.; his death, 354

Bost, Etienne (T.'s brother): born, xxi

Bost, Jenny (Pattey) (T.'s mother): her life and character, xvi; her thirteen children, xxi-xxiv; worried about T.'s baptism in icy water, 15; T. and S. answer her questions, 23, 98, 103, 134, 141, 164, 180, 209, 290-91; T. sends

her violets, 40, 92; prefers Julie
Bonjour to S., 85; learns from S.
about Minn., 130ff., 249-50; T. expresses love for, 133; asks for more
letters, 161; sends money, 169, 174,
295; receives legacy, 172; S. tells her
of housekeeping, 222-23, 238, 244,
291; urges T. to come to Europe, 294-
95; S. writes to her during T.'s visit,
299ff.; her sixtieth wedding anniversary, 326-27; her death, 327-28
Bost, John (T.'s brother): his career in
philanthropy, xvi-xii; success in
England, 170-71; wins Monthyon
Prize, 171; does not write to T. and
S., 174; T. cool toward, 200; founds
asylums, 369n12, 373-74n1
Bost, Julie Adèle ("Mimi," the Bosts'
eldest child): born, 147; S. sews for,
158; is one year old, 166; speaks
French, 209; distressed at Alice's
death, 258, 264; married, 329; moves
with parents to Pomona, Calif., 333;
works for Red Cross and Allied war
relief, 347
Bost, Marie (T.'s sister), xxi: her death,
xxi, 368n1no.1; her illness, 117; S.
writes to her about marriage and travel
plans, 127-28
Bost, Paul (T.'s brother), xxi: marries
Alice Trew, xxiii; a misfit in the
Victorian age, xxiii
Bost, Samuel (T.'s brother), xxi: marries
Sophie Laguerre, xxii
Bost, Sophie Alice, see Bost, Alice (the
first Alice)
Bost, Sophie (Bonjour): a representative
yet untypical pioneer, xi-xiv; family
background and education, xix; courtship and marriage, xx, 81-86, 104-05,
119, 121, 124-27, 128, 130; feelings of
exile, xx, 136-37, 299ff.; hardships and
sorrows, xxi, 158-60, 237; teases T. at
age thirteen of fourteen, 81; works as
governess in Scotland, 97; scolds T. for
using "tu," 106-09; in love with
another man, 122; travel plans, 126-27;
brings Marie Moseman to America,
130; arrives in St. Paul, 130; on house-

keeping and cooking, 131-32, 137-38,
153, 186, 204, 208, 222-23, 228-29,
232-33, 244, 303-04; recalls her
father's death, 155; on making maple
sugar, 157, 160, 204-06, 208; on
sewing and embroidery, 157-58, 190,
243-44, 291; first wedding anniversary,
161; befriends Mrs. Cleaveland,
164-65; on flowers and gardening, 166;
on Marie Moseman, 183, 184, 199-200,
232, 258, 304-05; her legacy from sale
of "Les Parcs," 184, 197; wishes for a
piano, 186; on Mimi and Alphonse,
188-89, 209, 224-25, 250, 258-59,
264-65, 272; on new frame house, 189,
212-13, 222-24, 226, 228, 229-30,
232-34, 237-38, 272-73; wishes for
sewing machine and clothes wringer,
199; on family's reading, 209; fears
T. will be drafted, 213; tells of Sioux
uprising, 214-18, 220-24; on scarlet
fever epidemic, 224-25; tells of a
family picnic, 231-32; on Chanhassen
neighbors, 252-53; takes in boarders,
253, 288-90; visits Minneapolis, 264-
66; gets clothes wringer, 272; bene-
ficiary of T.'s life insurance, 272; her
brother Alphonse in Minn., 283, 292-
94; eleventh wedding anniversary,
287; adopts Powers baby, 291-92; runs
farm during T.'s trip to Europe, 297,
299ff.; fights plague of caterpillars,
307; tends bees and orchards, 307-08,
318; in despair over hailstorm, 309ff.;
on T.'s return, 312-13; and death of
Powers baby, 314; gets sewing
machine, 317-18; suffers from
"rheumatism," 321, 330, 348, 350;
lives in Excelsior, 323ff.; moves to
Pomona, Calif., 333; works for Red
Cross and Allied war relief, 347; in
good health on her eighty-second
birthday, 348; tells Elisée of T.'s last
illness and death, 355-56; descendants,
357. See also Children)
Bost, Sophie (Laguerre) (wife of T.'s
brother Samuel), xxiii
Bost, Sophie (Vivien) (wife of T.'s
brother Etienne), xxiii, 52

Bost Theodore: a representative yet untypical pioneer, xi-xiv; emigrates to America, xv, xviii-xix, 4-5, 7-8, birth and early life, xvii-xix; stays with Fivaz family, xix; his teaching posts, 9-11, 12-25, 28-29, 262, 267; baptism, 15-16; is attracted to Minn., 23; trip to St. Paul, 26-31; roadbuilding with Capt. Dodd, 33-35, 37-38, 41-50, 52, 54, 60, 62-63, 65-66; sells lumber, 53, 61-62, 64-65; buys claim near Chanhassen, 65-71; lives alone on claim, 72-129; considers marrying Marie Narbel, 74, 76, 80-81; becomes a U. S. citizen, 80; father favors his marrying S. Bonjour, 80-81; impatient for S.'s decision, 82-84, 93-95, 96-98, 100, 104-5, 111, 113-14, 116-17, 119, 121-24; courtship of S. by correspondence, 85-86, 106-09; describes his log house, 87-88, 102, 104, 107; describes his claim, 89, 91, 98-99, 138-40; enters local politics as a Republican, 99, 246, 283-84; his mastery of English, 99-100; works as tax assessor, 104, 245-46, 251; describes his claim shanty, 112-13, 116; considers marrying A. Maxwell, 114, 119-20, 122-24; his proposal accepted by S., 124-28; marries S., 130; his first months with S., 130-46; wants abolition of slavery, 181, 184, 218-19, 227-28, 235, 241; tries to buy lime quarry, 196-98, 201-03, 207, 239, 242, 247-48; builds new frame house, 199, 213, 223-24, 226, 228-34, 237-38, 272-73, 319-20; grows fruit trees, 208, 212-13, 263, 268-69, 272, 276, 280, 289, 293, 302, 309-12, 319, 333, 335-36; is Justice of the Peace, 209, 219-20, 256; keeps calm during Sioux War, 212, 214-17; takes up beekeeping, 238, 253-54, 262, 266-74, 280-82, 284-85, 289, 304, 307-08, 314-15; falsely accused of misconduct in office, 270-71, 273, 275, 277-78; sells forty acres, 274; wins prizes at fairs, 284; is vice president of Carver County Agricultural Society, 284; wins prize for essay, 286; takes in boarders, 288-90; trip to Europe, 295-313; is foreman of grand jury, 315-16; raises sheep, 316-17; is partner in general store, 321-27, 329; moves to Excelsior, 323, 325; learns of mother's death, 327-28; father's death, 329; celebrates silver wedding anniversary, 329; buys new farm near Excelsior, 329; moves to Pomona, Calif., 333; views on World War I, 344ff.; final illness and death, 355-56; descendants, 357. *See also* Child(ren); Health (T.'s)

Bost, Theodore Charles (son of T. and S.): born, 275, 278-79

Bost, Théophile (T.'s brother), xxi, xxiii: marries Eliza Baker, 99-100, 102-3

Bost, Timothée or Tim (T.'s brother), xxi, xxiii: marries Isabella (Bella) Lennox, xxiv; lends T. money to buy partnership in store, 322; T. learns of death of, 345-46

Buffalo, N. Y., 29-30

Bull Run (First Battle of), 191, 193, 204, 370n14

Burlington, Vt., 12-16

Butler, Gen. B. F.: favored by T. for President, 242

Cadier, Hélène (daughter of Ami Bost, Jr.), 354, 377n9

Calhoun (Lake): drownings at, 162-65, 369n6

California: S. and T. move to Pomona, 333; T. comments on climate of, 334-35; T. discusses Indians, Mexicans, and Basques in, 334-35; 3 churches flourish in Pomona, 343; T. describes farming in, 353

Carver County Agricultural Society, 284

Carver, Minn., 99, 252

Caterpillars: plague of, 307

Champlain (Lake), 12, 78

Chanhassen, Minn.: T.'s sketch map of, 75; origin and meaning of name, 86, 366n11; T.'s sketch maps of his neighborhood, 97; the Bosts' neighbors in, 98-99, 133, 140, 160, 366-67n5; T. walks to Minneapolis from, 118; Rev. C. B. Sheldon preaches in, 132; T.'s sketch of township of, 140; T. is tax assessor for, 251; draft takes men from,

254; T. returns to, for Thanksgiving,
265, reference to Alice's grave in, 270
Chaska, Minn.: T. searches for claim near,
67, 69; T. gets bank draft at, 174;
Bosts sell maple sugar in, 204; hysteria
in, during Sioux War, 212, 214; T.
hauls sand and bricks from, 228, 319;
Moravian church and academy established in, 247; development of, 250; T.
foreman of grand jury in, 315;
Alphonse runs errands in, 320
Cheeseman (ex-minister and stonemason):
accidentally starts prairie fire, 156-57;
makes barter deal with T., 172-73, 176;
and Northfield lime quarry, 196-97,
198, 201-2, 207; his wife terrified by
Sioux, 214; leases Mrs. Cleaveland's
farm, 215; background, 369n1
Chicago, Ill., 29-30
Child(ren): S. and T. expecting their first,
133-34, 135-37; birth of first, Julie
adele ("Mimi"), 147, 149-51; delights
of first, 154; S. feels well while expecting second, 183; birth of second,
Alphonse Ami, 187-90; news about,
188-89, 264-65, 265-66; S. recalls
euphoria after birth of Alphonse, 194;
S. expects third, 233; birth of third,
(Sophie) Alice, 241; death of first
Alice, 257 ff.; birth of Theodore
Charles ("Dodi"), 275, 278-79; birth
of second Alice, 315, 317; birth of
Edward, 329; are growing up, 329-30;
study music, 331-32; their marriages,
careers, moves, 333; death of "Dodi,"
333, 336
Chippewa Indians: T. describes, 53, 90,
216, 220; T. compares with Calif.
Indians, 334
Christmas murders at New Ulm, Minn.:
T. learns of, 274, 374n4
Church and state: separation of, in France,
339
Civil War: T. critical of North, 181, 191-
93; S. fears T. will be drafted, 182; T.
impatient for action, 183; first Bull Run
a fiasco, 191; Minn. raising four regiments for, 193; S. comments on, 199,
206-07; T. comments on, 200-201,
203-04; T. espouses Northern cause,

209; going better for North, 212; T.
sees slavery as main issue, 218-19;
drags on, 227-28, stakes of, as seen by
T., 227-28; new draft of men for, 235;
T. expects Northern victory, 241, 244-
45; T. angry about Southern treatment
of prisoners, 251-52, 256; Bosts' continuing anxiety about, 254-55; end of
hostilities, 257
Claim (T.'s): T. searches for and purchases,
67-70; T. takes possession of, 72; T.
describes living arrangements on, 72-73;
sketch and description of, 75, 138-40;
T. describes clearing of, 91-92; T. pre-
empts, 109, 112-13, 117; costs of
clearing, 175, 177; T. sells forty acres
of, 274. See also Preemption
"Claim fever" in Minn., 44-45
Claim Shanty (T.'s): T. describes, 112-13,
116; S. describes drawbacks of, 137-
38; T.'s sketch shows location of, 138-
39; T. and S. plan to move back to log
house, 145. See also Log house
Clear Water Lake, 100
Cleaveland, Arba and Clarissa (neighbors
of Bosts), 100, 102; 366n11, 367n8:
multiple drownings in Lake Calhoun,
160-65, 369n6
Clothes wringer: S. wishes for, 199; T.
buys one for S., 272
Clothing: S. tells of sewing and embroi-
dering, 157, 189-90, 219; S. defends
extra work on, 243; women's fashions
in, 243. See also Sewing machine
Coillard, François: recalls Ami Bost in
memoirs, 340, 377n7
Colfax, Schuyler: T. supports for Vice
President, 283
Cooking: S. tells of plans and achieve-
ments, 132; S. on tea and coffee substitutes, 204; S.'s cooking praised by
Boissonnas, 208
Copperheads: T. denounces, 235, 248
Cory, Rev. Isaac, 376n6no.1
Courtship in America: illustrated by Max-
well girls, 114; long engagements not
common, 122-23
Coutouly, Mme. and son Edouard: writes
to, 143-56
Crimean War, 32, 73, 247, 362n6, 365n2

Crops: damage to, 104; S. grows Swiss flowers and vegetables, 131; not worth marketing, 142; damaged by frost, blackbirds, 152
Cudrefin, Switzerland, 5, 39, 52
Culpepper Court House (Battle of), 212

Debts: T. pays off, 261-62
Democrats: T. opposed to, 99, 110-11, 240, 244, 247-48; T. critical of Wilson and, 351-52, 355
Descendants of T. and S., 357
Doctors: T. lacks confidence in local, 170, 178, 191
Dodd, Capt. William B.: T.'s association with, 33-34, 42, 47-52, 54, 60, 63, 65-66; killed in New Ulm by Indians, 225; roadbuilding activities of, 363n4
Donnelly, Ignatius, 283
Douglas, Stephen A., 18
Dreyfus Affair: T. comments on, 336; summary of, 376n3no.2
Dubuque, Iowa: mail routed through, 110

Election of 1864: T. looks forward to, 242, 247; T. triumphant at Republican victory in, 248-49
Election of 1868: T. supports Grant and Colfax, 283-84
England: T. critical of pro-Southern policies of, 200-01, 209-10, 216-19, 227, 235, 247, 255
Episcopalians, 114
Europe: T. thinks of returning to, 114; T. visits in 1870-71, 295, 297-313
Evangelical Association: 320, 375n5no.1
Excelsior, Minn., 73, 240: T. tries to fetch Dr. Snell from, 178; scarlet fever epidemic in, 224; T. gets lumber from, 226, 228; economic growth of, 250; religion in, 287; Bosts move to, 321, 323, 325; summer visitors bring trade to, 326-27; T. gives money for academy in, 331
Exchange rate: dollars to francs, 178, 370n6

Farm: T. and S. think of moving to another, 175-76, 184-85

Farming in America: Pastor Fivaz on, 3, 5-7: T. discusses, 10-11, 13-14, 16-17, 19, 50-51; T.'s advice to E. Coutouly on, 143-46; in Calif., described by T., 353
Farming in Minn.: T. on climate and crops, 89-90; hurt by Panic of 1857, 148; S. discouraged by problems of, 151, 158-60, 161-62; T.'s health a handicap for, 162; depressed state of, 162, 170; problems with animals, 167; Civil War brings better prices, 172, 174; low farm prices, 174; hurt by high taxes and prices, 189; horses replace oxen, 234; bad weather causes setbacks, 234, 276; Bosts become self-supporting, 246; various difficulties in 1872, 314
Feller, Mme. (Swiss Baptist missionary): runs grande Ligne mission in Quebec, 9-10
Fencing: T. makes progress with, 173; Cheeseman helps with, 172-76
Fivaz, Pastor, xix, 3, 5-7
Flowers and Gardening, 166
Fondation John Bost, xxii
Forbel, Pastor, 63
France: T. denounces Napoleon III, 209-210, 256. See also Napoleon III
Frémont, Gen. John C., 242
Freudenreich, Baron de: befriends T. in Minn., 32-33, 35, 49, 51
Fruit trees: T. orders from Wisc., 208; T. plants more, 212-13, 268, 272, 302; T.'s do well, 263, 302; bring welcome income, 280; in Calif., 333, 335-36
Fruits and berries, 131
Furniture: T. makes, 77-78; Bosts buy from Mrs. Cleaveland, 165

Galena, Ill., 30
Garibaldi, Giuseppe: T. hears rumor about, 192
Garland, Hamlin: writes of pioneer life, xii
Geneva, Switzerland, 46, 57
Germans in Minn.: T. critical of, 230
Gladstone, William E.: T. cites a speech by, 218, 372n9
Goepp family: taken in as boarders by

Bosts, 288-90, 375n4no.1; tries to find post for T. in St. Louis, 290

Grand jury (Chaska): T. serves as foreman of, 315-16

Grandchildren of T. and S.: their service in World War I, 347, 352-53

Grande Ligne (Quebec): T. teaches at Swiss Baptist mission in, 9-10, 15-16, 20-21

Grant, Ulysses S.: T. an admirer of, 245, 283

Great Britain, 11. See also England

Hailstorm (1871): destroys orchard on eve of T.'s return, 309ff

Health (S.'s): feels well during pregnancy, 183; plagued with "rheumatism," 321, 330; still spry except for "rheumatism," 348

Health (T.'s): has headaches, xvii-xviii, 270; loses weight, 131; suffers from fatigue, pains in side, 147, 153, 156, 165, 191, 238-39, 278-80, 283; catches whooping cough, 165; has insomnia, 177; advised to give up farming, 198; feels better, 205, 228, 245, 278; hopes for medical exemption on account of hernia, 211-14; ill in summer of 1865, 278; ill in winter of 1866-67, 278; goes to Europe for, 297, 302; fails to get aid in Europe, 306; has eye operation, 342; ailments in old age, 347, 348; final illness, 355-56; normal weight, 361n6; convalescence at Pointe-aux-Trembles, 364n22

Hedding Institute (Ashland, N. Y.): T. appointed to faculty, 22; reasons for T.'s leaving, 26-27

Hennepin County, Minn., 269

Hinds (husband of Anna Maxwell), 133

Hired help: hard to find, 183, 228. See also Moseman, Marie; "Old Mike"

Hole in the Day (Chippewa chief), 220

Homeopathy: T. studies, 4; T. treats self by, 91; Alice treated by, 258; system of, explained, 362n1no.1

Homestead Act, 16-17

Hotels and boarding houses, 12-16, 32

Housework: S. tells of, 153, 186, 228-29; S. hopes for machines to ease, 244. See also Boarders; Clothing; Cooking; Hired help; Maple sugar and syrup

Housing, see Claim shanty; Log house; New house

Hunting: T. goes with party to Clear Water Lake, 100-101

Hutchinsons ("The Singing Hutchinsons"): verse from a song of theirs, vii, 372n4no.1; killed by Indians, 216

Illinois: Compared with Minn., 240

Indians: S. has bad dreams about, 214; panic in Bosts' neighborhood at approach of, 214-15; T. keeps calm despite, 215-216; T. writes of war with, 216-17; S. fears for children, 217-18; S. looks back on war with, 220-22; S. notes their just complaints, 222; S. fears new raids, 224, 229; Dodd killed by, 225; thirty-nine executed at Mankato, 225; removal of, 242. See also Chippewa; Hole in the Day; Little Crow; Sioux; Winnebago; Yankton

Insurance: T. insures life for S.'s benefit, 272

Ireland: T. thinks of going to, 10

Ironclad ships: in Civil War, 207, 209, 371n9; the Arkansas, 212, 372n1no.1

Isolation: S.'s feelings of, 136, 160

Johnstone, William: marries Alice Bost, 333

Jones & Bost (general store in Excelsior): T. offered partnership in, 321; Tim advances money for, 322; T.'s partner Jones, 323, 325; summer visitors bring trade, 326-27

Justice of the Peace: T. appointed, 209; T. has problems as, 219-20, 266

Kansas-Nebraska Bill, 17, 367n14

King (inventor of patented beehive): sells rights to T., 269

Land: clearing, fencing, and planting of,

141; T. clears and breaks, 147, 159

Land boom in Minn.: collapse of, with Panic of *1857,* 366*n*3

Land Office: T.'s problems with, 112-13, 117-18

Land speculation: T.'s neighbors active in, 100, 112

Langdon family (neighbors of Bosts), 259

Lime quarry (Northfield, Minn.): discovered by Cheeseman, 196-97; attempts to buy, 198, 207; hopes for, 201-02; Rev. Sheldon advises T. on, 202-03; T. still thinks of, 239, 242, 247-48

Lincoln, Abraham, 191, 192, 242, 245, 249, 354, 373*n*4no.1

Little Crow (Sioux chief), 220

Livestock: T. loses cow and calf, 112; acquisitions and problems of, 155-56; T. loses another calf, 180-81

Log house (the Bosts'): T. describes, 102-03, 107; T. and S. plan to return to, 145; inconveniences in winter, 222; problems with mice and insects in, 223; layout of, 366*n*12

Loneliness: S.'s for T. in *1870-71,* 137. *See also* Isolation

*Los Angeles* (relief ship): T. writes Elisée about, 349, 372*n*12

Los Angeles, Calif., 350

Lumber and lumber business: T. employed in, 53, 60-61, 64-65; wood sold to steamboats, 86; farmers get income from, 177

Marriage: T.'s thoughts on, 74-76; first thoughts of marrying S., 80-82, 85; T.

McKinley, Pres. William, 337, 354

Mails: carried by steamboats, 71; letter is lost in, 80; delays in forwarding, 110, 175; sent via Glasgow, 365*n*6; cost of, 368*n*3no.2

Mankato, Minn.: execution of thirty-nine Indians at, 225

Maple sugar and syrup: S. delighted with, 157; S. tells of making, 204-6, 208

Maps: drawn by Theodore, 75, 82, 83, 97, 138, 140

Marriage: T's thoughts on, 74-76; first

thoughts of marrying S., 80-82, 85; T. impatient for S.'s reply, 93-95, 97-98 107-08, 111; T. learns of Théophile's, 99; in Europe, 105; T. thinks of marrying Anna Maxwell, 114, 119, 122-23; questions S.'s sincerity, 119, 121, 124; S. accepts T.'s proposal of, 124; S,'s plans for, 126, 128; of T. and S. finally occurs, 130; S. refers to her wedding, 161, 369*n*4no.1; Bosts' eleventh anniversary, 287; S. before marriage, 361*n*11, 365*n*9

Maxwell family (neighbors of Bosts), 98, 107, 133, 250, 259: T. stays with, 111; T. critical of their young friends, 119; Anna ("Fanny"), 122-23, 133, 135, 167, 368*n*19; their difficulties, 136; Mrs. Maxwell, 148, 150, 160, 205, 221, 237, 259, 278; help Bosts, 148, 150, 259; try to scare away blackbirds, 152

Mendota, Minn.: T. vague about location of, 35, 363*n*6

Methodists, 58, 172, 287, 343; T. is critical of, 24-25

Mexicans: in Calif., 334

Mieliton (fictitious person invented by Dodd), 49

Mill Springs or Somerset (Battle of): T. hails Union victory at, 204, 371*n*8

Minneapolis, Minn., 311, 322: a fine city, 250; S. enjoys visit to, 262, 264; T. gives lessons in, 262, 266; State Fair held in, 284; railroad lines from, 285-86

Minnesota Territory: physical description of, 23

Minnesota Agricultural Society: T. wins prize offered by, 286

Minnesota River: flood damage along, 182

Minnesota State Fair: T. wins prizes at, 284

Minnetonka (Lake), 73, 78, 86, 294, 324: steamboat rides on, 294-95

Minnewashta (Lake), 86

Mississippi River: navigation on, 30, 35, 68, 105; falls at St. Anthony,

118, 266, 281

Moore family (neighbors of the Bosts),
98

Moseman, Marie, xx: accompanies S. to
America, 130; is satisfied and helpful,
162, 183, 199-200, 241; has grown up,
184; stays home to watch house, 232;
grief-stricken at Alice's death, 238,
258; sleeps too soundly, 260; works
for Powers family, 293; her wages,
304-05; goes with Bosts to Calif., 333;
her death, 333

Mosquitoes, 42-43, 115

Music: Ami Bosts's, 105, 340; Bost
children study, 331-32; T. recalls
childhood songs, 342

Napoleon III: denounced by T., 210, 256,
371n10, 372n5no.2

Narbel family, 74, 76, 365n3

Nature and Scenery: in America, com-
pared with Switzerland, 59; Lake
Minnetonka, 78-79; upper Mississippi
and St. Lawrence, 86; an outing in the
Big Woods, 86-87; T.'s excursion to
Clear Water Lake, 100ff.

Neighbors: in Chanhassen, 133, 140, 160,
366-67n5; influx of Germans, 252-53

New England, 13

New House: Bosts plan for, 189, 199,
212-13, 223-24; building of, 226, 228-
30; Boissonnas helps with, 231; well is
dug for, 232; Bosts move into, 233-34;
pleasures of, 234, 237-38; photo of,
sent to parents, 272-73

New Ulm, Minn.: Christmas murders at,
274, 374n4; settled by German
Turners, 374n2

Newspapers, 58-59, 73, 115, 209, 277,
285

Nichols, Rev. Henry Martyn and family:
drownings at Lake Calhoun, 162-65,
369n6

Normandeau, M. and Mme.: teach at La
Grande Ligne, 10, 15-16

North, John Wesley: declines to finance
lime quarry, 196-97, 371n4

Northampton Colony: some members
settle in Chanhassen, 365n30,

366n5

Northfield, Minn.: T. attracted by, 195ff.;
limestone quarries near, 370n2. See
also Lime quarry

Officeholding: T. finds drawbacks in,
270-71; T. and Powers falsely
charged with abuse of, 273, 275,
277-78

"Old Mike" (Bosts' neighbor and hired
man), 191, 205, 228, 253, 261, 278,
370n13

Oxen: T.'s first use of, 88, 91-92; use of,
to break land, 159, 167

Palmerston, Viscount (British Prime
Minister), 216, 372n7

Panic of 1857: hits Minn., 134, 141, 148

Pearson, Thomas B., 22

Pepin (Lake): T. first sees, 31

Perrot, M.: sends Bosts money, 169-70,
369n11

Piano: S. wishes for, 186

Pierce, Pres. Franklin: T. critical of,
18

Pointe-aux-Trembles (Quebec): T. con-
valesces at, 57, 66

Pollens, Louis, 64

Pomona, Calif.: Bosts move to, 333,
341

Pope, Gen. John: leads troops against
Indians, 221

Powers, Albert (infant son of Mr. and
Mrs. George M. Powers): taken in by
Bosts, 291-92; dies, 314

Powers family (neighbors of Bosts), 99,
133, 152, 155, 181, 205, 214, 246,
248, 251-53, 255, 259, 261-62, 270,
275, 277-78, 291, 366n5: death of
Mrs. Powers, 291-92

Prairie fire: burns T.'s stable, 115;
destroys stable and hay, 156-57

Preemption: explanation of process,
366n4

Presbyterians, 63, 343: and Woodrow
Wilson, 355

Pronier, César: T.'s friendship with, 293,
362n no.1

Railroads: travel by, 29, 83, 94; routes from New York to St. Paul 82-84; to Chanhassen, 145; in Minn., 105, 285-86

Reading matter: available to Bost family, 115, 209, 285

Red Cross: S. and daughters work for, in World War I, 349-50

Religion: revivals in America, 132, 134, 178-80, 274, 368n2no.1: T. is opposed to modernism in, 287

Remittances received by Bosts: from M. Perrot, 170, 174; from Ami Bost, 176-77, 181; from T.'s parents, 261, 264, 361n3; S. expects her legacy from sale of "Les Parcs," 184

Republicans: in Minn., oppose slavery, 99-100; T. active in politics with, 183, 211, 219, 234-35, 246; ill treated by Wilson, 351-52

Richelieu River (Quebec), 9

Ridgely (Fort), 221

Roads: T. helps build Dodd's road, 33-50; poor condition of, in vicinity of Chanhassen, 79, 231-32, 324

Rochat, M. (T.'s Swiss friend in Minneapolis), 286, 288, 375n2no.1

Roux, M. Mme.: teach at La Grande Ligne, 10

Russell, Lord John (British Foreign Secretary), 216, 372n7


St. Anthony, Falls of: T. disappointed on first visit to, 37; T. revisits, 118

St. Louis, Mo.: T. thinks of moving to, 289-90

St. Paul, Minn., 105, 146: T. arrives in, 26; T.'s early experiences in, 50, 52, 79, 91; rapid growth and development of, 66, 249-50

Salies-de-Béarn: elder Bosts living in, 95

Sampson, Hattie Brisbin (second wife of Alphonse Bost), 376n5no.2

San Francisco, Calif., 350

Sarver family (neighbors of the Bosts), 132, 168, 177-78, 187, 190, 214, 255; he helps T. cut down bee tree, 168-69

Savoyards, 19, 362n9

Scarlet fever: epidemic of, in Minn., 224-25

School district: of Chanhassen, T. lends money to, 142

Schools: Moravian academy established in Chaska, 247; T. gives money to found academy in Excelsior, 331

Scotland, 124

Seamans, Lula: marries Alphonse Bost, 333

Selkirk Colony, 105, 367n12

Sepoy mutiny, 216, 218, 372n6

Serrières, Switzerland, 61

Sewing machine: S. wishes for, 199; S. finally gets, 317-18

Shakopee, Minn., 67, 69, 72, 79, 146, 150, 154, 165, 194, 221, 228, 244: development of, 250

Sheep: T. raises, 316-17

Sheldon, Rev. Charles B., 132, 179, 196, 202-03, 250, 287, 317, 333, 369n2, 373n8

Sioux Indians, 54, 90: uprising in 1862, 216, 220; T. compares with Calif. Indians, 334

Slaves and Slavery, 18, 19, 62, 99, 110, 120, 181, 183, 227, 235, 245, 247

Slidell and Mason (Confederate envoys): T. comments on, 199-200, 371n5, 373n10

Smithtown, Minn., 78

Snell (doctor in Excelsior), 178-79

Snelling (Fort), 211, 214, 216, 220

Sonderbund War: fighting qualities of Swiss in, 192, 370n15

Spain, 11, 19, 22

Steamboats: travel on, 30-31, 39-40, 94; carry mail, 71; on Minnesota River, 84, 94

Stone (neighbor of Bosts), 317

Storekeeping: in Excelsior, T. a partner in Jones & Bost, 321ff.

Suchard, Philippe, 35, 363n5

Swiss: as better fighters than Yankees, 192; young immigrants often discouraged, 260-61

"Swiss Connection," 363n2. See also Freudenreich, Baron de; Rochat, M.


Tax assessor: in Chanhassen, T. works as,

245-46, 251

Taxes: too high, according to T., 104; T. and neighbors in arrears with, 372n8

Teaching (by T.): at La Grande Ligne, 9-10, 15-16, 20-21; in Burlington Vt., 12-16; in Ashland, N. Y., 22, 27-29; in Minneapolis, 262, 265; possibility of post in St. Louis, 289-90

Thonon, Switzerland, 59

Toupoint (youthful friend of T.), 64

*Tutoiement*: T. scolded by S. for, 106-09

Underground Railway: praised by T., 18

Unitarians, 58

Vaucher-Veyrassat family (of Bellevue, Switzerland), xviii, 3-4, 98, 144, 151, 194, 275, 361n7

Vermont: T. lives in, 11, 13, 14

Vines: T. explains care of in Minn., 213, 254

Weather: extremes of in Minn., 79-80 103, 110, 113, 132, 152, 167-68

Wheat: Minn. prices compared with

French, 176; yields in Minn., 212

Whooping cough: Mimi and T. both have, 165-66; Alice dies of, 258; Alphonse has mild case of, 259

Wildlife in Minn., 101, 118, 180

Wilson, Pres. Woodrow: T. critical of, 350-51

Winnebago Indians: T. describes passage of, through St. Paul, 36-37; compared with Chippewas, 90; compared with Calif. Indians, 334

Winter in Minn.: inconveniences of log house in, 222; hardships of, 237; Mrs. Maxwell suffers during, 237; extreme cold of January *1864*, 239-40; T. depressed by length of, 331

Women: in America, 56; in Europe, 56; as farmers' wives, 74; French women defended by T., 120

Worcester, Mrs. (T.'s landlady in Burlington, Vt.), 12

World War I: T. comments on, 344, 350-51; Bost grandchildren in, 352-53

Yankton Indians, 215-216

Ralph Bowen, editor and translator of the Bost letters, is professor of history at Northern Illinois University. His teaching and research interests center upon modern European intellectual history and Franco-American cultural relations, and he has served as a Fulbright visiting professor at the Universities of Nantes and Nice.